Cultural Policy

Cultural Policy

Toby Miller and George Yúdice

SAGE Publications
London • Thousand Oaks • New Delhi

First published 2002

SAGE Publications Ltd
6 Bonhill Street
London EC2A 4PU

SAGE Publications Inc
2455 Teller Road
Thousand Oaks, California 91320

SAGE Publications India Pvt Ltd
32, M-Block Market
Greater Kailash – I
New Delhi 110 048

British Library Cataloguing in Publication data

A catalogue record for this book is available
from the British Library

ISBN 0 7619 5240 3
ISBN 0 7619 5241 1 (pbk)

Library of Congress control number 2002102290

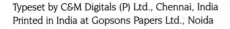

Typeset by C&M Digitals (P) Ltd., Chennai, India
Printed in India at Gopsons Papers Ltd., Noida

Contents

Acknowledgements

We wish to thank the following for their assistance: Ian Antcliff, Kay Bridger, John Caldwell, Briankle Chang, Stuart Cunningham, Talitha Espiritu, John Hill, Mariana Johnson, Linda Lai, Marie Leger, Andrew Lockett, Anna McCarthy, Eric Kit-Wai Ma, Robert Murphy, Robert Nixon, Chris Rojek, Sohnya Sayres, and an anonymous reviewer for Sage. This project derived in part from a doctoral seminar we taught together in the Fall semesters of 1998 and 2000, and our thanks are due to students in the class. We also wish to thank colleagues at *Social Text* over the years for their interest in cultural policy questions, along with a number of fellow-travelers: Tony Bennett, Andrea Frazer, Néstor García Canclini, May Joseph, Randy Martin, Ana Maria Ochoa, Tom O'Regan, and Vera Zolberg. Finally, our appreciation to all the workers who made this book.

Parts of what follows have appeared in different forms in *Emergences, Continuum, Global Hollywood, American Behavioral Scientist, Social Text, Culture and Policy, Southeast Asian Journal of Social Science, Film Policy, Communication, Citizenship and Social Policy, Oxford Guide to Film Studies,* and *British Cinema of the 90s.*

Introduction: The History and Theory of Cultural Policy

> Can it be denied that the education of the common people is the most effective means of protecting persons and property? – Lord Macaulay (quoted in Lloyd and Thomas (1998) 18)

Culture is connected to policy in two registers: the aesthetic and the anthropological. In the aesthetic register, artistic output emerges from creative people and is judged by aesthetic criteria, as framed by the interests and practices of cultural criticism and history. In this world, culture is taken as a marker of differences and similarities in taste and status within social groups. The anthropological register, on the other hand, takes culture as a marker of how we live our lives, the senses of place and person that make us human – neither individual nor entirely universal, but grounded by language, religion, custom, time and space. So whereas the aesthetic articulates differences *within* populations (for example, which class has the cultural capital to appreciate high culture and which does not), the anthropological articulates differences *between* populations (for example, which country sells new technology and which does not) (Wallerstein).

Cultural *policy* refers to the institutional supports that channel both aesthetic creativity and collective ways of life – a bridge between the two registers. Cultural policy is embodied in systematic, regulatory guides to action that are adopted by organizations to achieve their goals. In short, it is bureaucratic rather than creative or organic: organizations solicit, train, distribute, finance, describe and reject actors and activities that go under the signs of artist or artwork, through the implementation of policies. Governments, trade unions, colleges, social movements, community groups, foundations and businesses, aid, fund, control, promote, teach and evaluate creative persons; in fact, they often decide and implement the very criteria that make possible the use of the word, 'creative.' This may be done through law courts that permit erotica on the grounds that they are works of art; curricula that require students to read plays on the grounds that they are uplifting; film commissions that sponsor scripts on the grounds that they reflect national concerns; entrepreneurs who print symphonic program notes justifying an unusual season on the grounds of innovation; or foundations that sponsor the community culture of minorities on the grounds of a need to supplement (mostly white) middle-class culture with 'diversity'. In turn, these criteria may themselves derive, respectively, from legal doctrine, citizenship education, tourism aims, impresarios' profit plans or philanthropic desires.

The second understanding of culture appears in academic anthropology and journalistic explanations of the *Zeitgeist*. For instance, references to the cultures of indigenous peoples by anthropologists before land-rights tribunals are in part determined by the rules of conduct adopted by the state in the light of local political issues and international human-rights discourse. Similarly, references to yuppie dot-com culture by newspaper feature writers are in part determined by the rules of conduct adopted by their editors/proprietors in the light of local market segmentation and international occupational norms. In effect, we hear about these lifestyle/ritual practices because of such policies.

In addition to these highly deliberate practices, policy is often made unwittingly, through the permeation of social space by genres that invoke 'a particular kind of organization of audience' that may maintain or modify ideological systems (Vološinov 96–97) on an *ad hoc*, inconsistent basis. Performativity, rather than constativity, characterizes policy, and it is frequently made 'on the run,' in response to unpredictable pressures. In semiotic terms, both culture and policy have their *langue* (formal, rule-driven qualities) and *parole* (actual usage). Just as *parole* complicates *langue*, so there is inevitable overlap between the aesthetic and anthropological registers in cultural policy.

Delegates to *Mondiacult* 1982, a world conference on cultural policy run by the United Nations Educational, Scientific and Cultural Organization (UNESCO), agreed that:

> culture gives man the ability to reflect upon himself. It is through culture that man expresses himself, becomes aware of himself, recognizes his incompleteness, questions his own achievements, seeks untiringly for new meanings and creates works through which he transcends his limitations. ('The Mexico' 190)

Similarly, the Canadian Commission for UNESCO – operating in a First World context but from a position vexed by unequal cultural transfer with its elephantine Southern neighbor – calls for a 'proper cultural education' that can guarantee citizens will engage in both self-criticism and self-appreciation, in order to produce well-rounded individuals – a combination of maintenance and renewal through critical reflection (Canadian 81).

What are these 'UNESCrats' talking about, and does this axiom define the field of cultural policy? To historicize and theorize that question, our Introduction approaches cultural policy under seven headings: governmentality, taste, ethical incompleteness, alibis for funding, national and supranational projects, cultural citizenship and cultural policy studies. This is a prelude to the heart of our book: those cultural knowledges and practices that determine the formation and governance of subjects. For as well as being a book that seeks to summarize the current state of play in discussions of cultural policy at a very general, international level and this is *also* an intervention into that knowledge that urges a particular theoretical and political orientation. We position ourselves within the committed norms of cultural studies rather than the objective claims of orthodox policy research. Our book seeks, in other words, to articulate knowledge with progressive social change, with social movements as primary *loci* of power, authorization, and responsibility. More conventional research articulates knowledge with social reproduction, with governments as primary *loci* of power, authorization, and responsibility. Whereas our project is concerned with transforming the social order, the alternative seeks to replicate it – a struggle between cultural policy as a transformative versus a functionalist sphere. Our starting points are therefore theory, history and politics, rather than efficiency, effectiveness and description.

The Rise of Governmentality in the West

Michel Foucault's concept of governmentality is key to the actions and claims of Western states in the cultural domain, both historically and today. Foucault uses the term to explain 'the way in which the modern state began to worry about individuals'. An example is that even as eighteenth-century Revolutionary France was embarking on a regime of slaughter, public-health campaigns were also underway. This paradox was an ongoing, Janus-faced 'game between death and life' that the state constructed for itself as a benevolent despot ('Conversation' 4). Foucault offers a history of this emergent modern sovereignty in an ironised mode via his use of the 'barbarous but unavoidable neologism: governmentality', a word originally coined by Roland Barthes to describe variations in market prices and responses by the state (130).

Foucault identifies a series of problems addressed at different moments in European economic and political organization, beginning with five questions that were posed across the sixteenth century: 'How to govern oneself, how to be governed, how to govern others, by whom the people will accept being governed, how to become the best possible governor'. These questions emerged from two historical processes: the displacement of feudalism by the sovereign state, and the similarly conflictual Reformation and its counters. Daily economic and spiritual government came up for redefinition. The state emerged as a centralizing tendency that sought to normalize itself and others. Religious authority, embroiled in ecclesiastical conflicts, lost its legitimacy to vouchsafe the sovereign's divine right of rule. The monarch was gradually transformed into a manager, rather than the embodiment of immanent rule (Foucault 'Governmentality' 87–90).

From that moment on, governing required a double movement. The sovereign discovered how to run his life, and treated his dominions according to these lessons. And the father learnt to run his family like a principality and train his minions to carry their docility and industry into the social sphere. In turn, the family's forms of life influenced conduct away from the home. This backwards and forwards motion of public and private, of imposed and internalized norms that shuttled between work and domesticity in search of civic peace/control, came to be known as the 'police'. Pedagogy extrapolated from the ruler's self–knowledge to the rule of others, and policing transferred this motion into the head of the household and also back onto the street (91–92). Put another way, we might see this as the economization of government, a complex movement between self and society in search of efficiency and authority.

With the upheavals of the seventeenth century, such as the Thirty Years War and rural and urban revolts, new modes of social organization arose. In eighteenth-century Europe, the concept of 'the economy' spread beyond the domestic sphere. What had been a managerial invention, dedicated to forming correct conduct, transformed itself into a description of the social field. By now, the government of territory was secondary to the government of things and the social relations between them. Government was conceived and actualized in terms of climate, disease, industry, finance, custom and disaster – literally, a concern with life and death and what could be calculated and managed between them. Wealth and health became social goals, to be attained through the disposition of capacities across the population: 'biological existence was reflected in political existence', through the work of 'bio-power'. Bio-power 'brought life and its mechanisms into the realm of explicit calculations and made knowledge-power an agent of transformation of human life'. Bodies were identified with politics, because managing them was part of running the country. This history is still relevant to contemporary life. For Foucault, 'a society's "threshold of modernity" has been reached when the life of the species is wagered on its own political strategies' ('Governmentality' 97, 92–95 and History 143).

The foundations of classical political economy date from around this time, and are generally associated with a libertarian championing of the market. But as Michael J Shapiro's study of Adam Smith has shown, the very founder of the discourse theorized sovereignty beyond the exhibition and maintenance of loyalty – government was also required to manage 'flows of exchange within the social domain' (Reading 'Adam Smith' 11). The physiocrats and Smith identified a transformation in the status of the government from a basis in legitimacy to a basis in technique, specifically the ability to distinguish 'what is free, what has to be free, and what has to be regulated', notably in the areas of crime and health (Foucault 'Problematics' 124–25.) Science and government combined in new environmental-legal relations, under the signs of civic management and economic productivity. So when the British Parliament required smallpox vaccinations for all children from 1853, this was simultaneously a landmark in medicine and in public regulation of the body politic. Two years later, Achille Guillard merged 'political arithmetic' and 'political and natural observations' to invent demography, which had been on the rise since the first population inquiries in seventeenth-century Britain. The new knowledge codified five projects: reproduction, aging, migration, public health and ecology (Synnott 26; Fogel 312–13). Cultural policies became part of this duty of care. For instance, at the turn of the twentieth century, the British state introduced a policy of 'Education for All'. The subsequent Education Act of 1902 mandated school-pupil visits to museums as part of its curricular requirements (Coombes 124).

The critical shift here was away from an autotelic accumulation of power by the sovereign, and towards the dispersal of power into the population via the formation of skills. The center invested people with the capacity to produce and consume things, insisting on freedom in some compartments of life and obedience in others (Foucault 'Problematics' 125.) Governments wanted people to manufacture goods by the most rational allocation of resources available. Hence, governmentality was other-directed and instrumental, and its target was the whole population. At the same time, philanthropy was also developing in Europe – the beginnings of today's third sector, inbetween the private and the public. Neither profit-making nor state-based, it was occupied by an array of elites that were interested in social reform, and operated beyond the immediately self-interested norms of politics, but in a governmental mode (Donzelot 36, 55–57, 65).

The model of the household as an economic matrix continued across the first half of the nineteenth century, despite its provincialism in an internationalizing, post-mercantilist world, until the externalization of the state created new industries and modes of production. The new duality – empire and economy – expanded the purview of governments beyond the sovereign and the household. The population had displaced the prince as a site for accumulating power, and the national economy had displaced the home as a site of social intervention and achievement that became both international and local (Foucault 'Governmentality' 98–99).

Clearly, then, the emergence of modern capitalism was connected to the rise of the sovereign state, which was concerned to deliver a docile and healthy labor force to business; but not only to business. Cholera, sanitation, and prostitution became the business of government in the modern era through 'the emergence of the health and physical well-being of the population in general as one of the essential objectives of political power'. The entire 'social body' was assayed and treated for its insufficiencies. Governing people meant, most centrally and critically, obeying the 'imperative of health: at once the duty of each and the objective of all' (Foucault 'Politics' 277). This idea of fitness to perform expanded to include education and hence culture.

Of course, before the emergence of governmentality, cultural policy had long been a symbolic and a highly pragmatic topic. The uptake of English as a national language occurred after 1400, when writing in Latin and French were disavowed. This was a national language policy at work, animated by the desires of Henry IV and V to reinforce their dubious legitimacy by encouraging national unity in the Parliament and citizenry. And from the first days of her empire, Queen Isabella's functionaries established Castilian as a language of conquest and management. Indeed, Antonio de Nebrija, the imperial grammarian, wrote in his *Castillian Grammar*, published in that fateful year of 1492, that 'Language is Empire' (11). By the mid-fifteenth century, Italian nobles were establishing instant libraries, employing copying scribes. This marked the advent of an industrial process for producing symbols of power. Already, we can discern the two great wings of cultural policy flapping energetically: subvention and training. Princely galleries of sixteenth- to eighteenth-century Europe developed into places of lavish decoration, designed to impress local and foreign visitors with the grandeur of regimes and their scions, through décor and iconographic representations of individual rulers (Duncan *Civilizing* 22). The doctrine of Robespierrean France in the 1790s was, in the Abbé Grégoire's words, 'to erase dialects and make French universal' (quoted in 'How Multilingual?'). In 1850, 20% of French citizens could not speak French. The full armature of a press and compulsory education was mandated to rectify this failing. At the same time, in the immediate post-Independence period, Latin American statesmen wagered that curricula underpinned by grammars devised from empirical observation of New-World Spanish – in contrast to the Latin-based grammars of Spain and Europe – would maintain national unity (Bello 'Prologue: Grammar' 101–102). And at the moment of Italian reunification in 1870, Massimo d'Azeglio commented in sponsoring language policy that 'we have made Italy: now we must make Italians' (quoted in Shore 'Transcending' 474).

Once language is shared, other forms of cultural production follow suit – for along with speech can come geographical representation. Imperial cultural policies varied between the exclusion of languages (the outlook of the British and the Dutch in their colonial 'possessions'), language assimilation (Spain under Franco, France today, the US in the 1920s, Pakistan in the 1950s and 1960s) and a pluralization of equal legitimacy for different languages (contemporary Canada, Peru, Paraguay, Nigeria, and Austria) (Schmidt 57–63). The struggle for making meaning continues to this day, as new (sub)national entities like the Basque Country and Catalonia seek to standardize their own national languages as top priorities for autonomous governments (John H Fisher, 1168, 1170, 1178; Phillipson 8; Urla 822; Bolton and Hutton; Nathaniel Berman). Croatian cultural policy goes so far as to tease apart any remnants of Serbian that might 'contaminate' the new national language. And when the Soviet Union broke up, its former republics had two choices in dealing with their sizeable Russian-speaking minorities: either propound a cultural nationalism that marginalized the Russian language and set religious, racial and linguistic criteria for citizenship (as per Estonia and Latvia); or adopt a civic policy that offered entitlements based on territory, fealty, and labor (which took place in Ukraine and Kazakhstan) (Laitin 314–17). The Estonian government must now deal with a sizeable Russian minority, which it alienated by initially adopting a hard-line nationalism. The government is trying to defuse the situation via Russian-language schools and cultural groups.

The artistic corollary of these forms of linguistic governance is a project that seeks to educate the citizenry into a set of tastes. We might say, then, that taste formation is cultural policing or cultural policy. To engage the philosophical correlatives of this shift, we turn now to the Western cosmology of taste, which appears at the same time as modern Western government.

Philosophizing Taste

In his *Critique of Judgement*, the eighteenth-century philosopher Immanuel Kant conceives of taste as 'conformity to law without the law' (86). He means that aesthetic activity, if properly monitored through education ('examples of what has in the course of culture maintained itself longest in esteem' (139)), produce an effect and a 'knowledge' in the human subject derived from universally valid 'morally practical precepts' that are independent of particular interests. They 'rest on the supersensible, which the concept of freedom alone makes cognizable' (Kant 11). According to Gilles Deleuze, Kant's *Critique of Judgement* is tantamount to a new 'Copernican revolution', whereby the foundation of knowledge 'no longer has a theological principle, but rather, theology has a final human foundation' (Deleuze 69). Moreover, the presumably universal character of this foundation is, for Kant, identified with the public sphere, which locates the social in *bourgeois* modernity: 'Taste as a kind *of sensus communis*' or '*public* sense, i.e. a critical faculty which in its reflective act takes account (*a priori*) of the mode of representation of everyone else, in order ... to weigh its judgement with the collective reason of mankind' (Kant 151).

Across a century or two of economic modernity, other, more revolutionary thinkers pick up on the importance of this kind of identification for collective loyalty. Karl Marx writes that: 'it is impossible to create a moral power by paragraphs of law'. There must also be '*organic* laws supplementing the Constitution' – i.e. cultural policy (*Eighteenth* 27, 35). These organic laws and their textual efflorescence come to represent each 'epoch's consciousness of itself' (Althusser 108). Antonio Gramsci theorizes this supplement as an 'equilibrium' between constitutional law ('political society' or a 'dictatorship or some other coercive apparatus used to control the masses in conformity with a given type of production and economy') and organic law ('civil society' or the 'hegemony of a social group over the entire nation exercised through so-called private organizations such as the church, the unions, the schools, etc') (204).

Raymond Williams applies Gramsci's concept of hegemony to culture, defining it as the contention of *dominant* versus *residual* and *emergent* forms. Hegemony is secured when the dominant culture uses education, philosophy, religion, advertising and art to make its dominance appear normal and natural to the heterogeneous groups that constitute society. The accomplishment of this 'consensus' instantiates what then appears to be an 'ethical state', which deserves universal loyalty and transcends class identifications (Lloyd and Thomas 114–18). These practices necessarily reference historical change in order to legitimize changes of taste and power. Residual cultures comprise old meanings and practices, no longer dominant, but still influential. Emergent cultures are either propagated by a new class or incorporated by the dominant, as part of hegemony. These manoeuvers find expression in what Williams terms a 'structure of feeling': the intangibles of an era that explain or develop the quality of life. Such indicators often involve a contest – or at least dissonance – between official culture and practical consciousness. Further, Williams insists on the importance of community life, the conflicts in any cultural formation, the social nature of culture, and the cultural nature of society.

The notion of the popular was used by Gramsci in his diagnosis of the rise of fascism in 1920s Italy, and as part of his program for moving Italian politics in a more revolutionary direction. In his estimation, progressive Italian intellectuals of the day were out of touch with key social forces, particularly the 'popular masses'. It was necessary to construct a 'national-popular' consciousness or 'collective will' amenable to revolution. Language was most important as a means of 'collectively attaining a single cultural "climate"' necessary for constructing a hegemonic project. For Gramsci, a language compelling to the popular classes (including artistic and cinematic language) was perhaps the most strategic instrument of a bid for hegemony, which had to reach down to the people who could bring revolutionary change. His view was premised on the tenet that 'all men are intellectuals' insofar as they 'participate in a particular conception of the world … and therefore contribute to sustain a conception of the world or to modify it, that is, to bring into being new modes of thought' (Gramsci 348–349, 9). Institutional or party intellectuals thereby transform common sense into good sense, which then should guide the popular – cultural policy at work.

National cultural policies are, then, a privileged terrain of hegemony. They provide a means of reconciling contending cultural identities by holding up the nation as an essence that transcends particular interests. In keeping with the negotiated conflict that lies at the heart of hegemony, the cultural domain produces challenges from those sectors that the contingency of history has moved into contestatory positions. David Lloyd and Paul Thomas give the example of English working-class radicals of the 1820s and 1830s who rejected cultural criteria for citizenship and political representation (i.e. education), on the grounds that there is a 'close relationship between being represented, being educated and being appropriated' (61). Other examples are rival sectors of the industrial and commercial *bourgeoisie*, and (more recently) new subject positions: immigrant, anti- and postcolonialist, gender and ethnically based, and so on. Frequently, attempts to assimilate anthropological difference are mounted under the sign of aesthetic unity – hence the tight link between language policy and teaching on the one hand, and literature and the audiovisual media on the other. Literature has been a central strut of public education, as a training in both language and in norms. It embodies the public sphere by offering public discussion of the private life of the *bourgeoisie* (Habermas *Structural*), serving up exemplary individual lives to be emulated (or abjured) and providing a *mise-en-scène* of the predicaments that face an economic class-in-the-making as it devises forms of ethical legitimacy.

In keeping with the project of governmentality, the emergence of a philosophy of taste in the eighteenth century displaced social authority from religion and the theocratic state, assigning it to the social as a privileged terrain where conduct would be regulated in the modern age. Looked at from this vantage point, we can see that the pedagogy and exercise of taste are premised on the authority of a monitorial function, internalized within the subject through culture. This developmentalist logic reasons that when a people's sense of taste is removed from sensory interests, their taste will approximate purity as part of 'a transition on that part of our critical faculty from the enjoyment of sense to the moral feeling' (Kant 156). Despite disclaimers, Kant says the development of universal taste constitutes the 'link in the chain of the human faculties *a priori* upon which all legislation must depend'. Taste is not given – it depends on cultivation through a sentimental education, premised on what Matthew Arnold was later to recommend as a principle of social regulation.

Arnold, a nineteenth-century British poet, cultural critic and schools administrator, identified productive goals for culture through policy, such as putting poetry onto the elementary-school curriculum and campaigning for a national theatre (McGuigan *Culture* 55). For Arnold, culture is neither autotelic nor accidental, but 'a study of perfection. It moves by the force, not merely or primarily of the scientific passion for pure knowledge, but also of the moral and social passion for doing good'. By opposing *Culture and Anarchy* in his 1869 classic, Arnold defends a liberal education against a purely utilitarian training for industrial production. But he does envisage culture instrumentally, as a 'practical benefit ... [a] great help out of our present difficulties'. Culture counters social 'anarchy' not only by mitigating the modern tendency to break down traditional ways of life, but also by correcting the shortcomings of the three classes: the Barbarians (the aristocracy), the Philistines (the middle class), and the Populace (the working class). His notion of culture eschews the specific interests of industrial classes, particularly the working class: 'Culture does not try to teach down to the level of inferior classes; it does not try to win for this or that sect of its own, with ready-made judgments and watchwords' (70). Instead, culture is the 'pursuit of our total perfection by means of getting to know, on all matters which most concern us, the best which has been thought and said in the world' (6). More specifically, culture can produce *national consolidation*, secured by state institutions. Neither Philistines, nor Barbarians, nor the Populace alone may exercise the 'authority which we are seeking as a defense against anarchy, which is right reason, ideas, light' (85). This authority can only be found in the 'best self', which gives the three classes their unity and harmony. That self is embodied in the State, the 'organ of ... our national right reason' (94–97). *Culture and Anarchy* seeks to demonstrate how the 'cultural values of the modern state' function, arguing that culture is central to authority's mission of preventing anarchy by helping to design the modern person, the liberal individual. Arnold wants an architecture for this person that can define and develop individuals who comprehend the need for an authoritarian antisepsis to populist excess.

An aesthetic of truth and beauty is, as per Kant, the internal monitor within each person that provides a collective, national, categorical imperative. Its very *ethos* of singular appreciation becomes, ironically, a connecting chord of national harmony, binding individual goals to an implied national unity. For Arnold, 'culture, self, and state' form a trinity of modernity, in the service of enlightened authority. Elsewhere, he writes that 'culture is *reading*'. This elevates interpretation to the level of a cultural requirement for citizenship that is learned via public education (Lambropoulos 173, 175–76, 179, 191).

Arnold had counterparts elsewhere. Domingo F Sarmiento founded public schooling in Argentina after the motto 'civilization or barbarism', delineating educated creole citizens from indigenous-*mestizo* peoples. One could move between these categories, but only through the work of a new, educational culture, rather than an inherited, analphabetic one (García Canclini *Hybrid* 112). In Chile, Andrés Bello founded both the educational system and the Civil Code with a view to producing ideal national citizens. He had been exiled in London from 1810 to 1829, where he conducted research on language, literature, and law at the British Museum, and collaborated with British intellectuals like James Mill, whom he assisted in editing Jeremy Bentham's papers. This earned him the suspicion of Simón Bolívar and other revolutionary leaders who mistakenly took him to be a monarchist. While it is true that Bello designed and implemented his liberal educational and civic projects within the conservative context of Chile in the first half of the nineteenth century, his work was also adopted in many other, more republican contexts. His prominence, moreover, stemmed from his role in formulating a model of international order that echoed Kant's 'Toward a Perpetual Peace', which was incorporated in the charter of the Organization of American States in the twentieth century.

Bello charted out a double method for constructing the nationhood of Chile and the 'emergent nations' of America. While he accepted the epistemological advances of European historiography and science, he nevertheless rejected 'excessive servility toward the science of civilized Europe' (Bello 'The Craft' 183). That is, American nations had to arrive at self-understanding not by applying European knowledge to local circumstances, but by applying the 'independence of thought' characteristic of scientific and historical methods: they must gather data, establish facts, and arrive at a philosophy of history through 'synthetic induction' (Bello 'Commentary' 170 and 'The Craft' 177). This construction of the nation through a new history relied on freedom to think for oneself, outside the prestige of European knowledge. The journal he founded, *El Repertorio Americano* (1826), '[gave] preference to everything related to America' (5).[1] Bello, moreover, placed little value in abstract philosophies, 'generalizations which say little or nothing in themselves to the person who has not looked on living nature in the paintings of history', that is, in the sources themselves ('The Craft' 183). The people best positioned to carry out this historical research, he argued, are the Americans themselves ('Address' 132), not for essentialist reasons, but because the 'sources [are] closest to us', and because it was a historical and political necessity for Americans to construct nations. In the process, Bello envisioned a civilizational maturity expressed in (Latin) America's additions to the European reservoir of knowledge ('El *Repertorio*' 6), thus bringing it much closer to the universal history in whose name it (unilaterally) spoke. In any event, Bello took heart in the conviction that historical certainties are also dated, and that new knowledge continually reshapes the past and the present from which it is constructed ('The Craft' 184).[1]

Although he does not cite Kant, Bello derived his notion of freedom from the paradox, elucidated by the German philosopher, that law operates as 'the hindering of a hindrance to freedom' (Kant quoted in Balibar 119). He also concurred with Kant that 'juridical constraint morally educates individuals', that the self-education of the people 'proceeds from the pure idea of the law as from an interior directive' (Balibar 120, 127) – all the more reason to include the law-governed template of grammar in his popular education program. For Bello, 'the spoken word is insufficient'. The ability to read and write becomes a qualification for citizenship: 'to preserve, in safety and order, the few or many affairs in which they will engage'. Literacy is necessary for 'the study of the Constitution [which] must form an integral part of general education ... in order to grasp the organization of the political body to which we belong' ('On the Aims of Education' 113, 115). Obviously, this was both a necessity and a utopian aspiration at the time that Bello wrote, for only a very small percentage of the population in Chile could read and write ('Report on the Progress' 144). Nevertheless, the will to impose literacy was symptomatic of the will to control alternative knowledges rooted in oral cultures (Mignolo) and different ways of life resistant to governmentality.

'Standards of taste', to use the phrase that *bourgeois* critic Hilton Kramer wielded in the recent US culture wars, are part of hegemony, a key means of differentiating and stratifying society. The value projected by aesthetic hegemony is ultimately premised on a series of exclusions, which are clearly recognized as such by those who stand to lose out. Social harmony is bought at the expense of those whose tastes are not only aesthetically unacceptable but, more importantly, potentially contestatory. Thus, when artistic practices are not perceived as contributing to the prevailing order, hegemonic actors use the law to quash them. Any person, object or practice deemed offensive to prevailing standards of taste has no legitimate place within the public sphere, as Henry Louis Gates, Jr. argued a decade ago in defense of the US rap group 2 *Live Crew* when one of their albums was banned as obscene. Gates contended that the group's threatening cultural *ethos*, not obscenity *per se*, brought on court action ('Two'). Part of this *ethos* was a racially-inflected opposition to governmental authority and conventional morality. Taste was an index of, and a cloak for, racial style and subjectivity.

The tasteful citizen has, therefore, never been universal in practice. The history of aesthetics finds a feeling, sensate romantic (perhaps male?) figure who can locate and luxuriate in the radiance of an object of beauty. This romantic soul's 'other worldly' take on the sublime is transferable to his lesser co-nationals. No longer the processual quality that derives from the specific meeting of a will and a text, transcendence detaches itself from a particular human agent and becomes a quality of the object observed, the text. Now, the aesthetic is an object (that text) and no longer a practice (the romantic soul and the text). As an object, it becomes available for redisposal as a method of pedagogic formation. New people are to be formed through the experience of being led to the aesthetic sublime in interaction with this text. This is the moment when they are brought into the cultural fold, when the twin registers of the anthropological and the aesthetic merge. But as the next section demonstrates, this merger is never permitted to reach a climax. It is an ultimately unattainable desire.

Shaping and Managing Ethically Incomplete Subjects

Clearly, then, the merger of governmentality and taste finds cultural policy dedicated to producing subjects via the formation of repeatable styles of conduct, either at the level of the individual or the public. Jacques Donzelot brings the terms together in his concept of policing, alluded to earlier. It describes 'methods for developing the quality of the population and the strength of the nation' (6–7). For middle-class reformers in nineteenth-century Western Europe, teaching the working class to value the nation was the best bet for avoiding industrial strife and class struggle. That process began by improving urban life, and proceeded to instill collective investment in the patrimony (Lloyd and Thomas 18). Policing was conceived as a struggle between reason and unreason for 'the public mind'. The irrational aspects of subjects would be made known to them as a preliminary to their mastery of life and its drives. Journalist Norman Angell's speech in acceptance of the Nobel Peace Prize for 1935 represents policies informed by such anxieties. He calls for public education to demonstrate the subject's ethical incompleteness to itself, so that this indeterminacy can be worked on in the interest of social harmony: 'First, the ordinary citizen and voter must acquire a greater awareness of his own nature, his liability to certain follies, ever recurrent and ever disastrous' (quoted in JDB Miller 56, 59). In other words, the way to produce well-tempered, manageable cultural subjects who could be formed and governed through institutions and discourses was to inscribe ethical incompleteness in two-way shifts between the subject as a singular, private person and as a collective, public citizen that could govern itself in the interests of the polity.

Cultural policy, both elite and popular, is much concerned with the legitimate interests of the polity. So, for example, the newly emergent and triumphant *bourgeoisies* of nineteenth-century Western Europe wanted a *laissez-faire* ideology that favored *new* kinds of privilege, based on market success. They also sought a national ideology that connected these monetary freedoms to social control via national identification and the ethical uplift of art – a Kantian-Arnoldian formula (McGuigan *Culture* 55). As monarchical systems were gradually displaced by democracies, leaders needed legitimacy in order to tax the populace and hence finance a standing army (Borneman and Fowler 490).

No surprise then for Jean-Jacques Rousseau to insist that '[I]t is not enough to say to the citizens, be good; they must be taught to be so' (130), or that the Preamble to the US Constitution specifies the need 'to form a more perfect Union' and 'to ensure domestic tranquility'. Similar heads of power endorsed cultural subvention in Revolutionary France, where the *Declaration of the Rights of Man* was distributed to all schools in 1793 to help children distinguish between public and private virtues, conceptualize female citizenship, and contemplate the rights of the child. Anxieties about the revolution's future, which were close upon reformers by that year, generated numerous publications for young people, designed to create a new kind of public person. Instruction in citizenship appeared in manuals, non-religious catechisms, and alphabets. These texts established a close nexus between political and ethical principles. The citizens of tomorrow were expected to know their *Rights of Man* in the same sense – and with the same purpose – as they could recite and live out codes of manners and lists of facts, or recognize a variety of typefaces. But unlike other manuals of conduct, such as the variety that flourished in the nineteenth century, the revolutionary primer addressed a reader who would constitute a new social order, not await integration into an existing one.

Cultural policy in the Third Republic in France aimed to instantiate a republican sentiment via drama. Where early Revolutionary theatre made the occasion of performance into the originating text – with the canon residing in the pleasures of the populace, rather than in an inviolable textual classicism – this was quickly displaced by a core of tracts to uplift the citizenry, as per the aesthetic elitism described earlier. Jules Michelet used drama as an article of education to connect people who were otherwise dissociated from one another. The theatre was 'le meilleur espoir de la rénovation nationale' [the best hope for national renewal]. By the 1880s, the Ministry of the Beaux Arts encouraged the construction of 'the people' as a national entity, utilizing their comparatively recent literacy and enfranchisement in a double move of allegiance and participation that would bind them to the Third Republic, even as it spoke to their drives for pleasure and accessibility. The same period in Britain saw an intimate connection between calls for a national theatre as a conduit to public contemplation of the state of the nation and subsequent self-improvement (Kruger).

Where eighteenth-century Europe saw the emergence of the human being as the center of the new sciences, with the promise of new freedoms through self-knowledge, the nineteenth century's 'mature' capitalism required a specialized division of person and labor in all areas of life, with New York its center. By the middle of the twentieth century, the international center of cultural gravity had passed from Europe to the United States – or was 'stolen' by it (Guilbaut). A crisis emerged between the logics of civility and management because of an overcoded economic rationalism whose apogee was 'technocratic centralism', to use Julia Kristeva's summary. There seemed to be a lack of fit between the logic of developing technology and the values it was supposed to serve. C Wright Mills introduced 1959 readers of *The Listener* to the 'post-modern period'. Postmodern because freedom and reason, the joint inheritances granted to liberalism and socialism by the Enlightenment, had 'virtually collapsed' before the overweening priority given to a rationality dedicated to efficient centralization (Mills 236–37, 244).

By the time US cultural critic Christopher Lasch published *The Culture of Narcissism* twenty years later, this postmodern turn sounded more like a post-mortem for the American character. Lasch attributed the turn for the worse to 'quite specific changes in our society and culture – from bureaucracy, the pro-liferation of images, therapeutic ideologies, the rationalization of the inner life, the cult of consumption, and in the last analysis from changes in family life and from changing patterns of socialization' (32). Mass culture had hastened the turn away from rational citizenship and toward a society of the spectacle's trade in images, as per emulation of black ghetto *patois* and taste by 'middle-class society'. This expressed a 'widespread loss of confidence in the future', whose only palliatives were living for the present through self-indulgence (67–68). Lasch discerned a 'pathological narcissism' of the 'performing self' in the rise of aesthetic populism, the waning of affect, the escalation of self-consciousness exemplified by parody and historicism, the erosion of authority, the displacement of artistically unified work by texts comprised of differences, and above all the abolition of critical distance (Jameson). This culture of narcissism resulted from a 'bureaucratization of the spirit' through government programs that had established criteria for social service Lasch (90). People became 'connoisseurs of their own performance and that of others', with the 'whole man' fragmented into multiple identities (93) that pre-saged cultural politics based on race, gender, sexuality, and so on.

As you will see, unlike Lasch, we welcome many of these postmodern developments – not least because we lack nostalgia for the supposed organi-cism of an anterior time, – which is really code for a period when subordinated groups 'knew their place'. Nevertheless, it has to be acknowledged that cultural policy's synergistic complex of government programs, media representations, and market lures, has accommodated itself to, and in the process blunted the radical potential of, this repudiation of the well-rounded individual. Cultural policy always implies the management of populations through suggested behavior. Normalization has different performative forces in different times and places, variously enjoining universal adoption of *bourgeois* manners or stratifying access to cultural and other material resources on the basis of other demographic categorizations (e.g. the five pan-ethnic groupings characteristic of the US census, media and consumer markets, and political voting blocs). Such normalizing power sets an ideal that can never quite be attained, yet must be striven for.

The notion of 'ethical incompleteness' is premised on instilling a drive towards perfection (as the best possible consumer, patriot, ideologue or Latino). The process inscribes a radical indeterminacy in the subject, in the name of loyalty to a more complete entity – the nation. Cultural policy finds, serves, and nurtures a sense of belonging, through educational and other cultural regimens that are predicated on an insufficiency of the individual against the benevolent historical backdrop of the sovereign state. These regimens are the means of forming a collective public subjectivity, via what John Stuart Mill termed 'the departments of human interests amenable to governmental control' (68).

Some of this is done in the name of maintaining culture, to preserve ways of being a person or ensure governmental control over a population in terms of ethnicity, age, gender, faith, or class – though the last two are rarely cited as justifications for state intervention. These regimens can also manage change, often by advancing new modes of expression. Whilst there are superficial differences between a collectivist *ethos* and Mill's individualistic utilitarianism, they share the precept that ethico-aesthetic exercise is necessary for the responsible individual (Lloyd and Thomas 121). 'Good taste' becomes both a sign of and a means towards better citizenship. This ethico-aesthetic exercise also has a postmodern version: culture is the legitimizing ground on which particular groups (e.g. African Americans, gays and lesbians, or the hearing-impaired) can make a claim for resources and inclusion in the national narrative, if only to decenter it (Yúdice 'For a Practical'). They do so by calling up the alibis used to privilege specific cultural forms on behalf of the totality of the social.

Funding Alibis

Of course, the ideas of a universal philosophy of taste and a technology of ethical incompleteness for imposing it, still have to contend with competing social politics, even within dominant classes. Crucially, cultural policy raises difficulties for ideologues on behalf of the supposedly non-paternalistic state that simply allows its citizens the opportunity to determine their own cultural wants and needs. If cultural-capitalist societies identify themselves as sources of free expression, as evidenced in the absence of a state that seeks to direct the work of art, what should be their governments' stance on culture? Should they adopt one at all? Western cultural-capitalist countries are wont to take two rhetorical positions here. The first offers the market as a system for identifying and allocating public preferences for culture, denying the state a role other than as a police officer patrolling the precincts of property – deciding who owns what and how objects should be exchanged. The second identifies certain artifacts as transcendentally laden with value, but vulnerable to the public's inability to remain transcendental in its tastes. This latter position encourages a *dirigiste* role for the state, one that appears to coerce the public into aestheticization and is routinely accused by certain critics of 'cultural magistracy'. Nevertheless, it would be misleading to argue that the market and the state do not work in tandem in many situations. In some cases, cultural-capitalist and *dirigiste* roles operate together, as the market is declared the proper venue for the culture industries, while heritage, particularly that of indigenous peoples and minorities, is administered by the state. There is also an increasing monetarization of heritage, across the First and Third Worlds, led by governments. Heritage tourism schemes involve capitalist enterprises, state assistance, and international financial institutional investment by agencies such as the World Bank, the Inter-American Development Bank, and kindred organizations, in collaboration with third-sector, non-governmental organizations (NGOs).

Ronald Dworkin divides the public subvention of culture between 'the economic and the lofty'. The economic approach suggests that community support for culture is evidenced through the mechanics of price. The lofty approach suggests that a command culture is necessary, because market processes emphasize desire rather than improvement, and hence favor pleasure over sophistication. We could name this false taste consciousness. Markets fail to encourage and sustain art's function of defining and developing universal human values and forms of expression, because popular taste is ephemeral. Of course, conventional capitalist logic is opposed to the deployment of public funds in the service of an ethically derived set of preferences – the contested presumption that 'it is more worthwhile to look at a Titian on a wall than watch a football game on television'. As most people supposedly prefer the latter – a preference that can be quantified through preparedness to pay for the right – it is paternalistic to force them to subsidize the former as part of their generic tax burden on the grounds that timeless art can in fact only survive if the *poloi* are required to admire it. Art may, however, be reconceived within the economic wing of this Manichean divide, as a public good that makes a collective contribution to the aesthetico-intellectual functioning of a community, via the mutual impact of popular and high culture. On this view, art can be subsidized so long as it contributes to the community. Insofar as it does, it parallels popular culture's impact. And both art and popular culture contribute, one to intellection and the other to fun. The idea is to allow the market to gauge popular taste, and the state to ensure the continuation of elite taste and heritage appreciation – a method of keeping unpopular history alive and at the forefront of culture. As Gordon Graham (770) poses it: 'Sport, though valuable, is essentially a release and distraction. Great art is directly concerned with human experience and its ennoblement' – an opposition between pleasure and enlightenment. This notion of culture as fun (via the market) and progress (via the state) is central to much cultural policy.

The contribution of the aesthetic to the collectivity can be assessed in two ways. Beatriz Sarlo argues, as per Lasch, that in contrast to the speed and ephemerality of popular, consumerist culture, aesthetico-cognitive culture requires slow processing and critical thinking, which are ultimately necessary for the proper functioning of the polity. Sarlo laments the disappearance of a serious engagement with the aesthetic dimension in recent English, US, and Australian cultural studies. In her view, a symbolic practice's semantic density and formal complexity endow its producers and interpreters with a critical faculty that cannot be delivered by more popular forms of cultural expression, such as pop music, television, celebrity performance and cyberculture. They lack the 'excess' which escapes the rationalization of distribution or the logic of the commodity, a logic to which, she argues, cultural studies practitioners have capitulated.

But if this were the case, then the US, as the epicenter of the audiovisual, would presumably lead the way in a popular incapacity to appreciate, for example, the performing arts. But this is not so. Consider the data comparing them with sport and cinema:

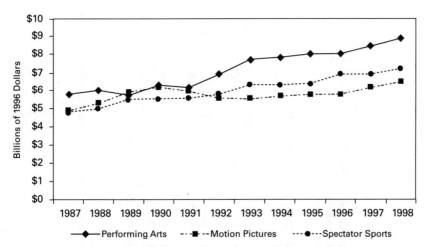

Source U.S. Department of Commerce Bureau of Economic Analysis

Figure 1 *Admission Receipts for Performing Arts Events, Motion Pictures, and Spectator Sports in 1996 Dollars: 1987–1998*

So, in place of these critiques by Lasch and Sarlo, we turn here to Walter Benjamin's insight that 'turning points of history' are accompanied by challenges to the optical and tactile 'apparatus of perception' (240). Following this reasoning, semantic density and formal complexity do not constitute the only practices that shape cognitive faculties. New habits of sensorial appropriation, such as those fostered by the cinema (Benjamin's example) can hone critical faculties in an analogous manner, although not necessarily in conformity with the cognitive skills developed in previous historical periods. There are different

Admission Receipts to	1997 $ Millions		1996 $ Millions		1995 $ Millions		1994 $ Millions		1993 $ Millions		1992 $ Millions	
	Current	Constant	Current	Constant	Current	Constant	Current	Constant	Current	Constant	Current	Constant
Specified Entertainments (change from previous year)	**23,192**	**19,185**	22,060	18,891	20,218	18,246	18,973	17,821	18,108	17,803	16,559	16,559
	5.1%	**1.6%**	9.1%	3.5%	6.6%	2.4%	4.8%	0.1%	9.4%	7.5%	5.1%	1.8%
Performing Arts	**10,380**	**8,583**	9,317	7,980	8,711	7,864	8,175	7,680	7,795	7,665	6,796	6,796
	11.4%	**7.6%**	7.0%	1.5%	6.6%	2.4%	4.9%	0.2%	14.7%	12.8%	13.5%	10.0%
Motion Pictures	**6,540**	**5,414**	6,237	5,419	5,970	5,385	5,592	5,248	5,220	5,131	4,991	4,991
	3.4%	**-0.1%**	6.0%	0.6%	6.8%	2.6%	7.1%	2.3%	4.6%	2.8%	-5.4%	-8.5%
Spectator Sports	**6,272**	**5,188**	6,416	5,492	5,537	4,997	5,206	4,893	5,093	5,007	4,772	4,772
	-2.2%	**-5.5%**	15.9%	9.9%	6.4%	2.1%	2.2%	-2.3%	6.7%	4.9%	6.4%	3.0%

Source: U.S. Department of Commerce, Bureau of Economics Analysis

Research Division Note #69
National Endowment for the Arts
September, 1998

Figure 2   *Admission Receipts for Performing Arts Events, Motion Pictures and Spectator Sports: 1992–1997*

cognitive styles, and they do not all rely on a high-aesthetic training. Certain styles have little to do with the internal workings or complexity of a practice. They are more connected to interactivity (as in theater and stadium sport) or citationality (parody, pastiche, and sampling, which were mainstreamed in the digital age). The value of these alternatives does not ensue from density or complexity, but from the ways in which interaction and citation are organized – part of which, of course, also relates to the impact of the state, the market, and the media on cognition, via education and the interpretive techniques that inform cultural policy.

Dworkin charts a third way to support culture, beyond the market and culture-crats. In their place, he proposes 'a rich cultural structure' to undergird the social world of both the contemporary moment and its imagined descendants, allowing for old and new cognitive registers. This structure is valuable not because it produces pleasures of the moment, fleeting joys of fashionable accessibility, but because it generates complexity and difference; for in differ-ence can be found the flexibility to produce pleasure at *other* times and places, through an audience protected from the ephemerality of fashion. Dworkin denies that this is an imposition of uplift. Deflecting potential charges of pater-nalism, he appeals to a notion of trusteeship. This trusteeship conserves the historically contingent (in terms of taste), in order that currently unfashionable options for pleasure can be made available to future generations. Diversity is supported over popularity or excellence, because it is a rubric of difference rather than taste or value (Dworkin 221–33).

Dworkin's move submerges the loftiness of training inside a heritage-inflected economism. Yet its exchange between excellence and difference presumes a capacity to differentiate between structure and content, singularity and normalcy, repetition and innovation, which in itself involves a training in distinction – cataloguing people and their preferences. As categories and valencies are themselves historically and politically derived, these differentiations can never be reduced to innocent technical calculation. In other words, Dworkin still presumes to know the difference between what does and does not matter to an era. Just as the apparently timeless horizon of truth claimed for free-market economics is bounded by a definite history, so this attempt to broker a *rapprochement* between non-interference and cultural magistracy secrets an inevitably tight connection between artistic work and social scaffolding.

Be that as it may, Dworkin's reconciliation of the 'economic and the lofty' references a dilemma for cultural policy almost everywhere, as part of the need to elaborate the nation to itself. The Australian Labor Party's 1986 policy *Platform*, for instance, maintained that the 'basis of Australian society lies to a significant extent in the strength of its own artistic and creative expression. Government has a responsibility to encourage the development of an Australian culture'. In 1992, as the North American Free Trade Agreement (NAFTA)/Tratado del Libre Comercio (TLC) was about to be signed into law, the Mexican government created a National Council for Culture and the Arts (CONACULTA) to allay any fears that the Agreement might lead to a loss of sovereignty – the director of CONACULTA arguing that 'the solidity of our culture is the substrate of our identity ... and the bulwark of our sovereignty' – and to modernize Mexican society by capitalizing on the cultural diversity necessary for success in a globalizing world (Tovar y de Teresa 17, 19–20). As we shall see, these claims have been repudiated by officials who approach cultural policy from the special relation between localization and globalization (World Commission on Culture and Development; Intergovernmental Conference).

A similar concern for a governmental role in fostering culture as a means of furthering a national project is evident in the 1965 law enacting the United States' National Endowments for the Arts (NEA) and Humanities (NEH). The legislation states that '[i]t is necessary and appropriate for the federal government to help create and sustain not only a climate encouraging freedom of thought, imagination, and inquiry but also the material conditions facilitating the release of this creative talent'. Looking back a quarter of a century later, a Congressional sponsor of this legislation, John Brademas, maintained that 'the arts are essential' because 'art and artists make an immense difference by enriching our lives as individuals and building a culture that illumines and enobles us'. He argued that art would 'nurture the creativity of our nation'. The evidence given in support of this assertion was a quotation from Robert Motherwell, who declared that cultural creativity gives renewed focus to discovering real selves: 'an artist is ... a person skilled in expressing human feelings' (quoted in Brademas 95, 104–05). Such a statement need not be in opposition to the more overtly programmatic economic or political goals revealed by the NEH's quasi-religious 1985 *Annual Report*:

> The humanities are vitally important to the educational and cultural life of our nation, constituting as they do the soul of civilization, which has been formed over the course of the centuries. Preserving and transmitting this tradition serves to nurture and sustain our national character, helping to make the United States worthy of its leadership in the world. (quoted in Stimpson 34)

This Olympian mission reveals a significant fit between a humanistic faith in renewal of the social order through expression of the artistic *persona*, and a more vigorously confident aesthetic underwriting of military and economic power. No wonder George Bush *fils* could speak with such chilling certainty of his binary view of good and evil as civilizational markers in the aftermath to September 11, 2001.

Early in the Cold War, US cultural sponsorship claimed that freedom inhered to American modern art, in contrast to the command culture of the Soviet Union. The end of the Cold War required a new legitimizing narrative, discernable in the cultural sector's current claim that it can solve US social problems: enhance education, salve racial strife, reverse urban blight through cultural tourism, create jobs, reduce crime and perhaps even make a profit. Much as in classic cases of governmentality, artists are channeled like service providers to manage the social. And just as the academy has turned to 'managerial professionals' who bridge traditional liberal professions, 'a technical body of knowledge, advanced education ... professional associations and journals, codes of ethics – and corporate middle management in the business of producing students, research, outreach, institutional development, etc' (Rhoades and Slaughter 23) – so the cultural sector has burgeoned into an enormous network of arts administrators who mediate between funding sources, on the one hand, and artists and communities, on the other. Like their counterparts in the university and business worlds, they must produce and distribute the producers of art and culture. As per Dworkin, they are simultaneously clarifying, abetting, modifying, and countering market tastes.

This is often contested terrain, as social movements call on the state to maintain the varying identities that comprise its citizenry, and conservatives insist on a more assimilated unity. Proponents of cultural citizenship argue that social identity is developed and secured through a cultural context where collective senses of self are more important than individual ones, and rights and responsibilities can be determined in accordance with cultural membership rather than the individual (Fierlbeck 4, 6). For some critics, this flexibility can be achieved through a doctrine of cultural rights. For others, it is a by-product of universal access to education, a 'primary condition of free and equal citizen participation in public life' (A Rorty 162). This latter position opposes public funding to sustain specific cultural norms of familial or religious origin, calling instead for a curriculum designed to generate cosmopolitans who learn about their own country's public life and their 'global neighbors' in a way that does not adjudicate between identities as workers, believers, or any other forms of life that exist alongside one's culture of origin (A Rorty 164). Such a position is a collectivist flipside to human-capital arguments about liberal individuals maximizing their utility through investment in skills. Each is fundamentally concerned with efficient and effective social life.

National and Supranational Identities and State Projects

Having established the historical and philosophical trace of cultural policy, we now turn to its history in a national and supranational world. Nations and regions frequently declare their cultural specificity in order to legitimize and materialize unity, sometimes through decentralization and sometimes via centralization. So the Federal Republic of Germany put individual Landers in charge of cultural policy. Each Lander has a ministry for the arts. But the French system is centralized. A national Ministry of Culture employs many thousands of bureaucrats across archives, museums, performance, film, music, dance, books, and heritage, supplemented by over 20,000 private associations dedicated to culture, many of which receive state assistance (Home 'Structure'). Prior to Canadian confederation, the 1850s saw pressures to impose cultural protectionism in the shape of a tariff on books, as a means of promoting national identity through locally-produced literature. One might consider this in the same light as the proliferation of Canadian Government investigations of cultural nationalism since the Second World War (numerous Royal Commissions and policy reviews, going to such matters as the need for locally owned, locally textual culture industries) and major surveys of public opinion on cultural identity over the same period. These instruments represent an anxiety about putatively 'discrete' national entities in the face of a homogenizing multinational/US superforce. But they are also about industry policy – through a substitution effect that seeks to displace one source of production (foreign) by another (local), alongside an ideological effect.

Similar forces were at play in the most vibrant Latin American economies and societies of the 1920s and 1930s – Argentina, Brazil, and Mexico. They were characterized by corporatist pacts between state-aligned elites, who promoted import-substitution industrialization (ISI) and developmentalism, and an equally state-aligned popular nationalism that sought state welfare. The origins of the huge bureaucracies that provided support for a 'national-popular culture' can be traced to this paradoxical situation, which recreated the Western European entities that had been most responsible for supporting culture: education, radio, film, and ethnographic museums. 'People's culture' was disseminated from these venues, not outside the market, but within the culture industries, which were controlled and sometimes subsidized by the state. The most salient examples are *samba* and carnival in Brazil, and radio and film *rancheras* in Mexico. The nationalization of *samba*, for example, involved the intervention of the Vargas regime in the 1930s in the music industries, in various social institutions like carnival and 'popular' networks (Raphael; Vianna). This produced the very culture in whose name such arts were supposedly undertaken. In the process, the state became an arbiter of taste.

As we have seen, such taste formation is inevitably about forms of life as much as forms of art. For example, David Birch argues that the discourse of pan-Asian 'values' was invented across the 1970s and 1980s to protect oligarchical and monopolistic power structures in South-East Asia that felt threatened by the popular-cultural corollaries of international capitalism and their message of social transcendence, whereby commodities are said to animate a new world, a new life. 'Asian values' became a distinctive means of policing the populace in the name of an 'abiding' idea of personhood that was in fact a reaction to the growth of capitalism and participation in international cultural exchange, while press freedom was constrained in the name of nation-building (Birch 'Constructing' and 'An "Open"'). 'Asianness' became an alibi for domestic social control.

The exercise of authority has come to rely on the ability to enunciate a partial past, an account of history that births the present in an appropriately linear way and can be made to identify the concerns of the public (established in part through constitutive exclusions) with its collective heritage. We draw here on Tony Bennett's understanding of history as 'the locus through which the representations of the past circulated by the institutions comprising the public historical sphere are brought into contact with the historical record in order to be either corrected by it or allowed to change with it'. Historians act as referees for example, in discussions over museums, heritage sites, and historical miniseries (Bennett *Outside* 50, 290 n. 17, 163–64). It follows that cultural policy produces zones of public memory and learning, organized by rules and colored by debates in historiography, that regulate the past, in a way that is determined by the concerns of the present.

Re-engineering history is the principal means by which Mexico charted a new and more inclusive national identity as it broke with a nineteenth-century, post-colonial but Eurocentric, legacy. The revolutionary Mexican Constitution of 1917 ushered in a new national project of mass education to jumpstart the economy, incorporate the masses, and create a large educated and nationalist middle class capable of resisting the power of *caudillos* (local bosses) as well as national and foreign oligarchies. Education projects embodied artistic expression in the muralist movement, identified with *los tres grandes* (the three great ones): Diego Rivera, Clemente Orozco and David Alfaro Siqueiros. Muralism infused the public face of Mexican identity with strong indigenist features. This movement was engendered by José Vasconcelos, who was appointed in 1920 by Presidents Huerta and Obregón as Director of the Departamento Universitario y de Bellas Artes, which included the Secretaría de Instrucción Pública y Bellas Artes (subsequently Secretaría de Educación Pública or SEP). Cultural and educational policy were intensified and further institutionalized in the 1930s under the populist president Lázaro Cárdenas, with a greater focus on incorporating indigenous populations, expanding arts education, defending national patrimony, and regulating the film industry (R Johnson 136).

This (re-)engineering of history is usually contested terrain, for all the efforts of governments. The well-documented struggle between Jewish leaders to construe the Holocaust as a uniquely Jewish event, Ronald Reagan's identification of the Soviets with the Nazis (even as he attempted to appease the Jewish community in the US) and conservative Germans' claims that Nazi soldiers were also victims, exemplify such contestation (Friedman). And consider the struggle over cultural appropriation that broke out in Canada in the early 1990s. Native Canadian writers were concerned that their 'voices' had been subject to 'theft' by whites. The Canada Council's Advisory Committee for Racial Equality in the Arts responded by issuing guidelines on the concept that attacked 'the depiction of minorities or cultures other than one's own, either in fiction or non-fiction' (quoted in Coombe 209). The Council decided that it would no longer issue grants to authors who crossed the boundary between cultures without the active participation of the 'other'. Writers replied to this *force-majeure* collaboration derisively, claiming the autonomy of art from politics and the need for an unfettered expression of the imagination in order to unleash Romantic genius. On the other side, the Council showed signs of an Orientalist commitment to an essential Native Canadian identity, unchanging and universally distributed by virtue of race. This biological/customary status supposedly stood beyond history (and hence lacked the ability to change its circumstances) (Coombe 209–13).

Other uses of national heritage to broker international deals abound. For example, in the 1990s, Taiwan decided to redirect the energies of its perfor-mance troupes when touring overseas. Instead of targeting the diasporic Chinese, such companies would look to open new markets via 'international publicity and cultural interflow', to quote the Ministry of Foreign Affairs (Wang). In the British case, the Arts Council of Great Britain, formed in 1945 under John Maynard Keynes, had, as its principal original task, the rescue of Covent Garden from war-time use as a dance hall, returning the venue to its musical origins as a Royal Opera. This stress on high culture and centralization in London continued as settled policy until the mid-1960s Labour government formed Regional Arts Associations, which devolved public culture (to Scotland and Wales in particular). By the late 1970s, the modernist and political nature of much publicly funded work drew strong objection from Tory hacks such as Kingsley Amis and Paul Johnson. When the Conservative Party came to power in 1979, one point of key resistance was Labour local councils, which used the language of economic development to promise cultural reindustrialization. The national government disestablished local political representation, putting an end to such initiatives, but retained and developed the principle of region-alized arts administration (McGuigan *Culture* 57, 64–65, 106). Many critics doubt the industrial and aesthetic efficacy of such moves. Consider *The Beatles* and Liverpool. The city's music, clothing, football, and voice became part of the fabric of youth culture across the world. But as Angus Calder notes, the city governors of the time were 'innocent of "cultural" objectives'. And its rich 1980s television drama was produced under a radical–left administration that concentrated on public housing rather than aesthetics (454). Now, the city's reformist local government uses culture to attract capital investment in heritage tourism; but there is no clear correlation with cultural innovation. Instead, policy is a mop for deindustrialized 'waste', with gentrification assisted by government. Here, the idea of building citizenship has been overdetermined by a search for building culture as a substitute for building ships – a way of quieting citizens whose lives have been buffeted by unregulated global capital. We turn next to the citizens who have been theorized and produced in this rootless world.

Citizenship and Culture in a Postnational World

The ideal of citizenship takes three forms: political, economic and cultural. Political citizenship encompasses voting, the capacity to appeal to represen-tative government, and guarantees of physical security that people are given in return for ceding the right to violence to the state. As developed through capi-talism, slavery, colonialism and liberalism, political citizenship has expanded its reach and definition exponentially since the eighteenth century, though it remains unevenly distributed across the globe. Economic citizenship covers employment, health, and retirement security through redistribution of capitalist profits and the use of the state as an agent of investment. Having developed through the Depression and decolonization, economic citizenship is now in decline, displaced by historic renegotiations by capital, the state, and their intellectual servants in economics since the 1970s to privatize economies. Cultural citizenship concerns the maintenance and development of cultural lineage via education, custom, language, and religion, and the acknowledgement of difference in and by mainstream cultures. It is a developing discourse, in response to the great waves of migration of the past fifty years and an increasingly mobile middle-class workforce generated by a New International Division of Cultural Labor (NICL). As we have seen, in its role as a custodian of nationalism, the idealized Western state endeavors to form cultural citizens who will be virtuous political participants through self-scrutiny and self-improvement. This pedagogic style may appeal to national objectives of economic or cultural growth, patriotism, educating populations into artistic appreciation, or 'unlocking' creative talent that awaits the opportunity to express itself.

Citizenship is taken as a given in all modern polities, although it does not function identically across or within different national formations, particularly in those non-Western countries where it was adopted as a construction of the postcolonial state and where polyethnicity has been a basis for discrimination. While Germany has recently expanded the rights of ethnically non-Germanic people born there, by eliminating ethnic criteria for citizenship, Croatia forecloses economic and political rights to Serbs on the basis of a renewed ethnocultural citizenship. Theocratic states, moreover, base eligibility to rights on the cultural criterion of religion, often limiting the citizenship rights of women. And what does it mean to foster self-improvement via education and museums when 90% of a country's population is illiterate? Literacy programs for example, in Mexican post-revolutionary cultural policy, address this 'lack', but do more to incorporate peasants and Indians into a language and labor regime than endow them with the motivation to 'improve'. It may be that the dissemination of liberal and revolutionary ideas embodied in cultural policy, founder in the gap between the juridical people and the empirical people, as per Kant's analysis of the nation in 'the character of nations'. This raises the question of what Roberto Schwartz calls 'misplaced ideas'.

We are not saying that the Third World fails to develop authentic or autochthonous cultural policies, but rather that their socioeconomic situation points to the gap between the juridical and the empirical, the ideal and the real, the utopian and the present. A Third World perspective on this may lead to an ethnomethodological view, according to which cultural policy, even in Europe and the US, is not really about fashioning well-rounded individuals, but about creating bureaucracies that deal with the problems that the very institution of policies create! What does it mean in theocratic states for the governance of subjects to be situated in 'cultural knowledges and practices'? What does cultural citizenship mean in a country like Colombia, which is divided according to different power groups, and what was the cultural formation of individuals under late twentieth-century Latin American dictatorships whose conduct was limited to orthodox norms, where disloyal subjects were 'disappeared' or visibly murdered?

Latin American mimesis deviated from its European models because it was permeated by indigenous or African-derived practices (e.g. in syncretic religious forms or the unique baroque designs of church decoration) and Iberians and creoles cultivated a high culture at a remove from metropolitan centers and partly beholden to the cultures of the lower classes by defining themselves against the latter. This would come to be seen by some Latin American intellectuals in the twentieth century as a source of cultural innovation. The Brazilian writer Silviano Santiago, echoing Jorge Luis Borges, has argued that by supplementing already existing models, the constitutively excluded (i.e. Latin Americans vis–à–vis Europe, or blacks and mixed-race people vis–à–vis creoles) have been able to appropriate, transform or debunk status models without fetishizing them. We have here a possible postmodern understanding of cultural policy as appropriation that characterizes Latin American cultural production at all social levels, although no cultural bureaucracies have yet shown the temerity to promulgate 'subversive simulation' as policy. More typically, the state endorsed the efforts of some colonial and postcolonial intellectuals to counter America's secondary status by appealing to what was presumed to be original and thus national: the sublime force of nature, or the greatness of Aztec and Incan civilizations of the past. But even here they were dependent on the pathbreaking research of European naturalists (von Humboldt) and ethnographers (Koch-Grünberg). And European intellectuals were always quick to put down these attempts at self-valorization. Cornelius De Pauw, for example, argued that all natural species in the New World were inferior to those of the Old (Gerbi). Many nineteenth-century historians derided Bolívar as a pale reflection of US independence heroes. Even Marx and Engels endorsed the annexation of Mexican lands and thought all of Mexico should have been taken by the US in order to bring it up to date historically, that is, to unleash the 'objective' forces of class struggle by imposing 'true' bourgeois rule, in the process creating a proletariat (Marx (1968) Karl Marx on Colonialism 18).

If nineteenth- and early twentieth-century mimesis was concerned with cultural and economic development, the contemporary manifestation is the discourse of citizenship rights. Despite its mission of instilling loyalty in citizens, contemporary cultural policy is linked by the left to citizen rights, a means of tying social-movement claims to actionable policy and a newly valuable form of entitlement that transcends class and is a guarantee against the excesses of both the market and state socialism. On the right, culture is subject to privatization pressures. Citizens and consumers continue their uncertain dance in the rhetoric of political philosophy, neoclassical economics and neoliberal policy mandarinism (Zolberg 'Paying' 396; Miller *Well–Tempered*). An additional division on the right exists between those who consider that citizens' responsibilities go beyond the self, and those who do not.

Traditional views of citizenship have been thrown into confusion by the extent of late twentieth-century immigration and multiculturalism (Feldblum 103). Whereas republican ideals assume a migrant subject who throws off prior loyalties in order to become a citizen, or nationals of the same country who put aside social divisions in the common interest, multiculturalism blurs the lines between liberal individualism and collaborative communitarianism. Of course, liberal individualism is also about the opportunity to accumulate wealth and resources. It is not just, or even primarily, about transcendence. On the other hand, communitarianism can result in bloody contests between communities that have different senses of whose identity is to be recognized and allowed to stand for the whole. And alongside the drive to *discipline* the citizen, is the disposition to *showcase* and *market* the citizen. The culture of pre-citizen eras is often advertised in heritage tourism (France's Notre Dame and Versailles attract more visitors than the National Assembly).[2]

This new form of citizenship may not locate fealty in the sovereign state, nor does it necessarily articulate with democracy, as subjects of the international trade in labor lack the access to power of native-born sons and daughters (Preuss 310). Liberalism assumes, with neoclassical economics, that people emerge into citizenship fully-formed, as sovereign individuals with personal preferences. Multiculturalism assumes, with communitarianism, that group loyalties override this notion. But where communitarianism assumes people find their collective identity through political participation, multiculturalism assumes, with liberalism, that this subjectivity is ordained prior to politics (Shafir 10–11). And cultural policy has seen a series of debates in which seeming polar opposites – the right versus multicultural arts – appear to be logo-centrically interdependent. Each group dismisses traditional aesthetics in favor of a struggle to use art to represent identity and social purpose (Yúdice 'For a Practical' 130). Multiculturalism stresses the need for a grassroots and marginal arts activism, focused on civil rights, and a combination of demographic and artistic representation and representativeness. Conservatism calls for an arts practice that heralds Western values and progress while obeying the dictates of religious taste.

Orthodox histories of citizenship postulate it as the Western outcome of 'fixed identities, unproblematic nationhood, indivisible sovereignty, ethnic homogeneity, and exclusive citizenship' (Mahmud 633). This history ignores the fact that theories of citizenship were forged in relation to the imperial and colonial encounters of West and East as a justification of extra-territorial subjugation, followed by incorporation of the periphery into an international system of labor. These conditions in turn led to cultural policy concerns with language, heritage and identity, expressed by both metropole and periphery as they exchanged people and cultures.

Bonnie Honig has shown that immigrants have long been the limit-case for loyalty, as per Ruth the Moabite in the Jewish Bible/Old Testament. Such figures are both perilous for the sovereign state (where does their fealty lie?) and essential (as the only citizens who make a deliberate decision to swear allegiance to an otherwise mythic social contract). In the case of the US, immigrants are crucial to the foundational *ethos* of consent, for they represent alienation from their places of origin and endorsement of the New World. This makes a national culture all the more fraught, for just as the memory of what has been lost (by choice) is strong, so is the necessity to shore up the 'preference' expressed for US norms.

In Europe, the creation of 'supranational citizenship' in 1992 problematized coupling citizenship to national culture. At the same time that this recognized a new international division of labor, equivalent moves limited the rights of guest workers. Consider the situation of those who, because of changed socioeconomic conditions, have turned into officially acceptable migrant-citizens, such as Asian Australians since the 1970s. Excluding and brutalizing Asians had been critical to developing a sense of Australian citizenship and national identity for most of the twentieth century. Asian Australians' latter-day take on citizenship is, not surprisingly, instrumental (Ip et al.).

In each case, citizenship is no longer based on soil, blood, or culture. Rather, it is founded on some variant of those qualities in connection with existing pressures on the capitalist labor market. The state is no longer the key frame of citizenship, in the face of new nationalisms and cross-border affinities that no single governmental apparatus can contain (Feldblum 96, 98–99, 101, 110). Supranational citizenship and identity are not only tied to a new international division of labor, but also to a new trading order, in which juridically established trading blocs like NAFTA/TLC, the Mercado Común del Sur (MERCOSUR) and the European Union (EU) make decisions that override national laws. In fact, awareness that the rule of law transcends the nation state can lead to a more compelling supranational identity, as witnessed by the exponential increase over the 1990s in the number of cases brought by individuals to the European Court of Justice and the European Court of Human Rights (Roger Cohen 'Trade Pact').

Of course, many migrant workers around the world are neither citizens nor immigrants. Their identity is quite separate from their domicile and source of sustenance, with equitable treatment guaranteed not by a sovereign state, but through the supranational discourse of human rights and everyday customs and beliefs that superintend the legal obligations of conventional citizenship (Shafir 20, 19; also see Robin Cohen). Activists in these areas frequently turn to cultural policy to assist in the maintenance and development of collective identities and their expression in artistic form – hence its importance for the left, and cultural studies in particular.

Cultural Policy Studies

What is the existing state of English language cultural policy studies? The *ur*-text on the economics of cultural assistance was published twenty years ago by Australian-based researchers, and it is twenty-five years since Herbert Gans' pathbreaking work on 'taste cultures' provided a multiple layered framework for intellectualizing the popular and its relationship to policy (Throsby and Withers; Gans *Popular* 121–59). 'Cultural policy studies' was named and undertaken in the 1970s through the formation of the Association of Cultural Economics and the Center for Urban Studies at the University of Akron. This was followed by regular conferences on economics, social theory and the arts, and major studies of policy and program evaluation produced at Canada's Institute for New Interpretive Creative Activities, the Cultural Policy Unit of The Johns Hopkins Center for Metropolitan Planning and Research, the Cultural Information and Research Centres Liaison in Europe, and Columbia University's Research Center for the Arts and Culture. Publications such as the *Journal of Arts Management, Law and Society* and the *Journal of Cultural Economics* have long provided a wealth of theoretical speculation and empirical reporting and have latterly established connections to the Washington DC think-tank Center for Art and Culture. Europe now publishes the *International Journal of Cultural Policy*.

These developments have led to queries about the relationship between a humanities and a sociological basis to the area: whether there should be, for instance, 'a social science aesthetic', and how the new proxemics of administration, politics, and the arts should be ethically and technically managed, along with the need for both 'historical analysis *in* policymaking' and 'the history *of* policy' (Towse and Crain 1; Alderson 5; Hendon et al. x–xi; Chartrand 'Subjectivity' 23–24; Peterson 'Foreword' iii, v; Graham 21). But in general, the social sciences side to the analysis of culture holds onto value-free shibboleths and has not affiliated with progressive social change.

By contrast, cultural studies has an overt political agenda about social movements and cultural worker's rights. Angela McRobbie calls cultural policy 'the missing agenda' of cultural studies, given that it offers a program for change (335). But Stuart Cunningham suggests that:

> Many people trained in cultural studies would see their primary role as being critical of the dominant political, economic and social order. When cultural theorists do turn to questions of policy, our command metaphors of resistance and opposition predispose us to view the policy making process as inevitably compromised, incomplete and inadequate, peopled with those inexpert and ungrounded in theory and history or those wielding gross forms of political power for short-term ends. These people are then called to the bar of an abstrusely formulated critical idealism. (*Framing* 9)

The notion that theory undergirds practice via a renewing critique taken up by bureaucracies has often seemed misplaced in the cultural field, where everyday academic critical practice eschews such relationships as either insufficiently aesthetic or too co-optive. Cunningham attacks this line of argument as failing to acknowledge, for instance, that public action on sexism in advertising and the status of women in the workplace have come about because of a shift from utopic critique to implemented policy. He calls for cultural studies to adopt a 'political vocation' that draws its energies and direction from 'a social democratic view of citizenship and the trainings necessary to activate and motivate it'. This 'new command metaphor' will displace 'revolutionary rhetoric' with a 'reformist vocation'. Its 'wellsprings of engagement with policy' can nevertheless avoid 'a politics of the status quo – a sophomoric version of civics', because cultural studies' ongoing concern with power will always ground it in radicalism. Cunningham uses cultural policy studies as a conduit to cultural rights, access to information held by multinational corporations, international organizations, the balance of power between developed and less-developed countries, and how all these developments have an impact locally (*Framing* 11). Jim McGuigan welcomes this turn in cultural studies, provided it retains radical insights by connecting to political economy's emphasis on public debate and citizenship rights (*Culture* 21).

At the same time as we support this preparedness to engage actually existing politics, there is a truly sordid history to academic participation in so-called democratic government. Consider language-spread policy and the part played in it by linguists, let alone the work of economic advisors (Robert Triffin acting as plenipotentiary for the US to the European Economic Community and then as a European delegate to the International Monetary Fund, just a few months apart, in the 1980s), political scientists (Project Camelot in the 1960s), biomedical researchers (relations with pharmaceutical companies), public-relations consultants (a critical concern of the professional associations), anthropologists (cultural-relativist defences of male violence in court), nuclear physicists (red-baiting of scientists), and communication studies. The very existence of communication research raises questions of ideological distortion, given the discipline's formation under the sign of war and clandestine government activity and later corporate and foundation support (God bless the CIA, Wilbur Schramm and Daniel Lerner).

In the US, university consultancies date to nineteenth-century museums, observatories, and agricultural-experimentation outposts, but the shop was really set up in the late 1950s. Considerable effort since then has gone into clarifying the significance of tailoring research priorities to contemporary political parties and corporations: 'pork-barrel science', as it is known. Paul DiMaggio and Walter Powell suggest a trend towards homologies between sponsoring and consulting bodies: when one institution depends on another for assistance, it tends to mimic its structures and reiterate its concerns ('Iron' and *The New*). Ralph Nader's Center for Universities in the Public Interest was set up because of such concerns, which are even evident to former supporters of government/college/industry relationships who have experienced the obstacles they pose to disinterested research outcomes (*Language Problems and Language Planning;*

Markoff and Montecinos 44; Ammon 6; Nisbet; Beauchamp; 'Special'; Winkelman; Rieff; C. Simpson; Sholle 132; Rowe and Brown 98; Ruscio 209; Stahler and Tash; Bowie 5, 7; deLeon 886).

The policy sciences, originally conceived as a connection between democratic and executive action, frequently degenerate into 'unrepresentative expertise' that lacks articulation with public life. John S Dryzek's review of policy analysis suggests that the animating subjectivity is either of 'clients or spectators', not active citizens, while Thomas Streeter points out that advocacy of a policy focus in cultural studies may be inappropriate in the US, where 'policy' connotes a pro-corporate position that turns highly contestable positions into absolutes, with consultant professors simultaneously performing objectivity and applicability. (For example, the policy and program management of US National Parks has consistently owed much more to bureaucratic *force majeure*, tourism money and 'development', than to ecological science) (Dryzek 117; Streeter 16 n.14, 133, 136; Sellars 3–4).

It is vital to understand the difference between distilling, invoking and reforming the public mind. The shift between policy analysis and policy service and advocacy is an important one. Public administration was the refuge of the worthy but dry academic, until public policy emerged as a site for carpetbagging academics in search of influence and consultancy clothing. A rich analysis of political discourse has come from both spheres. And the lessons of this literature should form the founding texts of cultural policy studies. These lessons provoke skepticism about the fit between the rhetoric and practice of policy, because animating logics are often spurious or counter-indicative. Most significantly, social research has cast serious doubt on the notion that policy works because of the utterance of actionable rather than expressive proposals. The literature demonstrates the error of aligning organizations and actors with their statements, their statements with their actions, or either with actual outcomes (Stark 514–15; Jobert 381; Colebatch and Degeling; Egeberg).

Of course, cultural policy studies does not have to be carried out on behalf of corporations and the government offices that back corporate welfare. Not all academic and intellectual involvement bends to the right. The Communist-based intellectuals and academics of the cultural front were important in keeping New Deal cultural policies from complete accommodation to Roosevelt's administration; leftists counterbalanced nationalist bureaucrats in the US's Good Neighbor Policy; antiwar and antiracist activists were instrumental in establishing new cultural institutions in the 1960s and 1970s; academics joined political and religious activists in the 1980s in strengthening the solidarity and sanctuary movements on behalf of Central American insurgencies against US neoimperialism, and their participation contributed to the decentering of the literary canon and the rise of multiculturalism through the dissemination of texts by indigenous and oppressed people; and today, there is increasing work on labor rights for graduate students and cultural workers. All of this academic and intellectual activism is not at odds with instituting policy, but is crucial to that end. Anthropologists like Néstor García Canclini in Mexico make policy recommendations that avoid the production and reception parameters fostered by corporate interests. Research with the US-Mexico Fund for Culture and other Latin American government and non-governmental initiatives is not designed to further the interests of corporations, but to intervene in such a way that citizen and cultural rights are respected over the interests of capital accumulation and traditional elites. Critiques of cultural policy studies can be too knee-jerk, putting into the same category radical-democratic actors like Sonia Alvarez (formerly of the Ford Foundation) and Tomas Ybarra Frausto (of the Rockefeller Foundation) with those who promote the interests of capital and the status quo from the reactionary offices of RAND, Olin, Brookings, etc.

Some of the resources to conduct research from a radical-democratic perspective come from foundations and NGOs, the newly fetishized buffers between state, religion, population and media – prescriptions for third-sector change that can magically mediate between citizen, government, and corporation. That could help us find ways of dealing with immense contemporary transformations, akin to the world-economic shifts of two centuries ago that birthed governmentality. Civil society encompasses the amateur institutions and informal associations that emerged with the European Enlightenment as alternatives to the compulsion associated with the state's rule of law and the other-worldly mysticism of organized religion. These new zones were both secular and voluntary, sometimes encompassing the new phenomenon of the market. Today, with states and markets frequently reinforcing and validating one another, non-religious, cultural civil society is transformed into a new third sector that straddles each but is beholden to neither. The US has two million such institutions, almost all of them formed since 1970. Russia has gained 650,000 since the end of state socialism, and Kenya births 240 a year. Most NGOs associated with aid are effectively regranting institutions that utilize state moneys in ways designed to avoid accusations of neocolonialism from the left and governmental waste from the right. So the US gives US$700 million annually to Africa through surrogates, and Médecins Sans Frontières derives a significant proportion of its budget from state agencies. Some bodies become captive of their real funders – so Congress' taste for good Christian souls holding the purse strings has led to the neologism RINGOs (religious NGOs), symbiotic relations with governments produce GRINGOs (governmental NGOs), and corporate self-modeling offers BINGOs (business NGOs) (*Economist*). No wonder the World Bank's claim that NGOs guarantee a mixed-Internet model for the Third World reads so spuriously (Nulens and Van Audenhove 459). This is clearly an attempt to sidestep the relationship of culture to state and market domination through a 'Third Way'. That appeals to cultural studies activists.

NGO rallying cries of expressivity and representativeness can make for real change. Consider how the place of indigenous cultures in official Mexican national identity was put into question beginning in the late 1970s, following pressure from indigenous groups and a cohort of anthropologists and sociologists who worked with them, like Guillermo Bonfil Batalla, Rodolfo Stavenhagen and García Canclini. They challenged institutionalized indigenism, because it restricted indigenous people to empirically erroneous and politically debilitating representations of their culture. Stavenhagen, for example, denounced assimilationist precepts within the ecology of Mexican identity as promoted by anthropological, museological and social-service institutions (5). Bonfil Batalla called for a redefinition of the researcher as a collaborator in the projects of subaltern communities. He proposed this collaboration as a necessary retooling for social scientists who were seeing their traditional functions disappear thanks to neoliberalism and privatization. These changes displaced the anthropologist from his or her function as a facilitator of national integration, as per a pact that had been struck between the state and civil society in the post-revolutionary 1930s (18–19). García Canclini, in turn, sought not only to refashion the organization, production, marketization, and consumption of popular culture, but also the creation of a new public sphere and even a new tourism industry from which to rethink and re-experience culture.

Such debates center key questions in cultural studies: identity, authenticity, authorial genius, Orientalism (or indigenism), the postcolonial and the state. Clearly, this is appropriate terrain for applying the insights of the most radical critics, with two questions always kept in mind: What do policy analysts have to offer without links to social movements? And what does cultural studies have to offer without ties to institutions? When we think about oppositional theory, Umberto Eco, Noam Chomsky, Jean-François Lyotard and García Canclini recur as signs. Some of their most famous work was born of cultural consultancy and state funding: Eco's TV semiotics for Italian state broadcasting ('Towards'), Chomsky's transformational generative grammar for the Joint Services Electronics Programs of the US military, Lyotard's report on the postmodern for the government of Québec (La Condition), and García Canclini's postmodern theory of hybridity from a report on indigenous crafts (Hybrid Cultures). These links to policy are more than investigations of how 'taste' becomes 'technique', or efforts to ensure the 'promotion of the good, the true and the beautiful', as the editors of a 1980s volume on comparative cultural policy would have it (Cummings and Katz 5; Ridley 11). Such instances encourage a positive view of engagement, provided that the paymaster is subordinated to radical-democratic politics. They suggest a space of intervention.

Conclusion

Albrecht Dürer's Enlightenment-era *Painter's Manual* proposed a rational cultural policy that would instruct young people in perspectival and geometric relationships, as per the Kantian ideal. But Stephen Greenblatt's gloss of Dürer's plans for civic monuments glorifying historical events indicates how contingent legislated meaning can be:

A victory over rebellious peasants calls for a commemorative column – after all, the fate of worldly rule, that is human civilization itself, depends upon this struggle – and yet the enemy is an object of contempt and derision. The princes and nobles for whom such monuments were built could derive no dignity from the triumph, any more than they could derive dignity from killing a mad dog ... the peasants, of course, have no titles to seize, and can yield up no trophies to adorn the victor's monument. Indeed, in the economy of honor they are not simply a cipher but a deficit, since even a defeat at the hands of a prince threatens to confer upon them some of the prince's store of honor, while what remains of the victorious prince's store can be tarnished by the unworthy encounter. (Greenblatt *Learning* 108–09)

Herodotus' fifth-century BC *Histories* begins with what read like today's options for treating the past: to recount 'the astonishing achievements both of our own and of other peoples; and more particularly, to show how they came into conflict' (43). This hope for cultural policy, that it could provide a radical contextualization of the present, such that our understanding of ourselves is itself subject to critical historicization via a questioning of each statement's conditions of existence, is one positive side to cultural policy for the left.

That turn will not be welcome to all, especially those inclined to critique for its own sake, as some higher good. For Colin MacCabe, 'almost all appeals to "policy", like its repellent semantic cousin "management", are appeals away from a reality which is too various and too demanding' ('A Post–National' 192). But getting to know cultural policy and intervening in it is an important part of participating in culture. Resistance goes nowhere unless it takes hold institutionally. The gains made in world culture by women and people of color have come·about through harnessing the work of social movements to critiques of state policies and programs in actionable ways. That must be our axis – social-movement access and governmental articulation. Much of what you will read in the chapters to come points up what happens when those links are not in place, and when the less utopic, inclusive side to the UNESCO remarks with which we began this Introduction are dominant. We hope that *our* work aids you to practice the arts of governmentality in order to further a radical-democratic cultural politics.

---

1 Bello is speaking of what we now call 'Latin' America, for until World War II, and even after it in some cases, Latin Americans referred to themselves collectively as 'Americans', and to Anglo-America as the US or North America.

2 Of course, we cannot limit heritage tourism to the citizen frame, especially since so many visitors are foreigners. Heritage accrues to those who are current citizens, which may be inaccurate historically, as in those countries where indigenous cultures are celebrated as national patrimony by the descendents of settler colonists.

1

The United States, Cultural Policy, and the National Endowment for the Arts

When we get control of that National Endowment for the Arts, you'll see how it ought to be done. You shut it down, fumigate the building and put the I.R.S. [Internal Revenue Service] in there – Pat Buchanan, Republican and Reform Party candidate for President, speechwriter for Richard Nixon, and CNN nightly commentator, 1999. (quoted in Roane)

This chapter addresses the great historical paradox of culture – that its principal exporter, the United States, claims to be free of any policy on the matter. In questioning this *donnée*, we examine the role of the state in culture, with particular reference to the National Endowment for the Arts (NEA) – its birth, attempted murder, and assisted-living resuscitation.

In 1965, the year that the Federal Government began to establish such domestic cultural institutions as public broadcasting and an arts endowment, the US already housed more museums than Western Europe, more libraries than any other country, and half the world's symphony orchestras (Moen 'Congress' 186). But the government's paper at UNESCO's 1969 Monaco Round Table on Cultural Policies began with the famous line: 'The United States has no official cultural position, either public or private' (quoted in Kammen 798, 795). Put another way, a profound American commitment to keeping the state separate from the production and restriction of meaning, notably evident in the free-speech guarantees of the First Amendment to the Constitution, saw the Federal Government purportedly decline to elevate, discriminate or even differentiate artistically. This paper's astonishing position, which bewilders both by its mendacity and its representativeness, has a long, bizarre lineage, and considerable ongoing resonance.

The *ethos* of democracy identified in Alexis de Tocqueville's eulogy to early nineteenth-century life in the US forcefully rejected European ruling-class accounts of civilization and how to stimulate it. De Tocqueville identified a widespread belief in the US that equality militated against artistic transcendence. There could be few patrons in an economic democracy, and so profoundly utilitarian a country as the US did not recognize the value of aesthetics. From the first, then, issues of migration and citizenship were critical to the relationship of government and art. An egalitarian philosophy, in keeping with upwardly mobile immigrants, supposedly flattened tastes through cultural relativism, denying in the process the age-old route to artistic distinction provided by a socially hierarchical rank order. Ennoblement was in the eye of the ennobled, rather than a universal quality. Practicality was preferred to artistry, in a New World driven by economic pressures to manufacture for the mass market, as opposed to a single, discriminating paymaster-patron. A utilitarian faith in the market allocating cultural resources was evident early on. So the relationship of the US Federal government and the arts began with copyright provisions authorized by the Founding Parents as a means of encouraging capitalist innovation (Van Camp 'Freedom' 53). When President John Quincy Adams asked Congress for money to start a national university, observatories and related programs in 1825, however, this led to accusations of political 'centralization' from Martin van Buren and John C Calhoun. De Tocqueville's account, and these tensions, have become touchstones of United States folklore and political culture (Filicko 221–23). There remains a special distaste for connecting culture to the state, other than in the service of dispossession and capital accumulation. Meanwhile, the entire fiction of the US as a sovereign entity of course rests on denying the link between archaeological artifacts and Native American ownership (based on the allegation that the burial sites and objects found in the North-East were Israeli or Phoenician). This is a clear and foundational instance of cultural policy (Nichols et al.).

Consider Hollywood: film and TV are crucial to US balance-of-trade figures (exporting US$36.8 billion in 1998) and ideological transfer. Hollywood is often cited as a case of a truly open market in which cultural creativity exists outside state policy. The US claims that its success is a function of satisfying the needs of audiences, not a consequence of policy. Indeed, the appeal to markets is superficially compatible with an audience-centered approach to dealing with the politics of recognition and diversity. Despite minimally adequate representation of US minorities, not to speak of other peoples throughout the world, US audiovisual policy, like US corporate culture more generally, uses 'diversity' for its own ends. As the saying goes, Hollywood favors one color – green (Crane; et al.; Gordon; Newfield; Yúdice 'Civil Society' 1995). The film industry is supposed to be a pure market of private enterprise and consumption, so it seems sensible to evaluate *laissez-faire* as an account of US screen production, to question whether this is a free market based purely on consumer demand.

The US government endorses trust-like behavior by film companies overseas, while prohibiting it domestically. The local film industry was aided through decades of tax-credit schemes, the old Informational Media Guaranty Program's currency assistance, and oligopolistic domestic buying and overseas selling practices that (without much good evidence for doing so) keep the primary market essentially closed to imports on grounds of popular taste. And after the Second World War, Hollywood's Motion Picture Export Agency referred to itself as 'the little State Department', so isomorphic were its methods and contents with Federal policy and ideology (Guback 'Government' 92–93, 98–99; Schatz 160; K Thompson 117–18, 122–23; Vasey 160, 164; Guback 'International' 156–57). Today, the US Department of Commerce produces materials on media globalization that focus on both economic development and ideological influence, problematizing claims that Hollywood is pure free enterprise and that Washington is uninterested in blending trade with cultural change (Ferguson 83–84; Jarvie 37, 40). Meanwhile, the Justice Department is authorized to classify all imported films, and has prohibited Canadian documentaries on acid rain and nuclear war as 'political propaganda' (Sorlin 93; Parker 135, 137). In 2000, the US had 205 state, regional, and city film commissions, hidden subsidies to the film industry (via reduced local taxes, free provision of police services and the blocking of public wayfares), State and Commerce Department briefings and plenipotentiary representation (negotiations on so-called video piracy have resulted in PRC offenders being threatened with beheading, even as the US claims to be watching Chinese human rights as part of most-favored nation treatment), and copyright limitations that are all about preventing the free flow of information (which the US is forever instructing less-developed countries to permit, in order that they might prosper). The 1990s Agreement on Trade-Related Aspects of Intellectual Property Rights (TRIPS) saw the US government insisting on a transnational deal that would suit Hollywood's interests. Clearly, then, Washington is intimately involved in screen culture, and claims for a naturally occurring diversity are specious. So at the overt level of cultural policy, the state continues to exclude discussion of its own screen subvention, but this hypocrisy hints at a more complex and layered history.

Despite all the rhetoric, and its international image, one might argue that the United States actually invented modern cultural policy in a Federal frame. The US Marine Band was formed in 1790 (J Alexander *Command* 72). The 1848 Treaty of Guadalupe Hidalgo, which dealt with the US seizure of Mexican territory, protected people caught in the annexation, via provisions that some argue included cultural maintenance via language. Native American activists read treaties with their forebears similarly, and ongoing debates about 'English-only' are a sorry history of racism and xenophobia (Schmidt 114). In 1872, Congress purchased Thomas Moran's painting of the Grand Canyon, which so engaged spectators that the area depicted was later secured for conservation. That same year, the US became the first nation to establish national parks. Legislation empowering the Federal Government to buy and maintain historic monuments dates from 1906 and 1935. In 1917–18, the US pioneered tax deductions for gifts to non-profit organizations. A Committee on Public Information was set up when the US entered the First World War, as a global advertising tool applied to militarism (Snow 16). The State Department's Division of Cultural Relations, created in 1938, and the Office of the Coordinator of Inter-American Affairs (OCIAA), established in 1940 with Nelson Rockefeller at its helm, promoted educational, cultural and scientific exchanges with Latin American countries, and provided aid to hundreds of US schools based there to woo the population to anti-Fascism. The activities of these offices also enabled a hemispheric trading bloc under US hegemony as a means to overcome the economic blight of the 1930s. A State Department reorganization in 1944 presaged changes in cultural policy for the postwar era – combating the New Deal at home and promoting American values against communism in Europe and Asia – thus resignifying Rockefeller's claim that cultural relations were 'the imperialism of ideas' (Ninkovich US 13; Rockefeller quoted in Ninkovich US 35–36).

In US Constitutional law, art has generally been regarded, at least since 1952, as a source of social commentary that can be translated into political speech. Protection of free expression is given to it on the basis that art can embody the social criticisms that the First Amendment was designed to enable. Neither mimetic nor counterfactual, art is claimed as a beneficial 'condition for imaginatively living' that can subvert the state in the interests of liberty, as per religion (Hamilton 107, 104–105, 88, 76–77). This disturbs those conservative libertarians who see art as a mystical form of life that beggars communicative norms and rationality.

Groundbreaking initiatives for the support of arts and culture include the Works Progress Administration (WPA) arts projects of the 1930s (which employed 40,000 artists), US advocacy of a UN cultural organization in the late 1940s (which became UNESCO), the United States Information Agency (USIA), dedicated to propaganda euphemized as 'public diplomacy', and the 1973 Comprehensive Employment and Training Act (CETA), whose important Artists-in-Residence program, which involved income-security provisions, led to unintended social critique (French 5; Sellars 7; Ninkovich US 3; J Alexander *Command* 73; Kammen 793–94; Joseph B. Rose 429; Dubin 198).

The Emergence of Cultural Foreign Policy

Rockefeller's labors established a pattern of overseas cultural policy that dominated for fifty years and set the organizational tenor for domestic activities from the 1960s. Cultural exchange, which was already being promoted within an 'idealistic' framework after the proclamation of the Good Neighbor Policy (GNP) in 1933, became an urgent security issue by 1939. Modest cultural and academic exchange programs were instituted in the 1930s to foster, as Assistant Secretary of State, Sumner Welles wrote, 'wider appreciation of the culture and civilization of other peoples' (2, 7). Welles was responsible for 'articulat[ing] a government policy on cultural relations', that is, institutionalizing within government the system of intellectual and cultural exchange established by philanthropic foundations like the Carnegie Endowment and the Rockefeller Foundation (Berger 51–52). As we shall see, this relationship between philanthropic foundations and government policy became the basis for establishing the Arts and Humanities National Endowments in the mid-1960s.

The US gave a salient international role to culture because of reports that Germany offered technical advice and scholarly exchange to Latin American countries. This threatened the Pan-Americanist work of US philanthropic institutions, signaling to the State Department that it needed to include cultural issues within the paradigm of security, as other countries had done. Great Britain, for example, created the British Council in 1934 as part of its defense against German nationalist propaganda throughout Europe. To similar ends, the State Department created the Division of Cultural Relations in 1938. The first chief of the Division, Ben M Cherrington, recollects justifying its programs in these terms:

> When Hitler and Mussolini's exploitation of education as instruments of nationalist policy was at its height ... our Government was determined to demonstrate to the world the basic difference between the methods of democracy and those of a 'Ministry of Enlightenment and Propaganda'. There was to be established in the Department of State an organization that would be a true representative of our American tradition of intellectual freedom and educational integrity. (quoted in Colligan 3)

Behind this expression of freedom, however, it was clear that the US needed to manage how Latin American countries understood US culture, which frequently presented unflattering images of them. It was thus necessary to weed out these stereotypes, as well as disseminate knowledge of Latin American ways of life, in order to manage political and economic matters in ways that did not appear to be coercive. The promotion of foreign policy objectives through private corporations and non-profit organizations like the Ford, Rockefeller and Carnegie Foundations became the *modus operandi* of US cultural foreign policy, later evident in the workings of the Congress for Cultural Freedom and other institutions of the cultural Cold War.

Rockefeller proposed the creation of an agency for cultural, scientific and educational diplomacy after a trip with other businessmen to Latin America in 1940, and Roosevelt asked him to take command of this initiative. Fascist and Nazi propaganda had secured the sympathy of presidents and political leaders in a significant number of Latin American republics, especially Argentina, Brazil and Chile, but also Mexico, an immediate neighbor. Latin American nationalism, and the concomitant proclivity for protectionism in matters of trade, against which US policy makers railed, provided a common ground with Axis ideology. As trade with significant partners like Britain was largely cut off during World War II, the US could strong-arm Latin American countries by blocking exports of capital goods that were needed for industrial development, as well as closing its own doors to imports from these countries. The US thus used commercial and financial programs to encourage Latin America to end collaboration with the Axis powers (Thorp 118–20). Because he had direct access to the President and could raise vast sums of money, Rockefeller was able to thwart attempts to limit his activities by certain State Department officials, including the Secretary of State. In little time, Rockefeller increased his budget from US$3.5 million to US$45 million, and oversaw a staff of five hundred assistants, including an intelligence operation.

Roosevelt had turned to Latin America out of expediency. He needed to link domestic recovery to an international agenda, but European governments opposed these relations, the US was racked by isolationism and the Japanese controlled Asia. As one historian put it, 'Latin American actions played an integral part in shaping worldwide strategy' (Gellman 17). This meant abandoning the US practice of only intervening in other countries' internal affairs when the commercial interests or property of US nationals were at stake. The first test was Cuba, where a *coup d'état* had toppled a hated dictator in 1933 and brought into power a military *junta*, then, under US pressure, a provisional president who was hostile to foreign ownership of basic industries (Gellman 20). That same year, Secretary of State, Cordell Hull was lobbied by Latin American delegates at the Seventh International Conference of American States to commit the US to stay out of the Caribbean and Central America. Hull also made a free-trade economic resolution that led to increased commercial activity between the US and its southern neighbors. Throughout the 1930s, the US faced various crises in which the policy of non-intervention was brought up, including the expropriation of foreign (including US) oil interests in Mexico in 1938. Hull and other cabinet members helped negotiate an agreement whereby Mexico would compensate property owners.

It was recognized by some that an economic program was not sufficient to achieve hemispheric prosperity or international peace. Given the administration's interest in Latin America, several cabinet officers developed expertise in the region and many Latin American scholars were recruited to provide analysis and policy design. Indeed, Latin American Studies was first institutionalized under the Roosevelt administration, providing a prototype for the area-studies model that emerged with the Cold War:

> Beginning in the early 1940s area-studies specialists were mobilized in the crusade against fascism, and then against Soviet totalitarianism. The North American area-studies specialists, writing in the post-1945 era, readily transposed the lessons of appeasement and the Nazi threat in Europe to the rest of the world, drawing the line against international communism around the globe. (Berger 70)

Since Latin America was not the focus of the war, the Office of Strategic Services (OSS), founded in 1941 and the precursor of the CIA, which not long after was to launch the largest cultural war ever, included few Latin American specialists. Indeed, as soon as the war ended, Latin American studies receded. It did not grow again until the 1960s, in the wake of the Cuban Revolution. But while Latin Americanists were not recruited into the OSS and the CIA in its early years, some of the most important scholars, intellectuals and artists were recruited by Rockefeller for the OCIAA. It is here that we begin to see linkages between important intellectuals, Ivy League academics and government

(Gellman 146), a mirror image of the social, political and financial brahmins who intersected in the CIA (Saunders 135–36). Indeed, there is overlap between the old-boy networks of inter-Americanists and Cold Warriors in the persons of Rockefeller, John Hay Whitney, René d'Harnoncourt, Lincoln Kirstein and many others. They traveled in the same circles: the Rockefeller and Ford Foundations, the Museum of Modern Art (MoMA) and subsequently the CIA.

When he ran the OCIAA, Rockefeller mobilized the press, radio and motion pictures to aid the war effort. He appointed experts on these industries to establish relations with their counterparts in Latin America and conduct research on production systems and audiences for these media. The press section became one of the biggest programs, providing features, photographs and cartoons for Latin American newspapers. It published *En Guardia*, a magazine patterned on the format of *Life* that reached a wide audience. The OCIAA also subvened *The Inter-American Quarterly* and *The Inter-American*, which lasted only until the end of the war. The Division of Radio was also a major priority. To counter the Nazis, who supplied seven hours of broadcasts per week, a Pan-American broadcasting station was built; it transmitted official speeches and educational programs in concert with private commercial programs like opera presentations. The OCIAA eventually doubled the peak output of the Nazi broadcasts, producing everything from news to popular music, all to enhance the spirit of inter-American solidarity (Gellman 152).

The most visible program was the Motion Picture Division, headed by Whitney, who was a trustee and vice-president of MoMA, a future secret agent and a front man for the CIA's news service, Forum World Features (Saunders 311–12). A patrician, like Roosevelt and Rockefeller, Whitney was also a sportsman, publisher, philanthropist, art collector and Hollywood mogul, whose most memorable production was *Gone With the Wind*, in partnership with David O Selznick. As a movie producer and creator of MoMA's film library, Whitney was well positioned to understand the persuasive capacities of film, which he put in the service of the war effort by bringing in public relations specialists and noted filmmakers like Luis Buñuel to analyze the propaganda value of German and Japanese films. Whitney was especially interested in the construction of ethnic stereotypes in order to formulate a program for revising Hollywood films, which were obstacles to gaining solidarity from Latin Americans for the US war efforts. We might say, then, that he was one of the first US intellectuals and *apparatchiks* to engage in a 'positive images' politics of representation. He was responsible for getting Hollywood to produce *The Life of Simon Bolivar*, *The Road to Rio* and Disney's *Saludos Amigos* and *The Three Caballeros*. Some production costs were borne by the OCIAA in exchange for free prints to be distributed in US embassies and consulates in Latin America. Whitney even accompanied GNP ambassadors Disney and the star of his film, Donald Duck, who made a guest appearance in Rio, and was also instrumental in modernizing Mexico's film industry, as part of his cultural diplomacy with the OCIAA (Kahn Jr. 145).

Other GNP ambassadors from the film sector were Carmen Miranda and Orson Welles. The involvement of popular-front intellectuals and artists like Welles was perhaps a carry-over from the New Deal Federal Arts Programs, when the left was wooed by government, and even had fellow-travelers like Roosevelt's Vice President, Henry Wallace. Welles' GNP film *It's All True*, about a group of fishermen who traveled over 2,000 miles on a flimsy raft to Brazil's capital in Rio to get the President's help in establishing a union to end abuses in their industry, was filmed in Brazil in 1941 and 1942. Welles departed from usual practice with this film as he became interested in the culture of Rio's poor, especially black Brazilians and their participation in carnival. His film thus became a liability both to the OCIAA and to his studio, RKO, which considered it would have no commercial value. The propaganda value was also compromised by revealing that Brazil was populated by so many black people. He was never able to finish the film project. Its undeveloped rolls were lost, then rediscovered in the 1980s and subsequently made into a film that reconstructs Welles' intentions and explains the difficulties he confronted.[1]

It is often noted that cultural Cold Warriors from the 1950s and 1960s used abstract art as an expression of freedom *vis-à-vis* the command culture of the Soviet Union, which promoted socialist realism. Abstract Expressionism seemed dubious to reactionaries brought up on representational art, but Rockefeller referred to Abstract Expressionism as 'free enterprise painting', and George Kennan, the architect of the State Department's brutal containment strategy for isolating the USSR after the War, called it the ideology of 'free art' (Ninkovich US 18; Rockefeller and Kennan quoted in Petras 52–53). Rockefeller himself was associated with the avant-garde, having been a trustee of MoMA, which his mother Abby Aldrich Rockefeller co-founded. In the earlier days of the OCIAA, contemporary art evoked, in addition to freedom *vis-à-vis* Nazism, entry into the modern world. Indeed, one of the ways in which Latin American countries and the US could show their commonalities was by demonstrating a shared modernity, in addition to endorsing claims to civilizational pedigree based on ancient heritages like those of the Aztec, Maya and Inca cultures. MoMA had a track record of exhibiting Latin American art. In 1931, it had showcased Diego Rivera's work in a one-man show. With the collaboration of Rockefeller and the OCIAA, MoMA took up Latin American art again with enthusiasm. In 1940 it exhibited both *Twenty Centuries of Mexican Art* and *Portinari of Brazil* (an important modernist painter who also had a strong social dimension); in 1941, *Industrial Design Competition for the 21 American Republics*; and in 1942, the *United Hemisphere Competition*. In 1943, it held the two most important exhibitions of that period: *The Latin American Collection of the Museum of Modern Art* and *Brazil Builds*.

Rockefeller put up the funds for both these exhibitions, covertly in the case of *The Latin American Collection*, by a 'timely gift' from an 'anonymous donor' (Affred Barr 3). US$24,842 was given under the name of the 'Interamerican Fund' (Buntinx 16). The foreword to *Brazil Builds* acknowledges the sponsorship of the Office of the OCIAA, naming its staff as the helmsmen who 'helped steer our course' (Philip Goodwin 9). As Gustavo Buntinx demonstrates, the curator of the *Latin American Collection*, Lincoln Kirstein, 'homologize[d] the artistic developments of Latin America with those of the United States' (20). This was no doubt meant to be flattering, but it also did violence to very different traditions of Latin American art. Kirstein's catalogue essay also made many mistakes, demonstrating too hasty a concern with showcasing Latin American art for the sake of political expediency. The politics of the GNP was, indeed, its motivating force (Buntinx 25). Latin American and North American modernity were exalted by Kirstein as examples of what Nazism found intolerable: 'It is art that Hitler hates because it is modern-progressive-challenging. Because it is international, because it is free' (Guilbaut 88; Kirstein quoted in Buntinx 25).

Like some other goodwill ambassadors, Kirstein's trips to Latin America were meant to gain sympathy for the American cause. In 1942, he traveled through Brazil, Uruguay, Argentina, Chile, Peru, Ecuador and Colombia to acquire the works that were exhibited in *The Latin American Collection*. Buntinx notes the problems inherent in this kind of cultural diplomacy. Kirstein was often forced to buy works for political reasons rather than artistic ones: the Peruvian indigenist painter Jose Sabogal had been badly treated by other museum officials and US cultural diplomats. Kirstein's purchase of a painting by Sabogal was therefore 'in no way determined by the specific artistic interest of the painting in question, but by densely intertwined political demands that went all the way from the State Department to delicate public relations with other museums, including the need to cover for the rather uncouth behavior of the American Embassy and the Rockefeller Foundation' (Buntinx 40).

A feature article on Rockefeller published in *Life* magazine in 1942 states that he 'accomplished more in a year and a half [at the OCIAA] than Herr Goebbels did in a decade,' and that the OCIAA 'stands as a convincing refutation of the theory that the Germans are the only people who know how to apply politically the kind of common sense that US businessmen invented' (Busch 80). The essay stresses that the OCIAA presumed if intellectuals could be persuaded to embrace a US point of view, then the politicians and the rest of society would follow their lead. The reason for this was that artists and intellectuals had the status of sports celebrities and pop stars in Latin America: 'The streams of exchange scholarships, traveling exhibitions of paintings and invitations to Brazilian artists to visit the US, have more point than is usually apparent to the US public. The fact is that pianists, painters and professors occupy in many Latin American countries the kind of prestige accorded in the US only to pugilists, dipsomaniacs or crooners' (Busch 88). The Office of War Information (OWI), created in 1942, also channeled funds through the division, establishing what one commentator called a 'shot-gun wedding of scholarship and war information [that] begot some dubious progeny: the mongrel mixture of culture and propaganda' (Wythe 171).

Culture thus took its place next to economic policy. The Division of Cultural Relations and the OCIAA were cultural analogues of the Inter-American

Financial and Economic Advisory Committee, established in 1939, the Export Import Bank, economically upgraded in 1940 to capitalize construction of the Pan American Highway, and the Inter-American Coffee Convention, which was drafted in 1941 (Thorp 121). This two-pronged policy of economic and cultural persuasion paid off. Mexico and Brazil allied with the US, in 1941 and 1942 respectively, Chile cut off ties with the Axis powers in 1943, and Argentina, the most recalcitrant, finally declared war on Germany and Japan in 1945.

As the war wound down, culture and information policy was reorganized. In 1944, a joint committee was created that included the head of the Division of Cultural Relations, a representative of the OCIAA, and a member of the General Advisory Committee, which was responsible for policy positions. Soon after, the OCIAA and the OWI were terminated; their activities persisted, however, in the State Department's Office of International and Cultural Affairs (1953). The culture and information agencies created during the war to manage Latin American affairs thus established a cultural policy legacy in the post-war era; they could be characterized as dress rehearsals for the Marshall Plan, the USIA, UNESCO, and the CIA's cultural Cold War. This future role was acknowledged by Assistant Secretary of State for Cultural Affairs, Archibald MacLeish, the head of the new avatar of the OCIAA and the Division of Cultural Relations, when he announced a bill in Congress in 1945 'to extend to the rest of the world [the US's] cultural activities as developed over some years in South America', to promote US interests against communism in Europe and Asia.

RC Lewontin has argued that only war or a major economic crisis can legitimize the state's intervention in the US – that it takes a catastrophe to overcome 'American antistate ideology' (17). The Cold War thus 'became the instrumentality of a vital national economic policy', channeling policy and institutional practice as evidenced in the growth of the university and its increasing receipt of federal and state subsidy (7). Rockefeller's claim that cultural relations were the battlefield of 'the imperialism of ideas' (quoted in Ninkovich 35–36) thus took new turns and twists after the Second World War, leaving Latin America out of the new lucrative agenda, which was the economic recovery of Europe under the Marshall Plan (1947). Of US$33 billion in non-military foreign-aid grants from 1947 to 1953, Latin American countries received a mere 3%, less than Korea, Belgium and Luxembourg (Berger 51; Bethell 128). The resources once earmarked for OCIAA and the GNP were now aimed at the reconstruction of Europe. The result was the deaccessioning of Latin American art at MoMA, which turned its attention to promoting the freedom presumably inherent in abstract expressionism as a means to counter the allure of Soviet cultural relations in Europe. Like several other associates of Rockefeller's OCIAA, Whitney and Kirstein also took a distance from Latin America to play a role in the CIA's cultural Cold War, fronting for covert money-laundering when necessary.

The Cold War partly explains the championing of 'artistic freedom' in 1965, and its abandonment in the 1990s. The creation of the NEA and the NEH can be considered the *dénouement* of a tale that began in the late 1940s and early 1950s, when post-war intellectuals during the Truman administration (1945–53) fashioned a cultural program to legitimize US world leadership, pitting artistic and scholarly freedom, as embodied in new abstract art and a rapidly expanding higher education system, against the totalitarianism embodied in the command industrial and cultural economies of the Soviet bloc.

Of course, not all these projects were bipartisan. In the 1950s, US conservatism took a turn against what was variously termed 'rationalism', 'statism' and 'collectivism' – legacies of the Roosevelt administration's use of government money and agency through the WPA to stem the ideological tide and social misery threatened and actualized in the Great Depression. Republicans reacted against the subsequent consolidation of centralized governmental authority in the Second World War, but were themselves divided between libertarians who championed rugged independence from the state (to whom collective social-movement thinking was bad and individual freedom was good) and God-botherers who reasserted the character of the US as a Christian nation (to whom the social collective and the free individual use was bad and the familial was good) (Himmelstein and Zald 174–75).

Many on the right concurred with liberal Democrats in favoring large-scale internal and external Federal action to counter the Soviet Union's model of state socialism. The aim was to better the USSR in every activity, in a way that was homologous, analogous and aetiological – battles on all fronts, from book bounties to bomb ballistics. Our favorite instance of this was an occasion when hearings of the House Committee on Education and Labor in 1954 found a New Jersey Democrat anxious lest the USSR 'picture our citizens as gum-chewing, insensitive, materialistic barbarians' (quoted in Kammen 801).[2]

By the time of John F Kennedy's presidency (1961–63), liberals clearly had taken up Cold War intellectual cudgels. North American international cultural policy was meshed very tightly with diplomatic, military and economic strategies. The belated decision to join international copyright regimes had as much to do with a Cold War cultural policy of using books to win over non-aligned readers as it was about opening new markets (Phillipson 11–12; Mokia; Graham). Indeed, the very connection between world economic and political leadership, on the one hand, and cultural leadership, on the other, is built into Public Law 89–209, which brought the NEA into being: 'The world leadership which has come to the United States cannot rest solely upon superior power, wealth, and technology, but must be solidly founded upon the worldwide respect and admiration for the Nation's high qualities as a leader in the realm of ideas and of the spirit' (23). The NEA and the NEH would extend this 'world-wide Marshall plan in the field of ideas' to the conflict-ridden terrain of 1960s America (Lewontin 11).

The CIA also became involved with covert funding of anti-Marxist (but occasionally pro-left) intellectuals through support for various journals, magazines and conferences that sometimes criticized the US, as a sign that their unremitting opposition to state socialism was the product of unfettered thought and speech. Its front organization from 1950 to 1967 was the Congress for Cultural Freedom, which maintained bureaux in thirty-five nations, produced twenty periodicals, employed dozens of *apparatchiks* and sponsored tours and prizes that would win the West for US values without admitting it was underwritten by state espionage (Saunders).

The influence of anti-communism on US cultural policy continues, supplemented by commercial concerns. The 1990s saw the US spending a few million dollars each year on the USIA, which sponsored radio and television propaganda, scholarly and community exchanges and information programs, all to follow the Agency's motto of 'telling America's story to the world' whilst claiming to do so via 'communication between peoples as opposed to governments' (Ninkovich US 3). But the urgency of this mission had gone – by 2000, the funds amounted to a quarter of the figure granted at the time of the Soviet Union's demise (Molotsky). The policy dualism of information and culture facilitated this mixed message – on the one hand, the Agency sought to correct negative images of the US through 'facts' as part of improving the nation's standing in the world. On the other, its cultural programs demonstrated the nation's ability to create great art that could transcend politics and economics. Public diplomacy served to answer critics of the Agency from both right and left. Conservatives, opposed to the idea of cultural policy and outraged by exchanges with state-socialist nations, were mollified by the notion that cultural exchanges were supported on a civil-society basis, while radicals had their critiques of propaganda deflected by the showcasing of works by minorities and others often excluded from the market canon of cultural production. This story has been refined in ever-more virulently anti-left terms with the generation of new media propaganda systems in Asia and the Caribbean since the end of the Cold War, with the Clinton era adding a strong emphasis on capitalism and open markets (Snow 13–14, 32–39, Ninkovich US 32). The USIA has latterly taken a turn toward multicultural rhetoric, which makes it compatible with progressive anti-racist politics. Indeed, support for diversity by US government agencies and non-governmental foundations is looked upon by certain left intellectuals and activists in Latin America as a ruse for encouraging the displacement of redistributive politics by a focus on recognizing identities.

'Fordism' Births the National Endowment for the Arts

We turn now to the domestic analogue of these developments, the storied and scarred history of the NEA. Rockefeller was also important as Governor of New York from 1959 to 1973, while his family's Foundation stimulated the creation of forty-five new local arts councils across the country between 1954 and 1959 (Richard Jensen). But critic John Kreidler attributes the creation of the non-profit US arts sector most centrally to the Ford Foundation's initiatives. The NGO arts grant was invented by W. McNeil Lowry,[3] vice president for

Arts at the Foundation from 1957 to 1976, as 'a vehicle for the long-term advancement of individual non-profit arts organizations, as well as a means for the strategic development of the entire non-profit arts sector' – leveraged investments rather than charity. Until Ford's initiative, almost all US cultural philanthropy had come from individuals. Ford put more than US$400 million into the arts during Lowry's tenure, to revitalize NGOs, decentralize them beyond New York City, create arts service institutions (e.g. the Theater Communications Group), and enhance conservatories and visual arts schools.

Ford saw itself as a catalyst rather than a perpetual funder. To this end, it invented the matching grant, a tactic to recruit new donors and establish a pattern of long-term support spread across many sources. Before this 'Ford era', only the Carnegie, Rockefeller and Mellon Foundations had entered arts philanthropy. But the idea of the matching grant spread throughout various funding sectors, including 'big government'. In the 1960s, US not-for-profit Foundations, principally Carnegie, Ford and Rockefeller, helped generate an x infrastructure of artistic diversity, at the same time as the Federal Government and state and private colleges stimulated development. The Ford model channeled high-art organizations towards a non-profit model, rather than the proprietary one characteristic of the pre-Ford era. The strategy has been a success. For example, in the pre-Ford era, there were only twenty to thirty arts organizations in the San Francisco Bay area. By the 1980s, there were over a thousand. This transformation was legitimized by economic studies of the time, which established that the performing arts were 'inherently prone to cost over-runs', unlike mechanically or electronically reproducible art. The very value of live performance – its mutability and uniqueness – set limits on its profitability. Expenses were high, with no prospect of economies of scale through increased production or adjusted inventory (Zolberg 'Paying' 402; Hirsch). So the market would not be sufficient to ensure a wide range of 'live' cultural production.

Two other philanthropic branches grew from Ford initiatives: foundation and corporate support. Foundations acquired specialized staff to formulate funding strategies and analyse grant applications. By the end of the Ford era, aggregate arts funding from foundations would surpass US$1 billion per year, over three times the aggregate budgets of state and national government art agencies. Corporate arts funding started later and was the fastest-growing sector of arts funding in the 1980s, spearheaded by Exxon, Dayton Huston, Philip Morris and AT&T. It has been more concerned with marketing than strategic development of the arts.

The burgeoning infrastructure of the arts in the post-War era was due not only to government and foundation money, but also to the emergence of artists, technicians and administrators driven not by funding or economic gain, but by their interest in producing art. The expansion of higher education in the 1950s and 1960s was another important stimulus. Artists, administrators and educators founded many arts organizations, not so much because of their interest in the market, but because they had the training and the desire. This happened at a time of significant shifts in social values, a peak in economic prosperity, the arrival of a massive baby-boom generation on American college campuses (8 million college graduates in 1960, 16 million in 1975, and 33 million in 1990 (Richard Jensen)), the momentary ascendancy of liberal arts education, and a marked increase in leisure time. The new generation was large, white and mostly affluent. It contributed to the creation of NGOs and arts audiences, providing labor for the expansion of non-profit health, environmental, educational and social-service organizations that received foundation and government funding. The expansion of free expression, and the complementary change in attitudes toward public service, were in tension *and* in tandem with a Cold War investment in opposing an American premium on individual freedom to the collective *ethos* of state socialism. Economic prosperity and the expansion of liberal-arts education also created a sizeable public of arts consumers.

From 1960, Kennedy, Lyndon Johnson (President 1963–69), and Richard Nixon (1969–74) were all worried that Rockefeller's wealth might buy him the Presidency. Rockefeller's support for the arts was an important means of product differentiation from his competitors. So they smiled on the public subvention of culture as a means of counteracting this, from the moment when Johnson signed the NEA and NEH into law in 1965, until Nixon muttered to HR Haldeman in the 1970s, after years of abuse from liberals, '[t]he arts are not our people. We should dump the whole culture business' (quoted in Kammen 796). For all Nixon's anxieties, the 1960s and 1970s were a time of burgeoning immigration and government cultural policy, mutually reinforcing signs that the US model of free traffic in persons and ideas could generate better, as well as fairer, outcomes than could command economies, despite Congressional opposition from many Republicans (Dittgen 279, 260; Richard Jensen). On the other side, the liberal Foundations, as per Dworkin's philosophy outlined in our Introduction, feared both market-driven and government-driven systems, so they sought a third way, pouring millions into partnerships *across* the three sectors. The matching grant was their model.

The NEA and NEH were conceived, among other reasons, to 'strengthen the connections between the Administration and the intellectual community' (quoted in Cummings 'Government and the Arts: An overview' 49). This recommendation was made, aptly, by the liberal intellectual Arthur Schlesinger, Jr. Since the nationalization of such goods and services as health care, and even education, were deemed to run against the American grain, the mobilization of freedom and resources necessary to wage the Cold War became the means to overcome this 'ideological antipathy' to state intervention. Indeed, to this day, many government policies have been cast in the rhetoric of war: the '"war" on cancer', the '"war" on disease', the '"war" on poverty', the '"war" on crime', the '"war" on drugs' (Lewontin 23) and the 'war' on terrorism. No surprise, then, that Public Law 89–209 states that: 'while no government can call a great artist or scholar into existence, it is necessary and appropriate for the Federal Government to help create and sustain not only a climate encouraging freedom of thought, imagination, and inquiry, but also the material conditions facilitating the release of this creative talent.'

Like anti-poverty programs, the NEA was aimed at ameliorating a society divided by race, ethnicity and gender. From the 1960s to the 1980s, the NEA took a series of initiatives to democratize the arts, developing inner-city arts after Watts and other riots, establishing the Expansion Arts program in 1971 to give institutional sanction to more 'populist' arts practices (again mainly in inner cities) and providing direct financing of storefront and church arts programs serving inner-city children in 1977 (Netzer *The Subsidized* 157; Marquis 93, 101). New York City's unions and its Housing Authority even coordinated classes on opera, ethics, symphonic music and choral work (Freedman).

But by and large, the US government used subsidies for cultural activism to channel the expression of opposition. Johnson's Great Society was a complex mechanism of crisis management, to deal with the deterioration of social control unleashed by migration to the cities and unemployment among blacks and other racial minorities, and a way of shaping blacks as an electoral constituency in urban centers, especially in the North, as Republicans made inroads among whites in the South. The federal strategy in the cities involved the creation of various service programs for inner cities: youth development under the Juvenile Delinquency and Youth Offenses Control Act; community center attention to mental illness under the Community Mental Health Centers Act; community action programs under Title II of the Economic Opportunity Act (the anti-poverty program); and urban renewal programs under Title I of the Demonstration Cities and Metropolitan Development Act and the Neighborhood Service Program. These programs elevated poverty to public prominence, as Democrats sought to empower blacks. Bypassing local governments, they made it possible for black activists 'to staff and control many of these agencies, much as Italians or Irish or Jews controlled municipal departments'. The new intermediaries between national government, communities and private social agencies, many of whom were selected from cadres of civil-rights activists and other 'young minority-group spokesmen', were drawn into an 'intricate mesh of interactive effects'. Government funding ultimately brought into the fold even those activists who initially used federal money for their own purposes (Piven and Cloward 261, 274).

The Nixon administration increased the budget of the NEA by several hundred percent in the 1970s, extending the Johnson administration's use of social programs to manage crises (Piven and Cloward). While artists may not have been his 'kind of people', the NEA served as the carrot to Nixon's stick in dealing with social activists and others 'responsible' for urban disorder, such as blacks and antiwar protestors. Where brute force fell short, incorporation into a bureaucratized cultural apparatus drained some activism away. By the late 1960s, it was evident that true empowerment of the urban, racialized poor had been headed off by the very mechanisms that had made organization possible. The swift institutionalization of 'alternative art spaces' followed a similar route, while the Business Council for the Arts and the Rockefeller Foundation argued for arts infrastructure as an alternative to the grave peril of 'leisure' in these areas (Brian Wallis 16; Martin *Critical* 90). Such anxieties clearly connect to the ethical incompleteness identified in our Introduction: being 'into' art kept the underprivileged population 'out' of strife.

The NEA generated enormous growth. In thirty-five years, the US went from having one hundred orchestras and dance, theatre and opera companies to eight hundred. Six hundred local arts agencies turned into 3,800, and the number of state arts *bureaux* increased from six to fifty-six ('National'). In the first twenty years of the Endowment, professional arts organizations grew by 700% (Bayles). Today, it is estimated that each dollar of NEA money provides a twenty-fold return in contracts, services and jobs (American 'Economic').

So how did the NEA become a problem in the 1990s? The answers lie in four adjacent domains: debates about sex and race; the government of culture; party politics and constitutional law; and critiques from the left. Each one is interlaced with the notion of what constitutes Americanness and how it should be governed: private enterprise versus centralized power; the separation of the state from the generation and suppression of meaning; and changes in national citizenship occasioned by migration, sexual subjectivity and their expression in cultural forms. For if in 1965 Johnson explained that: 'it is in our works of art that we reveal to ourselves, and to others, the inner vision which guides us as a nation' (quoted in Martin *Critical* 90), three decades later, the public face of that interior had taken a battering. Congressman Dick Armey referred to the Endowment as the 'single most visible and deplorable black eye on the arts in America' (CNN 10 July 1997). The remainder of this chapter examines what happened to Johnson's vision over the intervening years, and the implications for the future, situating the NEA in the history of US cultural policy, the arts activism of social movements and contemporary debates about citizenship.

Sex and Race

Since their President, Richard Nixon, had scored zero on *political* morality, post-Watergate Republicans proceeded to stress *personal* morality, targeting the left and social movements, notably civil rights and feminism, in areas of symbolic power. Corporations were major supporters of the growth of right-wing think-tanks from the 1970s, as arguments from the magazine *Commentary* and other periodicals about a left elite in and around government grew in appeal. Coors brewers, the Scaife family and the Hearst Foundation funded anti-arts groups, and 'Defund the Left' was on the letterhead of the Republican Conservative Caucus by the late 1970s. These reactionary forces believed that progressive politics was using public money to challenge conventional morality and inequality. During the 1997 Congressional debate on the Endowments,

Representative Duncan Hunter alleged on the floor of the House that NEA money 'goes to aging hippies ... to desecrate the crucifix' (quoted in Richard Bolton). He was referring to 1989 controversies surrounding Andres Serrano's exhibit at the Southeastern Center for Contemporary Art in Winston-Salem, which included 'Piss Christ', a 'blasphemous' photograph of Christ in the artist's urine, and a posthumous exhibition of homo- and auto-erotic photographs by Robert Mapplethorpe, of which more below. Republican Senator Alphonse D'Amato ripped a copy of 'Piss Christ' to pieces on the Senate floor, and his colleague Jesse Helms proposed a ban on public funding for 'obscene and indecent' art and any work that 'denigrates, debases or reviles a person, group or class of citizens on the basis of race, creed, sex, handicap, age or national origin' (Jane Alexander *Command*; Helms quoted in Dowd).

The cause was the offense that Senator and Mrs Helms took at the flagrant display of homoeroticism in an exhibition of Mapplethorpe's photographs, which was canceled by the Corcoran Gallery. 'This Mapplethorpe fellow', said Helms, 'was an acknowledged homosexual. He's dead now, but the homosexual theme goes throughout his work' (quoted in Dowd). It was not the art work *per se* that Helms found offensive, but the *ethos* conveyed by it (the aesthetic meeting the anthropological). Helms' objection to grants awarded to 'three acknowledged lesbian writers', without having read their work, bears this out. His target audience was the 175,000 members of the nationwide Christian Coalition, along with a network stretching across the National Right to Life Committee, the American Family Association, the Liberty Alliance, the Eagle Forum, the Family Research Council and the Christian Action Network (Richard Jensen; Jane Alexander *Command* 217). These controversies gave rise to the 1989 Jesse Helms Amendment, which forbade the Endowment from supporting 'obscene or indecent materials'. It passed with very few Senators present and was upheld in 1998 by the Supreme Court (Moen 194; Plagens B4). Meanwhile, chairing the NEA had become a position of such gravity that it was subject to intense surveillance – nomination and confirmation required FBI interviews with 'teachers, relatives, landlords', and anyone who had known nominees (Jane Alexander *Command* 21).

After the Serrano and Mapplethorpe incidents, vigilant conservatives in Congress protested the funding of the 'NEA Four' in 1990 – John Fleck, Holly Hughes, Tim Miller, and Karen Finley. Objections to the first three revolved around their dissemination of a gay 'attitude toward life', while Finley's 'unspeakable acts' of nudity sweetened by chocolate also gave 'offense' (Kramer). The artistic representation of consensual sex was imagined by religious mavens, anxious critics and rent-seeking cultural politicos as a threat disseminated from the arts community to the society at large. Helms and other moral monitors, like *New Criterion* editor Kramer, justified their attacks by arguing that in passing itself off as art, the political agenda of 'social deviants' had illegitimately shielded itself in the armor of aesthetic autonomy. (It is significant that the numerous sex scandals involving US military personnel these past few years have had no discernible impact on funding in that area: rape does not see an end to the military, nor do attacks on innocent gay and lesbian soldiers. The military continues to enjoy an autonomy denied by the arts.) The neoconservative agenda to dismantle the National Endowment was, unsurprisingly, part of a larger strategy to reverse the political gains made in the past two decades by gays and lesbians, racial and ethnic minorities, women and other subordinated and subaltern groups. With civil rights in retreat, the hitherto relatively protected sphere of the aesthetic was foregrounded as a terrain of political contestation. It provided *fora* to address crucial ethical concerns in ways that the mass media were disinclined to adopt.

The new contestatory movements provoked a counter-offensive by various sectors of the Right: fundamentalists (anti-obscenity and anti-abortion), nationalists (English Only advocates and anti-flag-burners) and political conservatives (anti-affirmative action and anti-civil rights). Having learned from the new social movements that the personal and the cultural were political, the Right declared itself the ideological foe not only of subaltern groups seeking enfranchisement, but also of liberal, humanistic expressions of universality (Bernstein 'Arts'). In what follows, we focus on the reasons why these political, moral and economic issues have converged on the aesthetic, paying particular attention to how conservatives attempt to maintain hegemony at the expense of gays and lesbians, who in turn have repoliticized their cultural practices.

The conservative backlash to the politicization of sexuality and other 'intimate matters' (D'Emilio and Freedman), reached its pinnacle with Helms' actions. If all these contestatory groups could challenge the sacrosanct category of the aesthetic by insisting on questions of 'content' – their lifestyle or group *ethos* – why shouldn't the Right also participate in the dismantling of the universal by advocating its own *ethos*: fundamentalism, homophobia and nationalism? If blacks and other minorities protested anti-defamation, why shouldn't the Right protest the defamation of *its* values? The very language of the proposed ban was a parody of civil-rights legislation and the rhetoric of subject positions around which contemporary social movements wage their struggles. Helms twisted the arguments to the advantage of conservatives. Recognizing that federally sanctioned public avenues of expression legitimize the current practice of making rights claims on the basis of group *ethoi*, he moved to close off those avenues. For two decades, feminists, gay and lesbian activists and racial and ethnic minorities had waged a politics of identity by which they sought self-determination over 'intimate matters' and participation in the public spheres where decisions on such matters are made. The conservative counterattack appropriated their language, ironically making it more difficult for these movements to set the agenda of public discourse.

The irony of Helms' actions was not lost on Kramer. In a *New York Times* article entitled 'Is Art Above the Laws of Decency?', Kramer pried open the contradictions of an artistic sphere falsely perceived as autonomous. '[I]s art now to be considered', he argued, 'such an absolute value that no other standard – no standard of taste, no social or moral standard – is to be allowed to play any role in determining what sort of art it is appropriate for the Government to support?' Against the likes of the Senators, artists and art critics who pointed out that 'freedom of expression' was protected by the Constitution – Christo, for example, wrote to the House subcommittee on civil rights that '[a]s an artist and a citizen, I feel that nothing may ever inhibit or threaten the First Amendment right of speech and dissent' (quoted in Glueck) – Kramer retorted that such freedoms do not guarantee public subvention. Knowing full well that the means of public participation of many subaltern groups had been facilitated by certain state agencies, most notably those dealing with the arts and education, Kramer argued for a public sphere in which the state did not intervene on behalf of any groups. This amounted to a re-privatization of issues that had entered public debate since civil rights, for without the resources provided by the state, many subaltern groups would not have a spitting chance against those corporate and Christian-right groups that 'privately' dominate the public.

Kramer advocated that public policy endorse only those expressions that meet the standards of cultural arbiters who answer to the public, arguing that the arbiters of public funding for the Mapplethorpe and Serrano exhibitions had been irresponsible in permitting 'false avant-garde' promoters of 'an attitude toward life' to be confused with the 'authentic avant-garde … which everyone knows no longer exists' (quoted in Glueck). Echoing the position of the Frankfurt School, more recent cultural theorists like Peter Bürger, and social critics such as Lasch, Kramer's diagnosis of art in late capitalist society is really a postmortem: art died because it was absorbed by the logic of capitalism into a pure commodity form. Another contributing cause to the demise of its autonomy is the 'famous "cutting edge" that looks more and more to an extra-artistic content for its raison-d'être' (quoted in Glueck). As artists themselves had abjured the sanctity of autonomy, it could only be 'sheer hypocrisy' that 'we are being asked to accept the unacceptable in the name of art'.

Now Kramer might allow any 'attitude toward life' in private. But even such a concession cannot save contemporary sexualized and racialized artistic practice, because he claims that the art world has failed to police the public/ private divide. Consequently, other arbiters of taste – the Congress – govern the 'autonomous' institution of art. The new arbiters must 'distinguish between art and life' because the art world no longer demonstrates that ability. The entry of 'life' into the hitherto protected sphere of art has made art a 'threat to public decency'.

Until the Endowment ran into political problems in the late 1980s, its awards had largely been protected by the concept of artistic freedom, based on this very separation. Analogously, the basic research promoted by the National Science Foundation was 'free' from the profit-oriented *ethos* of corporations. Over the long-term, however, science was expected to contribute to the economy. The cost was thus socialized under the control of entrepreneurial professors who had relative autonomy from ideological control. Similarly, artists were encouraged to conceive of themselves as professionals through a vast capillary network of arts administrations, linked to the NEA either through block grants to state arts councils or other forms of support. These decisions were perceived as relatively free from both government mandate and market criteria. The mechanism of this freedom was the peer review panel until 1989, when Congress intervened to increase its own oversight. The NEA was reauthorized in 1997 on condition that politicians have a say in NEA decisions (Gray 'Cuts').

There was significant opposition to this Congressional invasion of arms-length funding. Most, like an Olympian *New York Times* editorial from 1989, sought to protect 'the process carefully legislated to insulate art from crude politics' ('The Helms'). A liberal reaction would be expected from the *Times*. It was surprising when some alternative institutions stripped the art they exhibited from its political reality, as Susan Wyatt, director of the Artists Space in New York, attempted to do for the exhibition *Witnesses: Against Our Vanishing*. She alerted John Frohnmayer, then recently appointed to chair the NEA, to the potential controversy that artist and AIDS activist David Wojnarowicz might set off with his catalogue essay 'Post Cards From America: X-Rays From Hell', which excoriated Helms, Representative William Dannemeyer and New York Roman Catholic Cardinal John O'Connor for their opposition to safe-sex education. Wyatt's action led to a hasty withdrawal of funding, which was subsequently restored. The catalogue, however, was not supported, thus complying with the injunction to separate art from 'dirty politics'. The outcome demonstrated that even 'alternative' institutions cannot always be relied on to press the political-aesthetic claims of contestatory groups and social movements. They are, after all, part of the art world, and must look after their own assets.

The Government of Culture

As well as taking aim at civil rights-arts connections made by subaltern subjects, the religious right and the Republicans embarked on restructuring the cultural relationship between government, capital and society in an analogous (and ultimately bipartisan) fashion to what they did with social services, health insurance and higher education. These sectors were called upon to legitimize themselves in new ways. Part of this was to do with cost-benefit analysis.

The conservative attack makes it seem as if the change was purely a partisan, ideological one, leveled against obscenity or a 'gay attitude toward life'. But the change goes deeper, to the very fabric of what is understood by public culture and democracy. The budget cuts and the attempt to eliminate the NEA were meant to head off the possibility of an official cultural policy focused on democratization, to show the Right was serious about cutting public expenditure. Indeed, the change foreclosed the purpose of President Bill Clinton's Committee on the Arts and Humanities, which had called for a national reflection on American creativity, on the premise that 'a healthy cultural life is vital to a democratic society' ('President's' 1).

At the same time as the Republicans geared up to shut down the NEA, there was a gathering philosophical and aesthetic anxiety over socioeconomic rationales for cultural subvention and how to cordon off culture from profitmaking and politics (Zolberg 'Paying' 398). Whenever cultural organizations appeared to be building themselves as institutions rather than allocating resources to art, or were engaged in social critique, they became vulnerable. It suits those who maintain that the task of art is to speak with 'truth' and 'purity', and so indirectly influence public affairs to the good, to argue that it should not be funded by governments. Marci Hamilton maintains that 'the inconsequential size of the NEA budget' clouds a 'coercion of culture' behind 'benign assistance'. She claims that 'AIDS awareness and multiculturalism' have been favored by it. Such 'social goals' work to 'chill original artistic expression', with the avant-garde subordinated to policy categories (116). This argument says governments should not promote speech, but simply permit its free expression (which would logically entail an end to the Government Printing Office, the Congressional Record, campaign financing, and virtually all education (American Arts Alliance 'Myths').

David Boaz, Executive Vice-President of the right-wing think-tank the Cato Institute, addressed Delaware's Center for Contemporary Arts in 1995 from a similar perspective:

> there are only two basic ways to organize society: coercively, through government dictates, or voluntarily, through the myriad interactions among individuals and private associations.... [B]ecause art has power, it deals with basic human truths, ... it must be kept separate from government.... Take a typical American taxpayer. She's on her feet eight hours a day selling blue jeans at Wal-Mart. She serves spaghetti twice a week because meat is expensive, and when she can scrape together a little extra she likes to hear Randy Travis or take her daughter to see Mariah Carey. Now what gives us the right to tax her so that lawyers and lobbyists can save a few bucks on Kennedy Center tickets? (Boaz 541)

This is the right's populist side, arguing that removing the NEA would reduce the tax bill for over 400,000 working-class families (Policy.com 2). Such talk combines common-folk demotics with anti-élitism. It assumes government has nothing to do with democracy, while consumption has nothing to do with boardrooms; or put another way, that citizens have no power over the state, and company directors have no power over corporations. Other figures are in control: in the case of the state, shadowy bureaucrats and rent-seeking politicians; in the case of business, sovereign consumers. Some adherents to this argument also claim that the arts and their appreciation are part of individual human capital, at both supply and demand ends of the relationship. Arts laborers elect to work in the industry, foregoing accumulation elsewhere, and so are voluntarily offering discounted labor, for their non-financial benefit. Arts audiences add to their utility through aesthetic improvement. If they truly value culture, they will pay for it directly rather than through subsidies that burden others. Either way, there is no need for state funds in this human-capital argument, which sometimes also merges with libertarian discourses (Gary Becker).

Interestingly, many conservative figures dispute such neoliberal logic. As per Dworkin, they believe that core values integrate society and can be instilled through high culture, a process that is not supported by pure market structures: excellence is beyond the collective aesthetic grasp of the great unwashed, and the higher calling of the arts will be debased if left to the tastes of the American public. The NEA is misguided in seeking to broaden the audience to art and in encouraging politicized topics, but governments are right to fund the maintenance of a civilization's memory (Himmelstein and Zald 182). This thinking follows Friedrich Schiller's dictum 'to please many is bad' and Victor Cousin's 'l'art pour l'art'. The anxiety here, as per Hamilton, is that the Federal arts budget has a perverse multiplier effect, retarding artistic innovation, which must be free from economic and political constraints. Worse yet, on this reading, corporate and Foundation buyers look to the NEA's systems of peer review as a guide, which purportedly ramifies this 'groupthink' approach (Schiller and Cousin quoted in Cargo 216, 215. For more on such arguments, see Benedict; Smith and Berman; Hamilton 115).

Both these positions are linked to theories derived from nineteenth-century Romanticism that privilege myths of the solitary artist who rejects the old world of Europe in favor of transcendence through a self uncluttered by social standing or origin. This translates into a potent US myth via the Puritan *ethos* of self-reliance, which downplays the idea of decadence as a component of this rejection of convention. The myth can work both ways. It can be anti-governmental, and long for a restoration of individualism; or it can lament the impoverished intersubjectivity of electronic commodification and governmentality, emphasizing the loss of face-to-face community produced by the spread of microelectronic communication. In some sense, such a loss gives a reason to have an NEA, because 'live events will begin to seem like some of the few authentic experiences we have.... That is really what the Arts Endowment is all about – helping people connect with their families, their culture and their community' (Jane Alexander 'Our' 210–11).

Consider a similarly mythic anecdote to that told by Boaz from Cato. A few weeks after he braved the arts rentiers, then NEA Chair Jane Alexander talked with *bourgeois* rentiers – the Economic Club of Detroit. Her story is of being escorted through the city by two policemen 'since I had such a tight schedule and wanted to see as much as I could':

> One of the last places we visited was the Detroit Institute of the Arts which has a fine collection of African and Egyptian art and does significant outreach to the community, and one of the police officers became more and more

interested in the collection as we went through it. As we said our goodbyes at the airport, he said 'You got to me today. I'm taking my kids to the Mosaic Youth Theatre tomorrow night. I think they'll really like it, and the Museum, there's a lot there for them! I haven't been there since I was a kid, and it's changed. I can see my face and those of my kids reflected there now' ('Our' 210)

This anecdote references nineteenth-century elevation, and twentieth-century government delivering the opportunities for citizens to take stock of their lives against a backdrop of heritage.

Boaz and Alexander's stories, implicitly about the poor-white and poor-black working class respectively, embody and emplot the spectral category of popular support for arts funding – without properly engaging it. Poll numbers are solidly behind some form of relationship between government and the arts. A 1981 poll saw just 26% of Americans say government should not be involved in the arts, 24% approve participation by local government, 19% in support of the states being in on it, and 14% Washington. In both 1980 and 1992, about half the people polled were prepared to pay an extra US$25 in tax annually to help the arts. In 1990, 76% of the US population thought the NEA directed money to appropriate organizations, 69% disagreed with the proposition that it was wasting tax dollars, and 83% felt it served 'a useful purpose for American society' (all this at the height of the so-called 'culture wars') (Filicko 230, 237, 238). Seeing this level of public support suggests that a more credible explanation for the controversy lies in party ideology.

Party Politics and Constitutional Law

Immediately upon its election, the Reagan Administration's 1981 budget proposed a 50% cut in the NEA's vote. Reagan's faction of the Republican Party had long opposed UNESCO, in a move that was simultaneously ideological and an instance of *Realpolitik*: a belief in the wrong-headedness of state support for culture coalesced with the belief, mentioned earlier, that left-liberal forces depended on government funds, and hence could be destroyed by cutting off these sources. Pressure from a Democrat-dominated Congress saw half the NEA cuts restored that year and again in 1983 (Himmelstein and Zald 177–78, 171–72), but the way forward was clear should the Republicans gain control of the legislature.

The 1994 Congressional elections saw Republican takeovers of both Houses for the first time in decades. The Grand Old Party (GOP) swept to power in an anti-political, anti-professional wave of reactionary sentiment by white male Southern voters, hailed and codified by the Contract With America. Federal cultural policy went into crisis, with the GOP voting in the House of Representatives in the summer of 1997 to reduce the NEA's 1998 appropriation to US$10 million, which would have been used to close down operations. Representative Armey called on his Republican allies to 'vote for freedom, vote

	Fiscal year to which data relates	Spending (m U.S Dollars)
Central Government		
Kennedy Center for the Performing Arts	1995	7.5
Smithsonian Institution	1995	358.0
National Gallery of Art	1995	57.4
Institute of Museum Services	1995	28.7
National Endowment for the Arts	1995	162.3
Commission of Fine Arts	1995	0.8
Total Central Government		**614.7**
State Arts Agencies	1995	265.6
Local Arts Agencies	1996	650.0
Total Services		**$1,530.3**

Figure 3   *Direct Public Expenditure on the Arts in the United States*

for the children, vote for the parents, and vote against elite control of Art in America' (quoted in Arts-alert-usa) – and they did. The score was 217–216 to include the Endowment in a point of order for agencies that would not be reauthorized. Congress had previously cut the 1996 budget by almost 40%, from US$162.4 million to US$99.5 million, which followed fifteen years of declining purchasing power (Jane Alexander 'Our' 211).

Apart from ideology, what was being struggled over – in material terms? At its peak, the NEA budget amounted to no more that 66 cents per person (for a total of US$176 million). At its 1998 level, the figure was 36 cents per person (for a budget of US$98 million). Much is made of the comparison with Western European countries, where government ministries or secretariats provide the arts with an average of US$40 per person. But it is misleading to compare NEA funding with Western European ministries, because overall support for the arts in the US, including private donations, reached US$10 billion per year in the 1990s, more or less equivalent to the European norm, and total public support was quite significant.

In 1997, these energies were released anew when the House of Representatives voted to abolish the NEA (Gray 'House'). The Endowment was saved when the House-Senate conference committee deferred the NEA's death sentence for another year, but the Committee further reduced the budget and compromised the agency's autonomy by putting Congressional appointees on its decision-making bodies (Judith Miller). Some Republican members of Congress proposed that an amount equivalent to the NEA's 1996 disbursements of US$80 million should go to the states in block grants: 40% to arts agencies and 60% to school districts. At the same time, twenty-eight GOP Congresspeople

	Australia	Canada	Finland	France	Germany	Ireland	Netherlands	Sweden	United kingdom	United states
Main year of financial data	1993/94	1994/95	1994	1993	1993	1995	1994	1993/94	1995/96	1995
Per Capita Arts Spending (U.S. Dollars)	$25	$46	$81	$57	$85	$9	$46	$37	$26	$6
Total Government Arts Spending† (no. of U.S. Dollars)	$438	$1,272	$460	$3,275	$6,888	$33	$714	$496	$1,518	$1,530
Government Arts Spending as Percentage of Government Final Consumption Expenditure*	0.82%	0.93%	2.10%	1.31%	1.79%	0.43%	1.47%	1.02%	0.65%	0.13%
Government Arts Spending as Percentage of Gross Domestic Product	0.14%	0.21%	0.47%	0.26%	0.36%	0.07%	0.21%	0.29%	0.14%	0.02%
Government Final Consumption Expenditure (no. of U.S. Dollars)	$54	$136	$22	$251	$384	$8	$48	$48	$226	$1,142
Government Final Consumption Expenditure as a Percentage of GDP	17.79%	22.31%	22.31%	20.08%	20.75%	17.14%	14.33%	28.08%	20.46%	15.32%
Population (Millions)	17.7	27.4	5.1	57.7	81.2	3.6	15.4	8.7	58.4	258.2
Gross Domestic Product (no. of U.S. Dollars)	$304	$612	$98	$1,249	$1,913	$48	$338	$173	$1,105	$7,265
Per Capita Gross Domestic Product	$17,181	$22,321	$19,210	$21,651	$23,565	$13,428	$21,944	$19,845	$18,918	$28,158
Human Development Index Ranking	7	1	16	6	11	21	9	4	10	8

†Includes only direct government spending on the arts and not indirect subsidies such as fargene taxes from contributions to the arts.

*Government final consumption expenditure, measured by the OECD (Organization for Economic Cooperation and Development is used as an indicator of the over-all size of each country's public sector.

SOURCE: National Endowment for the Arts *International*

Figure 4   *Government Expenditure on the Arts and Museums*
Includes Federal, State, and Local Government Spending on the Arts

wrote to then-House Speaker Newt Gingrich, indicating their support for the NEA in the light of the '[US]$3.4 billion in revenue ... given back to the federal government' by the arts each year in Federal taxation, and the US$37 billion a year claimed by the industry as externalities. The Clinton administration threatened to veto the Interiors Bill, an omnibus supply package that included the NEA's wind-up vote, and the Senate wrote alternative legislation, restoring US$100 million to the Endowment. The upper house, long more favorable to the NEA, made it safe with an eventual budget of US$98 million, and that figure was retained during the summer 1998 vote. Many Republicans in the House of Representatives changed their minds in an election year, when the NEA was supported by 253 votes to 173. The US$98 million was just over half (56%) of the US$176 million allocated in 1992, the onset of the downward slide. When the figure rose to US$120 million for 2001, that was cause for great celebration – Chair William Ivey hailed it as 'a tremendous victory' (quoted in Southwick 'Budget').

This resigned glee indexes a restructuring of governmentality towards a new way of channeling conduct and enabling action. The new century would require new economic legitimation narratives for the arts, even as their wel-farist mission was conformed. It remains to be seen whether renewed support was a temporary, psephological reprieve, or a seriously rethought response to the Endowment's promise to cut the New York liberal art scene's hold on 25% of all funds – the NEA has a poor record of granting money outside the major arts areas (Rice 38). It was assuredly a major reversal for the reactionary Right, and a source of pleasure to those Republican funders who are patrons of the arts and/or businesses that thrive on art exhibits and theatrical shows (Seelye).

Why had matters gone this far? During the 1994 campaign, promises were made on the GOP side (quickly borrowed by the executive branch) to balance the Federal Budget. Once Congress was under its control, the far right estab-lished 'Conservative Action Teams', loose groupings of about sixty Congress-people. The NEA was their principal symbolic target, even though outlays on it were minimal. The other three aims (abolishing affirmative action, cutting taxes and balancing the budget) were substantive as well as symbolic in that they involved vast sums of money and held immense implications for a diverse workforce (Gee 10–11). In other words, while welfare reform was the principal item for discussion, high-profile minor cuts, such as the NEA, were also a pri-ority. But was the Endowment a meaningful contributor to the deficit run up by the Reagan administration's borrowing in the 1980s to fuel the military with-out raising taxes? Hardly. The NEA's budget has never exceeded the amount the Defense Department spends each year on military bands (US$183 million) (Schechner 7; Plagens B4; Jane Alexander *Command* 72). In 1996, Congress approved the purchase of 80 C-17 airplanes costing US$300 million each, 240 times the annual NEA appropriation, and voted the Pentagon US$7 billion more than it had requested (Jane Alexander 'Our' 211; Robert Hughes). Realistically, the Endowment seemed to represent easy delivery of a Contract With America item, one that posed no threat to the corporate welfare that underwrites companies, which in turn underwrite Republican (and Democrat) electoral expenditure.

We are seeing a coalition at work here between two wings of the Republican Party. One wing is composed of fiscal conservatives who want reductions in public expenditure and regulation. They are barely ideological, more accumula-tionist. The other wing defines the country's problems in expressly ideological terms – cutting budgets meets defunding the left in a way that does not hurt right-wing pork-barreling (Himmelstein and Zald 172–73). Virtually since its inception, the Endowment has had problems with Republicans and Southern Democrats in the House of Representatives, where opposition to government participation in culture matches a desire for expenditure patterns that assist constituents. House conservatives routinely recommend winding-up the NEA when Democrats are in the White House (Moen 188; also see Gilmore 138). By contrast, Senate Republicans are much more positive about the Endowment, recognizing the multiplier effect and boosterism of Federal arts expenditure on their state-wide electorates (Moen 'Congress' 187, 191, 199). Sometimes, attempts to cater to this diverse Republican reaction produce their own prob-lems. The recent shift by the NEA away from discipline-based review panels, such as dance, to issue areas (heritage, education, creation and stabilization) – designed to answer charges of revolving-door rent-seeking and the desire to shock – simply adds to the right's accusations of cultural engineering. In 2001, outgoing Chair Ivey proudly noted the Endowment's after-school arts initiatives that provided 'safe havens' for young inner-city people as part of an attempt to diminish interpersonal violence – a return to the homilies of 1965 that reinforced welfarist tendencies without engaging progressive politics.

Critiques from the Left and Ideas of Community

Dismantling the NEA has, of course, also been a part of the conservative culture wars, most specifically to counter multiculturalism, which had come late to the Endowment's priorities. By the 1980s, it was well known that minorities did not attend 'mainstream' art events in numbers even remotely approximating their distribution in the population. A 1978 study of arts atten-dance for the NEA estimated that only 7% of mainstream culture-consuming audiences were minorities (blacks, Asians and Hispanics constituted 20% of the population at the time). This figure is even smaller if the performing arts are differentiated from museums, which accommodate school visits (DiMaggio et al. (1978) 3, 29–33).

Until the so-called culture wars of the late 1980s, both liberal and conserva-tive voices in arts councils and arts institutions advocated greater efforts in minority audience outreach. Everyone agreed that the NEA was caught up in a form of cultural capital that appealed to upholders of Old-World norms as superior to US immigrant/popular culture. As late as 1990, in the midst of the obscenity controversies, the NEA under Frohnmayer made support of 'multicultural involvement [in] all grant-making programs in the arts' a priority, earmarking a 'specific portion of the Endowment budget for underserved populations' (Gilmore 138–39). But the 'democratization of culture' as measured in audience equity will only occur when access is facilitated by raising the educational and income levels of minorities and by programming art events that are 'culturally relevant' to the different constituencies in the population. For Gilmore, greater emphasis on diverse cultural traditions in arts programming will attract minority audiences (170); DiMaggio and Francis Ostrower believe sociodemographic profiles and educational attainment to be more relevant 'than … the effects of race on the participation of otherwise similar men and women' (100). From the perspective of audience equity, it is clear that the critiques of representations in the 1980s, which were eventually absorbed into the institutional world of galleries and museums, did not go far enough in dismantling the privilege that the art world reproduces, especially in class terms.

The NEA has found it difficult to attract minority applicants for grants, so profound is their alienation from organs of governance, which are seen to police them and service others (Gilmore 159). As we have seen, there is a right-wing split between those who favor a small role for government in the arts, to provide for the public what the market cannot, and those who think all art should be dictated by consumption. The left sees the arts in a far more transformative way, harking back to the ideals of socialist 'man' as a new being. Somewhere inbetween resides *Time* art critic Robert Hughes, who favors the NEA because it gives a 'sense of community with other citizens, … the creation of mutuality, the passage from feeling into shared meaning' (quoted in Plagens B5). That is a nice sentiment, but it appears to be at odds with much of the art world's allergic reaction to such talk as nationalistic and imperialist. The precise nature of this mission has also varied by genre. NEA-assisted performing organizations have done little for the general public. When classical-music orchestras hold free or 'accessible' events, these are cordoned off from the norm. Such one-off affairs do not inflect typical offerings and structures of power (Zolberg 'Paying' 399). While some sectors of the left, particularly radical multiculturalists, decry the élitism of the NEA and arts councils, they differ from populist conservatives in linking their call for the democratization of cultural production and consumption to the inclusion of historically excluded and subordinated minorities in decision-making over cultural provision. Not surprisingly, this sector of the left views such categories as heritage with a critical edge, as per the 1990s clash between African Americans and white southerners over the display of the Confederate flag on government buildings: one group's 'heritage' is an affront to another's.

The NEA's reaction to such pressures has been to call for a sense of citizenship among artists and the public that is concerned with collaborative endeavor outside politics – a renewal of volunteerism that has always been the nation's response to the negative consequences of market capitalism

(Larson *American*). This twee, folksy notion of people muddling through troubles together, without the powerful forms of knowledge, technology and compulsion available to corporations and governments, is little more than an appeal founded on emotionalism. In the arts field, its impact is laughable. Money holds art together, and voluntary grass-roots associations do not have those resources. There has been diminished direct corporate support for culture since the end of the art-market boom in the late 1980s and subsequent recessions. In 1991, about 12% of corporate giving went to the arts; in 1994, the proportion was 9.5%. Total donations to the humanities and the arts declined by US$270 million in the three years to 1995 (Jane Alexander 'Our' 211; Policy.com 1). Corporations can hardly be expected to step into the breach. Gingrich was sent a letter from one hundred and fourteen business leaders stating that 'the corporate world is not able to carry the entire burden of the cost of cultural access, awareness and education'. As Kevin Mulcahy ('Public Support' 28) suggests, without the NEA, state and community arts agencies might increase in importance, but would struggle with the still-unclear outcome of the general devolution of welfare payments to the states (for example, will the disemployed leave poor states for rich ones, once Federal assistance is no longer available?). The focus of new art forms on 'everyday life' may be left to the market, as NEA supporters rally around 'distant and difficult' art that transcends the quotidian in search of difference and newness (Danto 6), thus appealing to an elite.

As we have seen, the legitimation of art and culture classically claims that they provide uplift, a safe haven for freedom or inner vision, and a transformation through utilitarianism and entrepreneurialism. These trends are evident in the NEA's 1997 monograph, *American Canvas*, a synthesis of six town hall-like discussions with people from all sectors of society interested in support of the arts. *American Canvas'* vision of the privatization or partnership of education and art with corporate culture is consistent with a human-capital emphasis on employment skills. In what follows, we review some premises and examples of this vision.

The 1990s ushered in one new academic and cultural narrative – that the arts and humanities help to legitimize post-Cold War society. Conservatives and many liberals have sought to cut arts budgets in reaction against the apparent demotion of high culture, or attempted to reinstate the classics, fearful that Shakespeare will no longer be taught. In the process, they encouraged populist and cultural studies critiques of gatekeeping practices. The ensuing debates have often lapsed into reciprocal condemnations of 'special interest', thus emptying out the 'intrinsic' value that was assumed to be the province of art when the NEA was instituted. On the other hand, universities and arts organizations have increasingly resorted to a pragmatic defense of the humanities and culture. They characterize the arts as tools that enhance employability, acting as junior behavior-modifying partners to the science faculties, which produce profitable intellectual property. In the cultural sector, the arts become part of social-service rationales or economic development plans for communities, thus justifying subvention by corporations and foundations. The new legitimation discourse encourages partnerships between government, business and the third or non-profit sector.

This shift from the state to partnerships is a way of resituating management of the social squarely within civil society – a new transformation in governmentality. As Foucault argued, 'civil society is the concrete ensemble within which these abstract points, economic men, need to be positioned in order to be made adequately manageable' ('Lecture'). Contemporary neoliberalism reintroduces the expectation that 'institutions of assistance' will be situated within civil society rather than government. *American Canvas* characterizes this new pragmatism as the 'need to "translate" the value of the arts into more general civic, social, and educational terms' so that they can be more convincing to the public and elected officials (Larson *American* 81). This pragmatic legitimation is made even more forcefully toward the end of the report:

> No longer restricted solely to the sanctioned arenas of culture, the arts would be literally suffused throughout the civic structure, finding a home in a variety of community service and economic development activities – from youth programs and crime prevention to job training and race relations – far afield from the traditional aesthetic functions of the arts. This extended role for culture can also be seen in the many new partners that arts organizations have taken on in recent years, with school districts, parks and recreation departments, convention and visitor bureaus, chambers of commerce, and a host of social welfare agencies all serving to highlight the utilitarian aspects of the arts in contemporary society. (127–28)

.The acquisition of skills is a major aspect of the arts touted by *American Canvas*. In one section, a report by the Arts and Education Commission is quoted which states that the arts should be

> part of [students'] preparation for productive work [insofar as they] help ... build the specific workplace skills needed to ensure their own employability and their ability to make a solid economic contribution to their communities and the nation. The arts teach and enhance such skills as the ability to manage resources, interpersonal skills of cooperation and teamwork, the ability to acquire and use information and to master different types of symbol systems, and the skills required to use a variety of technologies. (Larson *American* 100)

The report goes so far as to suggest that the arts can be as tough as the times require, inculcating in students a cognitive 'muscularity', that is, 'wir[ing] children's brains for successful learning' (Larson *American* 102)

The basic premise here is that investment in the arts will provide a return. While the 'return' of a 1960s investment in art and culture was presumably the channeling of protest energies into 'creativity', today's notion of 'return' indexes a shift among economists to the concept of social capital: the arts should provide safer communities, increase the ability to learn and earn higher salaries and concomitantly contribute more to the tax base, and so on. This is an example of the conversion of non-market activity to market activity (Santana). The report is thus consistent with this new legitimation narrative in promoting self-esteem and tolerance of difference through art. Aware that he may have gone too far in this utilitarian direction, the author of the report apologetically points out that this approach may be 'understandable in these difficult, distrustful times' but cautions that it can 'ultimately subvert the very meaning of art' (Larson *American* 103, 109, 111).

American Canvas' two hundred pages have virtually nothing to say about art practices or meanings. Although the author, Gary Larson, sounds such cautions as the one just mentioned above, he nevertheless concentrates on the leverage the arts can gain from partnerships with business and social-service agencies. He is not alone. One arts activist, Syd Blackmarr, president of the Georgia Assembly of Community Arts Agencies, advocates folding the arts into civic activity. He is reported as saying: 'It is time for those who know the power of the arts ... to become members of the school board, the city and county commission, the planning and zoning commission, the housing authority, the merchants association, the library board'. 'The point', adds Larson, 'is not simply to underscore the relevance of the arts to those various civic concerns, but to tap the public funds that flow through these channels, some of which might be used for the arts'. Blackmarr is quoted again as saying that 'we must insist that when roads, sewers, prisons, libraries and schools are planned and funded ... that the arts are also planned and funded. We must find the line items, the budget categories, the dollar signs in all of these local sources' (quoted in Larson *American* 83). The 'we' here is the well-tempered citizen of Kantian-Arnoldian vision – an active participant in the social who nevertheless does so via knowledges and modalities derived from governmentality.

It is quite evident that the turn to schools and communities is made with an eye to the bottom line. The report moves glibly from renewing the idea of the artist-as-citizen who works with communities, to using those communities as springboards to urban revitalization and tourism. This is not, of course, a one-sided gain, for urban renewal projects are enhanced by cultural tourism. The report gives the example of the town of Lowell, which became a kind of theme park of itself, and the Philadelphia Museum of Art, which brought hundreds of millions of dollars to Philadelphia with the blockbuster Cézanne show in 1996. A participant in another town meeting for *American Canvas* said that the 'arts are a tremendous asset', offering some communities an edge in the competition for tourists (84–87). There is a utilitarian side to sober, even, temper.

The boundaries between economic, civic and artistic activities are blurred in these examples, to the point where several participants at the colloquia spoke of the fusion of the everyday and art without the slightest awareness that they were echoing the most radical dreams of the historical avant-gardes. This is not exactly the same as the commodification of art – as in the case of museum tie-ins: mugs, t-shirts, ties, posters, paper weights etc. Although not mentioned in *American Canvas*, the fusion of art with urban and community development is more in line with the international movement know as 'culture and development' – a concern with development that does not put communities at risk (culturally or ecologically) but contributes to the economy. The central concept in the culture and development movement – promoted by UNESCO, the World Bank, the Inter-American Development Bank and the Rockefeller and Ford Foundations – is civil society, understood as the self-organization of communities (World Bank). Yet it is evident that this self-organization can no longer be understood as an autonomous process. Now it is in partnership with global NGOs and the non-profit sector as well as capital, in keeping with Foucault's insight about the intersubjective side to civil society that we mentioned above.

Blurring the private and the public has been accompanied by realignments of right and left on the political spectrum. Many civil-society activists in the US and around the world who were once very critical of capital are now spearheading these partnerships. As progressives move away from class struggle and anti-imperialism, and as capital – at least those sectors of it that have branched into cultural marketing and point-of-purchase politics – sometimes espouses environmentalism, anti-racism and anti-sexism, community arts activists see themselves as working on behalf of social justice. This is certainly the tenor of *American Canvas*, which oscillates between radical statements and more conservative accommodations. We read, for instance, of one organization that put on an exhibit that included gay and racial civil rights artwork and then invited a cross-section of the community, including conservatives, to discuss how it might be contextualized to be acceptable to all. We see here the notion of partnership extending from public and private, or economic and civic arrangements, to an embrace of political adversaries. The director of this community organization in Winston-Salem waxed enthusiastic that 'suddenly, these people were all partners rather than adversaries' (quoted in Larson *American* 70).

This cooptation has irritated the left, even those activists who see art as crucially intricated with the social and hence useable for political ends. They question whether the project of radical democracy has been aided by US Federal policy. The NEA has assuredly assisted official, institutional culture, whether at the level of the Metropolitan Museum of Art or local galleries. But its criteria for funding require incorporation, boards of directors and auditable books. Schedules must be made a year in advance, and a range of nominated communities addressed: 'In short, be coopted or lie' (Schechner 8). Richard Schechner suggests American performance has lost its vibrancy because of such bureaucratization and reportage. ACT UP, the best avant-garde around, gets no money from corporations or the state: 'Now we are in the final act of *Death of a Salesman* and Willy is realizing he's been had. It's not just that the NEA is shutting down or redefining itself, it never was that big a deal in the first place' (Schechner 9). This new governmentalization has subordinated the arts to administrators, planners, managers and entrepreneurs, who have increasingly sought to make business and culture compatible, regardless of their ideological proclivities. Indeed, arts administrators have pretty much resigned themselves to the entrepreneurial *ethos* that accompanies partnerships with private enterprise. This marriage of progressives and capital was written into law in 1997 when Congress allowed the NEA for the first time to solicit funding from the corporate sector (J. Gray 'Cuts').

Conclusion

Future US arts policy will probably see heightened cultural commodification, the shrinkage of arts organizations, and decreased assistance to minorities, unless the growing black, Latino and Asian middle class funds cultural diversity through philanthropy, corporate giving or a marriage of culture and economics. This is certainly the direction of Jesús Chavarría, influential editor of *Hispanic Business* and a major actor in Hispanic philanthropy (Chavarría). Business support will increasingly require product placement. For example, the NEA announced a 'record' tied grant in 1996 for school arts education from H.J. Heinz. The trade-off? Mr Heinz announced a contest for school children to redesign the firm's ketchup label during class, and Alexander proudly referred to ketchup as 'the nation's favorite condiment' (market surveys showed salsa had in fact displaced it, but NEA license was presumably as artistic as it was commercial). During her tenure, the Endowment also welcomed and publicized tiny contributions from Grand Marnier and Border's Books – not to the arts, but to the NEA itself – through its new Office for Enterprise Development ('Arts'; Alexander quoted in Winer).

Perhaps the US will move to a Federal cultural policy that focuses on its own agencies: the Kennedy Center for the Performing Arts, the Library of Congress, the Smithsonian Institution and the National Gallery of Art, leaving indirect assistance to its continued subvention of *bourgeois* taste (Cargo). Other possibilities include block grants to the States, national grants to large organizations or merging the NEA with the National Endowment for the Humanities. It is a time of great flux: renewed American world economic power, built in part on cultural export, flails about domestically in that very area.

In 1996, then-NEA Chair Alexander referred to a tripod of arts institutions. The civil society of volunteerism and localism was one leg; a disinterested but concerned business community the second; and committed legislatures the third. With the global waning of governmental solutions to social issues, this US model of philanthropic and corporate underwriting is increasingly popular, both domestically and overseas. Charitable gifts in the US amounted to US$190 billion in 1999, or 2% of the nation's income, and 73% of residents gave a much higher percentage than in other countries. People with the lowest incomes gave the most away proportionally. Of the total, about 6% went to the arts, compared to 43% to religion and 18% to health and human services (Greenfeld Karl).

Private-public partnerships, driven by tax exemptions and plutocrats in search of cultural capital (Ostrow), have become internationally revered. The model is proliferating throughout Europe and Latin America, as the neoliberal push for reduced government expenditure merges with a democratizing influence that associates state-driven cultural engineering with command cultures (see Chapter 4). Proponents see the US model as a form of non-market, non-governmental interaction between elites and the social (Bloch-Lainé). The United States is increasingly developing and exporting a notion of corporate citizenship – essentially unaccountable, yet supposedly principled. The most powerful export derives from the idea that US private philanthropy and corporate support generate at least as much diversity and quality in the arts as could taxation revenue (Zolberg 'Paying' 395–96). At the same time, there are criticisms that the big Foundations' average annual gift (5.5% of assets) is insufficiently large to justify their tax exemption (Stehle).

To go on as we are, caught between undemocratic if liberal forms of foundation support, and welfarist but controversy-laden forms of state assistance, would permit liberal and neoconservative forces to push citizenship further into the unaccountable realm of civil society. This is implausible as a means of ensuring a devolved, plural and equitably distributed public culture. Consider these statistics about the work of US philanthropy. First, 40% of arts money comes from 0.07% of foundations. Second, 1% of arts organizations receive 32% of philanthropic money. Third, 65% of that money goes to just five states (Larson *American* 156). Why? Private agencies are only accountable to 'civil society' – their shareholders and boards of governance decide where money is allocated.

Corporate and foundation philanthropy is no way to democratize the arts, to make expenditure sensitive to the will of the people. Put simply, that will is concretely expressed in either purchasing (markets) or political preferences (government subvention). The NEA's decision-making panels should be selected from among local politicians, artists' unions, Congress, academics, small popular-culture businesses and community groups. And these people should also decide what happens to foundation funds derived from tax revenue foregone. The *largesse* of nineteenth- and twentieth-century plutocrats may be liberal or conservative – but it will never be democratically arrived at or dispersed under existing arrangements. But the notion of transforming the state into a major source of direct cultural funding will not fly in the United States, and is increasingly regarded as outmoded in the rest of the developed world. Neoliberal economic ideology is rolling back the state from participation in the everyday other than as a trainer in docility and consumption.

The present conjuncture consists of a struggle between conservative morals and contestatory groups that do not conform to liberal standards of taste. As a result of civil rights successes and new social movement inroads that threaten the hegemony of the patriarchal, white, heterosexual status quo, liberals lack conviction in universal categories of human value. They even find it hard to defend their political label, and often bracket questions of moral judgment. But contestatory groups on the left and the right have forced such concerns onto the political agenda. So aesthetics has been foregrounded, and *New York Times* editorials favoring reauthorization of the NEA argue that 'art touches the soul, civilizes us, and promotes access to a "universal language"' ('Art Agency'). A new and more convincing argument must be found. In a culture riven by increased social stratification, racial controversy and gender and sexuality struggles, appeals to the universal confirmation of human dignity through artistic practice and reception are unconvincing. The major arts organizations have more or less supported the status quo of propriety and market criteria.

Back in the 1990s, a poster for the performance art group The Guerrilla Girls stated: 'Relax, Senator Helms, the art world is your kind of place!' (quoted in Roberta Smith; also see Regen). Through indifference to the claims of sub-altern groups made via 'extra-artistic' means (Kramer's phrase again), the art world, out of expediency or outright fear, opted for policing the offending elements. Institutional self-censorship has become a corrective to those artists who sneaked through the cracks, advocating an 'attitude toward life' in their practice (Vance; also see Carr 'War'). As the *New York Times* editorial quoted earlier states, the NEA need not be scrapped, only 'cleaned up'. And that, in fact, is what successive NEA Chairs have done.

What, then, are feasible contestatory responses? To be frank, nothing viable is forthcoming from the institutions themselves, despite bold gestures like the late Joseph Papp's rejection of NEA funding for New York City's Public Theater. Through such a gesture, a moral point is driven home about the autonomy of the aesthetic sphere. But that can no longer be tolerated in a multicultural democracy where certain groups have been consistently stereotyped, cen-sored and/or excluded. Social injustice must be addressed directly, and not solely in terms of autonomous art. Viable responses may be found among the contestatory groups themselves, within which artists have chosen to work.

A painter friend of one of us, active in GLAAD (Gay and Lesbian Alliance Against Defamation), ACT UP (AIDS Coalition to Unleash Power), and Gran Fury (ACT UP's art collective) in the late 1980s and early 1990s, felt that his long-standing policy of boycotting arts organizations was vindicated by the NEA's public funding fiasco. Not that he had anything against the idea of an institutionally sanctioned public sphere in which freedom of expression is guaranteed; on the contrary, he argued, the problem is that arts organizations have only constrained such a public sphere, at least as regards art which pro-jects a gay 'attitude toward life'. Given the two complementary systems in which the art world operates – the market (galleries and auction houses tacitly supported by museum practice) and the non profit/public foundation (over-seen by 'expert' panels) – there is little chance that a truly contestatory art will be funded. These are systems of exclusion, and they work for the benefit of the status quo. His own practice – posters and other public works incorporating explicitly homoerotic reworkings of classical iconography in response to homophobic representations, especially around the AIDS epidemic – was not deemed acceptable at the time (except at AIDS art exhibitions, quite frequently sponsored by groups not involved with the conventional art world).

David Trend recommends transforming the material conditions of art institutions: their means of production, distribution, reception, publicity and so on. The groups engaged in challenges to this infrastructure – Feminists in eXile, Guerrilla Girls, Mothers of Medusa, V-Girls, PESTS, GLAAD and ACT UP – have not offered abstract or distanced deconstructions of representation. Instead, they work to open up new, 'unofficial' spaces both outside and within institutions, combating and stigmatizing representations, developing 'non-traditional audiences' and serving the needs of particular communities, while publicizing their practice for wider access. In the process, according to Trend, such groups served two important functions: 'coalition building' and 'recovering the "public" function of art'.

Social-movement politics does not have to mean minoritization. Rather, it can exert pressure upon the rest of society to come to terms with a given *ethos*, to change in relation to it. In the process, aesthetic practices break loose from the straitjacket of representation and act to change our circumstances by seizing the public realm. Thus Gran Fury's political-aesthetic practice:

> We consistently attempt to situate our work in the 'public realm' in an effort to include a diverse, non-homogeneous audience. Through appropriating dominant media's techniques, we hope to make the social and political subtexts of the AIDS epidemic visible and to incite the viewer to take the next step.

Not a bad metaphor for interventions in cultural policy more generally! By contrast, the late 1990s found the Endowment 'neutered', according to the *New York Times Magazine*, which contemptuously dubbed it 'a kind of National Endowment for Arts and Crafts' (Weisberg). When Clinton asked Congress to increase the NEA's budget by over 50% for his last year in office, and was rejected by the Republican majority on the House Appropriations Subcommittee, there was no talk on either side of culture wars or offensive textuality. Democrats argued that the Endowment deserved a reward for devolving grants away from New York and California, while Republicans said that the money was better spent on national parks (Healy; Southwick 'House'). Both perspectives were compatible with neoliberal policies. Clearly, the project of governing the United States and its empire through culture is ongoing, mediated, and always already prone to controversy.

As Gregg Bordowitz suggested at a culture and labor conference in 2000, the media politics of visibility characteristic of AIDS activism in the 1980s and earlier 1990s, particularly as conditioned by the culture wars, is not enough. There have to be direct challenges to, and if possible negotiations with, government and corporations in order to make a real change. The politics of the public sphere will make an issue newsworthy, but as many activists have learned, recognition will last a short while. Good old coalition-building and new forms of alliance, as in the anti-globalization movement, are needed to pressure governments and corporations. Moreover, Bordowitz goes to the heart of the mechanism that links value both in the cultural sphere and in the health and pharmaceutical industries, which have the power of life and death of HIV-positive people. It is the intellectual property regimes and the copyright and cultural property arrangements that the two spheres have in common. It is thus necessary to work not only at a grassroots community level, or a public-sphere media scale, but also in relation to those governmental, inter-governmental and corporate bodies that make decisions over the life and death of populations – precisely the medium of governmentality, as Foucault characterized it.

---

1 This section on Welles is based on Catherine Benamou's account in 'Orson Welles's Transcultural Cinema: An Historical/Textual Reconstruction of the Suspended Film, *It's All True*, 1941–1993'. Ph.D. Diss, New York University 1997.

2 Of course, we should not go overboard in stressing the significance of culture within the State Department. For many years, cultural diplomats were apparently selected from those in the foreign service who suffered from mental illness or severe physical disorders – also a feature of decolonizing powers, such as France, where intellectual enfeeblement and chronic professional failure were qualifications for cultural governance (Wieck 131; Ingram 801).

3 We are using the international terminology NGO for what is usually known as a non-profit organization in the United States.

2

The Culture Industries – Citizenship, Consumption and Labor

[A cinematograph film represents something more than a mere commodity to be bartered against others] – UK Palache Report (quoted in Political & Economic Planning 12)

La radio y la TV tienen la función social de contribuir al fortalecimiento de la integración y el mejoramiento de las formas de convivencia humana. – Ley Federal de Radio y TV de México [Radio and television perform the social function of strengthening integration and improving conviviality.] – Federal Law on Radio and TV, Mexico (quoted in M Lever 23)

Many studies of cultural policy exclude music, film and television because of their relationship to profit-making and the fact that they tend to fall under the rubric of communications rather than culture (itself an index of their great importance to capital and government). But it is precisely because of the dominance of these entertainment industries that nations institute cultural policies. In this chapter, we turn to the audiovisual culture industries within three advanced-industrial liberal democracies and a Third World region. All have mature and powerful commercial cultural sectors that exercise global influence. We focus on the networks of practices and institutions that generate and sustain their production, distribution and exhibition. These practices include technical training, tax breaks, local government assistance, copyright clauses, co-production treaties, regional economic-development programs, media education, archiving, ambassadorial services and censorship. They are planned and executed, mostly in an uneven and discontinuous way, through networks of agents, institutions and discourses. Their impact varies considerably, depending on political regimes and historical conjunctures.

Two subjectivities underpin debate over the audiovisual: the citizen and the consumer as agents of culture and government, representing competing claims for the nation and the market respectively. These subjects are mobilized in debates about cultural policy, free trade and the NICL. We study them at four spaces and moments: Miami today, Australia since the 1970s, Britain in the 1990s, and Latin America since the 1920s. In each case, there is a clear drive towards both a national-popular and the desire for a strongly commercial form of industrial organization, albeit with public support. Because these sectors are so closely tied to corporate and popular activity, they bring out in fine color the linkages and differences between citizens and consumers.

Citizen/Consumer/Worker?

There is a complicated relationship between the citizen and its logocentric double, the consumer. The citizen is a wizened figure from the ancient past. The consumer, by contrast, is naive, essentially a creature of the nineteenth century. Each shadows the other, the *national* subject versus (or is it *as*?) the *rational* subject. We all know the popularity of the consumer with neo-classical economists and policy wonks: the market is said to operate in response to this ratiocinative agent, who, endowed with perfect knowledge, negotiates between alternative suppliers and his or her own demands, such that an appropriate price is paid for desired commodities. The supposedly neutral mechanisms of market competition see materials exchanged at a cost that ensures the most efficient people are producing, and their customers are content.

The consumer and the citizen loom large in global discussions of textual exchange, with one supposedly exercising free will in buying culture, and the other in authorizing the state to use tax money to make culture. But commodities are always cultural, and cultural products are always commodities. Desire and fetishism, which inhere to a culture, condition the reasons for buying commodities, through advertising. The ratiocinative conduct of the consumer is also subject to a range of cultural conditionings premised on what fuels desire: fantasies that function on the basis of the erotic, racial otherness and power. Furthermore, insofar as it materializes fantasies in specific objects, commodity consumption serves for many people as a way of realizing themselves – hence the emergence of a consumerist and reception-oriented politics of desire amongst some racialized, gendered and sexualized groups.

There are two basic accounts of audiovisual subjectivity. In their different ways, each is an effects model, for they both assume the audiovisual *does* things *to* people, to citizen/consumers as audience members. The first model derives from the social sciences and is applied without consideration of place. We'll call this the *domestic* effects model, or DEM. It is universalist and psychological. The DEM concerns itself, analytically and critically, with such crucial citizenship questions as education and civic order. It views the screen as a machine that either perverts or directs the citizen. Entering young minds osmotically, it can enable or imperil the learning process. And it may also drive the citizen to violence, through aggressive and misogynistic words, images and narratives. The DEM assumes, then, two kinds of audiovisual impact on citizenship. On the one hand, it may promote 'good' conduct: (i) learning and self-control; (ii) training and the superego; or (iii) preparation and responsibility. On the other, it may induce the diametric opposite of each 'positive' effect: respectively, (i) ignorance and self-indulgence; (ii) guesswork and the id; or (iii) lassitude and selfishness. The DEM is found in a variety of sites, including laboratories, clinics, prisons, schools, newspapers, psychology journals, music companies, TV networks, film-studio research and publicity departments, everyday talk, program classification regulations, conference papers, parliamentary debates and state-of-our-youth or state-of-our-civil-society moral panics (see Buckingham; Hartley). It generates cultural-policy interventions in education and censorship.

The second way of thinking about audiovisual citizenship is a *global* effects model, or GEM. It is more relevant to our concerns in this chapter. The GEM is specific and political rather than universalist and psychological. It is at the heart of both 'mainstream' concerns with productivity and decline as well as 'minority' demands to eradicate gender, ability or racial stereotypes, on the premise that they provoke discrimination and even violence, and that the dissemination of positive images will lead to understanding. Whereas the DEM focuses on the cognition and emotion of individual human subjects via replicable experimentation, the GEM looks to the knowledge of custom and patriotic feeling exhibited by collective human subjects, the grout of national culture. In place of psychology, it is concerned with politics. The audiovisual does not make you a well- or ill-educated person, a wild or self-controlled one. Rather, it makes you a knowledgeable and loyal national subject, or a duped viewer who lacks an appreciation of local culture and history. Belonging, not psychic wholeness, is the touchstone of the global effects model. Instead of measuring responses electronically or behaviorally, as its domestic counterpart does, the GEM looks to the national origin of texts and the themes and styles they embody, with particular attention to the screen genres of drama, news, sport and current affairs. GEM adherents hold that local citizens should control local broadcast networks because they alone can be relied upon to be loyal reporters in the event of war, while reflectionist claims for the role of fiction are thought to mean that only locally sensitized producers make narratives that are true to history and custom. This model is found in the discourse of cultural imperialism, everyday talk, record industry and telecommunications policy, international organizations, newspapers, cultural diplomacy, post-industrial service-sector planning and national-cinema discourse. It has a long lineage. For instance, when John Reith became the first head of the BBC, his guiding tome, *Broadcast Over Britain* (1924), promised that the Corporation would be a bulwark against rampant commercialism (i.e. the United States and its successful cinema exports) and political extremism (i.e. the Soviet Union and Italy and their successful ideological exports) (McGuigan *Culture* 56). And in 1936, the League of Nations created an International Convention Concerning the Use of Broadcasting in the Cause of Peace that was designed to prohibit messages sent from one national radio system into another lest they foment social struggle or operate 'in a manner prejudicial to good international understanding' (Kevin McDonald).

The DEM suffers from all the disadvantages of ideal-typical psychological reasoning. Each massively costly laboratory test of media effects, based on, as the refrain goes, 'a large university in the mid-West', is countered by a similar experiment, with conflicting results. As politicians, grant-givers and jeremiad-wielding pundits call for more and more research to prove that the audiovisual makes you stupid, violent and apathetic – or the opposite – academics line up at the trough to indulge their hatred of popular culture and ordinary life and their rent-seeking urge for public money. As for the GEM, its concentration on national culture: (i) denies the potentially liberatory side-effect of pleasure in imports; (ii) forgets the internal differentiation of audiences; (iii) valorizes frequently oppressive local *bourgeoisies* in the name of national culture's maintenance and development; and (iv) ignores the demographic realities of its 'own' terrain.

As Alain Herscovici explains, neoliberalism facilitates the transformation of patrimony into property. The valuation of patrimony or private property in market terms is not something that takes place naturally – it ensues from political decisions. These conditions both shape and are shaped by insertion into the world economy, technological developments, the features of a given industry, national elites' demands, and how citizens' needs are translated into consumer demands. Of course, a citizen's need is not in itself a natural phenomenon but the result of 'filtering' through the force-field 'sieve'. Consequently, in a given conjuncture, such a need may be construed as arising from the masses (a sociopolitical construct) and in a different conjuncture, consumers' needs may be conceived as emanating from a multiplicity of demographic segments, in this case both sociopolitical and market constructs. In the former case, the nation state participates in the shaping of the mass public through public investment in a communications infrastructure and a distribution system that will provide equal access (Herscovici 55). In the latter, when the airwaves are transformed into private commodities responding to technological innovation, and market pressures that orient communication to demographic niches, content is tailored to those consumers who provide the greatest profits. Consequently, in contrast with mass communications that seek to ensure equal access (at least ideally), cable TV and other pay-per-view products widen the cultural gap between haves and have-nots, for there will be a marked difference in the entertainment and information consumed by differently positioned consumers. Moreover, the absence of a regulatory mechanism in the media market is conducive to the oligopolization of markets (Herscovici 56).

The transformation of communications systems by neoliberal processes (privatization, deregulation, and the elimination of services provided by the welfare state for both political and economic reasons) results in the recomposition and resignification of territories and publics. The transnationalization and (neo)liberalization of the culture industries imposes (i) the need to enter into a supranational economy, and (ii) restructuring to facilitate that entry according to a 'dialectic of uniformization and differentiation' (Herscovici 58). On the one hand, juridical protocols, technologies and administrative procedures are made uniform; on the other, the accommodation to transnational markets requires the generation of local differences to facilitate profitability for contents that will have uptake across borders: 'Each geographic space needs to differentiate itself and construct its media image in order to valorize itself in relation to the exterior and in that way insert itself into international networks; culture is amply utilized in the construction of that media image' (Herscovici 58–59). The fact that this valorization of localities and their contents is produced by generating differences (orchestrated by a transnational market environment) obliges identity formation to obey performative imperatives. In other words, differences cannot be thought *outside* the force field in which they derive their value. Consequently, it is possible to argue that differences are constituted within globalization processes (Lacarrieu 4–5).

Taking cognizance of this complicates our understanding of projects for laying claim to the local, for we become aware that difference is the mechanism or resource that enables valorization, even in civil society initiatives that have no direct links to the market. We are referring here to tendencies of absorption of those movements that, like the *sem terra* (landless) in Brazil or the Zapatistas in Mexico, seek to *participate* in the distribution of goods and services, be they of the state, the market or civil society. But there are also resistance movements, like the Mothers of the Plaza de Mayo in Argentina, that attempt to rescue or restore the memory of what the state and the market have made invisible and to which so-called civil society cannot give access through prevailing strategies of representation.

To understand this situation, we need to consider the New International Division of Cultural Labor. The idea of the NICL derives from re-theorizations of economic dependency theory that followed the inflationary chaos of the 1970s (Miller et al.). Developing markets for labor and sales, and the shift from the spatial *sensitivities* of electrics to the spatial *insensitivities* of electronics, pushed businesses to see Third World countries as more than suppliers of raw materials and look on them as shadow-setters of the price of work, competing for employment amongst themselves and with the First and Second Worlds. This development broke up the prior division of the world into a small number of industrialized nations and a majority of underdeveloped ones, as production was split across continents. Folker Fröbel and his collaborators christened it the New International Division of Labor.

Just as manufacturing fled the First World, cultural production has also relocated, though largely within the Industrialized Market Economies (IMECs). This is happening at the level of popular textual production, marketing, information and high-culture, limited-edition work, because factors of production, including state assistance, lure cultural producers. What might this analysis do for those working in cultural policy studies? We turn here to instances from music, film and TV that embody crises of labor, the state, the nation, transnational agencies and the border-riding rituals that seek to separate culture from commerce and nation from nation. They show the importance of (i) the global as discourse; (ii) the complex specificities of the cultural and the economic; and (iii) the need for a blend of political economy and cultural studies.

In an era of globalized music, film and television, the idea that audiovisual spaces should be accountable to local audiences, as well as far-distant shareholders, is a powerful one. Eurocentric worldviews on citizenship assume a liberal state that guarantees citizenship. This is not the case in many if not most countries of the world. And how much can be expected from citizens' appeals to national governments when: (i) for the first time, trade between corporations exceeds that between states; (ii) deregulation sees huge monopoly capitalists converging and collaborating; (iii) texts are designed to transcend linguistic and other cultural boundaries; and (iv) many societies deny or limit citizenship claims?

Citizenship assumes governmental policing of rights and responsibilities. Does this apply when a NICL is in operation, and deregulation or the protection of retrograde media *bourgeoisies* seem the only alternatives? To whom do you appeal as a person unhappy with the silencing of your local dramatic tradition through TV imports, but demoralized by the representation of ethnic and sexual minorities or women within so-called national screen drama or network news? In Mexico and Brazil there is an increasing critique of national media for these misrepresentative practices, and the sites for doing something about these concerns are predominantly governmental and transnational. Recognizing, however, that the media are increasingly international, García Canclini and others advocate a Latin-American cultural space (prioritizing the audiovisual) that maintains a role for national involvement in a supranational initiative that protects local production and consumption desires without ceding control to national or international *bourgeoisies*. What would that mean, when the US has already constructed such a site – Miami – on economic rather than anti-cultural-imperialist grounds (as detailed below)?

Of course, much of the push for a citizen address in popular culture is profoundly anti-democratic, in that it laments the passing of 'happier' times, when all was stable and resolved and a patrimony was, well, a patrimony. And like its supposed other, the consumer, the citizen is an ideal type. Countries like France and Australia are committed to retaining local audiovisual production for some democratic reasons, but they also have immensely powerful local media that benefit from protection of the culture industries. To tease out these contradictions, we favor a labor-theory-of-value approach to cultural citizenship. For bringing together the economy and textuality of the screen necessitates looking at the terrain of trade and work. In other words, we are arguing for an outlook on culture based on fundamental shifts in the division of labor, as well as psychological health or national consciousness.

Miami Music and Entertainment

We begin with Miami's music industry. Today's extraordinary boom in Latin migration to the US has seen a significant contribution to the NICL. It is a double-edged sword. On the one hand, traditional discrimination against Latin

Americans sees many people uncomfortable with Spanish-language threats to the hegemony of English as the national language. On the other, the sheer numbers of Hispanics in the country, and their economic contribution, are attractive to both state and business. As this section demonstrates, government has been a major player in this fraction of the NICL (as usual, without any recognition in media discourse, where all is attributed to private initiative).

Miami has many attractions for people who are seeking to work in entertainment, new media and related enterprises that do business in Latin America or cater to US Latino markets. Compared to Latin America it offers: economic stability; the most convenient location for those who travel tricontinentally in Latin America, Europe and the US; the lowest cost of living of the major concentrations of Hispanics in the US (Los Angeles, New York and Miami); excellent communications and mail services; a critical mass of production companies and technological production services (studios, laboratories and post-production and distribution facilities); high intellectual and artistic capital (composers, arrangers, producers, musicians, scriptwriters, designers, translators, universities and specialized training centers); attractive locations for film, video and photography; ancillary services (accountancy, advertising, banking, law, etc.); tax breaks and other government incentives for production and commerce; and a diverse cultural life (restaurants, bars, nightclubs, galleries, museums and beaches). Moreover, according to many people who have relocated there, it has the feel of a Latin American city without the crime, grime and infrastructural dysfunctionality. In other words, it is a First World city (Granado; Casonu).

The city's music and entertainment infrastructure has grown to the point that any imaginable service can be found in Miami, from producers, arrangers, backup singers, writers, sound engineers, technicians and film and video personnel to specialized musicians. For example, besides Criteria and Crescent Moon Studios, the Estefans plan to construct a US$100 million dollar record and film studios called, somewhat grandiosely, Studio City ('Studio City'; 'Comras'). Since the mid-1990s, Latin music has enjoyed robust growth unseen in any other segment of the music business, with a 12% jump from 1998 to 1999. The US Latin music industry's strong performance is, according to Hilary Rosen, President of the Recording Industry Association of America (RIAA), additional to 'the Ricky Martin/Jennifer Lopez phenomena, as these artists' recent English language recordings are not classified as Latin' (quoted in Cobo). In Miami Beach alone, more than one hundred and fifty entertainment companies have been established in the past five years (Leyva). Almost half these companies (among them SONY, EMI, Starmedia, MTV Latin America and WAMI TV) are concentrated in a five block-long outdoor mall – Lincoln Road – amid stores, restaurants, theaters and art galleries (Potts). Growth has been so rapid that from September 1999 to March 2000, another twenty-eight companies opened there. These new media firms provide movies, television, videocassettes, CDs, books, interactive games and theater and Internet sites (Gabler). Indeed, the building industry has received a potent shot in the arm from all this activity. Even real-estate companies have formed partnerships with entertainment concerns. For example, developer Michael Comras wagered on the continuing prosperity of Miami's entertainment industry by forming a special division within Miami International Studios to steer companies from Los Angeles and Latin America to Miami, and in particular to his own buildings ('Comras').

The synergy of all of this activity makes Miami a most attractive headquarters location for dot-coms that seek to break into Latin American markets and specialize in entertainment or financial information and counseling. For example, AOL Latin America, Eritmo.com, QuePasa.com, Yupi.com, Elsitio.com, Fiera.com, Aplauso.com, Starmedia.com, Terra.com and Artistsdirect.com offer music information and downloading along with services like web-page creation for musicians; Subasta.com provides on-line auctions; Sports Ya.com and Totalsports.com deliver sports news and electronic commerce; R2.com deals with the futures market; and Consejero.com and Patagon.com offer online stock transactions ('Spanish-language Web Sites Specialize'). These new enterprises are betting that the Internet market in Latin America will grow exponentially, following market studies like International Data Corp's which foresees nineteen million subscribers by 2003 (Graser M32). Brazil alone is expected to have thirty million users in 2005 (DaCosta). Since it is predicted that the Internet will revolutionize the entertainment industry, vast sums of money are being expended as part of a Darwinian gambit for survival. The Cisneros Group invested over US$200 million in its 50/50 partnership with America Online, and spent US$11 million on a media blitz featuring actor Michael Douglas just to launch its Brazil site (Faber and Ewing 46, 48). Similarly, StarMedia raised US$313 million in public offerings in 1999, much of which will be used for marketing and acquisitions (estimated to produce a loss of US$150 million in 2001 (García). Perhaps the most spectacular merger and acquisition was the deal between Spain's global telecommunications corporation, Telefónica, and Germany's global media conglomerate, Bertelsmann, to give Terra, Telefónica's Internet service provider, a shot in the arm by acquiring and merging with Lycos (Carvajal). This is the first purchase of a major US Internet company by a European corporation. While Terra is expected to make sizeable gains in Latin America, it is nevertheless a global initiative, with significant activity in Europe and the United States as well. Miami, easily accessible to these three regions, is thus the most convenient site for its headquarters. Together, these companies have carved out a piece of South Miami Beach that is now called 'Silicon Beach', via entrepreneurial and corporate activity dependent on government initiatives – cultural policy.

Miami has become the third-largest audiovisual production hub in the US, after Los Angeles and New York (LeClaire), and perhaps the largest *for* Latin America. This was achieved not by happenstance or convenience of location, but through very deliberate policy. Consider Miami Beach's wooing of industry. The Miami Beach Enterprise Zone offers incentives to businesses expanding or relocating there that include Property Tax Credits, tax credits on wages paid to

Enterprise Zone residents and Sales Tax Refunds. The Façade Renovation Grant program provides matching grants to qualifying businesses for the rehabilitation of storefronts and the correction of interior code violations (City of South Miami Beach). As a consequence of this promotional activity, Miami entertainment industries generated about US$2 billion in 1997, more than any entertainment capital in Latin America. They boast a workforce of 10,000 employees (García; Martín). By November 1999, volume had increased to US$2.5 billion (Leyva). Other Miami counties are also renewing their initiatives to woo the entertainment industries. To counteract the difficulties that producers and film companies encounter in dealing with the complicated bureaucracy of the numerous municipalities in the area that have their own regulations, Jeff Peel, Miami-Dade's Film Commissioner, is leading an initiative that includes his counterparts in other municipalities to change the bureaucracy and draw more film and TV business to South Florida (Jackson). The importance of entertainment in Miami is not only that it supplies most programming for the US Latino market, but also an increasing share of the Latin American market. Miami entertainment and new media are expanding to global markets ('Boogie Woogie').

The location of the largest free-trade zone in the US close to Miami airport has attracted more than two hundred corporations specializing in international trade since the 1980s. Dupont, for instance, selected Miami as their regional headquarters over Mexico City, San José, Bogotá, Caracas, São Paulo, Rio de Janeiro, Buenos Aires and San Juan (Grosfoguel 366–67). For Néstor Casonu, an Argentine who moved in his capacity as regional managing director for EMI Music Publishing from Buenos Aires to Miami, the city has given him business advantages over Buenos Aires and other Latin American cities, to which he can easily fly from Miami International Airport.

Entertainment and tourism nourish each other. The critical mass of entertainment companies situated in South Beach has transformed it into a major international promenade for the 'beautiful people' and those who yearn to walk in their wake. In the early 1990s, following Versace and all the glitz of fashion and entertainment celebrities, 'the beautiful people came to town'. As Neisen Kasdin, mayor of South Miami Beach explains, 'people wanted to be around them'. Together, these phenomena produced a synergy that increased exponentially the 'non-stop creation of new businesses in modeling, new media, broadcasting and electronic commerce' (quoted in Kilborn). And of course, this 'Hollywood East' or 'Hollywood Latin America' has spawned a self-congratulatory hype – embodied in Will Smith's 'Miami Mix', produced by Emilio Estefan at Crescent Moon – that belies local conflicts but does capture the spirit, and no doubt part of the reality, of what makes Miami so dynamic in the early twenty-first century.

This hype, and the commercial reality that largely corresponds to it, together provide the major rationale, along with South Florida's incentives, for business and political leaders' strategies to locate the Center of Hemispheric

Integration in Miami. As the rhetoric goes, only in Miami are there significant representatives from each country of the region. Furthermore, Florida sends 48% of its exports to Latin America, most of which travel through Miami. According to Luis Lauredo, US ambassador to the Organization of American States (OAS), Miami 'is a blend of the best of the cultures of the Americas, both North and South'. As a center of commerce, technology and communications, whose personnel are at the very least bilingual, it has a comparative advantage. This advantage is expected to increase with the 'expansion of its intellectual capital', mostly by way of immigration but also by targeted training programs at public institutions like the University of Miami (UM) and Florida International University (FIU). That FIU graduates more Spanish-speaking students than any other university in the US is not an expression of concern for Latinos as an underprivileged minority, but rather a strategy for reinforcing the business and high-tech sectors. This strategy ensues from the observation that, in the words of FIU's president, the most dynamic 'technological and economical urban centers are connected with major research universities' (Rivera-Lyles). As the site of business and trade summits, Miami is touted as a new world Brussels. Should the Free Trade Agreement of the Americas (FTAA or ALCA in Spanish) be situated in Miami, where negotiations have been held over the past couple of years and in whose Intercontinental Hotel its headquarters are temporarily situated, it is likely that the OAS and the Inter-American Development Bank (IDB) would move there. This opportunity will enable Miami to redefine itself when the embargo on Cuba is lifted, and tourism, still Miami's largest industry, is siphoned off to that island. The location of a critical mass of communications and Internet companies in Miami is already a step in this direction (Katel).

Latin Miami is no longer an exclusively Cuban city. There are hundreds of thousands of immigrants from Nicaragua, the Dominican Republic, Colombia, Venezuela, Argentina, Brazil and other countries. While some have been in Miami for a few short years, they already have national festivals. Argentina's first festival in May 1999 attracted 150,000 people. Several hundred thousand Colombians, both from Miami, other parts of the States and from the homeland, swelled Tropical Park in July 1999. While many have come out of economic necessity or for political reasons, quite a few have come to work in the entertainment and new media industries. Many come for both reasons: telenovela actress Alejandra Borrero and talk-show host Fernando González Pacheco both left out of fear of kidnapping by guerrillas and moved to Miami where they could continue doing television work (Rosenberg). The new immigrants to Miami fit neither the assimilationist nor the identity politics paradigms familiar to US scholars of race and ethnicity. While they maintain ties to their homelands and travel back and forth, they have also developed a new spirit of belonging to the city. Daniel Mato's research on the *telenovela* industry indicates that many new transplants feel comfortable in reflecting the reality of Latin American immigrants in the US (Yúdice 'La industria'; Mato 'Miami'). Some have developed a new sense of cultural citizenship and seek to reinforce local cultural institutions. Unlike most Latin American immigrants and Latino minorities in other US cities, most of the fifty people interviewed in March 1999 characterized Miami as an 'open city' that accepts new migrants. Not all new transplants are from Latin America; many people have relocated to Miami from other parts of the US and from Europe to take advantage of opportunities. There is a recognition that entertainment, the new media, design, fashion, tourism and the arts are helping to transform Miami, to give it the cultural sophistication it never had before. And Miami's cultural policy officials showcase this multicultural image.

In Miami, culture plays a 'innovation-creating' role. Indeed, the Miami Beach's Liaison for the Entertainment Industry was transmuted into an Office of Business and Economic Development (Leyva). This is because markets and identity go together in Miami's Latin-inflected multiculturalism. The effect of all this Latin cultural production in a US city, no matter how Latinized, is of concern to many Latin Americans, who fear that national and local cultures will be homogenized by the 'Miami sound machine', one of the reasons why even leftist media artists working with MERCOSUR are seeking to create a viable regional market (see Chapter 5). But hybridity and transculturation are the name of the pop-music game in all Latin American entertainment capitals (Yúdice 'La industria'). The results are not a flattening out of music but, on the contrary, its pluralization, observable in the rock of groups like La Ley and Maná, respectively from Chile and Mexico, or the 'ethnic' musics of Olodum and AfroReggae, respectively from Salvador and Brazil. Moreover, there is a constant flow of musical forms from Latin America into Miami via the musicians who go there to produce their records, and the influences that arrangers and producers introduce into their work. This emphasis on local taste markets is increasingly reflected in the organizational structure of some entertainment companies, especially the most global ones. Mato points out that some telenovela and serial production companies are selling modular formats that can be tailored to the demographic characteristics of audiences in different localities ('Miami' 6). Something similar is taking place in the corporate reorganization of MTV Latin America. Programming and marketing were completely done in the Miami office when MTV Latin America got started, with one signal for all of Spanish America in 1993, and another for MTV Brazil. In 1996, it took its first step toward regionalization by doubling the Spanish American signals, centering the northern one in Mexico City and the southern one in Buenos Aires. In 1999, it begin to produce programming in the regions, following the adage of 'I want my own MTV'. Rather than homogenization, a global corporation like MTV wants local relevance, in every locality. The next step will be to establish full programming, production and marketing offices in each of twenty-two countries. Its center of operations will remain in Miami, but content will be much more flexible and nomadic, with managers and producers moving or communicating between Latin American localities and the Miami office (Zel).

While Hollywood, maintaining control over all operations despite geographically fragmented territories, exemplifies the NICL, Latin entertainment industries in Miami, while not exactly counter-hegemonic, present some significant manifestations of production and distribution that are not fully, and maybe even not significantly, in the hands of US corporations. This last statement requires an analysis of the status of corporations like Sony or the Cisneros Group when situated in the US. According to Carlos Cisneros of the Cisneros Television Group (CTG), a subsidiary of the Cisneros Group of Corporations (CGC) that moved to Miami from Caracas, 'Miami is becoming a world production city ... no longer limited by region' (quoted in Moncrieff Arrarte). That is, relocation to the US, and especially Miami in the case of Latin entertainment, enables corporations from other places to use the US as a springboard to increase their global reach. CGC is (or was) a Latin American corporation. It has divested itself of all commodity production and distribution to concentrate on the media, which enhances the possibility that it can, at least in its executives' eyes, penetrate the US. Indeed, it aims to do so *culturally*. Gustavo Cisneros, CEO of CGC, claims that 'Latin American culture has truly invaded the United States. ... Our local content is going to make it to the United States. We planned it that way. So I wonder who is invading whom?' (quoted in Faber and Ewing 52).

Is this a delusion, or the manifestation of something else? As a complement to the NICL, we need also focus on new international networks and partnerships of cultural production, which while headquartered in places like Miami, are also structured like an archipelago of enclaves that cut across the developed and developing world. Does it make any difference, especially to the poor consumers of this cultural production, whether Hollywood or Latin CEOs reap the profits? Yes, for two reasons. In the first place, the relocation to the US means that these companies and the immigrant intellectual and cultural labor they hire pay fewer taxes in their countries of origin. Why shouldn't Buenos Aires or Bogotá increase its tax base as Miami does? In the second place, it does seem to make a difference that Latin American executives, producers, and arrangers produce culture that speaks to people throughout the subcontinent, even if that production takes place in Miami. The culture industries, as Mato writes, are not so much deterritorialized as trans-territorial ('Miami' 4, 6). Perhaps the problem is less this trans-territorialization than the various means by which these industries produce, or better yet, extract value. In Chapter 5, we examine a suggestion by Octavo Getino for incentives for regional production and distribution in the South, and regulatory legislation that will enable Latin American countries and regional pacts to reap a greater share of the value they currently hand over to enterprises in Miami. We know that globalization of the industry involves a reconfiguration of the labor force, so perhaps that might give a solid material backing to our discussions. Our task must be to expose the contradictions at the center of consumer-citizen rhetorics and strive for democratically accountable forms of intervention. The backdrop must be an awareness of our NICL and the complex interplay of social-movement cultural rights and commodification. The remainder of this chapter applies these precepts to examples of major public subvention of film, undertaken for both cultural-political and commercial reasons. Their histories are longer than Miami's compressed, high-tensile version. But each depends on the NICL, just as it does.

Australia – The Mixed Cultural Economy

Australia has a relatively stable experienced white-settler liberal-capitalist rule since decolonization in 1901, by which time the native peoples had already been subjected to dispossession and domination, and the white working class incorporated via a parliamentary-political wing. Australia has both the structural inequalities and the relative income and health security that have come to white Westerners via First World capitalist welfarism since the Second World War. In Australia, this welfarist attitude has blended with a highly utilitarian partnership between state and capital. A mixed-economy approach of public and private ownership has produced a vast system of radio and TV (hundreds of radio stations, five national TV networks, and cable and satellite options, in a country with just nineteen million people that is the size of the continental United States). The film area, however, has been less consistently successful.

In the silent period and up to the 1940s, the Australian film industry produced many features, despite numerous British and American imports and a monopolistic domestic structure. But the post-War period saw the local industry decimated, as imports flooded in and state assistance was not forthcoming. This became a matter of grave disquiet for local intellectuals, who regarded dependency on the two largest producers of English-language popular culture as a sign of national immaturity – for in television drama, books and music, the US and Britain shared the spoils. In the film area, US imports were totally dominant – Australia made no features between 1958 and 1966 and precious few between 1950 and 1970, although government documentaries were produced throughout the century. Two decades of cultural-nationalist critique eventually helped to generate government support, along with the rise of political leaders who sought to stamp Australianness on their public image, notably the Liberal (conservative) Prime Minister John Gorton (1966–71) and the Australian Labor Party (social-democratic) Prime Minister Gough Whitlam (1972–75).

One particular essay is often regarded as a point of origin for this critique. In a noted magazine piece from 1958, 'No Daydreams of Our Own: The Film as National Self-Expression', Tom Weir spoke of screen drama as

> the most important means for heightening a people's feeling of communal personality, bringing them the shock of recognition that Herman Melville was concerned to give when his own America was a dependent culture. ... [Film] plants one's feet on the ground. The workaday world is integrated with the

world of one's imagination. ... It is typical of the undeveloped personality of our [Australian] people that we have practically no indigenous films.

Ironically, Melville himself had strongly opposed the unquestioning devotion by the US literary establishment in the early to mid-nineteenth century to all things English, notably Shakespeare. He questioned the compatibility of this Eurocentrically cringing, import culture with the need to 'carry Republicanism into literature'. Yet his work betrays numerous tropes and debts to Shakespeare (Newcomb 94). This mix of indebtedness and *ressentiment* characterizes the relation of import to export cultures, which oppose taste to domination and market choice to cultural control – graceless antinomies.

In the collection he edited on *Australia's First Ten Years of Television*, a decade after Weir, journalist Mungo MacCallum argued that: 'Drama is as much part of a community's culture as its sport. In its range, from banality to brilliance, it reflects us to ourselves, helps us to know ourselves and passes on the information to the rest of the world. A community without drama is undeveloped, or maimed beneath the skin'. Similarly, just after the advent of Australian television, former radio and future screen drama producer Hector Crawford lobbied publicly for the protection of local TV drama as a means of constituting 'a consciousness of national identity and pride in our nation, and a regard for our own cultural ideas and patterns' (quoted in Moran *Images* 95–96).

As these remarks suggest, Australian commercial interests intermesh with the cultural remits of both regulatory bodies and state-owned broadcasters. At license hearings prior to the introduction of television to Australia in 1956, it was assumed that there would be no more than eight or nine hours a week of overseas programming on the commercial stations. But by the end of the first year of operations, technological developments meant that US TV series were available on film. These programs had already cleared their costs domestically and thus had very elastic pricing internationally. Nevertheless, audience figures for television diminished by the early 1960s, when the networks flooded the market with US materials. While the absolute number of viewers continued to increase with population growth and the distribution of sets, time spent in front of the screen was decreasing. Advertisers reconsidered their departure from print and radio. When allied to the licensing of a third commercial network in 1963, this led to a shortage of popular US product. The commercials sought an alternative to the quick fix provided by imports at the same moment as a 1963 Senate Select Committee called for the export of Australian screen texts to South-East Asian television to showcase the nation. In a move that consolidated these influences, the public broadcaster began to show more local drama, with a commensurate improvement in ratings, and a local-drama quota was imposed on the commercials in 1966, requiring thirty minutes a week of Australian-produced material. It institutionalized what market forces were already configuring.

At the same time, these arguments fed into a revived call for film support. In 1965, Sylvia Lawson argued for a halcyon period of neo-realism in the 1920s

Australian feature film that might be regained. She referred to the 'identity which a community's own film-making confers upon it as nothing else can. Now, when most of our diversions are processed and packaged elsewhere, we probably need it more than ever' ('Not for the likes of us' 154–55). This position stressed that the general Australian public was in some way lacking culturally. Those who had cultural capital migrated to pursue careers where they would be appreciated, in more sophisticated climes (O'Regan *Australian* 32). In 1969, the Australian Council for the Arts' Film Committee reported to the govern-ment that the need for public subvention was 'self-evident' because of the necessity for Australia 'to interpret itself to the rest of the world' (*Interim* 171). Journalist, advertising executive and producer Phillip Adams spoke of the need 'to dream our own dreams', making special reference to a famous cartoon from the Vietnam War period which depicted an Australian family watching a TV that was advertising the opportunity to: 'Have your emotions lived for you tonight by American experts'. Today, critic John McLaren maintains that 'the most important argument for supporting ... Australian film and television' is 'to carry on a continuing dialogue amongst ourselves if we are to understand ourselves and our place in the world' – methods of inscribing ethical incom-pleteness and loyalty.

In the early 1970s, consistent state aid to fiction cinema came, via public financing of films selected by culturecrats to stimulate a revival that would then, it was thought, be picked up by private interests. By the end of the decade, it was clear that entrepreneurs had not been drawn to the industry, while the 'improving' themes selected by culturecrats were losing their audience. Both industry policy and textual policy needed reform. The notion was to harmonize them through tax legislation to allow massive write-offs for private money, which would allegedly be more in tune with public taste. Meanwhile, direct state assistance to both film culture and less commercial projects would sustain new and innovative initiatives that directly addressed cultural concerns. But instead of articulating the industry more closely with its audience, the generous tax write-off generated a new form of middle-person. Countless films were made without any intention of securing exhibition, let alone audience approval. The real 'audience' was dentists, doctors and lawyers, who looked at the tax-avoidance prospectuses more closely than the screenplays. In 1988, the government returned to a model of direct investment, but in coordination with capital, including overseas sources (Jacka 'Film' 82–85, 88). The system had evolved into a mixed-economy model, just as in Australian radio and TV, which have a national public sector and a networked and local private one. Competitiveness and commodification are inscribed into public agencies and content regulations, and requirements to stress national culture are imposed as conditions of the subvention available to commercial interests (O'Regan *Australian* 15). The state system is inflected with capitalism, and the private sector is inflected with public service. What does this mean in textual terms?

Australian screen cultural nationalism has been remarkably constant in its themes since Weir's landmark essay, with ethical incompleteness a crucial assumption. Playwright David Williamson wrote to the national daily, the *Australian*, in his 1989 capacity as President of the Australian Writers' Guild:

> It is not to protect an industry, or even employment, that Australian content in commercial television is so crucial. It is for the sake of an Australian culture. We as children grew up seeing ourselves as exiles from real life which only happened in the rest of the world. That is not what we want now for ourselves or for our children.

In his history of Australian television drama, Albert Moran has noted an inconsistency between the discourses of Australianness mobilized in screen subvention and regulation and producers' and writers' rhetoric, as opposed to drama texts themselves. In the case of the former, great play is made of fiction's capacity to open up a multifaceted awareness of the country and its people. But the actual product is monomaniacally concentrated on white, middle-class, heterosexual nuclear families. The specificities of Australia in terms of geography, demography, history and social relations are marginalized (Moran *Images* 11). Protectionism and state subvention have provided *cordons sanitaires* for a very conservative cultural politics, other than on the state- and advertising-funded multicultural network, the Special Broadcasting Service, which along with the ABC draws just under 20% of viewers (Cunningham and Flew 'De-Westernising' 239). Governmentality has been applied, but mostly across a homogeneous view of the populace.

In any event, twenty years after the plaintive calls for local screen industries had borne fruit, it was still possible for a key academic text on Australian feature film to refer thus to Australians' multifaceted dependence on Hollywood: 'They feel second best with their own markets and culture, forced to second guess what their authentic indigenous culture should be' (Dermody and Jacka 20). For Lawson, the country remains 'a colony of Hollywood' ('General' 6). Why?

Commercial pressures to make local drama that can be sold elsewhere lessen the claim to a specific cultural address – the force of the NICL. And Australia has garnered a reputation internationally for making capable low-budget film and television, such that many Europeans held it up as an exemplar of how *not* to use public funds – to produce exportable (because cheap) palimpsests of US TV filler at the lowest common denominator (Cunningham and Flew 'De-Westernizing' 240). Such issues are addressed in the 1978 feature film *Newsfront*, which traces the history of competing newsreel companies and their coverage of current affairs in 1950s Australia. Towards the end of the film, expatriate Frank Maguire returns after time overseas, replete with an American accent. He is back to complete a Cain and Abel relationship with his brother Len, to kill not by force, but with the kindness of an export culture. Len has stayed with the local company. Frank offers him a job on an American-funded TV series that will be shot in Australia with US iconography. Len is tempted by the prospect of on-set control, but dissuaded by the prerequisites of American themes, and unimpressed by Frank's insistence that it will be an Australian series simply as a result of being filmed there. The crisis of conscience

Len faced in the 1950s has multiplied as Australia has become a key site for runaway NICL production from the US, with facilities designed to produce a national cinema incorporated into offshore Hollywood – irony of ironies that the director of *Newsfront*, Phil Noyce, now makes Hollywood action-adventure films (such as *Patriot Games* and *The Saint*). A latter-day beneficiary of the NICL, he has become a stereotype from his own text!

In the late 1980s, the then-Australian Broadcasting Tribunal (ABT) reconsidered television drama via what became known as 'the Australian look', which favored 'signs of place, accent, and idiom, or more diffuse but no less vivid ways of hooking into the social unconscious or social "imaginary" of a particular sub-culture' (Jacka 'Australian' 126). Instead of using production indices – the *locus* of creative control – as a means of determining the Australianness of drama, the ABT considered counting on-screen indicators: 'theme, perspective, language and character'. Many cultural critics and policymakers feared that the disrup-tiveness, newness and self-formative potential of TV drama would be lost under such a proposal. They were concerned that a Pan-Australianism constituted from essentialist protocols would preclude the emergence of local political concerns that, it was thought, magically flowed from the participation of Australian production personnel. The reflectionist assumption that drove the ABT proposal on localism presumed an empirically uncorroborated calibration between textual indices and Australian reality. At the same time, a purely indus-trial, non-textual model, as per runaway production and the *Newsfront* plot, can produce distinctly 'unAustralian' texts that are financially underwritten by a localist presumption.

Kangaroo (Lewis Milestone, 1952) and *The Return of Captain Invincible* (Philippe Mora, 1983) provide chronological and conceptual limit-cases of US screen investment in the Australian film industry. *Kangaroo* was the first of several Hollywood features shot in Australia during the 1950s. Twentieth-Century Fox dispatched a crew and most of the cast because its Australian-based capital reserves had been frozen to prevent foreign exchange leaving the country. Shooting took place in Zanuckville, supinely named to honor the studio head. A formulaic Western, the film failed, but then the need to use money lying idle was probably the sole reason for its coming into being. Three decades on, *Captain Invincible* represented another outcome of the state producing condi-tions for foreign film-making. Taxation incentives designed to make Australian cinema more attentive to the private sector saw the local Treasury subsidizing Hollywood to make a film set almost 'nowhere'. The text concerns a lapsed US superhero, played by Alan Arkin, who migrates to Australia and dipsomania following McCarthyite persecution, reviving his powers and sobriety to thwart a villainous Christopher Lee. Recut by its producers following difficulties obtaining US distribution, the text was disavowed by Mora and denied certifi-cation by the Australian government as insufficiently local by comparison with its original script. A court challenge against this ruling succeeded, but the tax haven designed to boost commercial production was politically and culturally compromised from that point. Governments in Australia have continued to provide risk capital for foreign moguls, but generally at the State level, although the Federal Government has a body named Ausfilm, resident in LA, which is charged with promoting the NICL (Department of Commerce 50).

When Dino de Laurentiis was choosing between Sydney and Queensland's Gold Coast as locations for a joint-venture studio with the Australian company Village Roadshow in 1987, one factor in selecting the latter was the then Queensland Film Corporation patching together an A$7.5 million loan at low interest and attracting A$55 million via a local share-issue. His company collapsed after the stock-market crash that year, and the space seemed destined to fail. Touted as a new Disneyland site or a multifunction polis, neither plan succeeded. But in 1988, a hundred and fifty-day strike by the Writers' Guild of America over creative and residual rights payments led to a chronic shortfall in new programs. Village Roadshow responded by refinancing its investment via Warner Bros and seeking foreign business. The first major TV series shot on the Gold Coast was Mission: Impossible in 1988. The Queensland Film Development Office immediately advertised the State to prospective producers like this: 'the production company of a recent American primetime television series found a diverse range of "international locations", from London to the Greek Islands in Queensland'. Village Roadshow-Warner Bros. announced a studio expansion in 1989. The state was ready to assist with a construction subsidy that became part of the studios' promotional material. Well might the Queensland Tourist and Travel Corporation refer to itself as the 'last frontier', replete with 'smiling locals'. For Stanley O'Toole, managing director of what later became the studio, Queensland was 'LA without the smog'. The studio is part-owned by Warner Bros. and named Warner Roadshow. The Pacific Film and Television Commission, formed to promote the State to international and Australian film-makers, offers a revolving fund for low-interest loans secured against guarantees and presales, rebates on payroll tax and subsidized crewing costs (Miller Technologies 141–81). In its thirteen years of operation, the studio has drawn NICL investment from CBS, Viacom, ABC, Fox TV, Disney TV, Disney Channel, Fox and Warner Bros., aided by Australian Government tax credits on labor of up to 10%. Total runaway production to Australia increased by 26% across the 1990s (Hanrahan; Monitor).

Of course, not all jurisdictions are so keen to be exploited. The producers of Baywatch, then screened in one hundred and forty-four countries, decided to move to Australia in the late 1990s. Beaches are public property there, and residents of Avalon in Sydney protested when their local politicians offered to sign the space over. But Queensland's Gold Coast stood ready to help out ('"Baywatch"'). Such neediness has seen Hollywood producers refer to Queenslanders as 'Mexicans with mobiles', which has become a sore point with the local Screen Directors' Guild (quoted in 'Australia'; Fitzgerald). The shooting of high-profile movies like Mission: Impossible 2 (John Woo, 2000) and The Matrix (Andy and Larry Wachowski, 1999) in Australia saw savings on LA prices of up to 30% (Waxman).

The NICL also works offshore from Australia itself. Consider the Grundy Organization. From the 1950s, it produced Australian TV drama and game shows licensed from the US. Then the company expanded to sell such texts across the world, operating with a strategy called 'parochial internationalism' that meant leaving Australia rather than exporting in isolation from relevant industrial, taste and regulatory frameworks. Following patterns established in the advertising industry, it bought production houses around the world, making programs in local languages based on formats imported from Australia that had originally drawn on US models. From a headquarters in Bermuda, the Organization produced about fifty hours of TV a week in seventy countries across Europe, Oceania, Asia and North America, until its sale in 1995 to Pearson for US$280 million. This exemplified the NICL off shore – a company utilizing experience in the Australian commercial reproduction industry to manufacture US palimpsests in countries relatively new to profit-centered TV. The benefits to Australia, where a regulatory framework had birthed this expertise by requiring the networks to support such productions as part of cultural protection, are unclear. As Greg Dyke, the Pearson executive responsible for the Grundy purchase and later head of the BBC, proudly put it, the typical Grundy program *Man O Man* 'has no redeeming social values' (Cunningham and Jacka 81–87; Moran *Copycat* 41–71; Stevenson 1; Tunstall and Machin 30; Dyke quoted in Short). In such cases, cultural policy merely underwrites local and international cultural *bourgeoisies*. On the other side of the ledger, the supposedly public broadcaster, the ABC, was faced with the need to cancel its highest-rating program, *SeaChange*, in 2000 because of difficulties in attracting overseas sales. What had started as a government service designated as addressing the needs of local citizens had turned into a body that relied on international money to amortize its production debt, as public-sector expenditure was displaced by the impost of marketability (O'Regan 'Knowing' 29).

By the late 1990s, cultural and communications policy had merged in Australia. Cultural questions were now so central to commodification that the much-touted (and government-led) knowledge economy was as much about textuality as industry. But in another sense, communications questions about bandwidth, delivery and technical innovation overdetermined textual meaning (Cunningham and Flew 'De-Westernizing'; Spurgeon). The ABT had been replaced by a more neoliberal regulator, the Australian Broadcasting Authority, which was dominated by engineering technicalities and profit margins rather than content, as doctrines of neoliberal evangelism and technological determinism decreed that the advent of cable and satellite services ensured textual diversity (Cunningham and Flew 'Policy' 54). For its part, film continued to lurch from some spectacular international successes (*Priscilla, Queen of the Desert* and *Muriel's Wedding*) to dozens of failures the new conservative government elected in 1996 diminished outlays to fund screen production; and policy formation was increasingly the province of the industry-oriented Productivity Commission rather than culture-crats – skills and training overdetermined text and meaning. Both systems saw ongoing mixes of public and private funds, more than ever under the sign of industrial development, despite claims about cultural localism. But unlike earlier periods, the commercial networks were winding down their support of Australian drama (O'Regan 'Knowing' 28, 34). Such tensions apply in equal measure to the UK.

The Film Industry and the British Government

> Let every part of Merry England be merry in its own way. Death to Hollywood. – John Maynard Keynes (quoted in J.P. Mayer 40)

It's quiz time: which British Government released a White Paper on the arts that welcomed a new generation's desire for 'gaiety and colour … informality and experimentation', as opposed to the 'drabness, uniformity and joylessness' of convention (quoted in Malcolm Barr 36, 40)? Answer: Harold Wilson's Labour Party in 1965 (Wilson was Prime Minister of Britain from 1964–70 and 1974–76). 'Cool Britannia' is not as new as Tony Blair (Prime Minister 1997–present) wants you to think. Blair's rhetoric references both Wilson's 'white heat of techno-logy' and his co-optation of youth culture. Like that previous incarnation, con-temporary policy is as much about developing tourism and cultural commerce as new cultural norms. The premise is that cultural creativity is the spawning ground of innovation. In a global economy, innovation rather than material resources or manufactures drives accumulation. On this premise, Blair's 'Cool Britannia', a cultural-economic project including multicultural artists as well as new media entrepreneurs, sought to transform London into the creative hub for trends in music, fashion, art and design, thus constituting the foundation for the so-called new economy based on 'content provision'. Britain's Creative Industries Task Force focused on 'those activities which have their origin in individual creativity, skill and talent and which have a potential for wealth and job creation through the generation and exploitation of intellectual property'. Michael Volkerling examines similar projects in Australia, Canada and New Zealand, and the model is being explored throughout the world. The focal role this policy accords to the state was not accepted by the ruling Conservative Party between 1979 and 1997. For unlike the Australian case, there was no cross-party bipartisanship on British film. Accordingly, this section examines continuities and discontinuities in British film policy of the 1990s under Conservative and Labour rule, demonstrating disagreement rather than consensus within the cultural-capitalist state.

A gradually accreted system of subvention had protected and stimulated the British film industry for fifty years from the time of the 1927 Cinematograph Films Act. The system operated under twin imperatives – as per the GEM, to deal with the cultural impact of le défi américain (in 1926, the Daily Express had suggested Hollywood was turning British youth into 'temporary American citizens' (quoted in de Grazia 53)) and to shore up the domestic industry. In the television area, the longstanding duopoly (1955–82) of a strong public broadcaster (the BBC) and an equally powerful commercial force (ITV), provided a rich tradition of localism, taking up resources that might have gone into film production.

Post-World War II offshore NICL Hollywood production began in Britain because of the 1948 Anglo-American Film Agreement, which required the majors to leave US$40 million a year of their receipts in blocked accounts (Nowell-Smith 139). This policy invited Hollywood to use the money to make films in Britain, and even after its abandonment, later state incentives continued to encourage 'runaway' production. Most major post-WWII forms of support rewarded successful films made in the UK with state aid, so *Superman* II and *Flash Gordon* cashed in on measures that had been designed to encourage local production (Hill *British* 36 n. 18, 43). But under Margaret Thatcher (Conservative Party Prime Minister 1979–90), the government was not interested in the screen as a site either of cultural diversity, or industrial development through state participation (Hill 'British Film' 101–05). The 1990s opened with the British film industry in a period of extreme fragility and uncertainty, and confronted by an indifferent Tory government. But the news was not all bad. As one critic put it, the 'lumpen-monetarist approach to this industry has swept away some of the humbug', though he warned that 'the effect will be purely negative if the elimination of an industrial policy for the cinema is not used as an opportunity to promote a cultural policy in its place' (Nowell-Smith vi). Has this happened? Or are we still dealing with public subsidies given to support unspecified claims about cultural maintenance, diversity and development? Was the commerce-culture demon of film policy under any sort of control in 1990s Britain?

Apart from sporadic support for local film culture, the period under review saw bald attempts at a purely industrial policy to exploit the NICL. Britain has been a major player in the NICL, as both a foreign investor and a site of runaway production. In reviewing foreign films made in the UK, the *Independent* newspaper ironically refers to '[o]ur green and profitable land', while David Bruce notes of Scotland that it 'has tended to be regarded more as a film location and source of stories than as a film culture' (vii). In one sense none of this is new, since Hollywood has long tapped the UK for people, locations, settings and stories. But from the 1980s, it became impossible to recoup the costs of most British feature films domestically, and the industry was forced to look outside. The stimulus of European co-operation in the early 1990s launched some new projects, but few were commercially or critically successful. In 1993, Britain joined Eurimages, the continental film fund of the Council of Europe, which supports documentary, exhibition, distribution and marketing through interest-free loans, but the Conservative government thought it poor value for money and quickly withdrew (Jäckel).

The necessity of finding employment for skilled workers and their employers made the industry a true welcome mat. In 1991, the British Film Commission (BFC) was formed by the new Conservative Government of John Major (Prime

Minister 1990–97) to market UK production expertise and locations, providing overseas producers with a free service articulating local talent, locations and subsidies, and generating a national network of urban and regional film commissions. In 1997, seven Hollywood movies accounted for 54% of the £465 million spent on feature-film production in the UK (Home 'Response'). In 1998, the new Labour Government opened a British Film Office in Los Angeles to normalize traffic between Hollywood and Britain by offering liaison services to the industry and promoting British locations and crews. The BFC announced Labour's outlook on cinema: 'set firmly at the top of the agenda is the desire to attract more overseas film-makers' (Guttridge; McCann; Hiscock; BFC quoted in British Film Commission). The government's decision to float the pound and free the Bank of England from democratic consultation contributed to a situation in 1998 where a strengthening currency raised costs for overseas investors and encouraged locals to spend elsewhere, with obvious implications for film.

One key agency, the London Film Commission (LFC), was formed in 1995 with a £100,000 grant from the Department of National Heritage to attract foreign film production. It subsequently obtained funding from Hollywood's overseas distribution cartel, United International Pictures and the Corporation of the City of London, but needed a bail-out from the Government in 1998 because it failed to attract sufficient private-sector money to continue operations. The LFC arranges police permits, promotes the city to overseas filmmakers and brings them together with local residents and businesses. Its defining moment was the first *Mission: Impossible* picture, when Commissioner Louise Jury proudly said of the film's Hollywood producers: 'They came up with all these demands and I just went on insisting that, as long as they gave us notice, we could schedule it'.

Regulations promulgated under Major decreed that films made in Britain counted as British, regardless of theme, setting or personnel. So *Judge Dredd* with Sylvester Stallone was 'British', but *The English Patient* with Kristin Scott Thomas and Ralph Fienes did too much of its post-production work abroad to qualify – until 1998, 92.5% of a film had to be created in the UK. At the end of that year, the Blair government reduced this requirement to 75% to encourage US production (Woolf). A 100% tax write-off is now available for film and TV production, provided that most crew members are EU citizens and half the equipment they use is owned by UK firms. Failure to qualify under these terms may still mean eligibility for a lease-back scheme, whereby a local company buys the film rights then leases them back to the producer (Department of Commerce 72).

What do film industry mavens make of this situation? Michael Kuhn, managing director of Polygram Filmed Entertainment (PFE), the dominant company in the British film industry across the 1990s, considered that 'Europe (when you talk about mainstream movies) is almost a vassal state to that Hollywood business'. He argued that only 'supra-national government institutions' could turn this around, absent a firm financial base to compete with Hollywood's mix of production and distribution and the United States' cartel-like discrimination against European producers. Ironically, PFE was taken over by the Canadian drinks conglomerate, Seagram, and later by the Euro-multinational Vivendi/Canal Plus – which in turn moved its CEO's head office to Manhattan!

The other side to British film and the state is the medium working as a cultural plenipotentiary overseas. Notoriously, the Foreign Office declined to fund black British films at the 1992 Carthage film festival because they were deemed 'not likely to be representative' and might 'give a bad image of Britain. ... After all, they're not exactly Howard's End' (quoted in Julien 61). At the first British-Bangla Film Festival, held in Dhaka in 1998, the British Council featured films with colonial echoes such as Mrs. Brown, Chariots of Fire, The English Patient and A Night to Remember, along with texts set in the contemporary world, and Bangla movies. A homogeneous image of heritage and tranquility was preferred in each case.

The TV-film nexus has seen the BBC allocate approximately £5 million a year through the 1990s. This is a tiny sum in film-industry terms, though the Corporation also buys TV rights to independently produced pictures (Street 22). Murdoch's TV satellite service BSkyB invested small amounts in British films and participated in film pre-sales from 1994 in order to fulfill obligations for European content (Hill 'British Television' 160–61). Toward the end of the decade, Channel Four purged its programming staff and started a film com-pany, Film Four Ltd, with funds freed up by the new opportunity to reinvest profits. The new firm was envisaged as a movie studio, but it had much work to do – in 1998, Channel Four films accounted for just 1% of UK box-office revenues. The following year, Film Four announced a London-based partner-ship for production and global distribution with Arnon Milchan and TF1 to make and sell British films (Dawtrey and Carver). It would be odd to rhapsodize Film Four's success as a commercial bridgehead, as increasing commercializa-tion does not bode well for the independent and minority sector's access to the channel or its charter obligation of multiculturalism (Dawtrey 'New').

The commerce-culture divide of British film can also be seen at work in the British Film Institute (BFI) during the decade. The BFI's remit of archiving and developing film culture extends to some production as well as policy inter-vention. At the start of the 1990s, the Institute produced a number of docu-ments favoring commercial rather than cultural films. It encouraged industry restructuring, investment incentives, and increased co-productions, as well as establishing a firm to sell British films internationally (McIntyre 'Vanishing' 103). During his tenure there as a welfare-supported management apparatchik and screen producer, Colin MacCabe argued that the BFI had demonstrated a 'long-term commitment to a national television and cinema which fully articulates the multitude of cultures that now constitute modern Britain', seeing the UK as the only European country 'genuinely harnessing the talents of a whole range of communities' ('Preface' ix, x). So culturecrat MacCabe claimed a continuing and impressive role for an inclusive film culture, while his commercecrat colleagues proposed a new agenda. Of course, the dividing line between them is not as great as this might imply. Both were concerned with cinematic specificity and commercial viability. This is clear from the breadth and overlap of their work, from UK Film Initiative pamphlets like *The View From Downing Street*, to the Museum of the Moving Image and BFI 2000.

Views vary greatly on the merits of British Screen Finance, a quasi-autonomous non-government organization formed in 1986 to assist commercially-oriented films. It has operated through state funds, BSkyB deals, left-over National Film Finance Corporation money, Channel Four and other stakeholders, notably the European Co-production Fund. Producer David Puttnam claims that it has linked well with Europe, brought on new talent and assisted unusual projects to secure funding (he lists *Orlando*, *Scandal* and *The Crying Game* as examples) (Puttnam with Watson 250). By contrast, director Isaac Julien suggests black film-makers are consistently denied support.

In addition to London-focused bodies, there is some vibrant but underfunded regional cultural policy via the Scottish Film and Television Archive and production agencies in Wales, Northern Ireland, and Scotland and cities such as Sheffield and Glasgow interested in boosting their cultural credentials. (Or not. Bizarrely, the Liverpool Film Commission advertises itself internationally as 'a lookalike for ... Nazi Germany, and cities of the Eastern block [sic]'). This work is funded by the BFI, local councils, arts agencies and the Scottish and Welsh Offices (Steven Goodwin; McIntyre 'Art'; Afilm.com).

The Scottish Film Council and Scottish Film Production Fund, founded in the 1980s, oversaw a Glasgow Film Fund with financial input from the Glasgow Development Agency, Glasgow City Council, the European Regional Development Fund, and Strathclyde Business Development. This patchwork of sources is typical, as is the decision to combine funds in high-end conventional narrative film-making via the NICL rather than locally textured, independent 'edge' cinema (McArthur 113). According to Bruce:

> Location shooting by overseas companies in 1995 ... [was] at a record level and Scotland would be appearing on screen in its own right, or doubling for somewhere else, all over the world. (Someone said that had there been a 1996 Oscar for 'best supporting country' Scotland would have won). (4)

When the various bodies amalgamated into Scottish Screen in the late 1990s, there were accusations that locally-derived public funds were lining the pockets of the English, and outrage when the board, comprised of TV executives and London-based Scots, voted to finance a project by their own Chair (Boyd).

A Northern Ireland Film Council began in 1989 on a volunteer basis as a forum dedicated to 'the development and understanding of film, television and video in the region'. The Department of Education funded the Council from 1992. It became a local site for disbursing screen-related Arts Council money and combining disparate funding streams, as well as a public sphere for debating the need to regionalize BBC production (Wilkins 141, 143). In 1997 came the Northern Ireland Film Commission, which sought to attract outside production. Andrew Reid, the Commission's locations officer, reported that: 'Producers come here expecting the place to be rubble. ... Instead they end up having a great time. And I can show them mountains, beaches and great scenery. They can't quite believe it' (quoted in Gritten). Five features were shot in the North in 1997, more than doubling the entire number made in the province since 1947 (Cowan and Wertheimer; Gritten).

Much of the money now available to these bodies, both directly and indirectly, comes from the National Lottery, launched in 1995 and now a major source of funds for film production. One idea floated under the Major government was to take £100 million from Lottery funds and match it with £200 million from financiers to start a major film studio, complete with share offering. The Arts Council under Labour nominated three mini-studios for lottery franchises – DNA, Pathé and the Film Consortium – and encouraged them to unify production, distribution and sales. The decision was by no means universally popular. In 1998, the government announced that £27 million would be allocated to film from the lottery, along with £20.8 million in annual direct grants (Woolf). Three years later, there had been virtually no critical or popular successes. Certain critics complained that 'whingeing cultural stars' had turned into 'greedy moguls' via a system that discouraged diversity and innovation (Tim Adler; Boyd).

Besides measures designed to stimulate film-making, other policies affect the industry. The deregulatory verve of the 1979–97 Conservative government did not apply to questions of public morality in quite the same way that it did to economics. Censorship increased through the Video Recordings Act in 1984 as part of the moral panic surrounding young people and popular genres, and the Criminal Justice Act of 1994 required censors to address horror, drug use, criminal conduct and violence following the James Bulger murder case (Richards 176; Miller *Technologies* 62, 199–200). On other fronts, copyright, company incorporation and industrial relations machinery also affect film-making, along with general measures designed to stimulate industry, such as the Enterprise Investment Scheme (KPMG 225–53; Hilary Clarke).

Each new wave of acclaim for British cinema in the 1990s was followed by regretful decline, to the point where the triumphs of 1997 and 1998 came to be seen not so much as vital signs but harbingers of cyclical failure (Johnston). When the Blair government came to power, it decreed a desire to double the share of UK box-office for British films. Within one hundred days in office, the new administration had appointed the country's first-ever Minister for Film, announced the three Lottery recipients, permitted Channel Four to spend more on film-making and introduced a 100% tax rebate for production (later problematized by EU rules). This was done in the name of 'helping the film industry to develop from a series of small craft businesses into a properly integrated modern industry' (Department for Culture). Plans included raising US$24 million annually for development, production and distribution via a voluntary levy on UK film companies, including subsidiaries of US firms, to form an 'All-Industry Fund'. But the idea was ditched toward the end of 1998, when it became clear that both television companies and Hollywood studios were loath to pay for it (Tim Adler). The government restructured film funding under the umbrella of British Film, a new amalgamation of the BFI, the BFC and the film section of the Arts Council of England (which administers the lottery) (Boehm). Meanwhile, four areas of weakness in the local industry were identified by the government's Advisory Committee on Film Policy: training, marketing, distribution, and development. Industry–government committees were set up to address such matters and provide points of liaison with sources of private finance (Dawtrey 'U.K.'). Critics of these plans saw them as adding bureaucracy to already strapped institutions; supporters claimed the new arrangements would streamline and co-ordinate the industry. Meanwhile, training had moved toward a corporatist model, via Skillset, a tripartite body with Puttnam as its titular head ('Northern').

Labour's 1990s rhetoric of modernization was in keeping with the government's broader industry policies (Paul Mitchell; Pratten and Deakin). The move toward import substitution and export-oriented cultural industrialization showed a preference for large, consolidated entities that could compete with one another. In the cinema, this has seen a populist, big-budget, apolitical model preferred to an artisanal 'poor' cinema articulated around social issues. According to Puttnam, 'strong cultural resistance can best be built on the basis of a firm understanding of the realities of the marketplace'. He insists on the need to 'get away from relying on cultural defense, and concentrate our energies on industrial success' (quoted in Tonkin and in Finney 8). Film Minister Tom Clarke argued for films that were '[m]ade with passion, fuelled by cash', and expressed his enthusiasm for 'large, vertically integrated companies with deep pockets'. But the aim of increasing the proportion of UK film receipts going to British cinema has proved difficult to achieve: market share fell by half in 1998 ('European Film'). Outsiders wondered whether direct state intervention via quotas and levies might be the way forward (Christie). Alan Parker, movie director and cherished author of the remark 'Film needs theory like it needs a scratch on the negative', was appointed to head a new Film Council in 1999, with the key *apparatchik* a BFI maven. It united the BFI, the Film Commission and Screen Finance (Dawtrey 'Parker' and 'Woodward'). Industry and culture no longer had any buffer zones between them, and the results were keenly awaited by critics. Meanwhile, 2002 saw the BBC outperform ITV for the first time, as Greg Dyke, the man who as proudly brought Grundy game shows to UK television, celebrated his first year in charge of a thoroughly profit-oriented 'public service'.

The Latinate Screen Sphere

We turn now to a somewhat different set of audiovisual projects – the struggles for the national popular in Latin American screen production of the twentieth century. Unlike the Australian and British examples, these struggles took place against a backdrop, and sometimes a foreground, of frequently violent systemic political change. But like our earlier case studies, the film industries of Latin America are characterized by weak industrial infrastructures, subordination to Hollywood, and success only in periods of considerable state support (Johnson 133): Argentine cinema during the Perón era (1945–55) and redemocratization during the transition from dictatorship (1983–1990s); Chilean cinema during the Allende government (1970–73), when it was included in a government agency; Venezuelan and Colombian cinemas spurred, respectively, by the state agencies Fondo de Promoción Cinematográfica (FOCINE) and Fondo de Fomento Cinematográfico (FONCINE); and of course the Cuban cinema during the governments of Fidel Castro (1959–present). These are attempts to produce modernizing forms of nationalism that could symbolically mediate between citizen and state (Burton-Carvajal 195–96). Across the 1990s, film policy was abolished in Colombia, transformed in Mexico and decimated in Brazil. US imports make up well over half of all films screened on the continent, and local exhibitionary quotas have fallen into disuse. Worsening economic conditions since the early 1980s have seen an ironically increased dependence on global neoliberal institutions and a diminished public role in the media (Johnson 129, 131, 136; Elizabeth Fox 192).

It was not always so. In the early years of the century, film industries emerged in Argentina, Brazil and Mexico, founded by private capital, but with little state protection and promotion. These countries, all of which had large domestic markets, established studios in the 1930s to take advantage of the interest of audiences in music: Chapultepec Studios, expanded by Nacional Productora (1931), and CLASA (1934) in Mexico; Lumitón (1932) and Argentina Sono Films (1937) in Argentina; and Cinédia Studios (1930) and Brasil Vita Filmes (1933) in Brazil. Most actors, directors and technicians had experience in Hollywood (King 465). These studios produced successful films in the 1930s and 1940s, based on music and other cultural features of a populist nationalism specific to each country: the melodrama of the Revolution in Mexico, and musicals and melodramas in Argentina and Brazil. Fernando de Fuentes' *Allá en el Rancho Grande* (*Over at the Big Ranch*) (1936), the most successful film in Latin America, took the macho singing *charro* (or cowboy) as its featured icon, drawing on the stereotypes of northern Mexico but also reworking Hollywood's Roy Rogers and Gene Autry. These *charros* and *mariachis* harked back to a prerevolutionary era when everyone 'knew their place'. Lázaro Cárdenas, the radical president who spurred agrarian reform in this period, did not interfere in the reactionary imagery projected by the industry because the films were highly successful exports to the rest of Latin America (King 467). Despite the popularity of Mexican cinema, Hollywood predominated even then. In the 1930s, Mexican films accounted for 6.5% of the domestic market, with Hollywood taking a 78.9% share. This period saw compulsory exhibition of local films: in Brazil from 1932, Mexico from 1939 and Argentina from 1944 (Johnson 136).

Like the *rancheras* and nightclub movies in Mexico, tango-based films underwrote the Argentinian industry in the 1930s, taking their cue from Paramount's successes with Carlos Gardel. José 'El Negro' Ferreyra teamed up with screen star Libertad Lamarque, using songs to punctuate the high points of melodramas. In Brazil, the musical vehicle was the *chanchada*, derived from vaudeville routines of Brazilian comic theater (King 468–69). These films incorporated singers already popular on radio and in popular theater: Paraguaçu, Noel Rosa, Gaó, Napoleão Tavares and Alzirinha Camargo. There was horizontal integration of the culture industries, as music, film and theater were brought together. Wallace Downey, director of *Coisas nossas* (*Our Things*, 1931), for example, was an executive at Columbia Records. Cinédia Studios produced the most successful hits, such as Gonzaga's *Alô, Alô Brasil* (1935) and *Alô, Alô Carnaval* (1936), featuring the Miranda sisters. Carmen Miranda was the biggest musical success of this period, with 'more than 300 records, five albums and nine Latin American tours, before she erupted onto the New York stage in 1939 and was immediately bought up by Fox' (King 469).

It might be said that the first major state-sponsored audiovisual industrial policy for Latin America actually came from the US. As we saw in Chapter 1, the State Department and the OCIAA courted Latin America's entry into WWII on the side of the Allies by re-engineering how 'Americans' portrayed 'Latins'. The State Department went so far as to boost film production in Latin America, sponsoring Hollywood connections, exporting technology – and denying raw film stock to Argentina as punishment for not supporting the Allies.

Successful local film industries were supported by private capital, for the state (Cárdenas in Mexico, Vargas in Brazil) 'did little to protect or to sponsor local production' (King 470). By 1942, however, Mexican government institutions like the Banco de Mexico complemented private initiatives such as Banco Cinematográfico. In these circumstances, the 1940s saw the emergence of Mexico's Golden Age of cinema, with a cohort of talented directors and cinematographers, a star system and strong union labor.

Argentine cinema came into its own in the 1940s, with the complex urban dramas of Luis César Amadori and Francisco Mujica. However, lacking strong nationalist symbols, except for the *gaucho* and the pampas, which gave rise to few films, there was no national-popular cinema equivalent to that of Mexico. Moreover, when state intervention came in the form of screen quotas, state bank loans for production and restrictions on repatriation of profits by foreign-owned companies, the censorship practices by the Subsecretariat for Information and the Press during Juan Domingo Perón's dictatorship (1946–1955) discouraged many film-makers and actors. Many went into exile, some to Mexico. Despite some notable film-makers (e.g. Leopoldo Torres Ríos, Torre Nilsson, Hugo Fregonese and Hugo del Carril), most production loans went to directors of mediocre B-movies. Perhaps the most important nationalist aspect of the screen in this period was political spectacle, on a par with that of Roosevelt and Hitler, as Perón mimicked the style and demeanor of Gardel, 'playing opposite' his wife Evita (Eva Duarte), who had been a minor actress.

Unlike the Mexican or Argentine industries, which could export their films throughout the continent and to Spain, the Portuguese language limited Brazilian producers to the domestic market. Indeed, no attempt was made to create a policy for a Lusophone market extending to other Portuguese-speaking countries until the 1970s, and that never amounted to much (Farias). The *chanchadas* of the 1930s, combinations of music, dance and comedy, continued to be popular in the 1940s. Atlântida, the premier producer of *chanchadas*, was financially successful, and increased its market share when it became part of the vertically integrated media empire of Luiz Severiano Ribeiro in 1947. This success was enhanced by domestic quota requirements imposed by the Vargas regime that year (Johnson and Stam 29).

The 1960s saw the politicization of cinema in most Latin American countries, both within and outside the state. The Cuban Revolution of 1959 was a powerful stimulus to leftist and anti-*dependista* thinking throughout the region; that also tapped into deep-rooted national-popular movements in most Latin American countries. As these movements played a role in the hegemonic process, their perspectives were relatively mainstreamed, to the point where social-science institutes, state agencies and independent productions all espoused 'popular culture'.

This term means something quite different from its connotations in Anglo-dominated nations, where the term 'popular' usually refers to the mass reception of commodified products of the culture industries. In contrast, Latin Americans strove to instill their work with the perspective of 'the people', an endeavor that was not without its shortcomings, particularly with respect to questions of representation and the actual experience of viewing. In addition to these questions, the often brutal backlash of conservative forces resulted in the eventual demise of popular and revolutionary initiatives in politics and culture as early as 1964 in Brazil, 1973 in Chile, 1976 in Argentina and so on. The model of the strong cultural state was notable in fascist Latin American military dictatorships of the 1960s to the 1980s, albeit in varied ways. The Argentine military kept control of TV during the 1970s and 1980s, but the Brazilian authoritarians of the 1964–85 period favored a state-run infrastructure with privately-held media companies as part of their modernization project, while Peru's 1968–80 dictatorship set out to broaden the media's interest in ordinary people. In each case, a technocratic elite was entrusted with the task of modernization (Waisbord 55; Elizabeth Fox 193). Latin American cinema in the 1960s and since cannot be understood apart from the concern with a revolutionary remaking of society, and the pivotal place of the popular in such endeavors. This is especially complicated with the democratization of the 1990s, where social-movement activism and clientelism are crucially intricated and conflictual, in ways that are unfathomable to Eurocentric discourses of Weberian public-service normativity (Krischke 111).

The construction of a national-popular will in Latin American societies faced similar challenges to those outlined by Gramsci (see our Introduction). Juan Carlos Portantiero, for example, considered Gramsci's analysis of 'Caesarism' and 'Bonapartism' applicable to Latin America nationalist populisms, particularly Varguismo in Brazil, Cardenismo in Mexico, Peronismo in Argentina and Aprismo in Peru. This situation results when a potentially catastrophic contention between social forces is intervened in by a third actor, for example the military, which brings into play an array of 'auxiliary [often popular] forces directed by, or subjected to, their hegemonic influence', and 'succeeds in permeating the State with its interests, up to a certain point, and in replacing a part of the leading personnel' (Gramsci 219–20). In this case, the popular forces do not, obviously, take power, but some of their agendas, particularly those that have been articulated with the third actor's ideological offensive against dominant forces, are incorporated into state policies.

Under the populist and developmentalist Brazilian governments of Getúlio Vargas, Juscelino Kubitschek, Jânio Quadros and João Goulart of the 1950s and 1960s, leftist intellectuals were able to insert certain demands into state policy, as part of their espousal of popular causes. In *Cinema: Trajetória no Subdesenvolvimento* (*Cinema: Its Trajectory in Underdevelopment*), Paulo Emílio Salles Gomes characterizes the era as one of widespread cultural renewal, which expressed itself in music, theater, the social sciences and literature (82). The formation of a public, composed of the urban middle class and not necessarily characterized by *mass* features, was crucial to political and art theater and cinema (Ortiz 103–104). This was the public for the first phase of Brazil's *Cinema Novo*, which sought to formulate a new visual and narrative language by exploiting its limited economic and technological resources experimentally, grounding itself in *auteurism* rather than the industrial model promoted by the Instituto Nacional do Cinema (created in 1966 under the military dictatorship). Gláuber Rocha, the film-maker most associated with the *Cinema Novo*, captures its essence in 'An Esthetic of Hunger', in which he upholds revolutionary violence against the hunger imposed by the colonizers of Brazil and other Third World countries. He includes 'Industrial Cinema' among the colonizers, for its commitment 'to untruth and exploitation'. In contrast, the thrust of *Cinema Novo* is to 'make the public aware of its own misery' and thus rise up against its colonizers (69–71).

The development projects of the 1950s and 1960s were a catalyst for popular mobilization. The intellectual context in which the anti-industrial *Cinema Novo* developed reflects this. In the mid-1950s came the reformism of the Instituto Superior de Estudos Brasileiros (ISEB), the Marxist Centros Populares de Cultura, the left-wing Catholic consciousness-raising movement and the Northeastern Popular Culture Movement (Renato Ortiz 162). Like Liberation Theology, these movements made an 'option for the poor', that is, the popular. They were targeted by the military coup in 1964 and its harder-line coup-within- the-coup of 1968 to 1973. The military formulated clear policies to modernize Brazilian society, to re-signify and transform the very notion and reality of the popular away from a perspective rooted in class and cultural struggles, towards a notion of popularity defined by consumer markets. Consequently, the Instituto Nacional do Cinema and Embrafilme (the national production company founded in the late 1960s) attacked the more radical exponents of *Cinema Novo*, particularly Gláuber Rocha.

While in its first phase (1960–1964) *Cinema Novo* produced realist films, in its second phase (1964–1968), it attempted to gain a mass audience without resorting to the industrial model. This was, according to film-maker Gustavo Dahl, 'the essential condition for political action in cinema' (2). The possibility of reaching a mass audience was frustrated, however, by the US film industry, which controlled distribution and exhibition. Consequently, *Cinema Novo* moved toward technical polish and production values, particularly in its third phase, which produced box-office successes for the first time. These film-makers generally tried to have it both ways: to continue the critique of repres-sion and underdevelopment, albeit allegorically so as to elude the censors, and at the same time take advantage of the new incentives, subsidies and screen quotas provided by the state agencies, Instituto Nacional do Cinema and Embrafilme. When many *Cinema Novo* directors went into exile (1971–72), Brazilian cinema began to flourish with nationally subsidized and protected popular films (in the market sense), such as the *pornochanchadas* or erotic come-dies. By the end of the 1970s, the authoritarian government's attempts to modernize culture had created a classic case of double-think: it courted huge amounts of foreign investment for development, which resulted in the mammoth foreign debt after 1973 that put an end to the 'economic miracle'. At the same time, its developmentalist efforts were couched in anti-imperialist rhetoric (Renato Ortiz 184), which translated directly into state protection for the film industry. Against the pressures of foreign media transnational corpora-tions and the US Motion Picture Export Association, the government fostered legislation that required movie theaters to screen Brazilian films at least 133 days of every year, and to include one Brazilian short with each foreign film. The result was that whereas thirty-two films were made each year between 1957 and 1966, by 1975 that figure had risen to eighty-nine, and by 1980 to one hundred and three. This rise in the number of films did not reflect the development of a critical cinema, but the authoritarian government's success in jump-starting a huge consumer market. Rui Guerra, another *Cinema Novo* film-maker, remarked at the end of the 1970s that the state was successful in translating the 'popular' into 'an alibi for better marketing' (101). Indeed, from this perspective, *Cinema Novo* was criticized for being 'elitist', since it catered to small audiences, in con-tradistinction to the 'universal communication' of the market (Renato Ortiz 168).

This translation of the popular was also quite evident in the emergence of the *telenovela*, television's most popular genre. Adopted from Argentine and Mexican models, the *telenovela* was melodramatic. Debates emerged in Brazil as to the value of the *telenovela* in reflecting the national reality. In the 1970s, non-alienated, realistic *telenovelas* were written and broadcast that interested *o povo* the people, thus demonstrating for some commentators that the market could meet the demand for national reflection better than other forms. This acceptance of the *telenovela* signals the emergence of a populist viewpoint, according to which a mass audience implies democratization, and a restricted public connotes élitist gate-keeping with considerable cultural capital. *Cinema Novo* was now criticized for creating a 'popular' cinema without the people.

Populism and nationalism were characteristic of cinematic developments in other countries in the 1960s and 1970s. In Argentina, Nilsson's urban-themed auteurism had received accolades from French New-Wave critics and thus had the greatest influence. However, by the mid-1960s there was political and intellectual resistance to Onganía's military dictatorship. Birri's 'national-popular' cinema, which in the 1950s sought to adapt neo-realism to the Latin American context and challenge commercial cinema's distribution and exhibition circuits, inspired a new generation. Its most salient exponents were Fernando Solanas and Octavio Getino, who made *La hora de los hornos* (*The Hour of the Furnaces*) (1966–68). Like *Cinema Novo*, the roots of this 'Third Cinema' lay not in Europe or North America but Africa, Asia and Latin America, including the worker-oriented populism of Peronism, an ongoing political movement that continues to arouse impassioned allegiance despite its turn to the right in the mid-1970s with Perón's return to Argentina and the succession to the presidency of his second wife upon his death. With the end of the fascist dictatorships of the 1970s and early 1980s, Argentinian cinema lost the bonds of intense censorship, but the advent of neoliberal policies of structural adjustment adversely affected state support, unleashing instead a multi-media alliance in film of government and private TV stations which had some popular success. Alternative projects had difficulty gaining support (Falicov).

Neoliberalism also played into the hands of a nationalist production *ethos*. The strategies of representation imposed by the NICL in Mexican cinema certainly do not make it into a viable vehicle for representing Mexican realities. In the 1960s, leading directors such as John Huston and Sam Peckinpah filmed in Mexico for the scenery, and Richard Burton, Elizabeth Taylor and their attendant *paparazzi* turned Puerto Vallarta into a tourist destination (Tegel). Durango was the site for over a hundred Westerns and genre films in the same decades, because it had non-unionized workers; but runaway productions shifted as other locations vied for studio attention ('Hollywood Heads').

The success of *Titanic* in the late 1990s saw Mexico again a key site for offshore production. Restoring Mexico to the Hollywood map gained James Cameron the Order of the Aztec Eagle from a grateful government, which offers Hollywood docile labor, minimal bureaucracy, a weak *peso*, many US-trained technicians and a new film commission that provides liaison services. It is a screen testimony to NAFTA, which has seen the annual average number of offshore productions in Mexico increase from seven to seventeen as the shipment of film stock and special-effects equipment is facilitated, especially for low-budget productions (LaFranchi; Riley). Local workers on *Titanic* in Rosarito, a *maquiladora* sixty miles south of the border, reported horrific levels of exploitation and mistreatment when the state forced out a leftist union in favor of management stooges. Mexico's new film 'union' even maintains an office in LA to reassure anxious industry mavens of its cooperativeness and to remain up-to-date on US pay rates – in order to undercut them (Sutter; Swift; Bacon). US-based Spanish-language TV networks frequently produce voice-overs for commercials offshore via high-quality phone lines, to utilize non-union labor (Porter). *The Mexican* was partly shot in Real de Catorce, the first location in San Luis Potosí used by Hollywood. Much was made of the fact that the production invested US$10000 on new water pipes and to tap a spring in an abandoned mine – doubtless so that its stars, Brad Pitt and Julia Roberts, would have the best *agua* each morning – and that the local grocer's sales increased 20% during filming. Meanwhile, construction workers were paid US$12 a day to match Pitt and Roberts' US$40 million salaries (Pfister). In 1999, a union carpenter in Hollywood earned US$275 for eight hours, and a union carpenter in Mexico earned US$216 for fifty-five hours. 'Mexico is becoming a "maquiladora" for movies of the week' (Riley) just as it is a low-cost cross-border site for auto assembly. It even offers non-mestizaje Menonite extras to compensate for the fact that 'the people look different' (Riley).

Not surprisingly, Rupert Murdoch cites approvingly the numbers of European workers invisibly employed in the making of *Titanic*: 'this cross-border cultural co-operation is not the result of regulation, but market forces. It's the freedom to move capital, technology and talent around the world that adds value, invigorates ailing markets, creates new ones'. How ironic that the workers submerged at the end of the credits (or not listed at all) should 'owe' their livelihoods to a boat sunk by invisible ice and business *hubris*. And that the ongoing livelihood of people in Popotla has been endangered by *Titanic* – since the production, the local catch of fish has declined by a third because of Fox's chlorination project (Pfister). Meanwhile, National Public Radio reported that Murdoch was asking the Mexican Government to offer financial incentives for runaways (broadcast of 24 March 2000), and the privatization of the film industry across the 1990s had decimated local production (Riley). This is some distance from the national popular, and Mexico may be a model for other Latin American countries.

Conclusion

[I want to … ensure that film-making in the UK remains a pleasurable and profitable experience for overseas companies.] – UK culture minister Chris Smith (Department for Culture)

Clearly, audiovisual policy across sites shares a dilemma – the commerce-culture relationship. There is always a struggle between (i) the desire for a viable sector of the economy that provides employment, foreign exchange and multiplier effects; and (ii) the desire for a representative, local cinema that transcends moneymaking in search of the opportunity for a society to reflect upon itself through drama, as per the less profit-oriented work of Leopoldo, Tracey Moffatt, Derek Jarman, Julien, Mike Leigh, Solanas, Jane Campion and Sally Potter.

To facilitate the struggle, we need to utilize contradictions on each side of the discursive divide between the consumer and the citizen, criticizing both neo-classical accounts of consumers and DEM/GEM takes on citizenship. We must beware falling for the rhetoric of citizenship adopted in discriminatory and exclusionary ways (think always of the *non*-consumer, the *non*-citizen, and their fate), and require each part of the consumer-citizen divide to illustrate: (i) the history to their account of either consumption or citizenship; (ii) the relationship between multinational capital, democracy and diversity; and (iii) the role of the state in consumption, and of corporations in citizenship. Lastly, we must look to minority, indigenous and migrant interests any time we are told consumers are unmarked, or that citizens are at the center of culture within borders.

Colin McArthur's requirements for a Scottish film culture reference the controversies well: 'a historically specific grappling with the contradictions of the ... past and present, a set of recurrent themes and styles discernibly amounting to a *collectivity*' (1115). The burden of democratic government – to address a population in all its life-forms – must animate policy. If it does not, we shall see 'rootless *Titanic*-style movies, free of geography, culture or humor, that play as well in Prague as in Peoria'. In the UK market, for example, that makes for plenty of Mr Beans and Mr Bonds, but very few Ms Potters or Mr Juliens (Hibbin).

Behind the rhetoric of national representation lie sectoral interests. Beneath the shroud of the free market, reside signs of political significance. Citizen and consumer meet at improbable crossroads that necessitate political action, as the following quotation from Michèle Mattelart, an intellectual working with Salvador Allende's 1970–73 socialist government in Chile, indicates:

> How will commercial logic be aligned with the social logic governing the interests of groups, the widening base of audiovisual production, the participation by citizens in the choice of technologies, and the definition of their use? Is a 'local product' one that would permit a particular collectivity to express and to reappropriate its sounds and images, compatible with the international market? Is there an 'alternative' product that could be international yet not in the mould of a transnationalized mass culture? (430)

This dilemma is an ongoing one for activists in the entertainment sphere. Intellectuals functioning as critics of the state to generate additional artistic freedoms or opportunities always walk a fine line. They must navigate between promoting a chauvinistic nationalism and protecting an indolent *bourgeoisie* on the one hand, and ensuring a local, democratic specificity to audiovisual culture on the other. And the spectre of neoliberalism looms largest of all, a kind of implicit deflator of cultural policy claims. When the Hollywood studios won a case in the Mexican Supreme Court in March 2000 against a Federal Film Law provision that required subtitles rather than dubbing for feature imports, on the basis that this discriminated against the 20 million Mexicans who do not read because of age, sight, language or literacy issues (Tegel 'Hollywood Gets') the stakes were brought into sharp relief. Even as the US cynically pretended to speak on behalf of an excluded group that would probably never be wealthy enough to become consistent film audiences, in order to increase exploitation of existing consumers, the hypocrisy of the Mexican state's commitment to an inclusive cultural nationalism was exposed. The Australian High Court had just decided that television programs from New Zealand counted as local under the terms of the two countries' trade treaty, thus subordinating culturalist protection to the precepts of customs-union commerce (O'Regan 'Knowing' 30–31). The uncertain dance of *laissez-faire* and screen production continued.

3

Command Cultures and the Postcolonial

[R]emoving the appendix and taking aspirin have no national form. This is not the case with the arts: with them the question of national form does arise. This is because art is the manifestation of people's lives, thoughts and emotions, and it bears a very close relationship to a nation's customs and language. – Mao Tse-Tung, 1950s (85)

Under the slogan of 'national culture' the *bourgeoisie* of *all* nations ... are *in fact* pursuing the policy of splitting the workers, emasculating democracy and haggling with the feudalists over the sale of the people's rights and the people's liberty. – Lenin, 1900s (On *Literature* 82)

There was this myth among dissidents in communist times that ordinary Czechs were secretly reading Proust. Our market research showed Czechs were not refined intellectuals at all. They weren't interested in Proust at all. No! We discovered what they were: beer-drinking, working-class Catholics. – Vladimir Zelezny, 1990s (quoted in 'The Disappearing')

The title to this chapter is awkward. We wanted to avoid the connotations of the signifiers 'totalitarian' and 'authoritarian', as used by *bourgeois* social science and media to link forms of social and governmental organization that were quite distinct (for example, the liberal state socialism of Hungary in 1956 and the fascist National Socialism of Germany in 1938). This association is very much alive: in 1999, the New York Times joined Nazi and state-socialist German culture in assigning them to 'history's dustbin' (Roger Cohen 'Exhibiting'). Such essentialization is more about the desire of the West to differentiate itself from alternatives by lumping them together, than it is an accurate category.

At the same time, something does link such governmental norms. The notion of a non-market form of cultural provision always already centers the state in planning, creating, policing and revising cultural practice. Hence our borrowing the idea of the command economy, and redeploying it to describe the provision of culture. We are confronting head-on the presumption that market-based forms of Western cultural production are 'natural'; that, for example, Stalinism 'overwhelmed and deformed an art that otherwise – if granted its own integrity – would take on the forms and social functions of the arts in the West' (Rueschemeyer 31).

In the second half of the chapter, we consider postcolonialism, the other crucial alternative to Western capitalism, which intersects with command-cultural models and profit-based ones. The postcolonial has a special purchase both on imperialist and neo-colonialist forms of capitalism and national self-formation. Of course, countries on the periphery have exchanged ideas and goods for a millennium. Networks of information and trade connected the Pacific, Asia, the Mediterranean and Africa until the fifteenth century, when the slavery, militarism and technology of European imperialism began to wipe out these routes. Intra-continental communications came to rely on Europe as a conduit. New ideologies came too: racial supremacy and the conversion mission of Christianity (Hamelink 223–24) made culture and information into imperial concerns.

The *laissez-faire* economy animating the preconditions for fascism and state socialism emerged at the global core of world capitalism in the eighteenth and nineteenth centuries. Countries outside Europe and North America came to be colonial and semi-colonial plots, with huge limitations on their political and economic sovereignty imposed by imperializing states and internationalizing corporations. With the decolonization of Latin America early in the nineteenth century, and elsewhere in the mid-twentieth century, the need of countries on the periphery of the system to progress beyond agrarian economies domestically, while competing internationally, produced a more planned approach to all kinds of development, including culture. Educational policies were designed to produce a citizenry capable of speaking to other peoples and trading with them. As the experience of postcolonialism is so longstanding in Latin America, as are traditions of command and commercial cultures, we devote the majority of this chapter to that region.

We think there is enough in common with non-market cultural provision, past and present, to justify situating it as a genuine alternative to capitalist democracies. It is certainly problematic to identify command cultures with comprehensive cultural control. State-socialist support was spread across a wide variety of methods: interest-free loans, stipends, commissions, teaching posts, contracts and political organizations (Toepler 7). So we clearly distinguish between cultural policies that proclaim an egalitarian, worker-oriented world and those dedicated to chauvinistic nationalism and the heroization of conquest and domination. The first of these we typify as state-socialist, the second as fascist.

State-Socialist Cultural Policy

[T]here will ever be hysterical intellectuals to raise a howl about ... [communist cultural policy], which degrades, deadens, 'bureaucratises' the free battle of ideas, freedom of criticism, freedom of literary creation, etc., etc. Such outcries, in point of fact, would be nothing more than an expression of *bourgeois-intellectual individualism*. – Vladimir Ilyich Lenin, 1920s ('Party' 180)

Culture was important from the first days of the 1917 Russian Revolution. It formed a 'third front' behind politics and economics. The Bolsheviks' governing assumption was that an entirely new category of personhood could be generated from socialist precepts and practice (Timothy O'Connor 51, 61). To this end, Lenin called for literature to 'become Party literature' in opposition to 'the profit-making, commercialized *bourgeois* press, to *bourgeois* literary careerism and individualism, 'aristocratic anarchism' and drive for profit'. Art would articulate with the ideology of social democracy, not the mechanics of capitalism ('Party' 180). Culture must serve the animating interests of the proletariat's dictatorship – and be dedicated to withering away class exploitation, through the vision and programs of the Communist Party (Lenin 'On Proletarian' 383). The vanguard did not believe that socialist art would emerge spontaneously from the workers. Leon Trotsky, who briefly held the title of Cultural Commissar, argued that while the proletariat would 'put its stamp upon culture' during this necessary period of dictatorship, that would not amount to a fully-fledged 'proletarian culture', which could only emerge following a 'series of historical changes'. Once mass literacy produced a familiarity with and a mastery of '*bourgeois* culture', the necessary preconditions would be in place to generate 'a mass culture, a universal and popular one' (Trotsky 192–93).

The question of national culture has been a complex one for Marxism, given its analysis of class struggle and solidarity as global, and the nation as a mystifying force that stands in the way of international worker unity. Lenin, for instance, regarded national languages as hindrances to the dominance of the most significant languages of commerce, which the majority should be able to speak in order to prosper, as opposed to clinging on to old cultural norms (*On Literature* 81). But addressing these issues in the mid-1950s, Mao argued that state socialism had produced content inflected both by socialist principles and 'national character ... national form and style'. Whereas science defied national specificity in its falsifiable search for understanding, the arts necessarily manifested everyday life via history and language. By the same token, the Marxist *credo* of development, that progressive politics should line up with progress in all parts of the social world, meant that state socialism must acknowledge the achievements of the West and its *bourgeoisie*, in a critical way that would produce exciting hybrids, 'neither Chinese nor Western' (84–85, 87–88). And Stalin (later facetiously nominated by the English literary-studies journal *Critical Quarterly* as the 'world's greatest linguist') excluded language from the general notion of culture as a superstructure determined by an economic base, because of its organic and comparatively non-ideological relationship to the history of everyday life (3–5). Like its capitalist counterpart, state-socialist cultural dogma has been about creating and tending political subjects *and* ensuring economic growth.

These complexities – themselves the product of a conflict-based form of theorization – meant that dialectical play, rather than a totalizing domination, characterized state socialism, albeit with the repressive influence of a state elite hemmed in by global capitalist militarism. State socialism's legitimation narratives have depended on nationalism as much as leftism. So the remarkable art treasures accumulated by the Czarist regime soon provided a legitimating body of national history for the Bolsheviks, which ran counter to their early links to a Russian avant-garde of cultural workers and theorists. This produced a quandary typical of state socialism's complex connection to earlier forms of power and authority versus new models (Groys 144–45). Proletkult, an organization dedicated to identifying and promoting proletarian cultural production, began just before the 1917 Revolution and was well placed a few months later to argue for the re-disposal of *bourgeois* norms by an emergent factory class. The contradictions of this position (how could vanguardism speak for an organic emergence, and how could spontaneous proletarian culture be recognized?) worked against the group. Nevertheless, anti-vanguard associations from below paradoxically charged Proletkult with élitism (these bodies included the wonderfully-named Union of the Militant Godless – where do we sign on?). Anatoli Lunacharksy, Proletkult's leader, went on to run the Commissariat of Enlightenment until its dissolution, along with many other institutions, in 1928–29, when Stalin reconfigured state and Party infrastructures (Fitzpatrick 20, 91, 94). The desire to re-forge alliances with the intelligentsia, pushed the state away from a hard line on traditional high culture.

Whereas the first years after the October Revolution were undoubtedly militant (as per the Cultural Revolution of the 1920s) it is no surprise to find the Soviet Union of the 1930s dissolving proletarian arts organizations, returning to Czarist educational systems, placing curricular attention on Russian rather than proletarian history and valorizing high culture. Jewelry and art plundered by the Czars were rearticulated as valuable once they had been 'returned' to the oppressed classes under the custodianship of the state (Groys 153). These were outcomes of the negotiation between 'the Stalinist regime and an emergent middle class' that saw the intelligentsia bought off with professional autonomy and power, in return for loyalty. The laughable endorsement of Pushkin as a socialist novelist *avant la lettre* was the low-point of this *rapprochement* (Barker 25), while the fact that the non-Communist Maxim Gorky was the ultimate cultural arbiter of Soviet letters in the 1930s signified a turn towards inclusiveness and the rule of professionalism rather than ideology. Traditional institutions of cultural production, such as the Bolshoi Theatre, were given power, whilst the Union of Soviet Writers exercised authority over literature relatively autonomously from the regime (Fitzpatrick 8–14, 248). The power of artistic creators meant, for example, that museum shows were chosen by the Union, not by curators and educators (Groys 159). This is not an argument for creative freedom under middle-period Stalinism – it is an argument for the hegemony of professionalism. Either way, it was not good news for pluralism, as consolidation of authority in the Artists' Union after 1932 was done in the name of destroying 'alien elements' and 'elitist withdrawal and loss of contact with the political tasks of contemporaneity' in favor of 'Socialist construction' (Central Committee).

By the mid-1930s, socialist realism had been endorsed as the only acceptable genre of cultural production. As enunciated by Andrei Zhdanov, socialist realism focused on those 'active builders of a new life' who would be 'the chief types and chief heroes of Soviet literature'. Workers, collective farmers; engineers and Party members should be depicted in a way that was 'optimistic in essence', in keeping with the genre's debts to 'the only progressive and advanced class' (410–11). There were three pillars of this policy: (i) *klássovost* (the relation of art to the proletariat's struggle with the *bourgeoisie*); (ii) *partúnost* (identification of art with the Communist Party); and (iii) *naródnost* (the relation of art to common humanity). Contradictions emerged between them, as the Party sought to enunciate and police proletarianism and common humanity (Brighton 25). Each strut privileged an active versus a contemplative life, which led to difficulties in other domains of arts policy. Museums were derided by some as symbols of consumerist pleasure where aesthetic transformation could never occur in line with proletarian principles and needs. A sociologically-inclined, reflectionist school of art criticism, prominent in the 1920s, associated artistic movements with movements in capital (so impressionism was equated with the financial *bourgeoisie*). Because this damned so much work that could otherwise be attributed to a developing history of artistic achievement, it was displaced by a form of critique that articulated art history with a double-declutching mix of national and class heritage (Groys 145, 153, 155). Early plans for statuary were about international and proletarian rather than merely national commemoration, and featured popular participation. This changed with the post-Leninist years, initially via a mausoleum trend for the deceased leader. Then, of course, Stalin's cult of personality was created. His personal distance from the people mixed with an iconographic ubiquity, via huge statues. After the development of the Eastern hegemony following World War II, the Soviet Union required Warsaw Pact nations to create statues marking their liberation to state socialism, until the USSR's post-Stalin reforms of the late 1950s (Michalski 107–09, 114, 118, 97, 125, 131, 138, 141).

The mature Soviet model of cultural policy rested on four struts: regionalism, centralism, urbanism and workerism (Rubinstein et al. 3). The first three of these were designed to ensure local and national sensitivities and the fourth to carry out the revolutionary, working-class mandate: control *of* labor *by* labor. Each sector had performing arts institutions (in the USSR's heyday, six hundred permanent theatre companies) and quasi-state authorities that funded cultural production, as well as a Theater Workers Union of 50,000. A comparison of the economics of the performing arts in the US and the former Soviet Union in the 1980s is quite surprising, given prevailing assumptions about command economies. The USSR's musicians received only minimal subsidy, but did not go into major debt, unlike their equivalents in the United States. Box-office receipts meant that the Soviet state did not have to engage in subvention, given price controls. Drama presented a different picture, with major public investment. Interestingly, administrative costs in each case were much higher proportionally in the US. So much for state-socialist bureaucracy as top-heavy!

The USSR also allowed a variety of schemes for arts funding, such as tax deductions and exemptions as well as direct support (Rubinstein et al.). So much for state socialism as necessarily centralized and financially inefficient!

The basic orientation given to people growing up in the Soviet Union was that culture was about more than entertainment. Commerce was considered secondary to uplift, as both a measure and an allocator of taste. High Stalinism blended popular and high culture in a contradictory *mélange* of improving literature and state-socialist versions of the Hollywood musical. Readers' clubs, instituted in the 1930s, may not exactly have policed everyday reading habits, but an internalization of ideological and material duties and failings was intense and successful. Forms of self-monitoring and habits of thought were critical, as well as censorship from without (Barker 14–15, 17, 24).

This complex relationship to tradition and modernity affected other state-socialist countries. Consider Czechoslovakia, where socialized literary production began in 1948 when large state combines displaced smaller publishing concerns. Centrally-located publishers produced children's books, translations and national literature with an eye to what the Ministry of Culture described as either 'progressive cultural world traditions' or the 'national literary tradition'. Access was democratized via mass literacy campaigns and distribution, while content was pre- and pro-scribed (Smejkalová-Strickland 199). Following the Soviet Union's brutal invasion to curb the 1968 'Prague Spring', literary production split between three zones: 'state-controlled, officially-published literature; "self-print" texts produced within dissident circles; and exile literature published abroad'. There was cross-fertilization between these zones. As in the West, prestigious firms were dominated by authors and editors who were themselves intellectuals. And they all referenced the state – the first zone, because it was dependent on the ideology and finance of state socialism, the other two because they relied on opposition to the regime for their intellectual coherence (Smejkalová-Strickland 198, 196, 200). Once democracy and fully-fledged capitalism came to the country, dissident intellectuals either joined the entertainment world or lost influence. The political-economic system they resisted had, ironically, sustained them ('The Disappearing').

The PRC has also gone through several distinct cultural-policy phases. Its initial incarnation saw domination of everyday life by the centralized production and distribution of a culture that was designed to produce ideological fealty. The present moment is a mixture of openness, based on the desire for incorporation into world capitalism, and protection, based on twin desires – to maintain traditional forms of life and ensure Party control. 'Foreign cultural materials' are only welcome if they 'abide by Chinese laws and regulations' (Wong). This means that while Party cadres are still formally in charge of censorship and cultural production throughout the nation, their influence over the quotidian is significantly compromised by budgetary reductions and the private proliferation of satellite dishes, VCRs and TVs throughout rural China.

Nevertheless, doctrines of 'building a spiritual civilization' and 'ideological and political work' remain strong, and directed at the revival of traditional religion (derided as 'feudal', like *feng shui*) as much as Western commodification. The tendency to use culture as a policing device of the everyday that we noted with reference to Western-Enlightenment doctrines (as per Arnold and the NEA) is strong – cultural-policy officials may, for instance, designate particular cities as 'civilized', while individual households and citizens are eligible for '10 Stars of Civilization', which range from questions of hygiene and birth control to duty and respect for law (Thøgersen). 'Art for art's sake' has surfaced among urban artists in reaction to both central control and the desire to deploy culture for social change (Keane).

After its creation following the Second World War, the German Democratic Republic (GDR) drew on Germany's national history to distinguish cultural production from the West. Martin Luther, Frederick the Great and Goethe were all buried in the East, and their figures were used widely in monuments and portraits. Weimar, where Goethe was born and Friedrich Schiller, Franz Liszt and Walter Gropius lived, became a key tourist site (Roger Cohen 'The Sorrows'). The GDR's cultural policy was based on a requirement that contemporary artists participate in the creation of a new social order. Local specificities saw an immediate post-World War II preference for artists who had refused to toe the line of the Nazis and had suffered exclusion or persecution. This helped to produce an impressive initial diversity under the new government, but social-ist realism quickly grew dominant until Stalin's death in 1953. A certain liber-alization at that time permitted painting and sculpture that were indebted to impressionism, expressionism and the decorative. But there was always intense pressure on cultural producers to follow Party logics, albeit with a mediating protection guaranteed through (quasi-obligatory) membership of the Artists' Union (Rueschemeyer 33–34, 36–39).

Broad-brush socialist-realist symbolism always looked *Kitsch* to Westerners ('see it now: woman tractor-driver meets hammer-wielding man') and became an object of parody within post-state socialist nations of the 1990s, but principally among those who have grown to adulthood these past ten years. The quality of 'manufactured sentimentality' still resonates with many others (Sabonis-Chafee). Certain forms of state socialism are of course scrupulously anti-intellectual, as per the Cultural Revolution in China (1966–77). When the Khmer Rouge ruled Cambodia between 1975 and 1979, they executed or starved 80% of the classical dancers who bore the country's cultural tradition (Turnbull AR6). And a similarly anti-intellectual cultural policy has obtained in the Union of Myanmar/Burma since it became socialist in the mid-1970s. Literacy has been a major focus, but universities were peremptorily shut down a decade ago.

On the other hand, cultural devastation awaited those who dropped socialism in favor of capitalism and the NICL. A trend towards commodification is equally clear in both countries that cleave to state-socialist principles and emergent capitalist states. In Hungary, participation in the capitalist world-system was sufficient in the early 1980s to find national parades organized around not state-socialist symbols, but the Rubik Cube, chosen for its export success and international recognition to sit alongside commercial popular culture from the West (Karnoouh 135). The Socialist Republic of Vietnam triumphed over US imperialism in 1975, but suffered terrible destruction of its national infrastructure and economy. Since that time, it has established a multivariate cultural policy that follows socialist principles, articulating social development of the working class and rural dwellers and a balance between economics and culture. The central Ministry of Culture has control over studios, colleges, museums and theatres, via government departments that specialize in music, dance, the fine arts, film and research. There is also a devolved system of cultural councils across the country. At the same time, the 1990s saw the country join the world capitalist system. Vietnamese cultural production shifted from a focus on socialist ideology and regionalism towards commercial applications.

Central Europe's embrace of market principles has had a devastating impact on cultural infrastructure. The Czech Republic is an oft-cited instance of privatization without mass unemployment. But that story hides major declines in labor force participation (Gitter and Scheuer).

In 2001, Wesley Snipes and a cadre of Hollywood film-makers arrived in Prague to shoot the action film *Blade 2: Bloodlust*. The formerly state-owned Barrandov studio, one of Europe's largest production facilities that employs five hundred skilled workers and has eleven sound stages and on-site laboratories, welcomed the estimated US$10–15 million this production brought to the studio. Prague's weak exchange rate and base of cheap skilled laborers makes shooting there 30% less costly than in the West, and six of the seven majors had shot there in the year and a half prior. Film production service companies with ties to US and British clients facilitated an influx of production, beginning with commercials in the mid-1990s, then British and US TV-movies, mini-series and feature films. Productions include the mini-series *The Scarlet Pimpernel, Dune* and *Mists of Avalon*, and the feature films *Messenger: The Story of Joan of Arc, Dungeons and Dragons* and *The Bourne Identity* (Meils). The government permits producers to set off fireworks in the downtown area in the middle of the night, and diverts air traffic for hours in the interests of 'quiet on the set' (Krosnar et al). The NICL facilitates the free movement of screen capital into cheap production locations, contains labor mobility and undermines labor internationalism – all brokered on the exploitation of skills and facilities developed under state socialism.

The decision by the Czech government to sell 75% of the studios was opposed by the local film-makers union, who pointed out its illegality – the process was begun in 1991, two years before the passage of a law ending the state monopoly on film-making. In 1994, directors who had made films under the previous regimes, and who called for retention of a national cultural policy, were told 'Don't even think about it' by Prime Minister Vaclav Klaus, under whom domestic films dropped to 2% of the studio's output. Such world-renowned artists as Jiri Menzel and Vera Chytilova were excluded from film-making (Hames).

Another story has been told from within by one of the privatization's architects, Michael Millea, who joyously relates going to Prague with the US Agency for International Development (USAID) to find that: 'the former Czechoslovakia was carpetbagger heaven' (489). Millea may have been referring to Hollywood film-makers, but of course *he* was the carpetbagger wonk in this story. The plan to privatize was predicated by USAID on data about US studios that correlated favorable exchange rates and comparatively low budgets with decisions to shoot offshore. Based on the Agency's projections, the successful purchase offer proposed translating Barrandov from nationally-framed texts to US ones, extending even to converting studio space into shopping centers and hotels for visiting crews. The competing plan, drawn up by film-makers that favored domestic production, was rejected by the Agency. Millea concludes his essay with the triumphant observation that the shooting of the first *Mission Impossible* film in Prague indicates 'capitalism has taken firm root in the Czech Republic' (504).

'Capitalism' immediately led to lay-offs for 85% of the studio's employees. After London, Prague is today Hollywood's 'second center' in Europe. At 2001 prices, labor was 40% cheaper than in LA – union painters are paid less than US$3 an hour, for example, while extras 'command' US$15 a day to Hollywood's US$100 ('Hollywood on the Vltava'; 'Hollywood Cashes Runaway Checks'; Hejma; Holley). A studio manager boasted in 2000 of 'one artist working on set-building for the last two months who's been earning about as much in a week as his British counterparts earn in a day and he just happens to be a famous Czech sculptor', while a non-union workforce meant that injuries to locals did not require compensation (quoted in I'Anson-Sparks). This is a terribly exploitative end to state socialism. Essentially, skills that were developed under a public system are now being used up by private 'enterprise'. Fly-by-night capital has moved in to exploit extant technical capacities without any intention of training a new cohort. Like the disastrous human experimentation in privatization by Chile, Britain and Argentina during the 1980s, this was a one-off benefit to government, a gift to international business and a disaster for workers.

Fascist Cultural Policy

Until the moment when National-Socialism took power, there existed in Germany a so-called 'modern art', that is, to be sure, almost every year another one, as the very meaning of this word indicates. National-Socialist Germany, however, wants again a 'German Art', and this art shall and will be of eternal value, as are all truly creative values of a people ... we will wage an unrelenting war of purification against the last elements of putrefaction in our culture. – Adolf Hitler (424, 426)

Nazi Germany (1933–45) inherited a Federal structure of cultural policy and centralized it (Ismayr 45–46). This was part of a more general nation-building strategy, with specific effects in the arts. The leaders of the National Socialist Party mobilized international looting by the military (of 250,000 items) as a means of developing impressive personal art collections that then served as both gifts and markers of distinction between elites. Their sense of cultivation animated a mutual participation in the formation of arts policy, often in unco-ordinated and conflictual ways that made an impact across the administration of museums, the control of arts workers, the expropriation of texts and goods and the conduct of magazine publishing. There was a cosmic ambivalence towards the interplay of tradition and modernity – the regime was torn between heroizing the past and privileging the latest and most innovative forms of life. National chauvinism won out in the late 1930s, as modernization in art (i.e. modernism) came to be associated with Jews and other enemies. An intensifying ideological campaign associated all forms of high art with Aryanism, and promoted a muscular militarism. The regime's iconography was increasingly in step with Hitler's investment in monumentalist architecture. He firmly believed that the cultural 'means and institutions of communication' had been taken over by 'Judaism', with 'so-called art criticism' a key element to this conspiracy (Hitler 423). The state banned such criticism – only descriptive prose was allowed, and unacceptable artworks were removed from view rather than criticized. Unusually, the negative side to Nazism went beyond suppression. A *Degenerate Art* show toured Germany in 1937–38, identifying the unacceptable face of modernism and other 'non-Aryan' forms from the Weimar period that were also said to represent the tastes of unrepresentative museum professionals rather than the public at large (Petropoulos 5–9, 51, 53). Cultural policy centered the ineffability of German heritage versus the ephemera of modernism, distinguishing sturdy stability and moralism from 'decadent' newness and fashionability (Hitler 424). Internationally, the Nazis supported cultural institutions in friendly regimes. Across Latin America in the 1930s and 1940s, they funded German-language education, public libraries, and scholarly exchange (Ninkovich US 11).

Hitler favored allegorical art that took ideal-types and reconfigured them as symbols of cultural norms. So portraiture was not as important to the regime as architecture. The latter borrowed from nineteenth-century personifications of mythic urges, such as the Muses, and physiocratic iconography, via homo-eroticized labor. Monuments were derided if they were associated with monarchy or democracy. The purifying *ethos* of war was represented in temples to martyrs of the Party and nation. Offices and auditoria were designed to maximize the sense of awe on the part of observers, a kind of gigantism of the senses that merged mystic pantheism with technological display. The *Autobahnen*, for instance, were never seen as practical means of transportation. Rather, the freeway system metaphorized the titanism of German labor. The War reduced the resources available to such buildings and saw a turn in cultural policy towards a cult of Hitlerian personality (Michalski 93–94, 96–97, 99–101).

For its part, the *nostrum* used to be that Italian Fascist cultural policy (1922–43) was 'based on an unchanging theoretical foundation or on a totalitarianizing mission' to obliterate difference. But the roster of influences on it runs the gamut from modernism to futurism to nationalism, and much of its impetus was simply to do with modernization – for example, dealing with the fact that a minority of citizens actually spoke Italian (Marla Stone 14; Berezin 364). On the one hand, the Futurist Movement spoke of technology and newness as signs of a vigorous modernity that would make Italy a world leader in applied knowledge and aesthetics, once it threw off the restraint of the church and embraced a nihilism that could be merged with the desire for progress. But on the other hand, fascism was dedicated to clerical structures of authority and a glorious past, to a history of Ancient Rome as the paradigmatic site of both warrior heroism and artistic achievement. This battle of tradition versus modernity was never resolved within the regime, although in terms of access to power, the Futurists were barely in the race, not least as their own libertarianism turned them away from actionable policy proposals and program management. Mussolini's first education minister was Giovanni Gentile, a conservative philosopher who ordained a return to the classics and the neglect of science and technology. This strategy was based on a notion of community with the existing state and nation, rather than the presumption that citizens would identify with innovation (Berezin 360). The classics would lead pupils to appreciate the country's dominant past and instill patriotism – hence also the formation of an Italian Royal Academy. Mussolini himself veered between instructing artists to focus on heritage issues and urging them to address the modern world. This amounted to a double bind, not only about themes, but also about methods. Part of the Futurism versus tradition divide concerned the appropriation of trends from elsewhere, because the notion of a glorious past as the touchstone of culture militated against international influences (Ferme; Palma and di San Luca 69).

The outcome was a form of 'aesthetic pluralism' during much of the Mussolini era, with relative state tolerance of diversity and culture-worker tolerance of the regime until the late 1930s. During the lead-up to the Second World War, certain tendencies within the Fascist Party pushed for the appropriation of Nazi methods of central control and the rejection of all non-Fascist outside influences, in favor of a militant nationalism that glorified state violence. This culminated in the creation and growing power of the Ministry of Popular Culture (Palma and di San Luca 69). Audience and artistic responses to this tendency were extremely negative (Marla Stone 179–80, 220–21, 256).

Latter-day fascists have encountered similar contradictions and splits. George Papadopoulos, dictator of Greece from 1967 to 1973, planned just the kind of Romantic return to former greatness that characterized Mussolini's evocation of ancient Rome. Papadopoulos announced, for example, his intention to rebuild the Colossus of Rhodes, one of the ancient world's seven wonders, as part of his slogan 'Greece is risen'. But this was always a tenuous hold on heritage. Aristophanes' plays, for instance, were banned because they criticized governments ('George').

A Hitler-like cultism has arisen among many beleaguered anti-democratic leaders. Islam has not generally endorsed figurative art, because the creator's form is neither knowable nor representable. But cults of personality were introduced in Egypt under Gamal Abdul Nasser and Iran under the Pahlevi, which featured the ruler's face as a key icon. Under Saddam Hussein (known in Islamic South-East and south Asia as 'the lion of the Gulf' for standing up to US militarism) Iraq has seen a vast investment in cultural policy, with Baghdad transformed via the addition of huge avenues and monuments dedicated to national glory. Prior to his ascent to power in 1968, the city had two public monuments. Hussein's monuments go beyond his own form. Perhaps most spectacularly, a US missile that destroyed the Saddam Tower in 1991 was retrieved, melted down, and cast into unpleasant portraits of anti-Iraqi leaders. George Bush the Elder and Margaret Thatcher look up, agonized, at the feet of a gigantic sculpture of Hussein ('Monumental'). That awkward link, between the cultural geography of Western Fascism and Eastern anti-democracy, leads us to the complex category of the postcolonial, with initial reference to Latin America.

Latin America

> [T]he Ministry of Culture positions itself between the Nicaragua we inherited – dispossessed and distanced from its own identity – and the Nicaragua of the new man, owner of his own culture, owner of his own values ... the people will cease to be simple receptors of cultural values and will become makers of culture. – Nicaraguan Ministry of Culture, 1981 (quoted in Whisnant 239)

Cultural policy in Spanish America and Brazil has been marked by conquest and colonization, from the beginning of the fifteenth century to the first decades of the twentieth, a full century after independence. Some would argue that the colonialist legacy – especially the subordination of indigenous, African, and mixed-race peoples' popular culture, and non-European religious forms – has endured to this day. On the other hand, the salience of state support for certain popular forms and practices since the early twentieth century – Mexican muralism, Brazilian samba, Cuban son, magical realism and testimonial narratives – bears witness to unique transculturated (Renato Ortiz) or hybrid cultures (García Canclini) whose significance cannot be adequately captured by the double bind of Eurocentrism and postcolonial nativism.

Hybridity, we shall see, was at first an affliction, to be contained – impossibly – by the theocratic Iberian colonial state, whose ideal subjects were constituted through repression. But by the early twentieth century, hybridity was becoming the very sign of Latin American modernity, against the citizen-defining Enlightenment and positivist narratives that had taken root there in the nineteenth century. Two apparently antithetical manifestations developed that would provide highly original cultural practices in the twentieth century. On the one hand, various trends in literary and visual cultures deconstructed European styles and philosophies by demonstrating how they become inoperable or fantastic in Latin American contexts. Latin Americans have characterized this process as manifesting the 'truth' of Western ethics at the margin of the West. As such, these deconstructive discourses – e.g. the 1960s literary 'Boom de la literatura latino americana' and artistic styles like Brazilian *tropicalismo* – are touted as expressions of Latin America's cultural maturity.

On the other hand, various populist regimes recognized that the vernacular culture of the working masses would provide the symbolic cement of the nation, necessary to push forward a new stage of economic development. The populist 1930s to 1960s provided the imagery for what has been accepted at home and abroad as emblematic, even stereotypical of Latin American national identities. The popular classes were idealized on the airwaves and the screen, in part to coopt their increasing demands, sometimes effectively and often violently, against the state and *bourgeois* society. Aside from cultural cooptation, they were also met with brutal repression by military governments, with the neoimperialist aid of the US.

By the 1980s, two decades of acrimonious battle between authoritarian regimes that upheld the rights of traditional elites and international capital and countervailing socialist visions of incorporation of the masses had left these nationalist and sometimes socialist utopias frayed beyond repair, with the partial and temporary exceptions of Cuba and Nicaragua. Ultimately, utopia was reined in by a new democratic discourse within a neoliberal world context that projected citizen ideals, through recourse to a theory of civil society in which all differences are recognized and incorporated. Many national cultural policies were reengineered to take account of and foster what were now perceived to be, or projected as, multicultural societies. At each step of this history, culture or its imputed absence has provided a model of human worth to legitimize or to contest the status quo.

In many ways, this represented a powerful continuity with five centuries before. From the earliest days of empire, signifying practice was a critical area of struggle. In 1513, one of the early Spanish excursions to destroy pre-Columbian civilization was subject to serious ideological retooling by a theological committee. It provided the *conquistadores* with a manifesto that was translated for the Indians. It was a world history told through the anointing of Peter as Christ's vicar on Earth, which was used to justify later Popes dividing up the world. The document concluded with a chilling warning of what would happen in the event of resistance to imperial conquest: Indian women and children would be enslaved, their goods seized, and culpability laid at the feet of the vanquished. In its careful attention to ideology, its alibi in divine nomination, and its overtly political use of non-combatants as symbols, this is a remarkably modern text. Of course, its superstition (Christianity) is non-modern, but the text's mode of address is incantatory and reasoned in its brutality – fire and the sword will prevail, so follow the direct line of reasoning from God and you will be spared. The Aztecs and Incas whom the Spanish subsequently overthrew had shown no such desire for cultural justification in destroying the civilizations *they* had found. And unlike other conquerors, the Spanish did not present themselves as superior – simply as selected by God's delegate (Brown 203–05).

When the Spanish colonized Cuba in 1512, they immediately banned *areíto*, a native dance story-form. By 1518, with conquest complete, the ban was reversed, as *areíto*'s narratives were deemed useful for stimulating and appeasing slave labor (Martin *Socialist* 142). Despite efforts by several Spanish and Portuguese priests to protect the Indians, acculturation to Christianity was achieved both by brutal extirpation of native beliefs, including the decimation of Indians and their temples, and totalitarian indoctrination. Native texts recorded during the period of the Spanish conquest register a note of profound despondency, not only at the destruction of lives and works of civilization, but more importantly at the loss of a guiding vision, whether epistemological or cosmological. The missionaries, who numbered in the thousands only fifty years after the conquest, engaged in ethnographic work, devised grammars, translated indigenous and Christian texts and established common languages among heterogeneous Indian peoples (e.g. Nahuatl throughout New Spain (Mexico), Quechua and Aymara in Peru, Tupí in Brazil). They also created missions in which indigenous customs were re-engineered in accordance with the spectacular *mise-en-scène* of Christian texts, with rousing music and chants and terrifying images. The purpose was to instill a visceral receptivity to belief as an educational crusade. Since writing was to be an instrument of revelation, the novel, a vibrant new genre in sixteenth-century Spain that de-ecclesiastized knowledge, was prohibited by law in 1532 and again in 1543 from importation or publication in the colonies. The authorities feared that fictitious characters might confuse the native peoples into thinking that the stories told in the sacred scriptures were also fabricated. Meanwhile, by making use of the very indigenous customs that were to be eradicated, missionary priests laid the groundwork for a rich syncretism that gave New World Christianity its own flavor, but was not valorized until the emergence of strong nationalist identities long after independence.

There was, of course, cultural opposition to colonial authorities, ranging from armed resistance to desertion, carnivalesque subversion and high cultural confrontation. Town dwellers organized *mascaradas* or carnivals, which inverted elite values and practices and occasionally erupted into riots. And early on, Indians of noble lineage, like Garcilaso de la Vega the Inca, a *mestizo* of double royal lineage, and Felipe Guamán Poma de Ayala, a Christianized Indian of noble, Incan lineage, contested Spanish accounts of Indian history and culture. They claimed a privileged knowledge that enabled them to write a truer history of their native Peru, wielding this knowledge moreover to criticize European historiography as it relates to Peru, in Garcilaso's case, and the colonial administration, from whom Guamán Poma sought restitution of his family property. This opposition was neutralized by censorship and the encouragement of self-monitoring. It should be remembered that the Inquisition imposed itself as an external epistemological and moral monitor to ensure compliance. Colonial authorities prevented the publication of the detailed ethnographic research of Fray Bernardino de Sahagún (Historia general de las cosas de Nueva España) and others, because it was thought to subvert Christianity. Guamán Poma's Nueva Corónica y Buen Gobierno, which deftly masked Andean ideas in European expressive forms (Adorno), was not published until the twentieth century. The porousness of the color line, and the religious and cultural syncretism that accompanied it, fueled anxieties among the many Iberians and creoles who sought to enforce European moral standards. According to one Inquisition dossier, the music, dance and performance of the lower classes (non-whites and poor whites) were 'lewd and provocative of lasciviousness, causing grave ruin and scandal to the souls of Christendom and in prejudice to the conscience ... and [an] offence to edification and good customs' (Rivera Ayala quoted in Burkholder and Johnson 241).

Popular culture, dismissed as in Renaissance and Enlightenment Europe by church, state, and the upper classes in colonial society, was both a site of abjection and potential contestation. In contrast to Europe, however, this hybridized and syncretized culture went on to constitute a key foundation of Latin American national identity, incipiently and precariously with nineteenth-century Romanticism. Then it was embraced/coopted by many populist states in the early to mid-twentieth century. In contrast, the high culture of the Iberian colonies – mostly religious and literary – is considered a pale reflection of European culture by most scholars. Within this derivativeness, there are flashes of brilliance, such as the baroque poetry and treatises of two seventeenth-century Mexicans, the nun Sor Juana Inés de la Cruz (1651–1695), who was ultimately silenced by the Church hierarchy, and the de-frocked Jesuit mathematician, historian and geographer Carlos de Sigüenza y Góngora (1645–1700), whose writings, when not in the service of the state, took the form of elaborate, dazzling digressions. According to Jean Franco, the discursive excess of these writers was in part a refuge from church authority as well as an artistic undermining of the usefulness of their texts for church or government.

The ascendancy of the Bourbon royal family to the Spanish throne at the beginning of the eighteenth century brought about a transformation in administration, the economy and intellectual and cultural life for creoles and Iberian elites. Under the progress-minded monarch Carlos III (1759–1788), trade with the colonies, hitherto restricted to Spain, was opened up to other European countries, and liberal reforms were implemented. Enlightenment ideals of rational and scientific inquiry generated a spate of scientific missions which reinforced the emerging national sentiment of creole elites, fanned by republican and revolutionary ideas in the US and France. Naturalist missions like that of José Celestino Mutis' Botanical Expedition of New Granada (what is now known as Colombia) (1784–1817) created a new goal of empirical self-knowledge that would lead, it was believed, to progress. In the process, many colonial subjects, Indians included, learned new techniques of representing nature that would influence illustration, painting and archaeology. In New Spain, Carlos III established a Naturalist Commission in 1787 to collect and study the flora, fauna and minerals of the region, and a botanical garden in which to house the collection.

The Spanish crown commissioned Count Alexander von Humboldt and French botanist Aimée Bonpland to go on a five-year expedition (1799–1804) to study topography, produce climatological data, and gather plant specimens in Cuba, New Spain, and the Andean regions. The findings of this expedition were published over the next three decades, reawakening European interest in the New World and fueling nationalist imaginaries among Latin American writers and artists. As Latin Americans fought their wars of independence, also in keeping with Enlightenment premises, and subsequently became embroiled in numerous civil wars among competing *caudillos* or economic/political bosses throughout the first half of the nineteenth century, a spate of traveler-reporter artists and scientists spread over the continent under contract to expeditioners (Catlin) – a European postcolonial cultural policy at play. These visitors included the likes of Johann Mortiz Rugendas, who produced over 5,000 drawings and paintings in the twenty-six years he traveled throughout Mexico and South America; Jean-Baptiste Debret, who applied his training at the Ecole des Beaux Arts and as an engineer to catalogue the natural and social landscape of Brazil for the Imperial family[1] and founded the Imperial Academy of Fine Arts in 1826; and Charles Darwin, who got his start as a naturalist in the company of artist Conrad Martens and sea captain Robert Fitzroy on the HMS *Beagle*. The objective of these expeditions was to map the terrain in order to provide valuable information for expansionist colonial and imperial enterprises such as the South Sea Company. They also provided numerous samples for the emerging science and museology of natural history in the metropoles.

The work of these European writers, artists, and scientists was, paradoxically, consistent with new initiatives to create national, even nativist histories in the wake of independence in the first three decades of the nineteenth century. Bello argued that Latin American countries would not be truly independent until they consolidated independent cultures, based on local practices, not on European models. Like the traveler-reporters, Bello catalogued and analyzed local linguistic expressions and designed a totally original grammar that broke with the custom of patterning linguistic structure after the classical languages. He also planned a new historiography in which European theories would have no modeling role, arguing that history must be grounded in a series of events and social and natural structures that, unlike the European case, had not yet been recorded in Latin America. Before there could be a mature nation, there had to be a people defined by a common culture. It was the task of the historian and the linguist to gather the repertoire of practices that formed the archive of the nation ('las republicans;' 'Craft'). The problem, of course, was that there were varying populations, and they presumably had little in common with each other. Consequently, philosophical notions of history had to take a back seat to the historical particularity grounded in narratives of local life and customs. This archive would underpin and give symbolic coherence to the nation.

Militarily and politically, the territories that came to constitute the nineteen ·Latin American countries were racked by dissension. Moreover, it was clear that a Bolivarian confederation was not feasible. Projects for the construction of a national identity were thus projected from local centers of power: Mexico City, Caracas, Bogotá, Lima, Buenos Aires, Santiago and so on. In most cases, national identity was to be constructed in republican terms, searching out the local meaning of citizenship. While republican ideas were readily importable from Europe, the most interesting intellectual-bureaucrat-politicians attempted to tailor these models to the peculiarities of the local society. Of course, Latin Americans had even greater difficulty resolving the divide between the juridical people and the empirical people (Kant 'The Character' 225; Balibar 110), since in addition to class differences, there were pointed racial and geographical resistances to being subsumed in national entities controlled by one of several competing interests. The first post-colonial cultural policies, aimed at reconciling these differences by the construction of a *pueblo* or people, relied heavily on educational policy to overcome such resistance.

Many intellectuals and statespeople were involved in designing educational programs aimed at producing patriotic, productive and well-behaved citizens: Simón Rodríguez, Bolívar's tutor, in Venezuela; Bello in Chile; independence heroes like Manuel Belgrano and Bernardino Rivadavia and the future president Domingo Faustino Sarmiento, in Argentina; the leader of the political reform and first post-civil war president in Mexico, Benito Juárez, born a Zapotec Indian but raised by a powerful creole; and even the still-colonial Cuban intellectuals Antonio Saco and José de la Luz y Caballero in the first half of the nineteenth century. Bello stands out in the first half of the nineteenth century for the enormous breadth of his programs, which included not only educational policy, particularly language and literary studies, but citizen-formation study, as designed and implemented by him in a new Civil Code. Bello is also exemplary of the influence that the English constitutional/governmental model had on Latin American educational and civic policy. As in Europe, post-independence reformers sought to mobilize domestic life through 'technologies of responsibilization', providing moral training for children (Nikolas Rose 74). In Bello's social-welfare blueprint, the university was the control center of this responsibilization, with the sciences – statistics, medicine, public hygiene, morality, etc. – applied to Chilean society ('Prologue: *Ideological*' 132). The university oversaw the training of teachers, who in turn would instill respect for the law until it filtered down to the home, the only site where the 'feminine … formation of the heart' could take place:

> Impressions of infancy exercise a power over all people which usually decides their habits, their inclinations, and their character. And since the period when these impressions establish their sway is precisely that period when we know

no guides to conduct other than parents, it is obvious that we owe to them this part of the exercise of our faculties, which would come too late were it delayed to the age when we were ready to receive public education. [However,] if the generations are successively improved with the help of public education ... the day will come when we can generally make a beneficent and philosophical use of parental authority. ('On the Aims of Education' 111–12)

In a country like Chile, where the popular classes were composed of various races and classes, education was seen by Bello as the means to 'change customs' and acculturate the masses into well-being. In other words, education operated as the intermediary between government and civil society ('customs, laws, moral and political antecedents'). Bello also understood the limits of his blueprint for progress. Whether and to what degree a nation could progress depended on 'a fortunate combination of circumstances', whose most successful example was provided by the United States. This did not mean that Chile or other Latin American countries could simply emulate the US, since 'each nation has its features, its aptitudes, its method of moving forward ... and no matter how great and beneficent the influence of some nations on others, it will never be possible for one of them to blot out its peculiar character and adopt a foreign model; and, we insist, this would not be suitable even if it were possible' ('Government and Society' 289–90). Consequently, each nation has to devise specific means to well-being, recognizing what it can and cannot change. This brings us back to Bello's insistence on a university that produces knowledge about and for the nation ('Prologue: *Ideological*' 132).

Similarly, the educational project of Bello's one-time associate, Domingo Faustino Sarmiento – a liberal (mercantilist) Argentine intellectual, exiled first to Uruguay and then to Chile during the dictatorship of Juan Manuel de Rosas (1829–52), who represented the conservative interests of regional landowners – was shaped by the presupposition that it would have a civilizing effect on the rural and urban working classes, many of whom belonged to Rosas' Federalist gangs who 'terrorized the educated elite into reluctant collaboration' (Halperin Donghi 110). From Rosas' cultural-nationalist point of view, compulsory education (which was extended to girls), institutionalized by Rivadavia in the early 1820s when he assumed the presidency, was a means to Europeanize the country (Chávez). Europeanization, Rosas feared, would drain the Argentine man of his energy. If administered by the state, it would favor demogogues, who might subvert morals and public order (Newland 41). When Sarmiento returned to Argentina in 1855, he was named head of the Department of Schools. From this position, he reinstituted public education, in the direction of Horace Mann (which he had studied on a research trip in the 1840s, sponsored by the Chilean government under Bello's recommendation, to gather the best models for educational policy). Contextualized by the Rosas dictatorship, Sarmiento, who would become president in 1868, hoped that education would shape civilized citizens and thus drive a wedge into the political bond among these 'barbarians', as he described the Federalists in his renowned *Facundo: Civilization and Barbarism* (1845), a sociologico-literary essay and critique of the *caudillo* or political boss Facundo Quiroga, and by extension, the dictator Rosas.

Although, contrary to Bello, Sarmiento opposed grounding education on the foundation of grammar, he nevertheless sought the same result: citizens respectful of the law and capable of contributing to the modernization and progress of the nation. For Bello, grammar was the underlying control mechanism of language. As such, it maintained order in the relationships of ideas ('Prologue: *Ideological*' 86) and in the common language of Spanish America, which he feared would fragment into 'irregular, undisciplined, and barbaric dialects' like those of the European dark ages, which persisted in the provincial languages of contemporary Europe and 'hamper[ed] the spread of enlightenment, the execution of laws, the administration of the State, and national unity' ('Prologue: *Grammar*' 101–02). Sarmiento, in contrast, characterized this focus on grammar as 'retrograde, stationary, [and characteristic] of a rhetorical society' ('Ejercicios' 50; Ramos 35). He opted instead for a *progressive* account of language, society, and nature 'always on the march toward, perfectability' ('¡Raro descubrimineto!' 97; quoted in Ramos 36).

Despite this apparent difference, which was the subject of a heated debate between Bello and Sarmiento in the early 1840s, their ultimate goals did not differ greatly. In *Educación popular* (1849), the result of the above mentioned educational research commissioned by Bello that took Sarmiento to Europe and the US, he outlined an educational plan geared to progressive social change. A rational, utilitarian, scientific education would lead to economic betterment, which in turn would aid moral skilling by making the masses more respectful of property, thus furthering social stability (*Educación* 27; Tedesco 28, 64). Consequently, education was aimed at the popular classes and focused on agriculture and mining, in contrast to the humanistic education characteristic of the colonial period. Sarmiento's advocacy of utilitarian education was not wholly at odds with Bello's own project, which was stratified according to class: humanistic education for the upper classes, which prepared them for the professions and public office, and basic education for the masses, in order to reduce the number of poor people by training them for productive labor. For Bello, moreover, basic education, which included rudimentary exposure to grammar, literature, and the sciences, would 'instill habits of virtue' leading to the welfare of all ('On the Aims' 111). Francine Masiello notes that this 'welfare of all' was premised in large part on moral instruction provided by the family. Sarmiento echoed Bello in affirming that 'men form the laws and women shape our customs' (quoted in Masiello 54).

The creation of industrial schools was only half of Sarmiento's educational plan for the modernization of Argentina, the other half being European immigration, as his rival ideologue, Juan Bautista Alberdi, advocated. Alberdi had criticized Sarmiento's idealism in assuming that institutionalized education would generate citizens who could fortify industry and commerce. For Alberdi, it was the other way around: infrastructure – commerce, rail and shipping transport, civil, commercial and maritime legislation, constitutional and representative government, and so on – was needed to generate productive citizens. 'Industry', wrote Alberdi, 'is the social tranquilizer par excellence ... moral inculcation is arrived at more easily by productive work habits than by abstract education' (90, 80). He took a materialist point of view, according to which the economic base generates culture and ideology, not vice versa.

The premise is that ideological or cultural struggles may not change political or economic structures, but they can generate 'original' cultural expression (Schwartz 20). If there is not a class or social inflection to this ideological struggle – because, for example, few inhabitants have access to it – then it will characterize only the cultural production of elites and affiliated middle-class sectors. In the nineteenth century, the vast majority of the population was outside this conservative-liberal ideological struggle. Most were illiterate and lived in rural communities, although they were very much affected by the rapid increase in agricultural, livestock and mineral trade, whose increase European nations, especially Britain, expected to be the outcome of independence. The nineteenth century is characterized by commercial reorganization, incipient infrastructural development (especially communications and transport), foreign (mostly British) investment, and massive increases in population, mostly due to immigration in the later decades. The population of Buenos Aires, for example, grew 500% in thirty years to half a million in 1880. By the end of the nineteenth century, the elites' perceived need for policing and public hygiene were no longer 'out of place', but a pressing call to contain the unleashing of moral, cultural and epistemological differences brought about by large demographic changes: immigration in some cities and manumission in others. Education and civilization were a means to 'domesticate the barbarians' and provide 'internal policing of the population', according to Sarmiento (*Obras iv* 402, 340).

Despite the social (often characterized as 'developmental') gap between Latin American and European societies, Bello and Sarmiento considered their respective countries as part of a European family of nations. To remain a part of this family, civilizational policies had to be implemented. Bello, for example, contrasted 'Europe and our fortunate America with the sullen empires of Asia, where the iron scepter of despotism presses on necks already bowed by ignorance, or with African hordes, where man – scarcely better than the brutes – is like them an article of trade for his own brethren'. What makes (Latin) America fortunate for Bello is the cultivation of letters, which for him constitute a direct lineage from Greece and Rome ('Address' 126). 'Letters' do not refer primarily to literature as we now know it, but to the function of writing in colonial and postcolonial bureaucracies. According to Angel Rama, who pioneered a Foucauldian interpretation of the rationalization of knowledge via writing, *letrados* (men of letters) had a decisive role in enabling the concentration of power in the state. The seat of power, the city, especially the diverse population residing in it, was given order by the *letrados*. Subsequent historical periods saw the emergence and incorporation of new subjects into the *letrado* class but, according to Rama, as 'keepers of souls' in their pastoral and educative function, they also effected a *trahison des clercs* by limiting social inclusion (45, 73, 96, 122).

In Argentina and elsewhere, cultural policy was also consolidated under Auguste Comte's tutelary philosophy of positivism. Its major tenet, that order and stability were necessary for progress, seemed tailor-made for countries coming out of civil war. Positivism was a handmaiden to the so-called liberal regimes that triumphed in the second half of the nineteenth century, as they were fully integrated into a neocolonial order in the world economy under British hegemony. While their economies and elite cultures were no longer oriented to the Iberian metropolises as in the colonial period, they neverthe-less maintained a similar dependent relationship to the industrial centers of Europe, especially Britain and France (Halperin Donghi 118). Under free-trade policies implemented throughout Latin America, commerce increased expo-nentially (fifty-fold in Argentine agricultural and livestock exports since the beginning of the nineteenth century) and urban populations exploded. Immigration created a need for public employees, which increased the ranks of the middle classes, and the ideology of 'progress' took root throughout. European standards of policing and public hygiene were instituted in the larger cities (Buenos Aires, Santiago, Caracas, Mexico City and Rio de Janeiro), wedding a call to order with the *desideratum* of progress.

Throughout Latin America in the post-Independence period, this positivist program entailed the conquest of barbarism by civilization. It was carried out violently through genocide, and culturally through educational and museolog-ical policy. In the Mexican context, where genocide was less of an option, given the number of indigenous peoples and the mixed-race or *mestizo* character of the population, civilization entailed the transformation of Indians into citizens, although this was largely seen as an impossibility for most of the nineteenth century. Educational policy was oriented instead toward the creation of a class consciousness appropriate to realizing Mexico's potential as an advanced civilization. According to Gabino Barreda, the positivist intellectual to whom Benito Juárez entrusted the plan of a new educational system, Mexico was embroiled in disorder from 1810 to 1867, when Juárez, who represented the Reform movement, took over the presidency. This movement opposed the conservative forces – the church and the military. The reformers represented the *bourgeoisie*. They adopted positivism as a doctrine. Consequently, the new educational system under Barreda was in the lineage of Comtean philosophy. Barreda and other positivists expected that the future of humanity was at stake in Mexico. The struggle against Maximilian and the French was a strug-gle to save all humanity: 'The soldiers of the Republic in Puebla saved, like the Greeks in Salamis, the future of the world by saving the republican principle, which is the modern standard of humanity'. Indeed, Mexico kept the onslaught on republicanism from spreading north to 'the United States through Mexico' (Barreda quoted in Zea 45–46). Barreda's educational system would shape liberal intellectuals and political leaders toward progress and thus enable it to withstand the encroachments of the US. As early as 1833, José María Luis Mora had envisioned such an educational system, but conservative forces then ruled the country.

The positivists went so far in their crusade against the conservatism of Catholicism to make Protestantism the official religion of Mexico. President Juárez had said: 'It is hoped that Protestantism will become Mexicanized, conquering the Indians; they need a religion that will obligate them to read rather than to spend their savings on candles for saints' (quoted in Sierra 423). The subsequent president, Lerdo de Tejada, even invited Protestant ministers to Mexico, but they failed to win over Mexicans, who found their ideas totally foreign (Zea 49). Barreda opted to suppress the teaching of religion altogether, so the ecclesiastical rites introduced by Comte were not reproduced in Mexico.

While positivism had no place for indigenous peoples, the reaction to this US-oriented political philosophy soon embraced two contradictory tendencies: Hispanic values associated with the supposedly Roman and Greek classical legacy of Iberian culture, on the one hand, and the valorization of *mestizos* on the other. The embrace of Hispanic values was a reaction to US imperialism in 1898; the valorization of the people hitherto regarded as barbarians was a response to revolution and industrialization in the early twentieth century. The Hispanic legacy is best exemplified by José Enrique Rodó's *Ariel* (1900), an educational program for the formation of Latin American intellectuals on the model of aesthetic education. It was designed to produce leaders whose internalized, Kantian lawfulness-without-law would produce a politics founded on 'disinterest'. The valorization of the *mestizo* is best exemplified by José Vasconcelos' *The Cosmic Race* (1925), which also turned positivism on its head by proposing an 'aesthetic selection' over and above 'natural selection', taking the *mestizo* as the race of the future, shaped by aesthetic plasticity.

Most Latin American cultural policies from the 1930s on may be considered variants on the policies of Western capitalist countries. Many cultural institutions in the region were modeled after the French, with centralized academies and ministries. Nevertheless, the specific history of Latin America, particularly the dictatorships in the 1960s and 1970s, generated forms of cultural support that resembled those of fascist command cultures. Subsequent to the dictatorships, and with the spread of neoliberalism in the 1980s, the US model of support has been increasingly influential. Under the aegis of Cuba, which led tricontinental Third World solidarity in the 1970s, many leftist activists operative in Latin American governments did at least espouse solidarity with postcolonial nations. With waning Cuban influence, that solidarity diminished, although as we will see, regional integration projects challenge the cultural hegemony of the US and communications and entertainment conglomerates.

Throughout the 1920s and the 1930s, in the wake of the First World War and the Mexican and Soviet revolutions, a new wave of cultural policy seized the Western world. Reconstruction and the creation of a 'new man' were on the agenda. A new subjectivity was also needed to meet the challenges of capitalist modernization, which required the incorporation of the masses. For example, with the new Mexican Constitution in 1917, a national project of mass education was undertaken in order to jumpstart the economy, incorporate the masses, and create a large educated and *nationalist* middle class capable of resisting the power of *caudillos* and national and foreign oligarchies. The principal instrument of this policy was mass education, including artistic expression as embodied in the muralist movement, which infused the public face of Mexican identity with strong indigenist features. This movement was engendered by Vasconcelos, Director of the Departamento Universitario y de Bellas Artes, which included the Secretaría de Instrucción Pública y Bellas Artes (subsequently Secretaría de Educación Pública or SEP). Cultural and educational policy were intensified and further institutionalized in the 1930s under the presidency of Lázaro Cárdenas, with greater incorporation of indigenous populations, the expansion of arts education and defense of national patrimony.

The history of national cultural policy undertaken by the Mexicans had a parallel development in other Latin American countries. This history was largely circumscribed by import-substitution industrialization in large Latin American countries, and the rise of viable mass media that enabled the consolidation of a national identity. New cultural institutions were established as a complement to economic modernization: ministries of education and the arts; museums, radio and broadcasting bureaux; and artists unions. It was the task of these institutions to consolidate national cultures. Mexico's Instituto Nacional de Antropología e Historia (1939) and Instituto Nacional de Bellas Artes (1946) mirrored the hierarchical structure of the ruling Partido Revolucionario Institucional, which governed for seventy years until the election of Vicente Fox of the Partido de Acción Nacional (PAN) in 2000. From the 1930s to the 1980s, and in many respects even today, the culturecrats in Mexico City determined all cultural activity, linking it to state policies on tourism, education and development.

In Brazil, São Paulo industrialists, united in the powerful Federation of Industries in the state of São Paulo (FIESP), also sought to consolidate a particular national universal from their emerging economic capital. The University of São Paulo was established in the 1930s along with a range of cultural institutions that paralleled these industrialists' faith in modernization. They constructed social and political networks to promote their theories of progress, liberalism and industrial rationalization for a modernized Brazil. As John Wineland writes, 'São Paulo's incipient bourgeoisie, many first generation European immigrants, attempted to advance a modernism and modernity aligned with the industrial and cultural centers of Europe that predated the Vasconselos-styled cultural machinery of the populist dictator, Getulio Vargas (1930–1945) by almost a decade'. Modernism/import-substitution industrialization is characterized by such institutions as the *Museu de Arte do São Paulo* (1947), founded by the 'William Randolph Hearst of Brazil', Francisco de Assis Chateaubriand Bandeira de Mello; the *Museu de Arte Moderno de São Paulo* (1948), established by immigrant industrialist Francisco Matarazzo Sobrinho; and the *São Paulo Biennial* (1951), also founded by Matarazzo after the Venice Biennial.

This intense institution-building in both Mexico and Brazil was tied to large capital-political interests in the respective countries: the Grupo Monterrey in the Northern industrial capital of Nuevo Leon, Mexico, and as already mentioned, the São Paulo industrialists. The public-private organization of the cultural sphere begins as early as the post-World War II period. Import-substitution industrialization soon transformed into developmentalism, with heavy doses of foreign investment. A culture of modernization characterized the emergence in the 1950s of the São Paulo Biennial and the construction of Brasilia, as well as Mexico's 'economic miracle', which saw the rise of an art market, the organization of exhibitions by foreign corporations and governments, particularly the US, and the shift to an international style. Concurrently, strong labor and socialist movements emerged to contest the state's articulation of high and popular culture. By the 1960s, both governments resorted to outright repression: the 1964 coup in Brazil and the 1968 Tlatelolco massacre in Mexico, preceded by a spate of workers' strikes.

We see here the limits of governmentality. What could not be governmentalized had to be eradicated. This is particularly the case in the struggle over the popular. To get a sense of what that struggle involved, one must look at other institutions, especially the culture industries. It could be argued that a story of museums and galleries cannot be properly told in the absence of their counterparts and the influences that one had on the other. The two major Latin American networks, Televisa (founder of the Centro Cultural de Arte Contemporáneo) and Globo (founder of the Fundação Roberto Marinho) had a hand in the administration of both high and popular culture.

The 1960s represent the crystallization of a common cultural consciousness among so-called popular sectors and leftist intellectuals, with the potential to create an alternative hegemony that threatened to change the 'equilibrium' between political and civil society within the state. In the countries of the Southern Cone, Brazil and Mexico, it is not possible to speak of hegemony as an equilibrium between political and civil society. Renato Ortiz, for example, writes of the 'precariousness of the very idea of hegemony among us' (65). Instead, what characterized these countries was a pact between state-aligned elites who promoted import-substitution industrialization and developmentalism, and an equally state-aligned popular nationalism that sought state welfare, delivered in corporatist forms from the 1920s and 1930s. As we wrote in the Introduction, the origins of 'popular culture' in Latin America can be traced to this paradoxical state, which recreated those sectors most responsible for supporting that culture: education, radio, film and anthropological institutions. By the 1960s, the influence of mass culture in the intellectual and political sphere caused a crisis at all levels, including the high arts. This is the period of the Jovem Guarda and Tropicália in Brazil and the government's fight against rock music in Mexico (Zolov), accompanied by the emergence of an important new critical genre that has offered a certain oppositionality and embodied alternative projects for visual culture: the *crónica* (chronicle or feature article) and *testimonio*, practiced by writers like Carlos Monsiváis and Elena Poniatowska. The rearticulation of popular culture, the emergence of a youth-oriented mass culture, and new cultural critical expressions such as the *crónica* converged in the work of artists like Hélio Oiticica and Felipe Ehrenburg.

Whereas the dictatorship in Brazil eradicated the cultural and political upsurge, the Mexican state largely absorbed it – *cronistas* like Monsiváis and artists like Ehrenburg were eventually accorded their place in the funding system. In the 1960s, the practice of these writers and artists largely conflicted with those of the sanctioned spaces of the art world and institutions that meted out prestigious literary prizes. However, by the late 1980s, and certainly in the 1990s, there would be a *rapprochement*, when a turn to civil society arose from the democratization movement in Brazil and popular forms of organization in the wake of the 1985 earthquake in Mexico. Ironically, there was ultimately a convergence between a scaling back of governmental investment in popular sectors and the development of a civil society that 'organized itself', to paraphrase the title of a book by Monsiváis. This shift was accompanied by a major transformation of cultural policy, the Plan Nacional de Desarrollo Cultural of 1989. Co-responsibility and decentralization are its main objectives, by which is meant a formalization of the civil society *ethos* that characterized both the self-organization in the wake of the earthquake and entrepreneurial activity in the cultural world.

In the wake of Mexico's economic crisis during Miguel de la Madrid's *sexenio*, or six-year presidential term, which saw a decrease in funding for education (but less so for culture, a fact that is revealing about the importance of cultural subvention as a form of legitimation for the state) President Salinas sought to bolster cultural support on new terms. Rafael Tovar y de Teresa was named president of the National Council for the Arts and Culture (CONACULTA), established in 1989 as part of Salinas' new cultural program to reconcile Mexicans with a new modernization project. In his account of the project, Tovar y de Teresa suggests that modernization entails trade deregulation, political liberalization and institutional decentralization, which have social and cultural effects that must be offset. Tovar tells the story of 'the close connection that a modernization project recognizes in and maintains with culture' (20).

Culture here is the terrain of negotiation around the social and political changes wrought by the acceleration of capitalist development. Faced with the threat of homogenization and the erosion of sovereignty, Tovar y de Teresa advocates a 'return to roots' for culture as a 'point of reference, unique and unsubstitutable, for the assumption of changes in such a way that our national identity is not put at risk' (12–13). To this end, he invokes the concept of *patrimonio* or heritage, whose preservation and dissemination is the first of the six functions of CONACULTA. At the same time, however, the point of the new cultural program is that the state must open the notion of heritage to the ethnic and social diversity that was overlooked by centralized corporatist programs in the past. Democratic participation was to be enhanced in two ways: first, by the decentralization of cultural institutions; and second, by encouraging the private sector to invest in culture through tax incentives (103). The National Fund for Culture and the Arts (FONCA) was established in 1989 to serve as the pivotal institution between government, the private sector and the cultural community (59–60). The ratio of state to private investment in culture through FONCA went from $125,000 to $0 in 1989 and $7.2 million to $16.5 million in 1993.

In Brazil, two days after taking office in 1990, president Collor de Mello announced a number of decrees that effectively extinguished all government-generated support for the arts. The changes he made included the abolition of the Lei Sarney, a law initiated in 1985, which offered tax incentives for industries that supported cultural production, the reorganization of the Ministry of Culture into a secretariat of the Ministry of Education, and the termination of the National Arts Foundation (Funarte), the Scenic Arts Foundation (Fundacen), the Brazilian Film Foundation and the National Film Distributing Company, which were reincarnated on a smaller scale in the minimally funded National Institute of Cultural Activities (Catani 98). Under Collor, the Lei Sarney was re-defined in the Lei Rouanet, written by a renowned intellectual, Sergio Paulo Rouanet, author of, among other things, books that offer a Foucauldian-inspired critique of the Habermasian public sphere.

After Collor's impeachment and the interim presidency of Itamar Franco, Fernando Henrique Cardozo, elected in 1995, sought to attenuate strong challenges from the left. Like Salinas in Mexico, he used cultural policy, in particular the Lei Rouanet, both for shifting cultural iniatives to a more entrepreneurial private-oriented program and for decentralizing support. 'Culture is good business', was the Brazilian Ministry of Culture's slogan in 1998, in accord with a refurbished Lei Rouanet under Minister of Culture Francisco Weffort. As part of its efforts to shift support in a more private direction, the Ministry of Culture generated numerous statistics to prove that cultural investment spurred export earnings, created jobs and fostered national integration. At the same time, however, the new incentive laws put into place a system whereby support for cultural projects is largely up to corporate sponsors, who decide, usually on the basis of the projects' marketing value, which ones they will underwrite. The Ministry of Culture is left the limited task of deciding on projects' eligibility for support under the incentive laws. The result has been the emergence of a new kind of cultural entrepreneur, and new kinds of not-for-profit corporations that broker cultural projects (Ottmann). Most of the funded projects date to *cultural marketing*, which is the title, in English, of a special trade journal that was born simultaneously with the Lei Rouanet.

According to cultural ministry documents, the objective of this shift has less to do with fiscal thrift than with a philosophy of giving greater responsibility to civil society, largely under the guardianship of the private sector. Indeed, the well-developed public-private system of US cultural support has served as a model for restructuring the Brazilian (and the Mexican) system. Wineland refers to various meetings at which semi-private, para-state corporations like Arte-Empresa: Parceria Multiplicadora, sponsored by the Serviço Social do Comércio (SESC), and the Serviço de Apoio ás Micro e Pequenas Empresas (Sebrae), have become powerful middle people in São Paulo's cultural funding processes, sponsoring meetings with American executives to discuss corporate philanthropy. At one such meeting were:

> representatives from the automotive, tobacco, information, electronics, cosmetics, audiovisual, petroleum, chemicals and food and beverage industries, as well as a number of marketing executives. Also present was AT&T vice-president and director of the Business Committee of the Arts, Timothy McClimon, who represented the 'American example' of how to properly include the arts in a corporate marketing philosophy. (Pompeu quoted in Wineland)

The public good heralded by the new corporate philanthropy is most often rhetorical, for these societies, which have never fostered a thriving public culture, are interested either in the cultural capital generated by sponsorship of the traditional arts or, increasingly, in the emergence of culture as a resource for the generation of profit. This is the case with most cultural heritage and tourism projects, many of which are financed by the Inter-American Development Bank and the World Bank. The impact on art, dance, film and popular culture programs, not to speak of critical cultural practices, has been quite marked; on the other hand, banks and some large corporations have financed their own cultural foundations, which do cultural marketing exclusively for the parent corporation, and deduct most if not all of the amounts invested from their taxes. And despite the claims to decentralization, the successful projects tend to be concentrated in the wealthiest states, especially São Paulo, Rio de Janeiro, Belo Horizonte and Rio Grande do Sul, to which – with the exception of certain tourist-attracting states in the Northeast like Bahia – much of the Ministry of Culture's resources traditionally went.

Whereas the Mexican reformers had to contend with a more stubbornly rooted symbolic system of populism and social reform, leading to a centrally coordinated aesthetic strategy aimed at weakening revolutionary symbolism, Cardozo's regime couched the Ministry of Culture's program in a pragmatic, free-market approach embedded within the larger claims of Brazil's 'transition to democracy'. In neither case is there room for critical art and culture. The above-mentioned partnership schemes are wedded to new cultural programs, whereby the state is enjoined to pry open the notion of patrimony to the ethnic and social diversity that was overlooked by the centralized corporatist programs of the past. This legitimizes changes in forms of cultural support, largely preempting critiques from the more elitist arts, including tendencies that espouse social critique. There is sometimes a political standoff over the role of culture on the left political spectrum between leftist intellectuals and artists, on the one hand, and popular or populist politicians and local leaders. From the 1960s to the present, intellectuals and artists have customarily relied on cultural work as a legitimation of their interventions, while populists have tended to disqualify even critical culture by taking popular tastes as their compass point. The creation of a Latin American cultural space might contribute to taking attention away from this defeatist dichotomy. Criticality and an interest in the needs and struggles of popular classes would not need to operate from such a national(ist) framework.

There have been significant alternative models: the Cuban revolution is clearly the most successful episode in Latin American history of making culture at all levels accessible to the entire population. From the very beginning, students, artists and intellectuals (including many international sympathizers) were recruited (many enthusiastically volunteered) to work in the literacy brigades and upgrade primary education. These developments transformed Cuba into the best-educated country in the hemisphere. The reformulation of cultural policy began with an extension of the Dirección de Cultura (a section of the Ministry of Education) just weeks after the triumph of Castro. Many new cultural institutions were established, such as the Unión de Escritores y Artistas de Cuba (UNEAC), the subsequently renowned Instituto Cubano de Arte e Industria Cinematográficas (ICAIC), the Casa de las Américas (1959), the Consejo Nacional de Cultura (1961), the Escuela Nacional de Arte (1962), the Instituto Cubano del Libro (1967), and a myriad of other cultural institutions, such as the local Casas de la Cultura, the cultural centers of the Organos Locales del Poder Popular (Local Organs of People's Power, which are self-governing bodies), and research centers. This intense activity operated simultaneously on three fronts, all of which were characterized by direct links between the state and cultural production: training and access for the masses, professionalization, and internationalism.

On the first front, the Casas de la Cultura and the cultural centers of the Organos Locales del Poder Popular have had an enormous impact in providing hands-on practise in the arts and heritage, above and beyond arts training in the schools and arts and media programming on television. There are 259 Casas de Cultura distributed throughout Cuba's 169 municipalities, offering classes in ballet, modern and folk dance, music and the visual arts, in order to 'cement citizen interest and participation' ('Escuelas vocacionales de arte'). The purpose of these centers, according to the Ministry of Culture, is that 'art penetrate into all spheres of life, including the industrial sphere' (Hart Dávalos 13). This latter point has received a great deal of attention in Cuba with the creation of professional schools across the arts and culture industries. Its cinema school counts among the best in the world. Indeed, Cuba produced so many arts professionals, that by the mid-1980s, they began to work outside the country, not necessarily because they wanted to 'leave the revolution' (although in many cases that was also true), but because the economic crises, due both to bureaucratic inefficiency and the US embargo, forced them to earn a living elsewhere. Starting in the late 1980s, a Cuban visual arts boom lifted the Latin American art market. And since the mid-1990s, the global music industry has sought to capitalize on the country; 11,000 professional musicians, who remained largely untapped in the global marketplace. The film *Buena Vista Social Club* is a good example.

Cuba has also exerted enormous influence on a third front, internationalism. In the late 1960s and throughout the 1970s, it promoted Latin American left culture and tri-continental anti-imperialist solidarity between Latin America, Africa and Asia. The very styles developed in film (especially in documentary-based works), music (the revolutionary *nueva trova* or new troubadorism), and propaganda posters, spread throughout Latin America and many other parts of the world. Cuba hosted meetings for Third World intellectuals, and became a central actor in anti-imperialist culture. Casa de las Americas, an intellectual and cultural center that hosted conferences and symposia, administered literary prizes and published books of revolutionary-cultural relevance in the hemisphere, became a potent force field for Latin American intellectuals and writers. Other centers dealing with visual arts (e.g. Centro para el Desarrollo e Impulso de las Artes Plásticas Wifredo Lam), music (Centro de Investigación y Desarrollo de la Música), film and broadcasting (ICAIC and International Film and Television School, founded by the Colombian Nobel Prize writer Gabriel García Márquez) also extend Cuba's influence in these venues. Contemporary Cuban cultural production also involves a powerful artists' union, that is central to encouraging members to criticize the very hegemony of the union in their work. Key themes of much theater include struggles against counter-revolutionaries. Since 1968, this has been a formal ideological front that works by anthropological investigations and narrativizations of workers' lives (Martin *Socialist* 141, 130).

Since the fall of Sovietism in 1989, and the adoption of neoliberal policies by all Latin American countries, Cuba's influence has waned considerably. Indeed, this epochal change has made the contradictions in Cuban culture even more glaring. On the one hand, there is an extensive network of people's culture, but on the other, many venues are closed off to ordinary Cubans. This contradiction emerged as Cuba turned to tourism to gain access to dollars, which intensified the implantation of capitalism via direct foreign investment in the 1990s, especially in oil exploration (by foreign companies) and tourism (Caivano). Even the Havana Biennial, originally designated to showcase artists from the Third World and in opposition to the mainstream art market, ended up becoming a clearing house where collectors and galleries could find new 'subaltern' stars (Camnitzer). The flow of dollars has resulted in increased corruption, prostitution and a two-speed society: access to the new trappings of modernity, for foreign capitalists, tourists, and upper-level party members, and long voucher lines for a limited variety of staples, for the vast majority of ordinary citizens. Many receive remissions in dollars from US-based relatives, yet it is against the law to use those dollars to buy from non-state-sanctioned markets. This represents a long strand of duality between the utopia and the actuality of revolutionary fervor, doctrine and practice.

It could be said that revolutionary Cuban cultural policy began with Fidel Castro's speech 'Words to the Intellectuals' (1961), in which he asked intellectuals and artists of all ideological persuasions to collaborate in a new cultural revolution that would put the welfare of the people above individualism and particular ideological interests. Castro promised a space to artists and intellectuals of 'opportunity and freedom ... within the revolution'. Most observers of cultural developments in the newly revolutionary state will remember the phrase: 'Within the revolution, everything; against the revolution, nothing' (Castro 16). This premise would have many opportunities to be tested, as a number of writers and artists were judged (often without due process) to fall astray of that dictum. The most notorious case was that of Heberto Padilla, a well-known poet and journalist who returned to Cuba in 1959,. like another more fortunate writer, Roberto Fernández Retamar, to work with the revolution. Increasingly vocal in his criticisms of the revolution's cultural policies, and especially its bureaucrats (those who oversaw whether or not an intellectual's work was 'against the revolution') Padilla was imprisoned, provoking a loud outcry for his release by most of the Western world's liberal and leftist intellectuals, including Cortázar, Fuentes and Sartre. When he was released, he published a self-critique. It emphasized his 'errors' so much that most readers suspected that he had been forced to write it, as he himself indicated afterwards. The 'Caso Padilla', as it is known in Latin American intellectual history, is exemplary of attempts by Cuba's cultural policy *apparatchiks* to 'rectify errors' (as former Minister of Culture Armando Hart Dávalos (15) characterizes the process), taking a hard-line route to perfecting the ethically incomplete. At the same time, Cuba's ideals are lofty inscriptions of an internationalism and egalitarianism that have inspired the democratic side to modernity for two hundred and fifty years.

Just such polyethnic, leftist internationalism also has a powerful history in Nicaragua, with its residue of indigenous people's culture prior to the arrival of the Spanish in the early 1500s, the *campesino* culture of *mestizo* survivors, the mass-produced popular culture of US-dominated nineteenth- and twentieth-century capitalism ('from baseball to Boy Scouts'), and an elite Eurocentric culture of the same period. These tendencies survived the US-based Somoza tyranny of the twentieth century, which almost entirely neglected the development of public cultural institutions, while its export-oriented agricultural policies devastated the cultural norms of the peasantry (Whisnant 3, 436).

When the Sandinistas came to power in 1979, overthrowing Somoza, they prioritized culture as a route to creating and sustaining a revolutionary consciousness in the population. Budgets for the arts comprised as much as 0.5% of total public expenditure. The new Ministry of Culture established regional Centers for Popular Culture (CPCs), culture brigades and poetry workshops. The twenty-six CPCs were designed not to carry culture to the countryside, but to sustain and develop what was already happening there. There were also six locally-funded *casas de cultura* (houses of culture). The ideology underpinning these programs was complicated: on the one hand, to generate loyalty to the regime and engage in political re-education; on the other, to emphasize local traditions and concerns. These twin aspects used articulated through the dual heritage of the Somosa dictatorship and US cultural exports, as Sandinista theoreticians enunciated a mission to build revolutionary unity by resuscitating the traditional popular culture that had been suppressed by the dictatorship and supplanted by multinational commerce. Between them, these institutions supported workshops in the plastic arts, painting and theatre, in addition to photography shows, seminars, film festivals, dance, poetry readings and sporting events. At the same time, the Sandinistas' Marxism meant that they endorsed a third aspect, alongside central government provision and local initiative, via a worker-based organization, the *Associacíon Sandinista de Trabajadores Culturales* (ASTC). The ASTC's six unions of writers, artists and performers were created by the state to assist with training, materials, international exchange and military arts development. But the *Associacíon* often behaved more like an academy of the elect than an anti-élitist democratic site, insisting on aesthetic autonomy and individualist creation myths over an instrumental governmentality. The insurgent war in Nicaragua, illegally backed by the US government, drew resources away from the cultural area as the struggle progressed through the harrowing 1980s. The Nicaraguan Institute of Culture, which the Sandinistas had set up at arm's length from the state, became a critical arm of culture after they handed power to a pro-capitalist government in the 1990s. It now solicits money from around the world and articulates art with the market rather than democracy (Whisnant 201–03, 268, 236–39, 241, 269; Martin *Socialist* 80–81, 74).

When the Sandinistas traveled to all corners of the newly liberated Nicaragua in the late 1970s, enthusiastically seeking to empower the inhabitants through educational and cultural integration, they found to their chagrin that certain linguistic and cultural minorities, such as the Miskitos, considered this integration an imposition. The experience of the Sandinistas repeats that of other postdictatorial and postcolonial states from the 1950s to the 1980s, where national integration chafed against the desire for local cultural autonomy. If cultural ministries were created to bring about national integration, it was soon discovered that subministries and other offices had to be created to deal with minorities, many of which had organized as insurgents, social movements, and NGOs, and sought national and international recognition. Cultural diversity is probably the most salient issue in the current period, in which the questioning of national identities has proliferated. This questioning does not ensue, however, only from minority perspectives. It is also spurred by the market and the media, which traverse all territories.

The mediation of this diversity, increasingly located in governmental and non-governmental institutions, is known as multiculturalism. Whether by design (Canada and Australia) or default (the US and Britain), multiculturalism is the area where cultural diversity plays itself out in postindustrial liberal democracies. Multiculturalism has also been adopted in some developing democracies in Latin America, going against the grain of the normative *mestizo* melting pots projected by governments and social scientists from the 1930s to the 1960s. Democratization after the fall of the dictatorships (particularly in the Southern Cone) and authoritarian democracies (Mexico and Peru) of the 1960s to 1980s was characterized by sundry social movements that translated the concept of human rights into civil and cultural rights, seeking the recognition of full citizen status for women, indigenous and other ethnoracial groups (Afro Latin Americans).

All Latin American countries now characterize themselves as multicultural, and have implemented policies to recognize their diversity. Chile, for example, recently revamped its cultural policies along three axes: decentralization, giving due recognition to all cultural and territorial identities that have contributed to national heritage; the integration of the arts and traditional and new media cultures into the curriculum at all levels, on the premise that cultural knowledges and practices enhance perceptive and critical faculties as well as reinforcing citizenship; and special attention to the marginal and disadvantaged, who can find inclusion through cultural citizenship. To this end, the Ministry has designed a program for training cultural catalysts of community creativity (managers, administrators, fundraisers, planners and educators) (di Girólamo 8–16, 24).

Catalyzing cultural citizenship is of crucial importance in a country like Colombia, which is racked by violent divisions. In 1991, a new constitution replaced the traditional twentieth-century imagined melting pot with a vision of society comprised of a pluriethnic, multicultural citizenry. Aside from designating special rights for indigenous peoples, which have also been implemented in other Latin American countries (most recently in Mexico, in 2001), the new Colombian constitution laid the foundations for Afro-Colombian communities to mobilize as a social movement for recognition of their identity, claims to territorial rights, political autonomy, the defense of their environment, and control of natural resources within their territory (Grueso et al. 202). The claim to a particular culture and identity was the major legitimizing feature of this movement. While this expansion of cultural rights, and other rights on that basis, proceeded more or less smoothly, Colombia's unique cultural policy for the establishment of peace has had a more fraught history.

It is well known that aside from regional diversity and the claims of indigenous and black groups, Colombia is also riven by armed conflict among guerrillas, paramilitary groups, narcotraffickers, and the military, as part of the US-financed war on drugs. Mediating diversity is thus a life and death issue. To this end, the government shifted its understanding of cultural policy from a traditional system of provision to a 'communicative process that permits the transformation of social relations through a new politics of identity and recognition' (Ochoa). For instance, 'CREA: An Expedition Through Colombian Culture', a series of festivals or 'cultural encounters' brought together creative artists and artistic products (oral poets, written literary forms, rock and folk musicians, video productions and food) from every locality. They ultimately converged in the capital, making it possible for Colombians of many different walks, including the above mentioned contending groups, to get to know each other, under the only peaceful circumstances that some have ever known (Ochoa).

Ana Maria Ochoa points out that despite the rhetoric of decentralization, for a country to 'encounter' itself, at least in the Colombian case, has entailed a certain centrality, beginning with the hub of cultural policy in the capital, and ending in the public sphere, on capital. Important as this program has been, it raises the need for a monitoring function open to representatives – especially local artists and/or cultural promoters – from the various localities, to mitigate the centralized character of policy-making.

The Postcolonial

The Government sees the need to continue playing a supportive role in arts development ... blending the best of East and West. ... [F]ollowing the reunification with our motherland, we need to go through a gradual process of getting to know our national history and culture so as to achieve a sense of belonging. – Hong Kong Legislative Council, 1998 (Home 'Response' and 'Long')

This multifaceted history of two centuries of independence in Latin America is matched, in complexity if not time, by the postcoloniality of those nations that gained their freedom in the last fifty years. Contemporary Western art is in many ways beholden to categories established as part of nineteenth-century empires, which separated culture as high civilization from culture as custom. The former became a sign of progress, and the latter an object of scientific analysis. The categories elided with imperial appropriation of artifacts and their classification as both signs of the essence of human organization, and alternative textual forms to be appropriated and redisposed via the market. This period also saw the emergence of copyright for artistic forms, rather than ideas or customary material manifestations (Clifford; Coombe 219–20).

In Southern Africa, precolonial performance was 'part of the common festival', and all members of the society participated (Mda 3). Under colonialism, Africa was widely construed as a place where the light of European culture would shine on darkness, gradually enlightening a supposedly primitive, savage space of brutal, uncivilized people. But the images of Africans in British public life were not as seamless and straightforward as this might suggest, given ethnographic collections in national and regional museums and the importation of African men and women for privately-funded public exhibitions. Rather than simply illustrating superiority, the detail and frequency of these sites and representations suggest that their function was to give the British citizenry a shared cultural self – in some senses a contradictory one, given the avant-garde uptake and redisposal of African art norms. In the Indian case, much was

139

made of the work produced at art schools that the British set up in large Indian cities (Coombes 2–3, 6, 65, 111, 196).

Many ethnographic collections were obtained by primitive accumulation. In 1868, the British stole everything they could find in Magdala, then the capital of Ethiopia. The loot included hundreds of illuminated bibles, manuscripts, books and assorted treasures from a Coptic church, which went to the British Museum, universities and royal libraries. When Mussolini invaded Ethiopia seventy years later, he did the same to the entire country: the booty covered the gamut from paintings and crosses to obelisks and airplanes. The British government ceremonially returned cheap parts of its plunder over the next century whenever it needed political favors from the Ethiopians. In the late 1990s, a society of Addis Ababa academics lobbied for the return of all such treasures, but war between Ethiopia and Eritrea provided an alibi for the former colonial victors to delay restitution ('Let's').

Protestant missionaries in colonial Africa sought to turn spoken African languages into orthographies. This was not just to do with representing speech in written form. It was also an attempt to control and reform native speech. These churchpeople and their governmental equivalents were much exercised in the nineteenth century by multilingualism, popular memory and heritage. British and Belgian colonial policy was to teach primary-school pupils vernacular literacy for the first half of the twentieth century, while France and Portugal taught only their own languages (Irvine). Language policies were critical aids to imperial rule and neocolonial 'enterprise' over the past century, as critical linguistics, Afrocentric language planning and examinations of triad anti-languages have shown. Complicated legal debates have taken place since the 1920s in international courts over attempts by former colonized peoples – such as the Flemish, Poles and Irish – to assert their linguistic uniqueness (Mazama 3; Akinnaso 139–41, 143).

Right across Africa, language has perhaps been the most significant aspect of cultural policy, given the proliferation of tongues across and within nations. Desires for national unity have encountered problems with minority rights caused by boundaries that were drawn by colonial administrators and intra-imperial diplomats, rather than being generated by popular action or democracy. Some of these problems are intractable, given that the continent has several thousand languages. Since independence, most African states have adopted language-status planning, imposing one or a small number of indigenous languages as official national forms of communication. Tanzania and Somalia stand out as relatively successful sites, but most countries have not unified, not least because of the complex choice between a European colonizer's language and a particular tribal one. The former may offend some groups less than the latter, which implies a shift in local dispositions of political power. Elite groups are also compromised, as their cultural capital and self-formation are embossed by the language of the former European ruler. Against these forces, there remain strong anti-colonial feelings, and the desire for a public manifestation of unity and history (Akinnaso).

The question of language use has been of great significance to ex-colonial powers. Until the 1990s, ruling-class Latin Americans had French as their second language. Today, a third of the continent's Presidents have attended college in the US, and English is dominant. As part of turning Latin America away from NAFTA and towards Europe, the French have called for a program of educational exchange ('French'). Conversely, radical Afrocentric approaches to language are concerned to displace Eurocentrism with forms of life more in keeping with continental traditions. The idea of language policy is itself questioned as an aspect of Western modernity, associated as it is with domination and oppression of people by central authorities (Mazama). Sri Lanka's national adoption of an official two-language policy in 1943, mixing Tamil and Sinhala, quickly saw Sinhala dominate because it had many more speakers, and 1956 saw its adoption as the sole official tongue (Akinnaso 153). In the revolutionary society of Jaffna, a separatist Marxist/Nationalist state of Sri Lanka, attempts have been made to legislate away Tamil-English bilingualism as part of a rejection of both a colonial past and the national government's authority (Canagarajah).

Apart from language, artifacts have been crucial to heritage-building. In the second half of the twentieth century, many Third-World regimes built temples to Western culture as a means of demonstrating their modernity and of attracting military and financial aid (Duncan *Civilizing* 21). The Gambia is a typical example of the dilemmas faced by such a postcolonial state. On gaining independence from Britain in 1965, it began a program of national legitimation. The National Archives were founded that year. In 1974, a preservationary Monuments and Relics Act was passed. A decade later, a National Museum was established to house materials. The relevant government department, the Ministry of Education, Youth Sports, and Culture, concentrated on developing teaching facilities and specialists, a critical need given the absence of a university system. The cultural budget went on a National Troupe dedicated to maintaining the *griot* repertoire of precolonial days. The idea of a cultural policy as such developed in the 1980s, with the aim of linking nation-building to tourism. The emphasis was still on heritage rather than the development of new forms and practices (Hoover).

In South Africa, white-settler domination of politics and economics for more than a century was widespread and brutal. Cultural production was important to both orchestrating and resisting this oppression. With a turn to democracy in the 1990s, the word 'resistance' was displaced by 'reconciliation', with associated changes in art practice and fashion. Some forms of exchange between urban centers and rural regions have been criticized as Romantic assertions of a timeless pre-colonial past, but practitioners defend this as a new partnership that draws on tradition and innovation (Mda 1–2, 4). The new South Africa is also dedicated to the commodification of culture. The Government's 1995 Report for the Ministry of Arts, Culture, Science and Technology stresses the role of the arts 'in the revitalization and regeneration of both industry and tourism', in accord with the state's Reconstruction and Development Programme (quoted in J.J. Williams 110).

In wealthier neo- or post-colonial contexts, the story is very complex. For example, the British combated the Triad secret societies in Hong Kong after the Second World War on two fronts, notably after the 1956 riots. The societies' technically criminal activities were prosecuted, and their forms of cultural communication were outlawed as embodying a rejection of the social – offering an alternative to colonial society. This had implications for the work of the island's Television and Entertainment Licensing Authority and what it was prepared to see represented once TV arrived in the 1970s. There was persistent rejection of texts and performances featuring Triad 'slang' (Bolton and Hutton 159–60, 166, 168–71). But there was no positive cultural policy, in the sense of planning, subsidizing or generating cultural production, from the time of Britain's takeover in 1842 until shortly prior to its departure in 1997. Hong Kong was a symbolic *entrée* into mainland markets, not a place to encourage the arts. By the 1950s and 1960s, the population expansion and economic growth of the Crown Colony saw its Urban Council construct a City Hall with library, museum, theatrical and concert facilities. As per the anxieties of nineteenth-century urbanizing Europe, this task was conceived alongside the disposal of waste, the provision of latrines, the management of abattoirs and parkland recreation. In 1973, the Council was freed from British control and given financial independence. In 1977, it founded the Hong Kong Chinese Orchestra and the Hong Kong Repertory Company. The Government decided to involve itself again, and appointed a Commissioner for Recreation and Culture in 1980 and a Council for the Performing Arts two years later, to fund ballet, classical music and an arts festival. The Regional Council embarked on devolved cultural development, with the formation of auditoria across the New Territories on the mainland. Along with the need for Hong Kong to be a global city in terms of all the services that implies, this was also conceived as a means of reassuring people who were anxious about the handover. Cultural infrastructure signaled stability as much as innovation (Ooi).

Cultural policy since 1997 has been similar to the century and a half of colonial rule – neglect followed by activity. Toward the end of British control, demands for transparency in politics and administration spread to the arts, with cultural workers calling for accountability from civil servants. The Urban Council opened its meetings to public scrutiny in 1991. Anxiety about an Orwellian centralization by the PRC was cited to preclude a more definite cultural policy (Ooi). The post-handover Legislative Council's Panel on Home Affairs instituted a Sub-committee on Long Term Cultural Policy. In seeking the basis for a cultural policy, it turned for comparators to large, economically advanced cities: New York, Vancouver, Toronto, Sydney and Singapore (Home 'Structure'). The Council also instituted arts education in the schools. For the first time, teachers obliged their pupils to visit museums, as part of the state's requirement that they 'develop students' creativity and aesthetivity'. This was also designed to connect young people to the PRC. On the business front, the Hong Kong Tourist Association undertook feasibility studies on bringing in foreign finance via performances (Home 'Response' and 'Long') and sought to bind tourism to culture.

Across South-East Asia, as we saw in the Introduction, cultural maintenance has frequently been a device for retaining power and creating new markets. The Association of South-East Asian Nations, primarily an economic bloc, has a Committee on Culture and Information that shares knowledge of overlapping and differentiated cultures in the region and preserves public memory of history. South Korea set up a Ministry of Culture and Information in 1968, as a site for systematizing state law and policy in the area, with a concentration on identity. In 1972, a Five-Year Plan for Culture/Art Promotion was set in motion, with a strong emphasis on traditional cultural practice (Kim 45). Over the 1980s, this shifted to devolving new cultural production from Seoul to the regions 'as an instrument for strengthening the competitive capability of culture, tourism, and regional economic growth' (Yim 1; also see Kim 46).

Singaporean cultural policy began in 1955 when the People's Action Party founded a Singapore Arts Council, modeled on the British version. Future global attention was always on the agenda, with arts festivals designed to appeal to tourists. Since the late 1970s, business has been linked to government via the Singapore Cultural Foundation (Low). The Singapore Tourism Board called this 'art for business's sake' (quoted in Susan Anderson AR6). A National Arts Council and the National Heritage Board report to a Ministry of Information and the Arts (a strong propaganda connection) (Home 'Structure'). In the five years from 1994, Singapore wooed individual artists and arts organizations (such as Cirque du Soleil) to move there through tax incentives – the NICL at play. Three museums opened after 1996, and the 1999 Singapore Arts Festival featured dozens of international troupes, hundreds of fringe performers and an ambitious sculpture exhibit across the city. A new US$265 million complex of the performing arts was also erected. These initiatives were designed to develop the worker-citizen. In the eyes of the National Arts Council's chair, Liu Tai Ker, '[a] person involved in cultural activities will be a more creative, thinking person, better in the work force' (quoted in Susan Anderson AR6). Total government expenditure on the arts rose from US$20 million in 1994 to US$36 million in 1998, with the number of art exhibitions doubling over the same period from two hundred to four hundred. Singapore now claims that it will be 'a global city of the arts' (Tsang 'Arts' and 'Intl'.). To signal the liberalism of the new Singapore, buskers are even permitted to perform (Low). The government announced a new cultural desire in 1999: 'dot com-ing the entire nation'. The same era saw the Singapore Broadcasting Authority aiming for 'a well-informed, culturally-rich, socially cohesive and economically vibrant society'. Those words mimic arts policy initiatives, blend with the commercial logic of the new media and provide an alibi for censoring the Internet as per the broadcast media, in the interests of national cohesion and what is officially designated as 'morally wholesome' conduct (quoted in Terence Lee 4).

Malaysia, a country moving from primary production to a diversified economy, has put resources into developing as export prospects such cottage cultural industries as *batik, songket* and weaving, in addition to deploying domestic cultural programs designed to 'improve the quality of life and to promote national integration'. It does so in accordance with *Rukunegara*, a doctrine of Malaysian nationhood, meaning the rule of law, faith in God, loyalty to the constitutional monarchy and morality. This is embodied in the National Cultural Policy, adopted in 1971. It emphasizes that *the* national culture is Malay, despite the proliferation and power of the Chinese, whose significance is acknowledged via various nods to ethnic pluralism. There are also several youth programs known as *Rakan Muda*, which favor 'a healthy lifestyle'. This is cultural policy as ethical technology, twinned with economic development. There are numerous tax deductions as incentives for the private sector to invest in culture. Internationally, the Voice of Malaysia carries a message of the nation's interests and tourist appeal throughout the region on radio.

Taiwan has certain similarities to Hong Kong. It defines itself against the PRC, but, has a more ambivalent attitude to the former colonial aggressor, in this case Japan, to which the island was ceded in 1895. Unlike both Hong Kong and the mainland, since 1949 Taiwan's Kuomintang state has stressed the need to safeguard traditional Chinese culture through language and 'national treasures' that could develop patriotism via fetishized displays, undertaken in the name of shared civilization and a mythic dynasty of origin. Since World War II, Taiwan has gone through several phases of cultural policy. Until the late 1960s, the state focused on purging the island of remnants of the Japanese occupation and suppressing ethnic Taiwanese culture, in favor of pre-state-socialist mainland norms and history. This was achieved via the imposition of Portunhua as a national language. From 1967 to 1977, a decade of 'cultural renaissance' saw the arts and education mobilized towards modernization and development, followed by 'cultural reconstruction' – the establishment of regional cultural centers and a national stress on both high culture and the classical past. So calligraphy was valorized, but folk medicine was not (Chun 72–75, 79–81). Since that time, the focus has been on preventing organic connections between the island and the mainland from leading to a popular desire for reunification. Localist realism and the Hakar and Taiwanese languages have been permitted to flourish, a stark contrast with their earlier suppression (Ping-hui 75, 77).

Thailand of course avoided colonization, but operates very much in the context of Western domination. The Constitution requires that 'the State shall promote and preserve the national culture', which it does through an elaborate archiving program, a national library, a large network of national museums, archaeology, 'traditional' arts and crafts, architectural preservation, performing arts, religion

(Buddhist and Brahmin influences predominate, with Buddhism officially promulgated), and morality (notably via the fetish of the family). An Office of the National Culture Commission licenses a fast-growing, 12,000-strong NGO sector in the cultural sphere.

Early in the new century, Thai environmental and pro-democracy activists publicized the arrogant despoliation they experienced when Fox was making *The Beach* in Maya Bay, part of the Phi Phi Islands National Park. The natural scenery was bulldozed in late 1998 because it did not fit the studio's fantasy of a tropical idyll. The government was paid off with a donation to the Royal Forestry Department and a campaign with the Tourism Authority of Thailand to twin the film as a promotion for the country. Meanwhile, the next monsoon saw the damaged sand dunes of the region collapse, as natural defenses against erosion had been destroyed by Hollywood bulldozers. All the while, director Danny Boyle claimed that the film was 'raising environmental consciousness' among a local population allegedly 'behind' US levels of 'awareness' (Justice for Maya Bay International Alliance).

The postcolonial dilemma of coming to terms with a past that is about the destruction of invading forces and complex ethnic histories is a central problematic for both command cultures and postcolonial states seeking to generate cultural policy as they deal with rampant neoliberalism. The embrace of market reforms oriented towards foreign investment has distinct cultural corollaries.

---

1 In contrast to Spanish America, Brazil gained its independence when Dom Pedro – whose father Dom João had transferred the court to Rio de Janeiro when Napoleon invaded Portugal in 1808 – refused the summons in 1820 to return the throne to the metropolis in order to prevent a reversal of the liberalized colonial policies instituted by his father and the opening up of trade. In 1822 he was named the constitutional emperor of Brazil.

4

Museums

When Millbank Penitentiary opened in 1817, a room festooned with chains, whips and instruments of torture was set aside as a museum.... Thus did a new philosophy of punishment committed to the rehabilitation of the offender through the detailed inspection and regulation of behaviour distance itself from an earlier regime of punishment which had aimed to make power manifest by enacting the scene of punishment in public. The same period witnessed a new addition to London's array of exhibitionary institutions.... Madame Tussaud set up permanent shop.... As the century developed, the dungeons of old castles were opened to public inspection, often as the centrepieces of museums. – Tony Bennett (*Birth* 153)

Museums are the last resort on a rainy Sunday. – Heinrich Boll (quoted in García Canclini 115)

[T]he Memorial Museum of the Chinese People's War of Resistance to Japan ... [includes] waxwork diorama reconstructions of Japanese atrocities against the Chinese. One such display shows a Japanese scientist in a white coat, intent on carrying out a gruesome bacteriological warfare experiment, plunging his scalpel into the living, trussed-up body of a Chinese peasant resistance fighter. But just in case this is not enough to drive the message home, the museum designers have added a refinement: a motor inside the waxwork of the peasant, which makes his body twitch jerkily. – Rana Mitter (279)

Consider the following setting. It's late spring, early summer 2000. New York City's MoMA is facing its greatest crisis. Workers are picketing the museum over MoMAnagement's refusal to come to terms with the local union over health care and job security. On the street outside, the protestors position a ten-foot tall inflatable rubber rat against a steel gate, preventing passers-by from seeing the Museum's garden sculptures. MoMAnagement responds by erecting screens to block those within from seeing the rat, presumably preferring that they look at scabs instead. Some little while later, courtesy of its need to get a land-use ordinance through a union-friendly city council, MoMAnagement caves in to the strikers. This anecdote captures the twin senses of museum labor. The first sense concerns the work done by people to produce art, as per the contribution of MoMA workers to the public. The second sense concerns the work done by culture on people, as per the aesthetic and political impact of the rubber rat (politicization) versus the sculptures (aesthetic contemplation).

This chapter looks at the institution that is most often connected with cultural policy – the museum. An institution of space, as opposed to the more mobile spheres of performance or the audiovisual, the museum is both static and dynamic, in that its monumentalism is matched by its fashionability. The United States has 8,200 museums, half of which have emerged over the past three decades (Cherbo and Wyszomirski 6). The number of visitors reached fifty million in 1962 and exceeded the overall population of 250 million by 1980, while France averages twenty million visitors annually (García Canclini 115). The year 2000 saw museums being built and extended in every major US city, while Paris' Pompidou Centre had just undergone a US$88 million restoration, Berlin had a new but exhibit-free Jewish Museum, and the Bankside Tate in London ('the Modern') opened on the site of a former power station and leant its name to paper coffee cups, Japanese chopsticks, bags, T-shirts and a line of clothing. Berlin began a US$1 billion plan to rebuild its Museums Island of five major sites, the US Smithsonian's National Portrait Gallery was shut for restoration and the Guggenheim announced that a US$800 million forty-five-storey cultural complex would sit astride its existing building. The spurt of building was because these established museums were bursting with objects and visitors. The Pompidou had been constructed to cater for 5000 visitors a day – three decades on, its average was five times that number. To pay for all of this, the Tate Modern, for instance, employed thirty-four fundraisers ('Museums'; Ellison). Meanwhile, Silvio Berlusconi was busily planning the privatization of all 3000 public Italian museums (Hennenberger).

The conventional binary of museum discourse opposes populist entertainment against *étatiste* instruction. But today we see 'simple warehouses of the past' transmogrified via 'insertion in cultural centers [and the] creation of ecomuseums, community, school and on-site museums' (García Canclini 116). In this chapter, we ask how the museum has changed across time and space, look at some fault-lines in museum politics, and report on a site visit to Western Australia's Fremantle Prison Museum.

History

The nineteenth century's proliferation of public art museums as cultural technologies was directly related to a new duty for the visual arts as agents of civilizing discipline. In terms of governmentality, the public museum embodied a critical shift of focus away from the intramural world of the princely museum. Prior to the Enlightenment, royal collections were meant to express the monarch's grandeur and induce a sense of insignificance in the viewer. But the public site of modernity called out for identification and a mutual, municipal ownership that hailed visitors as participants in the collective exercise of power (Turner *National Fictions* 60–62, 74–75, 98; Bennett *Birth* 166). The idea was to produce 'symbolic expressions capable of unifying a nation's regions and classes, to give order to the continuity between past and present, between one's own and the foreign' (García Canclini 116).

As García Canclini notes, '[t]o enter a museum is not simply to go into a building and look at works; rather, it is a ritualized system of social action' (115). That process of interpellation follows a fairly standard format. First, the implied visitor is given a proper perspective on the site's history and the visitor's place in it. And second – here, of course, is the rub, and the place where history and its public munificence really commence – a prior age is made known. For that past is compared, often unfavorably, with the moment when history is written – now. The subject of that history once occupied our own physical space, but is part of a transcended and either admirable or regrettable heritage. We can learn from it, but it is definitely over. The visitor is expected to understand that we now live in a better – or at least more knowledgeable – moment. This understanding activates a subset of cultural citizenship: historical citizenship. Historical citizenship emerges in the contemporary moment, but in reaction to the past. It knows that errors lie back there, before we knew. The past's commemoration in museum form is rendered as a strictly delimited ethical zone, a space that divides worthy and unworthy conduct. Tony Bennett's discussion of punishment instruments turns on the emergence of this ethical zone of the historical citizen, which sifts out the good, the bad and the sublime in past treatment of the population, noting discontinuities and linearities in a movement towards present, 'enlightened' standards.

This style of historical narrative is teleological – the latest epoch is always the most advanced. Successive French coups after 1789 saw the Louvre provided with at least one additional ceiling per change of regime. Each renovation explained past glories as precursors to the latest regime, and revised previous rulers' account of themselves. In 1793, the revolutionary state nationalized the French royal art collection to create the Louvre Museum as a space for public appreciation, of both the building and the art it housed. What had been a private site for generating regal grandeur and differentiation was turned into a public site for displaying the munificence of the people's government. Signifiers of luxury and aristocratic status became signifiers of national *Geist*, with heritage privileged over wealth (Duncan *Civilizing* 22, 27, 29).

Two relatively discrete political rationalities inform the museum. The first governs legislative and rhetorical forms. The second determines the internal dynamics of a pedagogic site. Certain difficulties emerge from the different dictates of these rationalities. The museum calls upon democratic rhetoric associated with access, an open space for the artifactually occasioned site of public discussion. But as a pedagogic site, it functions in a disciplinary way to forge public manners. A contradiction ensues between exchange and narration or reciprocity and imposition, such that an opportunity for the public to deliberate on some aspect of cultural history is opposed to an opportunity for museum magistrates to give an ethically incomplete citizenry a course of instruction.

This binary, or course, can itself be made more subtle. Consider the varied histories that underpin Holocaust memorials in the United States: to recall the dead, to remember the self as survivor or liberator, to constitute the US as the preserve of freedom *par excellence*, to draw tourists, to be a community center, to stress religious or ideological affiliations, and to obtain votes. All these decisions are made 'in political time, contingent on political realities' (James Young 58). Yet this 'political time' is rarely made explicit to visitors. Germain Bazin, an early curator at the Louvre, thought of the museum as 'a temple where Time seems suspended' and quasi-religious individual epiphanies could be experienced. Of course, these moments were directed from on-high via lectures on the value of the arts that positioned the state as the key point of articulation between work and subject (Bazin quoted in Duncan *Civilizing* 11; also see 27). But at least this spirituality was about secular publicness, not ecclesiastical mysticism!

The idea of publicness in museums can be politicized and bloody as well as democratic. Museums were imperial imports to most of the world, and sites in Hong Kong, Vietnam and Korea today are criticized for a monumentalism that continues to embody such politics (David Kahn). New Spain (later Mexico) ruler Carlos IV established Latin America's first Museum of Natural History in 1790 to display the latest scientific technology. These institutions not only served the purposes of the crown, but also the desire of the creoles to refute disparagements by European self-aggrandizers. After Latin American independence, the newly formed states invited scientists to 'discover' hitherto 'unknown' realities. Unlike the missionary work of the Church in the sixteenth and seventeenth centuries, these scientific missions did not aim to convert native peoples. Instead, they showcased Indians as part of national history, although those artifacts of indigenous culture not assimilable to ideas of grand civilization (e.g. a statue of the Aztec goddess Coatlicue that was deemed unworthy of comparison with Greek and Roman statuary) were closeted (Morales-Moreno 175–77). Nevertheless, to the degree that the objects selected for display gave New Spain and then Mexico a sense of history, they satisfied the pride of creoles and legitimized the state. Moreover, scientific missions produced new knowledge and understanding, consistent with Enlightenment ideas, of the realities of this different world, and mapped a range of hitherto unknown resources that might fuel the early phase of industrial revolution, charting new routes for extraction and trade. The creation of Argentina's Museo de Ciencias Naturales de La Plata, the continent's most important museum of natural history in the 1880s, was undertaken to differentiate a modern, immigrant-descended population from the Native Indian owners. Francisco P. Moreno, the founder of this museum, reconstructed Darwin's trip to Patagonia, gathering most of the objects that became the Museo's contents. Moreno sought to complete Darwin's reconnaissance to help order the still fragmented nation, bringing Patagonia into the fold of Argentina. This order and incorporation involved the conquest of Indians, exactly when Argentine president Julio A. Roca undertook the 'Conquest of the Desert'. Curiously, as the Indians were decimated, Moreno re-established a place for them in his museum, taking them as relics of the power of nature over the corrupting effects that civilization had on indigenous peoples. Indeed, Moreno literally housed a group of Patagonian Indians taken prisoner during the 'Conquest of the Desert' in the Buenos Aires Museum of Anthropology, giving the 'civilized' city dwellers a window into 'humanity in its infancy stage' (quoted in Grosman 110). When one of his Indian guides was killed by 'wild' Indians, Moreno had the body exhumed, stuffed and exhibited in the Museo (Grosman 115). The conquest of the wilderness (and of the Indians) went hand in hand with the nationalization of Patagonia and its mise-en-diorama in Moreno's museum: 'Moreno extends [nationalization] to his museum when he proposes the identification of territorial occupation as consolidation of the national state via the museum as tantamount to scientific development and progress' (Grosman 123). Moreno's naturalist excursions and the creation of his museum were transformed into an act of sovereignty (Grosman 139). One is reminded here of Theodore Roosevelt's invocation of the sovereign power of nature once it (i.e. the indigenous population) had been conquered, and indeed Moreno was Roosevelt's host and guide when the latter traveled to Patagonia.

Bennett argues that a museum politics must attend to contradictions inscribed in the institutional form of the public museum. One contradiction is between the museum as an instrument for universalizing claims of collective ownership of cultural property, and the museum as an instrument for differentiating populations. This results in a further tension between what a museum is in theory (collectively owned) and in practice (a *mise-en-scène* of constitutive exclusions). In turn, this leads to an unendable demand for access and use, as social movements press for a democratizing expansion of the collective. A politics of representational proportionality emanates from the contradiction between the space of representation associated with the premise of universality inherent in the institution of the public museum, and the fact that this injunction is impossible, due to its gendered, racist, classist or nationalist exclusions and biases.

Today, constitutive exclusions are wrought not so much by prohibiting entry or confining visitors, but by education. In both its arrangement of things and its instructions to the public on how to approach collections, the museum hails its audience as respectful trainees. Visitors are induced by example, exhortation, and even the physical layout of space to adopt certain *mores* and manners and relinquish others. They learn to look and not touch, to walk about calmly and gently, in effect distinguishing the graceful from the riotous in public behavior. These are modes of conduct, rather than reactions to art on a wall or in a display case (Bennett *Birth* 1, 7, 90–91, 97, 102–03) – but they are not universal codes, and they can alienate many sectors of the population.

The 1986 John Hughes teen movie *Ferris Bueller's Day Off* features a high-art diegetic insert, as otherwise unruly, fun-loving teens move respectfully around the Chicago Art Institute's impressionist collection, finding themselves to be maturing subjects, ready for college. Something similar is happening when German studies professor Andreas Huyssen takes his five-year-old son to a museum and the little boy is reprimanded for touching and leaning on art-works. Huyssen reads this symptomatically, as a sign of institutions seeking to reinstate the dissociated organic aura of art (178–79). These are really lessons in manners, part of the museum's mission as an ethical site. And this sense of an ethical control that excludes certain subjects, and privileges certain forms of conduct, systematically discourages attendance by audiences alienated from dominant cultural forms. For example, a 1987 survey of audience attendance in nine art museums in southern California found that minorities constituted only 15.2% of site visitors, but 47% of the region's population (Draper 54). Subsequent studies have borne out these figures. In Britain, 50% of the total population never visits museums, galleries, theaters or concert halls – although most support their existence, even as Blair-era policies have decreased the sector's annual budget decrease by 15% (Gilmore; Lister and Niesewand; Kennedy). The major US museums now prioritize 'blockbuster' shows and free-admission days, as a way of simultaneously avoiding charges of élitism and attracting corporate support.

The museum seeks to attract newcomers and draw reactions that can be taken back into the exterior world, following a temporary, voluntary enclosure of visitors that combines information with entertainment, and instruction with diversion. Museums stop us at the present, pointing out the hectic pace of the modern by freezing its 'unceasing dispersal of space and time' in the cali-brated space of an archive (Tagg 364). This complex relationship is further complicated by buildings that have prior lives. Britain's Imperial War Museum was once Bethlehem mental hospital ('Bedlam') but it now introjects and pro-jects a different form of madness and imposition. Yorkshire's Eden Camp offers visitors a brief stay behind the barbed wire that housed prisoners-of-war from 1942 to 1948, giving 200,000 people a year an exact experience of 'the condi-tions in which prisoners lived'. Nazi Germany's *Konzentrationslager* at Dachau is also a museum (Boniface and Fowler 105). And Corleone, a tiny Sicilian town known as a point of origin for *La Cosa Nostra*, renovated its convent into a museum about the Mafia in 2000 ('Sicilian'). As we shall see below, Western Australia's Fremantle Prison Museum achieves a physical unity between its former and current careers, performing successive functions of incarceration/correction and incorporation/education. In this sense, it has moved from dividing the rowdy from the respectable, in its initial incarnation, towards an ethical technology for demonstrating that process, and quietly replicating it as a mimetic space for exercising the mild-mannered gaze. This is the gaze of the decent person, who is being seen and heard as much as she is watching and listening, both at the time of her visit, and at later moments, when she narrates the visiting experience to others. Such museum visitors are interpellated as legatees of a national past and instruments of a collaborative national present.

At a conceptual level, museums are charged with bringing public attention to what has previously been concealed, to take the secrets of an elite into the populace at large. Instead of *ob*jectifying that population, as per the public executions of eighteenth-century Europe, the museum *sub*jectifies people, offering them a position in history and a relationship to that history. Since its original designation as a national institution by the French Revolutionary administration, the Louvre has been associated with virtuous government and elite beneficence disbursed from on-high. It has served as a model for the rest of Western Europe. By the end of the nineteenth century, the entire region had created public art museums as 'signs of politically virtuous states', and a series of American cities (Boston, Cleveland, New York, Chicago, Buenos Aires, Lima, Rio de Janeiro and Mexico City) followed suit. The Pennsylvania Museum was founded to embody the wisdom of the following precept: 'to rob ... people of the things of the spirit and to supply them with higher wages as a substitute is not good economics, good patriotism, or good policy' (quoted in Fraser 393). When the English Parliament first debated public art museums, discussion centered on how to prepare the people to appreciate the grandeur of art. An imposing architecture was deemed the best method of instilling awe (Duncan *Civilizing* 11, 32, 21). This can also have more specifically-targeted policy aims. Thailand's Narcotics Exhibition Centre, run by its Office of Narcotics Control Board, includes a wax model of a child being abducted by a methamphetamine addict as part of its warnings ('New').

The public museum's universal address has characteristically either obliterated difference, or caricatured it via racist and imperialist appropriation and scientism, sexist exclusion and mystification and class-based narratives of progress. The entire project of 'discovery' has also infantilized the visitor, for the principal characteristic of the museum era is a mastery over the physical environment and other countries. Scientific and imperial triumphs target more than the visitor, for they also infantilize those beyond such discourses or subject to them. This rhetoric of universal uplift runs into trouble when it encounters 'excellence'-inflected definitions of heritage and the aura of leading museums as prestigious clubs (Bennett *Birth* 97; Jordanova 22, 32; Clement Price 25, 30). The heritage concept has been overhauled following critiques of its élitism, which in turn has spread commodification down to the level of working-class heritage and 'locality-based, living history "experience" museums' that privilege the quotidian (Dicks 81–82).

As we saw in Chapter 3, from the 1930s to the 1950s, cultural institutions and museums in large Latin American countries merged in a twin project of national consolidation overseen by strong populist parties and industrial elites, exemplified in Mexico's Instituto Nacional de Antropología e Historia (1939) and Instituto Nacional de Bellas Artes (1946) and Brazil's *Museu de Arte do São Paulo* (1947), *Museu de Arte Moderno de São Paulo* (1948) and *São Paulo Biennial* (1951). Moreover, as we say in Chapter 1, there was a strong correlation between US government and capitalist-related projects, respectively the OCIAA and Rockefeller oil interests. It is no coincidence that these links converged on Rockefeller and 'his' cultural institutions, like MoMA.

Mary Coffey traces this process with reference to Mexico's Museo Nacional de Antropología, which was created in 1964 to shape the population's views of indigenous Mexicans as the source of national culture. The most-visited museum in the country, it articulates this version of a common origin via a radical separation of the ancient from the contemporary, with Indians relegated to scions of the past rather than emergent and present-day actors (Coffey 49–50). Latter-day critiques of *mestizaje* and *indigenismo* in Mexico and the emergence of new private institutions like the Monterrey Contemporary Art Museum (MARCO) suggest new purposes for museology that have less to do with national consolidation than with adapting to a discourse of diversity that is compatible with neoliberalism and free trade. In Brazil, cultural institutions have adapted to the possibilities opened up by MERCOSUR and urban development projects, as is the case with the impending agreement to site Guggenheim franchise museums in Rio and/or Recife.

In most other Latin American cities and in rural areas, however, traditional culture (and often [re]invented traditions) can ideally be central to sustainable-development projects, such as the Ecuadorean NGO, OMAERE. It seeks to strengthen Andean indigenous cultures through educational-touristic activities that produce knowledge as well as resources. OMAERE is dedicated to 'biodiversity, ethnobotany, the conservation of nature and the strengthening of the indigenous peoples and cultures of the world'. Its program, Valorization and Commercialization of Sustainable Products from the Ecuadorian Amazon Region, contextualized by a series of publications and audiovisual products, 'privileges the revalorization and protection of the knowledge of traditional peoples'. Similarly, RICANCIE, a network of ten Quichua communities in the high Napo Valley, consists of sustainable ecotourist development 'based on the cultural and natural heritage of these communities'. The program of the Yahcana Amazon Lodge offers its visitors 'participation in sustainable development and community health and education projects ... that will enable them to travel to another reality'. What is being sold is an experience 'in sharing the Amazon with one's eyes, ears and heart'. The Kapawi Lodge and Reserve's economic-cultural development project has made it possible for the fifty-two Achuar communities who provide an Amazon experience to substitute their traditional agricultural activity with ecotourism and crafts, to the point where income from these sources provides 45% and 21% respectively, of their total finances. Inevitably, this leads to political debate.

Controversies

Because museums carry the distinctive stamp of the modern as well as representing the governmental, they are never far from strife. In the UK, the seeming shift in tone from the Thatcher-Major era's emphasis on heritage to Blairite interest in the audiovisual has seen changes in how museum administrators understand their mission, blending the past with new technology under the sign of commodification (Chong 274, 277–78). When that desire for profit merges with pressure from social movements for inclusion in the public side to museum ideology, controversy ensues. Quantitative evaluation is undertaken by both sides, as account is taken of both revenue *and* representativeness, in search of what Anne Whitelaw calls 'statistical correctness' (34). And even as postcolonial critics assault such forms of thought as Egyptology, Egypt's Ministry of Culture relaunches the Egyptian Museum in Cairo as a multi-media site for just such fetishism ('Moving').

For its part, the century retrospective of German art held in three Berlin museums in 1999–2000 had to deal with the Nazi legacy. In titling the exhibit A *Century of Art in Germany*, the curators tried to duck issues of nationalism by including works by Picasso, Kandinsky, Warhol and others, alongside accounting for the country's past (Riding). Of course, anticipating critique does not necessarily deflect it. And when the ground was broken in Washington DC in 1999 for the future site of the Museum of the American Indian, destined for removal from New York City, there was great controversy. First, senior forces at the Smithsonian Institution, which houses the Federal Government's museums, had wanted the site for a 'Museum of Man'. Outvoted, they told African-American leaders that Native Americans had taken a site that would have been allocated to them, leading to bitterness between two disenfranchised groups (Hitchens). For if modernity promises secular transcendence, the pursuit of the good life and an inclusive state and civil society, while governmentality offers an ordering of that population in the interests of the nation, then highly symbolic sites like museums are caught in whatever contradictions may occur. The struggle between minority communities and mainstream art institutions, a struggle that governments and corporations cautiously negotiate via strategies to legitimize their own discourse of crossing borders, generates and signals shifting definitions of art and culture.

A prime example is the renowned National Museum of Mali. Founded under colonial rule in 1953 as a branch of France's Institute of Black Africa based in Senegal, the Musée Soudanais de Bamako served as an *entrepôt* for objects that had been taken from the Sudanese and were on their way to large museums in Senegal and France (Mali). The Bamako was left to hang onto duplicates. Stolen property was categorized through ethnographic and archaeological discourse, not art-historical knowledge. After de-colonization in 1960, the Bamako was nationalized as the Malian National Museum. Following two decades of minimal activity, it was reanimated by new policies of democratic access, use of local languages and regionalization, in the name of preserving, recording, and historicizing the people of Mali for themselves. This started with a physical redesign, with new architecture modeled on Mali villages. But two areas that have not developed are contemporary art and the representation of urban life. Holdings are minimal, due to a priority on forms of cultural history and anthropology that are holdovers from colonialism (Arnoldi 28–29, 33–34).

South African *apartheid* was served by museums dedicated to honoring Afrikaner trekkers and distinguishing them from the British, while differences between the original inhabitants were signified by separate displays for Xhosa, Mpondo, Venda and Zulu cultural practices. The gallery system privileged European high art. Black African artists were admitted to the canon in the late 1980s, but under conventional aesthetic categories and hierarchies. At the same time, ethnographic sites were deconstructed. The popular Bushman diorama at Cape Town's South African Museum was itself contextualized from 1989, allowing visitors to identify traces of historiographic enunciation. With the dismantling of the dictatorship, museums rushed to democratize their collections (Rankin and Hamilton 3–4, 6–7). Johannesburg's Apartheid Museum arbitrarily allocates each visitor a designation of white or black on entry, and they are treated accordingly. A private venture, this heavy anti-racism is mandatorily funded with the profits from a casino, a sign of the new links between private and public (Swarns).

All such cases of national interpellation, however inclusive, become techniques for governing through subjectification. Even the smallest indigenous groups can be inserted into transnational networks that have an impact on questions of identity and representation. This community was invited by the Smithsonian Institute's National Museum of the American Indian (NMAI) to participate in a discussion on 'Ethnic Identity, Community Museums and Development Programs' in 1995. Twenty-five other Latin American Indian groups were invited in what was meant to be the first event in the expansion of the concept of the 'American Indian' beyond the borders of the US. What makes this meeting interesting is that it raised many problems about the conceptualization of identity, ethnicity and nomenclature, problems that do not become evident until two or more systems of thinking about these issues come into contact.

The director, Richard West, explained that the groups were invited to educate the museum about the real meaning of the objects it housed. The Smithsonian took as its guiding premise that a museum should consult the people who provide the objects on exhibit (Barrera Bassols and Vera Herrera 23–24). The participants were told that the Smithsonian would use this knowledge in order to represent native peoples exactly as they wanted. This raised many concerns, and elicited doubts from some that their culture could really *be* represented. A Mam from Guatemala raised objections about the representativity of the collection, and said that 'we did not come to exhibit ourselves, we are not objects'. Another participant opined that preserving the bones of his forebears was counterproductive. A Shuar from Ecuador objected to the idea that the Museum wished to document indigenous cultures because they were disappearing. What was needed, he said, was to document culture for the cultural self-development of the community. The notion of a culture in disappearance was erroneous, 'surely put forward by an anthropologist' (Barrera and Vera Herrera 24–25). The most heated discussion, however, was about nomenclature, and the criteria for assuming Indian identity. Museum officials variously used the terms Indian, indigenous, Native American, tribal, people and community. This made some participants feel uncomfortable, as if it did not matter what they called themselves. One participant from Peru said that they only used the term peasant. Instead of *el día de la raza* (day of the race), they should celebrate *el día del campesinado* (day of the peasant) (Barrera Bassols and Vera Herrera 26). Mato observed a similar event, the Festival of American Folklife, organized by the Smithsonian's Center for Folklife Programs and Cultural Studies in 1994. He reported that 'the system of racial representations, conflicts, and transactions of U.S. society ... tends to racialize the lives of other peoples ... a very complex matter that must be examined in relation to workings of international and transnational agencies' (23).

The differences in systems of identity categorization were commented on with great concern. In the US, you can be an Indian on the basis of blood, even if you don't 'belong' to an indigenous community. For the NMAI, the problem of representativity is solved because 50% of its Board of Directors have at least 1/16 Indian blood. The participants expressed their view that such an institution should be administered by Indian communities. It is not enough, they argued, for the director to be a Cheyenne, which raised the question of what is important in the constitution of identity. Some groups considered participation, instead, as the way to determine belonging. Latin American Indian participants were not impressed by the racial component of the so-called ethnic minorities at the Smithsonian. They argued that this was not a blood or race issue, but a 'wide-ranging set of assumptions, presuppositions, beliefs, myths, values, experiences and ties that researchers themselves have defined as the "horizon of intelligibility" or "territory of meaning"' (Barrera Bassols and Vera Herrera 37).

Following the 1990s economic and social directive from governments and foundations in the US to reach out to new and non-traditional audiences, the Denver Museum of Art sought to involve that city's large Latino and Native-American communities in an exhibition of Aztec art, *Mexico: Splendors of Thirty Centuries*. To satisfy the educational requirements of such an enterprise, the museum offered seminars, involving volunteers from the larger Denver community, half of whom were Latinos. But the introduction of these new constituencies into the museum generated a whole new set of demands. Latino groups called for a say in the presentation of Aztec history, on the basis of a claim that they are descendants of that civilization. They also lobbied for an accessible rather than a scholarly catalogue, which was ultimately a boon since the 25,000 copies sold generated substantial profits. Native Americans also wanted influence over the exhibition, particularly the treatment of skeletal remains, which they hold sacred. Pressure from local minority communities involved the museum in an unusual negotiation with lending institutions in Mexico, which did not initially understand the inclusion of Hispanics and Indians in planning the exhibition (Stevenson 313). And because this was a costly event that highlighted relations between Mexico and the US, corporations wanted an association with the excitement of Aztec culture. The upshot was both cultural and economic, confirming García Canclini's arguments about 'cultural reconversion', whereby 'culture' is reconstituted in relation to a combination of political negotiations and marketing concerns: 725,000 people saw the exhibit, its economic impact is estimated at US$60–70 million, and a large percentage of the visitors came from Mexico. These facts gave two minority groups unprecedented leverage in negotiating with museum curators and boards, corporate executives, and governments over the display of their presumed heritage.

The exhibition was equally caught in a controversy over the exclusion of Chicanos and Native American artists, who, despite being citizens of the US, nonetheless contested the definitions of Mexican art and culture disseminated by this blockbuster showcase for Mexico's entry into NAFTA. Alternative exhibitions were held with the support of the Rockefeller Foundation and various progressive exhibition spaces. While *Splendors* was displayed at the Metropolitan, San Antonio and Los Angeles County Museums of Art in 1991, dress rehearsals started for the spate of exhibitions and other activities that countered the Quincentennial celebrations of Columbus' 'discovery' in 1992. Such counter-practices have also emerged in smaller communities. El Paso and Albuquerque in New Mexico set up gigantic monuments to their *conquistador*, Juan de Oñate, in 1998, on the four-hundredth anniversary of his arrival with enslaved Indian and African labor in search of mineral deposits. After defeating local Acoma resistance, Oñate had one foot of each Acoma man severed. Centuries later, he had been comprehensively euphemized and eulogized as the figure responsible for opening up the Southwest to agriculture and Christianity – not genocide and invasion. This commemoration was supported by ruling-class citizens who identify as Hispano (quasi-Spanish) against Native American, Chicano and Mexican identities. By supporting this statuary to Oñate, élites could differentiate themselves from working-class folk of 'other' races (Rodríguez and Gónzales).

On a related front, San Diego's Museum of Contemporary Art began planning a large exhibition in 1989 entitled *Dos Ciudades/Two Cities: The Border Project*. It lasted several years and generated a wide array of work about the shared territory of Mexico and the US. Immense controversy ensued following one exhibit, *Arte-Reembolso/Art Rebate*, which consisted of three artists handing out US$10 notes to undocumented Mexican workers crossing the border. Receipts for each note were to be displayed later on as part of the project. As the NEA had contributed about US$1250, this became an opportunity for hue and cry from both sides of politics, with front-page headlines ensuing and the NEA, as usual, capitulating to politicians by taking its money back, on the grounds that the funds had gone to non-citizens (Jane Alexander *Command* 45–46)!

At the same time as the 'culture wars', sex controversies were happening, a *Degenerate Art* exhibit, originally put on by the Nazis in 1937 to show the public the moral degradation of leftist modernism and Jews (see Chapter 3), was being recreated in Los Angeles by the County Art Museum, with NEA funding promised. Here, the already-risky National-Socialist strategy (citing material deemed unacceptable – akin to opposing porn by promoting its consideration in great textual detail) was itself troped in politically complicated ways. The NEA, which was credited with financial aid in the exhibition catalogue, withdrew money during the Helmsman's Senate hearings. Then the Endowment asked that the catalogue 'lose' the words 'censorship' and 'Nazi'. When Helms' inquiry was done, the NEA restored support, fearful of criticisms for buckling to conservatives (Burt 240).

Similar struggles over representing the past and occupying the present took place during the 1990 Into the Heart of Africa exhibit at Toronto's Royal Ontario Museum. The show adopted an ironical stance towards Canada's history of African colonialism, and the Museum's holdings as indices of that past. Its focus on artifacts and histories repatriated by colonizers was meant to encourage a critical view. But it angered black social movements across the city, as a Coalition for Truth about Africa demonstrated on a daily basis outside the Royal that the exhibit, curated by a white anthropologist, was racist and supremacist. The unintentional irony is that this was the first occasion when blacks had been targeted as visitors by the Museum in its seven-decade history – identified not as experts on this heritage, but as recipients of the Museum's interpretation (Mackey 404–05, 410–11).

Of course, contemporary art practice frequently goes beyond conventional definitional borders, to address a range of social issues, like colonialism, racism, and immigration. The Whitney Museum of American Art's 1994–95 Black Male: Representations of Masculinity in Contemporary Art imbricated these concerns with the very nature of labor conditions in art institutions. The exhibit brought people who left the third-floor elevator face-to-face with Fred Wilson's installation Guarded View (1991), which presents four headless black male figures dressed in guard uniforms of the Jewish Museum, the Whitney itself, the Metropolitan Museum of Art, and the MoMA. Of course, this very exhibit was primarily invigilated by African Americans! 'In your face' confrontations of the distinctions between museum labor and museum delectation are powerfully brought out by Wilson's text, its location and the power relations of the space, which ironically validated its commentary.

On occasion, such tensions can take spectacular flight: in 2001, a huge struggle between right and left took place in Paris' Rue Richepance, a street named after a Napoleonic-era soldier who quashed a rebellion in Guadeloupe by killing 10,000 ex-slaves. The Socialist Mayor, Bertrand Delanoe, decided to rename the area after slain slave leaders, but his conservative foes of course regard that very heritage 'patriotically' (Henley). And 1999 saw the New York art scene return to the controversies of a decade earlier, thanks to the Sensation show of British artists at the Brooklyn Museum. Whereas the UK exhibit had caused shocks because it depicted Moors murderer Myra Hindley, in the US – how predictable is this? – the problem was religion and sex. Chris Ofili's depiction of the Virgin Mother, which used dung and representations of women's genitals, riled local

Catholic God-botherers, and a City administration that was gearing a Senatorial campaign towards upstate Catholics, rather than the art-world mavens of New York. As an added teaser, public money was being used to inflate the value of a private collection owned by the high-reactionary Charles Saatchi, and the exhibit was supported by hidden contributions from him and his auction house, all of which made New York City Mayor Rudi Giuliani's bleatings a weird combination of high-conservative prudery and high-Marxist political economy. Meanwhile, the arts establishment generated cynicism amongst smaller, edgier presenters who had never been supported by the elite when in need of help over censorship questions, while Ofili and his team were careful not to show UK materials that really *would* have offended, such as his depictions of Michael Jordan and Tiger Woods superimposed on legshots from pornography (Barrett; Salz 'Chris' and 'At'; Pollock; C. Carr 'The Bad'; Ratman). The question of hidden subsidies led to further scandal when it was revealed that the Guggenheim's decision to showcase Giorgio Armani's clothes followed hard on his decision to give it millions of dollars. The Metropolitan Museum subsequently dropped plans for a Coco Chanel retrospective once it became public knowledge that her company had offered US$1.5 million towards the cost (Horyn). Great anxiety emerged at the venerable Detroit Institute of Arts that same year. For two days, the modern gallery featured a toy Messiah-with-condom, a stack of faeces, a urine specimen, and a nut with a racist term inscribed on it. In each case, the artist, Jef J. Bourgeau, was referencing other artists, including Ofili, to make a point about the fame these workers had attained. The exhibit was summarily removed, for fear of shocking the Detroit community (Meredith). Meanwhile, the New York Board of Regents was unimpressed by a proposed Museum of Sex 'because the term ... made a mockery of the institution of the museum' (Kimmelman E1). And in India, the Government ordered removal of a painting from Delhi's National Gallery of Modern Art that depicted a naked Icarus on the locally historic Ashoka pillar ('Indian'). These exhibition histories encourage us to walk away from the conventional binary of museum discourse of diversion versus elevation, indicating that the political-economic conditions of existence and interactivity at museums should be in our analytic toolbox. To exemplify such methods, we engage now in a site visit.

Fremantle Prison Museum

Thirty years ago, most prisons from the convict era in Australia were in disuse or had been transformed for other purposes. Since then, many have become museums, both major sites of national significance and small local-historical society displays. These two forms serve dual functions: the historicization of Australia, and the differentiation of contemporary penology from its 'uncivilized' past (Tony Bennett *Birth* 154–55). This relates to the sense of filling-in place and time in Australian social narratives, countering the popular argument that 'Australia has a blank where its historical consciousness might have been' (Bann 103).

For a dozen years until the closure of the Fremantle Prison in November 1991, a small Prison Museum existed there, its official mission 'to inform the public of the important part the prison system and prisoners throughout the State have played in the development of Western Australia and to emphasise the contrast between the historical attitudes to prisoners and the present pro-grammes devised to assist and help them' (*Policy* 23). We can discern here the two great wings of museum activity flapping energetically and demonstratively. First, the implied visitor is given a proper perspective on the site's history and the visitor's place in it. And second, a prior, non-Enlightenment age of dark-ness is compared unfavorably with today. Visitors learn of a time when there was no structural homology between crime and its punishment. This time was in our own physical space and is part of our transcended and regrettable heritage. We can learn from it, but it is definitely over. Such an understanding, that we now live in a better moment, activates historical citizenship. Fremantle Prison is rendered as a strictly delimited ethical zone of the historical citizen, who can sift out the good, the bad and the sublime in past treatment of prison-ers, noting discontinuities and linearities in a movement towards present, enlightened standards.

The citizen-addressee at a site such as Fremantle is in a complicated position. Consider the Western Australian State Planning Commission's 1988 Draft Conservation and Management Plan for the Prison. The Plan begins by divid-ing possible futures for the area into the grand binary of citizenship: 'OPPOR-TUNITY' and 'RESPONSIBILITY'. The Prison is announced as critical to the State's heritage, a 'cultural asset [whose] recycling is a major responsibility'. Virtually all colonial convict establishments around the world had been decommissioned and destroyed by 1988. In contrast, here was a functioning relic, 'possibly the State's most important heritage item'. So this zone describes the 1850s. The 1980s idea, following desires expressed by the City of Fremantle, was that the former gaol be an economic site once the last prisoners had gone, a 'city within a city' (*Fremantle Prison Management* 1–3). It emerged as a leased profit-making venture reporting to a Trust and a State government authority. In 2001, the Museum's web page describe it as 'Western Australia's premier heritage site' and 'a complex for community, commercial and government use'. The public adaptation of history – where a disciplining tenet of capitalism becomes both a commodity and a site for the controlled functioning of public memory – has corollaries in its historio-graphic bearings.

Here is the official description of the Prison's nineteenth-century architectural significance:

> As part of the changing attitude of Britain towards colonial administration, the Women's Prison indicated the new values attached to the imprisoning of women. It had its own walls, more intricate and delicate ornament, individual yards to cells and generally a less restricting environment. It was later adapted for use as a facility for the 'mentally confused'. (3.1)

The document describes incremental increases to exercise space, and the development of rehabilitation plans in the 1900s, once Australia has cast off from its constitutional status as a colony of Great Britain, and is free of direct associations of working people with forced convict immigration. Human labor is reconfigured as reusable and capable of ethical improvement. The state is coming to be loveable for its forgiveness and its powers of transmogrification, that special ameliorating capacity to build new persons where once dross alone resided. But we are, significantly, seeing this occur in buildings described as 'fine examples of the Royal Engineers' Georgian Style' (3.1). This exemplifies the regressive political project of 'a fabric-based heritage textuality' characteristic of Australian prison museums (Garton-Smith).

The actual use-and-exchange-value of 'the Royal Engineers' Georgian Style' as a site of human labor and human incarceration are lost in history. They have attained 'Architectural and Technological Significance' (3.1), i.e. sign-value. But such processes of reification always have targets for humanization, ironically enough. And here, we are told, the very architecture is a 'Demonstration of a way of life' (3.2), a central aspect – both material and cultural-cartographic – of Fremantle. The State Planning Commission advises that the Prison buildings 'represent a well integrated element in the fabric of the city' (3.3). This plan was promulgated in 1988, two hundred years after the English invaded Australia. That year, the Prison was 'occupied' (a quaint term to describe a reversal of control by people whose lives were contained within the Prison): set alight in violent protest at the conditions of everyday life. We find no reference to these conditions in the text; no reference to the tiny rooms, the pails for defecation, or the two open toilets amongst several hundred men left out in the elements for nine hours a day, each day of the year.

We can see more of the same in policies adopted by Western Australia's Building Management Authority (James Semple Kerr). The Authority allocates the Prison 'significance' on the basis of international and national comparisons and the thirteen reports written about it. This significance is again to do with the Prison's location amongst imperial and colonial public works: its degree of intactness, the symbolism of its development (acknowledging convict labor in an anonymous way), the authorship-functions of its (specified, named) engineers and governors, its artworks, and finally its landscape value (4). The document makes concessions to the complexities of a graffito that reads 'Jim Brown is well liked because he is gorgeous', supplemented by 'but not as gorgeous as Billy Little' – graffiti from a guard's watch-tower post (16). And the Authority endorses Aboriginal participation in determining the definition and preservation of the site's heritage (21). But it is ultimately dedicated to a reificatory and non-relational historicity.

What is implied about the ethical zone of the present? The Museum's visitor pamphlet calls this place the 'most wonderful monument of our history'. It says: 'We trust that you enjoy your visit'. The first 'We' ('our history') is the people of Western Australia, historical citizens who securely look back at the human cruelty and architectural grandeur of their predecessors. These citizens have not been prisoners, of course (although there may be convict lineage somewhere). The second 'We' ('We trust') is the managers of the Prison now, 'many of whom were prison officers'. Redundancy becomes a heritage-inspired line on a curriculum vitae. This is advertised as a means to 'maintain this most wonderful monument of our history'. Between these 'We'-categories, it becomes possible, within just fifty lines of writing in a pamphlet, to say what was just quoted, and to highlight spaces the Prison once set aside for flogging and hanging. That section of the document ends with: 'We trust that you enjoy your visit'. Meanwhile, for those interested in virtual touring, a convict database and a list of everybody hanged by the state are available on-line, all part of the administrators' desire to attain World Heritage Listing.

This ethical zone divides the rotten from the good, the past from the present, the oppressive from the enlightened, the contemporary law-abider from the historic law-breaker, and, critically, the museum visitor from the contemporary citizen. The zone operates via a strange structural homology; strange in that it might be expected to produce some identification with imprisonment and a sense of responsibility for the process. But nothing of the sort occurs for many visitors. The homology is what Barbara Kirshenblatt-Gimblett has dubbed the intercalculation of 'two different quotidians' (410). The prisoner's day is redisposed for the tourist, crushed into an hour. It becomes a voluntary sentence, undergone to differentiate the good from the bad in society and its governmental-carceral history.

A tour of the Prison reveals spaces dedicated to mass nudity, strip-searching, public showering and shitting, freezing cold, boiling heat and constant surveillance. Visitors are reassured at every point that this was the past, and are shown murals by prisoners telling Aboriginal stories, but they are not told the appalling statistics of the incarceration of Aboriginal Australians, who make up 3% of the State's population and 40% of its prisoners. On the trip there that one of us made, a guide referred to 'en suites' in the new prison contained in what she termed 'so-called cells', and one fellow-tripper said of the prisoners' art, 'so talented even though they were in here'. This was prior to a recitation of systems for murdering people in the gaol through capital punishment. No tasks confronted the contemporary citizen here. At Fremantle Prison, and in the domain of punishment now, there is no work to be done. Mistreatment of prisoners is a thing of the past, subject to progressive eradication up to November 1991. Then the *civiliter mortuus* (civilly dead) were transferred to a 'new-era' facility, more thoroughly, electronically, panoptic. Visitors to the Museum are, paradoxically, disarticulated from the materiality of what is done to prisoners in their name.

In the old Fremantle space, an ethical zone encourages consideration of how people were once 'treated' by the state. The zone values the contemporary and will not criticize it. Once we were wrong, which merely serves to confirm we are now right. The museum tells us this through a range of interpretative options:

Religion

The Prison is a shrine commemorating crime and justice, meted out in concert with the revised Judaeo-Christian ethic of nineteenth-century England: progressive incarceration. Redemption can be earned and granted. (It is significant that Father Brian Gore spoke to the question of Aboriginal incarceration at the decommissioning of the Prison.)

Psychoanalysis

The social represses its anti-social side. But this is not merely a suppression of sons who have transgressed the law of the Father-state. It represses guilt-laden reminders to those outside the gaol but inside the law. Why else would Western Australia need to lock up such a huge proportion of the Aboriginal population who have survived genocide?

Cosmetics

Georgian engineering, combined with prison graffiti and heritage historicizing, make for an aesthetic experience. They underwrite the essentially fetishized nature of a visiting experience designed to calibrate a social space so that it ceases to be connected to current penal practice, and is instead a *cordon sanitaire*, a cleansed, beatified and beautified object of architectural and commemorative interest.

Voyeurism

The gallows experience at Fremantle, with re-enacted furnishings, stories of interstate travel by anonymous hangmen, and the ghoulish delight-in-alterity expressed by visitors, is deeply fetishistic.

Jacques Derrida is quite right to require of a monument that 'imposes itself by recalling and cautioning' that it also 'tell us, teach us, or ask us something about its own possibility' (230). But museum officials have not read him. They call for 'pastoral care' and 'total immersion experiences' (quoted in Sorensen 66). For if we cannot escape either touristic commodification or ethical incompleteness, we might expect that museums reflect on their own history and *raisons d'être* as the price of our admission. In place of diversion versus elevation, interactivity at the site of the museum should be our underpinning philosophy. This would merge the 'resonance' and 'wonder' that Greenblatt commends as the way to comprehend museums: a compound that locates us in the present as part of our social formation, even as it asks us to pause and be struck with the singular occasion of our visit ('Resonance' 42).

Clearly, museums function as both national and international sites for formulating memory and generating tourism, as spaces of both national imagery and pride and monetary return. As such, they blend the patriotic and the neoliberal, in much the same way as the international organizations visited in the next chapter.

5

Transnational Cultural Policy

At this early stage in the WTO, we in developed countries should question why we are promoting a global trading order at all. Is it to make people in the world more like us, or more truly like themselves. – Chi Carmody, 1999 (238)

This chapter examines the global institutional framework for cultural policy: organizations affiliated with the United Nations and regional trading blocs. In an era of increasing immigration and textual trade, reflected in the NICL, the legal and economic arrangements determining the circulation of culture are frequently as important as national policies, while attempts by bodies such as the EU to create a united states of Europe have inevitably turned from a purely economic unity to a politico-cultural one.

Such concerns are by no means new, and they draw us back to the doctrine of ethical incompleteness outlined in our Introduction. The Sixth Assembly of the League of Nations, held in 1925, adopted a resolution that set out quite clearly the need for media policies that would deal with the propensity of citizens to act intemperately as a collectivity. '[T]he Press' was identified as a tool in the search for 'that moral disarmament which is a concomitant condition of material disarmament' via the 'tranquillisation of public opinion' ('Collaboration'). Twenty years later, this time as a reaction against the successes of Nazi propaganda, the United Nations, the League's successor, passed a resolution on freedom of information that stressed the need for a 'diversity of sources of news and opinion'. This was a *quid pro quo* from the media for the 'privileges derived from the people' via use of the airwaves and public trust ('Final'). In each case, there is a double quality to 'the people' – they are a device to legitimate policy and the object *of* that policy.

Contemporary international law is clearly committed to cultural pluralism as part of the equality of sovereign states; culture as a human right; and the value of diversity to the proliferation of competing ideas. The law is an important site for challenging the hegemony of neoliberal doctrine on this matter (Carmody 240, 242–43). Such sentiments were generated and promoted by the victorious West after each world war. But once they had been modernized and democratized to suit the Third World, these same precepts provoked intense controversy and the destabilization of international cultural diplomacy. 'Diversity' was reinterpreted away from the market and towards notions of equitable coverage of world news and exchange of world cultures (referred to as 'new equilibrium and greater reciprocity'), with racism and economic inequality particular targets ('Declaration' 177). The doctrine of free flow of information drew popular ire, as the South came to regard it as 'serving the interests of the most powerful countries and transnational corporations and helping them secure economic and cultural domination' (MacBride and Roach 4).

In the 1950s, modernity was set up by the First World for the Third as something to be striven for via the implementation of policies and programs by governments and capital in what were variously named 'developing countries', 'the Third World' and other teleological marks. This desirable condition was designated as a complex imbrication of industrial, economic, social and political development. The founders and husbands of this discourse were First-World political scientists and economists, mostly associated with US universities, research institutes and corporations, or with international organizations. Amongst the foundational premises of this modernity was the formation of nationalism and individual/state sovereignty as habits of thought. The 'modern individual' would not be prey to the temptations of Marxism-Leninism. Development necessitated the displacement of 'particularistic norms' of tradition by 'more universalistic' blends of the modern, as part of the creation of an 'achievement-oriented' society (Pye 19). The successful importation of media technologies and forms of communication would be a critical component in this replicant figure, with elite sectors of society trained as exemplars for a wider populace supposedly mired in backward, folkloric forms of thought that lacked the trust in national organizations required for modernization.

Apart from its unreconstructed narcissism, this set of precepts disavowed the existing international division of labor and the success of imperial and commercial powers in annexing states and/or their labor forces. A rather implausibly solipsistic policy model, it was initially supplemented from within the paradigm, by a more locally sensitive acknowledgement of conflicts over wealth, influence and status. Then it was comprehensively challenged from outside the paradigm, by theories of dependent development, underdevelopment, unequal exchange, world-systems history, center-periphery relations and cultural or media imperialism. Whilst these positions had disagreements and differences, they shared the view that the transfer of technology, politics and economics had become unattainable: the emergence of multinational corporations had produced a unified interest between business and government at the center in search of cheap labor, new markets, and pliant regimes on the margin of a globe spinning as a Northern Hemisphere top (Reeves 24–25, 30). Whilst there is clear evidence of the formation of indigenous *bourgeoisies* – frequently inside significant gender and ethnic boundaries – the general inequality of capital flows continues to dog most societies (Fröbel et al.). And these trends have their cultural corollaries/animations.

The export of modernization always ignored the way in which the very life of the modern had been defined in colonial and international experience, both by differentiating the metropole from the periphery and by importing ideas, fashions, and people back to the core. (Consider anxieties evident in the early instruction to the British Board of Film Classification that 'white men may not be shown in a state of degradation amidst native surroundings' (quoted in Martin Barker 11).) The model was also inflected with many of the assumptions of evolutionary thought, not only in its narcissism, but its very search for hidden unanimities that would bind humanity in singular directions and forms of development. That search enabled the owners of this discourse to observe themselves in an earlier stage of maturation, by investigating life in the Southern Hemisphere, and to police and coordinate what they found there, in keeping with a drive towards uniformity and optimality of human definition, achievement and organization (Axtmann 64–65).

The widespread reaction against racist and self-seeking – or at best patronizing – discourses of modernization has foregrounded the international capitalist media as critical components in both the formation of public taste in commodities, mass culture, and forms of economic and political organization in the Third World, and the links permitting ruling classes and states in the metropole to run the global economy. Examples include US export of screen products and distribution systems and dominance of international communications technology and infrastructure – the transfer of taste seems more profound and widespread than the transfer of the means of communication. A rhetoric of development through commercialism overtakes and decelerates the promotion of a local economy. The stronger the claim to the modern in, particularly, advertising, the weaker the allocation of resources to actual modernization. In avant-garde fashion, the postmodern cart-before-horse rhetoric of advertising appears in the Third World prior to its manifestation in the post-industrial states. Emergent ruling classes in dependent nations trade off local power against their own reliance on foreign capital and ideology (Reeves 30–35).

In the context of European reconstruction and US–USSR rivalry, accompanied by a cultural Cold War, the Non-Aligned Movement (NAM), sought a 'positive position' beyond being 'pro-communist or anti-communist', as Indian Prime Minister Pandit Nehru said at it foundational Bandung Conference in 1955. The NAM helped realize the 1960 UN Declaration of a 'speedy and unconditional end [to] colonialism in all its forms and manifestations' (United Nations). This entailed cultural decolonization within national frameworks. For many, cultural redefinition was crucial for changing the system of power relations between what came to be seen as the North and the South (Elmandjra). Such redefinition also entailed transforming the global flow of communications and information, especially since these were seen as necessary not only for sovereignty, but also for economic development. We might ask if this is still not the case when more than 80% of global communications, information, and entertainment distribution is in the hands of four or five conglomerates located in the North, notwithstanding their transnational web of administration. As García Canclini explains, the emergence of national media enterprises in Latin

American countries promoted 'modernization through import substitution and the upgrading of industry in each country [and] even the most internationalized agents at this point in time [the 1940s–1960s] – like TV and advertising – beckoned us to buy national products and encouraged the dissemination of local knowledge' (93). Now even Latin American media conglomerates like Televisa (Mexico) and Rede Globo (Brazil), not to speak of transnational cable and satellite companies, promote a global culture of consumption.

García Canclini has written that Latin Americans may be underdeveloped as producers of media, but they are *overdeveloped* as consumers. This statement should lead to a reconsideration of the old connection between culture and development. Not only has developmentalism not led to an improvement in distribution, it has worsened it. For all its enormous increase in trade and wealth creation, globalization has widened the income gap in comparison to the 1960s ('Nafta Widens'). Despite several decades of developmentalism, 'there persist marked ethnic, regional and national differences among Latin American countries. And we no longer believe that modernization will do away with them' (García Canclini 141).

The incorporation of newly independent states in the 1960s shifted the emphasis from using culture to foster Third World cooperation in the post-war period to enabling rational development. In 1969, UNESCO commissioned a series of *Studies and Documents on Cultural Policies*. While stating that UNESCO should not assume the role of 'defin[ing] the cultural policy of States', it did emphasize 'cultural development': (i) to integrate cultural policy into general planning; (ii) to emphasize the duty of the State to replace private initiative in the public sphere; (iii) to decentralize and delegate, nevertheless, the administration of culture to relatively autonomous cultural institutions; and (iv) to 'strengthen awareness of nationhood', especially in developing countries (UNESCO 'Cultural Policy' 11).

At the same time, a cultural imperialism thesis argued that the US, as the world's leading audiovisual exporter, was transferring its dominant value system to others, with a corresponding diminution in the vitality and standing of local languages and traditions, and hence a threat to national identity. Cultural imperialism is isomorphic to other forms of imperialism, in that it manufactures the transfer of taste rather than technology or investment. As Herbert Schiller expressed it, 'the media–cultural component in a developed, corporate economy supports the economic objectives of the decisive industrial-financial sectors (i.e. the creation and extension of the consumer society)'. US involvement in South-East Asian wars during the 1960s led to broader critiques of US intervention in anti-insurrectionist struggles of national liberation, and its 'interpenetration between the military-industrial complex and the communications industry'. It was noted that communications and cultural multinational corporations enabled the more general expansion of multinationals in addition to being substantial powerbrokers with links to military domination. Major studies derived from this insight looked at US control of world media, the role of international press agencies, TV program flow and village and corporate values. In Latin America, dependency theory emerged as a vital break from North American functionalist sociology and its attendant free-flow of communication paradigm.

Armand and Michèle Mattelart, veterans of Allende's experiments in demo-cratizing the media, and these anti-US paradigms, now argue that the cultural imperialism position was an enabling alliance of intellectual engagement rather than a sustainable theory. It served to mobilize people to think through the implications of the internationalization of textuality by drawing attention to the need for local audits of the relations between nations (especially small states), the US, and former colonizers, and to the significance of technologi-cal exports and transfers of taste. It is not surprising that this concentration on the inequality of exchange emphasized directions in flow rather than signs and their reception. But the accusation of cultural imperialism offered a way of bringing local culture to bear in resistance to the imperializing logics of neoclassical economics and its heroization of the sovereign consumer. It also exemplifies the export of theory itself from the Third World to the First (Mattelart and Mattelart 175–77). It is an enthymimetic shibboleth to argue that the founders of the doctrine believed in a simple effects model and were unaware of complex forces of internal *comprador* classes, post-colonial ties or interpretative audiences (Roach 49). In any event, the paradigm's rise and fall coincided with the centrality of UNESCO to world debate on the global, and so we turn now to that institution.

UNESCO

The United Nations Charter (1945) and its Universal Declaration on Human Rights (1948) specify unacceptable forms of discrimination against people by states, and UNESCO is charged with implementing global cultural policy for the UN. Language is included on the list, along with religion, sex and race. The retention of language is thus a human right, and this has led to numerous covenants, such as the 1966 International Covenant on Civil and Political Rights and the 1975 Helsinki Accords (Schmidt 146–47), and arguing struggles within the Organization over a Draft Universal Declaration of Linguistic Rights, an NGO initiative dating from the mid-1990s (Maffi).

In 1954, UNESCO enshrined its attitude to art and the state in *The Convention for the Protection of Cultural Property in the Event of Armed Conflict*. The *Convention* works from the assumption of a universal heritage in the form of art, such that its theft as a consequence of military action is a crime against humanity. *Contra* this proposition stands a cultural-nationalist view that people have a special relationship to art based on origin, not location or ownership. UNESCO's 1970 *Convention on the Means of Prohibiting and Preventing the Illicit Import, Export and Transfer of Ownership of Cultural Property* focuses not on the global demesne, but the property laws of specific sovereign-states. At different moments, postcolonial nations have called on each of these logics in their struggles with First World theft of artifacts. The fruitful contradictions between these positions come out in their incapacity to deal with emergent identities, where social change and hybridization bring into question either universalism or myths of origin (Coombe 220–23). In 1956, UNESCO put forward its 'Recommendation on International Principles Applicable to Archaeological Excavations', and in 1972 a *Convention Concerning the Protection of the World Cultural and National Heritage*. These instruments have suffered from prolix prose that is difficult to articulate with national legislation, and the absence of any mechanism of enforcement. Nevertheless, several museums have adopted similar codes (Whisnant 310). Salient debates revolve around the relative merits of art forms and customary traditions, interest in cross-cultural knowledge, the desire to own artifacts of other cultures, and global economic inequality (McNaughton 22). Disputes about cultural artifacts generally arise over three claims: restitution of objects to their original owners; restriction of export and import; and rights of ownership, access, inheritance, maintenance and interpretation. Ideas of universal ownership of a collective past contend with specific interests of indigenous peoples and capitalist investors (Warren 2–3). And the issues have spread internationally. For example, the market for Mayan artifacts, once essentially restricted to New York, Texas, and Los Angeles, now includes Japan and Australia, which are notorious sites for trafficking. UNESCO works closely with the International Council for Museums to deal with such lawlessness (Pendergast and Graham 58; Herscher 118–19).

The United States followed UNESCO practice in a 1970 treaty with Mexico and a 1981 compact with Peru on the return of stolen cultural property, followed by the 1982 Cultural Property Law and an arrangement with El Salvador (Whisnant 310–11; Hingston 129; Lou Harris 165). In 1993, the US Government imposed emergency restrictions on the importation of antiquities from Mali, principally artifacts from the Tellem Caves and clay sculptures from the inland Niger delta. The limitations were in accord with the 1970 *Convention*, but they were the first instance of a major First World art importer applying the ban to exports from an African country. Alpha Oumar Konaré, President of Mali at the time, once presided over the International Council of Museums. He emphasized the importance to the Republic of the struggle against illegal archaeology, appreciating the stand of the US given the prestige on the international museum circuit that goes with such holdings. In this instance, the very materials of a people, their customary and artistic heritage, had been placed within a market system of value connected to the seemingly benign operation of aesthetic relativism. The outcome was a blow to the artifactual history of a nation. Mali's sovereignty was then mobilized as a protocol by an international organization to prevent such losses. Prevailing museum policies in the US assisted this safeguarding. The cultural politics of the situation revolved around four material pressures: the desires of wealthy foreigners to own these objects; the poverty of traditional owners; a push towards global appreciation of cultural production; and the notion of cultural maintenance. It is telling that the US does not offer equivalent cultural protection to its own people, with the exception of Native Americans via the Native American Graves Protection and Repatriation Act (McNaughton; Clément; Zolberg 'Museum' 11; Messenger xv). And the decision to ratify the UNESCO protocols came after art dealers and collectors in the US had carefully ratcheted down the force of these provisions, protecting their investments and ensuring that prices for grand treasures would render them market entities, beyond the scope of public purchase (Harkavy). Again, an appreciation of the problem necessitates some attempt to comprehend the shifting politics of the market, nationalism, textuality and social meaning.

As noted earlier, UNESCO became the key site of these Third World claims in the 1970s, as the poorer nations' numerical majority enabled them to gain control of the Organization. It became the culturalist and Third World answer to Western economic and political domination. This in turn opened up the opportunity for a New World Information and Communication Order (NWICO), the cultural version of the New International Economic Order that the South was arguing for in the United Nations Conference on Trade and Development. NWICO addressed systematic inequalities in reports about the Third World as filtered by Western news agencies, the flow of TV programs, the lack of technology transfer in ownership terms even as there was increased penetration of that technology, and the impact of advertising in creating false needs amongst the poor (MacBride and Roach 6).

UNESCO sponsored a series of studies and conferences critical of multinational capital, arguing amongst other things for journalistic reporting that was sensitive to local issues rather than corporate news needs. This led to a backlash from First World journalists, media institutions, and governments, to the point where the reactionary Reagan and Thatcher regimes removed the US and Britain from UNESCO, battering its budget in the process. Weakened in turn by the neoliberal tide sweeping international organizations from the 1980s, UNESCO retreated to a much less powerful position on cultural policy, although it did convene a Global Decade for Cultural Development from 1988 to 1997, in the name of a multi-ethnic definition and appreciation of culture, and genuine diversity across business, education, and the state, plus the formation of cultural policy with an eye to the impact of globalization on the state and the market (UNESCO *Background*). But basically, UNESCO fell among the rubble of history. Other institutions, both old and new, picked up those ruins and commodified them.

GATT AND WTO

Cultural identity was not at issue. – World Trade Organization Decision, 1990s (quoted in Carmody 239)

In the 1986–93 round of talks towards the last General Agreement on Tariffs and Trade (GATT) the United States unsuccessfully took on the rest of the world in a debate over cultural trade, specifically film and television. The US argued from a *laissez-faire* position, that the revelation of consumer preferences should be the deciding factor as to who has comparative advantage in screen production – whether Hollywood or Bergen is the logical place for audiovisual texts to be produced. The US claims there is no room for the public sector in screen production, because it crowds out private investment, which is necessarily more in tune with popular taste. Both the active face of public subvention (national cinemas and broadcasters) and the negative face of public proscription (import barriers to encourage local production) are derided for obstructing market forces. The GATT's successor, the World Trade Organization (WTO), has focused initially on telecommunications and other industries, but is turning its oleaginous hand to culture, with just this agenda.

From its emergence in the late 1940s as one of several new international financial and trading protocols, the GATT embodied in contractual form central aspects of the First World's rules of economic prosperity: non-discrimination, regulations policed outside the terrain of individual sovereign states and multilateralism. It was born under the sign of North American growth evangelism, whereby standardized methods, vast scales of production, and an endless expansion of markets would be the engine of economic recovery and development for the Western European *detritus* of the Second World War. It is part of a long wave of restructuring capitalism.

The GATT stood for the paradoxically bureaucratic voice of neoclassical economics, dedicated to free trade in a way that transcended national interests and opposed state intervention. Officials worked like puritans ordered by manifest destiny to disrupt trading blocs and restrict distortions to the putatively natural rhythms of supply and demand, as determined by consumer sovereignty and comparative advantage. Needless to say, idealist, pristine forms of theorization routinely enunciate specific material interests. In this instance, a US agenda was suited by such arrangements until Japan and Western Europe became powerful economic agents capable of making some rules of their own. By the late 1980s, the seemingly transcendental nature of marginalist economics, which set up good/bad antinomies in the form of liberalism versus mercantilism, became a conditional argument, to be used as and when it suited the purposes of its self-interested enunciators (the US was extremist in one direction over cinema and television, in another on agriculture). The highly moral mode of the GATT itself became its legalistic ruination, as new forms of protectionism appeared, via non-tariff implements and industry policy, to match the varied positions of member-states.

As early as the 1940s, the US sought full coverage of cinema by the GATT, and inclusion of TV from the early 1960s, but other signatories insisted on exemption of the screen industries to permit quotas on foreign films, and early charters acknowledged the legitimacy of screen monopolies for cultural reasons. Clearly, the framers perceived a crucial distinction between culture and other

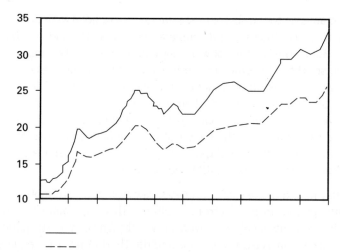

Total exports + imports as a percentage of the value of US GDP

Figure 5   *Growing importance of trade in the US Economy*

	1997	1998	1999	2000*	99–00*	90–00*
Exports:		Billions of Dollars			Percent Change	
Total (BOP basis)	257.2	262.7	271.9	295.0	8.5	99.5
Travel	73.4	71.3	74.9	84.8	13.3	97.2
Passenger Fares	20.9	20.1	19.8	21.3	7.9	39.5
Other Transportation	27.0	25.6	27.0	29.9	10.7	36.0
Royalties and Licensing Fees	33.6	36.2	36.5	37.7	3.3	120.3
Other Private Services	84.5	90.9	96.5	106.0	9.8	163.0
Transfers under U.S. Military Sales Contracts	16.8	17.6	16.3	14.5	−11.5	49.1
US Government Miscellaneous Services	1.0	0.9	0.9	0.8	−4.2	21.1

*Annualized based on January-November 2000 data.

SOURCE: Office of the US Trade Representative, 2001

Figure 6   *US Services Exports*

commodities (Jarvie 38–39; Carmody 255, 258). But the stakes grew higher over time. The services sector of the developed world expanded massively over the 1990s, to the point where it comprised 70% of gross domestic product in the industralized nations and 50% in much of the Third World, accounting for US$1 trillion a year in trade, perhaps a fifth of the global total (Drake and Nicolaïdis 37; 'A Disquieting' 55). The GATT was slow to notice this growth, in part due to neoclassical dogma, and because the technological limitations of the 'human' side to the sector (restaurants, for example) were not especially amenable to conceptualizing and enumerating what was frequently object-free exchange. But as the Western powers saw capital fly from their manufacturing zones, and sought to become net exporters of textuality, they discovered ways of opening up the area to bureaucratic invigilation. Trade in Services (TIS) was found to comprise, *inter alia*, film, television, and advertising production and distribution (Sjolander 54 n. 5; Grey 6–9). The Punta del Este Declaration of September 1986 put TIS at the center of GATT debates, because of pressure from the US (always the main player in negotiations) in the service of lobbyists for American Express, Citibank, IBM and Hollywood.

The Uruguay Round of the GATT (1986–93) saw related US attempts to remove state participation from electronic culture. This was almost universally opposed in the name of cultural sovereignty, with significant participation from India, Canada, Japan, Australia, Europe and the Third World. They equated cultural industries with environmental protection or the armed forces, as areas that were inappropriate for the operation of the market.

Western Europe's Community law enshrines freedom of expression through media access – the EU's alibi for putting quotas on US screen texts, along with the claim that the screen is not a good but a service. The EU opposed the idea that the GATT ensure open access to screen markets, on the grounds that culture must be deemed inalienable. To US critics, this was a smokescreen, with cultural rights secreting the protection of inefficient culture industries and outmoded *dirigiste* statism (Kessler; Van Elteren 'GATT'; Venturelli 61). A coalition of European artists, intellectuals, and producers also stood against the US.

Members signed a petition in major newspapers calling for culture to be exempt from the GATT's no-holds barred commodification (Van Elteren 'Conceptualizing' 47) in the name of a different figure from the consumer – the citizen (see Chapter 2 and the GEM).

Of course, American negotiators argued that the GATT must 'agree to disagree on motives – cultural sovereignty or business opportunity – and then start negotiating' (quoted in Miller *Well-Tempered Self* 100). The motivation was obvious: 'replacing national societies of culture with a global society of [alleged] efficiency' (Carmody 237).

In January 1995, the WTO replaced the GATT, taking over the latter's *detritus* of GATTocrats. The last gasp of the GATT came with the twenty-thousand page protocols, weighing eight hundred and fifty kilograms, that were agreed in Geneva in 1993, signed in Marrakesh in 1994, and ratified domestically by one hundred and twenty-five members and fellow-travelers the same year. Its effects are felt – through the WTO – beyond its life. The WTO has a legal personality, a secretariat, and biennial ministerial conferences. This machinery makes it easier for multinational corporations to dominate trade via the diplomatic services of their home governments' representatives, to the exclusion of environmental and other matters of public interest, which no longer have the *entrée* that GATT gave via recognition of NGOs. Multinationals now find it easier to be regarded as local firms in their host countries, and Third World agricultural production has been opened up further to foreign ownership (Lang and Hines 48–50; Dobson 573–76).

The WTO's operating protocols stress transparency, Most-Favored Nation precepts, national treatment (imports and local commodities are treated identically), tariffs versus other protective measures, and formal methods of settling disputes. 1997 was the WTO's first major move on cultural policy. It concerned the Canadian version of the US-based magazine, *Sports Illustrated*. The WTO ruled that Canada could not impose tariffs on foreign magazines as a means of enticing local advertisers to support local periodicals, signaling that it will not distinguish between cultural and other commodities – comparative advantage as judged by price should be the arbiter of where texts are produced. Not surprisingly, EU Ministers responsible for Culture and Audiovisual Policy met in 1999 to establish how to prevent the WTO from attaining jurisdiction over their programs, for fear of a roll-back of state support and an increase in US imports. As per the ultimate GATT round, the main claim was that heritage and creativity should be excluded from the WTO. French Minister of Culture Catherine Trautmann accused the US of intimidating prospective WTO members by offering entry in return for audiovisual liberalization (Venturelli 62, 66; Carmody; 'Culture/Audiovisual Council: Should'; Michael Williams 'Lines'). The new US move is to cluster cultural issues under the catch-all rubric of intellectual property, which saw it bring WTO cases against Greece for allowing the rebroadcast of US television programs without regard to copyright. This prodded Athens to legislate on TV copyright, then close down TV stations that broke the law (Venturelli 62, 66; World Trade Organization 51; 'Administration Settles').

Although the General Agreement on Trade in Services (GATS) (the WTO's protocol on TIS from the Uruguay Round) states that there must be easy market access and no differential treatment of national and foreign suppliers of services, it gives room to exempt certain services from these principles. This margin for manoeuver is utilized, for example, by the EU in setting quotas for films (Hoskins et al. 5–7). But since January 2000, the WTO has been conducting GATS 2000, a round of negotiations lasting until the end of 2002 that further addresses the liberalization of goods and services 'to entrench privatization and deregulation worldwide' (Gould) and rein in democratic controls over corporations across a broad swathe of business activity (Sinclair; also see Office of the US Trade Representative). One major issue is virtual goods, as audiovisual services are absorbed into concepts such as electronic commerce, information, and entertainment. The US has been like a child with a toy in the WTO, proud that it has filed more complaints than any other country, and has generally prevailed (Barshefsky). And just in case it should fail to destroy cultural policies through international trading institutions, it has lodged the EU on its internal 'Priority Watch List' for sanctions (USIA). Again, there is the sense of a child, this time keeping a list of most-hated peers and real or imagined 'meanness'.

Today, culture is not just a problem of political pressure – it is one more category for commodification. If the day comes when the United States complains that Japan's ideological objections to organ transplants are non-tariff barriers to the export of the American heart, or takes issue with the French for prohibiting patents on DNA maps on the grounds that they represent an inalienable human heritage, we shall see this debate played out again on less entertaining terrain. For this is the crowded hour of the *first* instance of economic versus cultural determinations; an hour we should all spend contemplating Daniel Singer's splendid oxymoron: 'GATT culture, that is to say, the resistible reign of merchandise' (56).

NAFTA/TLC and MERCOSUR

NAFTA began with a 1989 treaty between Canada and the US to open trade. As noted earlier, at Canada's insistence, culture was exempted from the Agreement, but the US retained the right to retaliate if it was used 'unreasonably', and Canada veered away from utilizing this clause. The same arrangement applies to the 1994 expansion of the Agreement into the Tratado de Libro Comercio Norte Americano with Mexico, though Mexican negotiators claimed that they were not concerned by the prospect of *le défi américain*. Indeed, according to then President Salinas, thirty centuries of cultural tradition dating back to pre-Aztec times would maintain Mexico's autonomy as it upgraded into the First World NAFTA bloc.

Since then, blockbuster US museum exhibitions like *Splendors* (see Chapter 4) have served government interests in the international arena, in this case NAFTA, at least at the level of 'high' culture. The artworks were meant to operate as a medium of negotiation, a form of cultural brokerage. This is evident in Octavio Paz's inaugural lecture for the exhibition, in which he reconciles the 'otherness' of Mexico's past, with the future (present) of its modernity: 'The radical 'otherness' of Mesoamerican civilization is thus transformed into its opposite: thanks to modern aesthetics, these works that seem so distant are also contemporaneous' (19). Not unlike advertising for tourism, catalogue essays for such exhibitions appeal to metropolitan indulgences in a 'comfortable exoticism', with all the luxuries of air conditioning, multi-lane highways and supermodern hotels. In one of those ironic twists that history can subject us to, Paz, who had produced some of the keenest insights into the rhetorical workings of power, became a spokesperson for free trade, the flipside to his assimilation of Mexico's otherness into a grand historical design. In *The Labyrinth of Solitude* and other works, Paz had written that revolution, love, and poetry transcend all antinomies in the self-realization of history. Now that role was bestowed on NAFTA, by his Op-Ed piece for the *New York Times*: 'NAFTA looks like the first step in a grand design. Its goal, therefore, is historical, transcending economics and politics. It is a reply to the terrible challenge of our historical moment, which is being torn asunder by the rebirth of the most ferocious nationalisms'. Purged of its communist specter, this new, neoliberal internationalism would resolve questions of national identity at a higher level. Thus, thirty centuries of Mexican culture could circulate as testimony to a new historical mission: entering the First World.

In capitalist Latin America, the post-dictatorship states of the 1990s settled on a form of regional cultural integration that would unite the continent as per MERCOSUR, the Latin equivalent to the EU that began in 1991 and has an annual Gross National Product across its membership of US$1 trillion (Burges; Galperin 631). This is a response to the realization that an exclusively national approach may hinder the formation of appropriate counters to local and multi-national cultural-commercial processes such as migration, textual piracy and transnational indigenous solidarity. Culture is more than a frosting to this economic community, because intense differences of ethnicity, race, language, and the experience of modernity cross the region. MERCOSUR's 1994 Colonia Protocol liberalizes cross-border investment within the organization, but largely excludes the culture industries, although Argentina permits much more foreign ownership than, for example, Brazil. In 1996, a Cultural Integration Protocol was adopted which sets out the legal infrastructure for cultural integration as a means of increasing economic integration by facilitating the circulation of goods for exhibitions and other cultural events, a writers' exchange, fellow-ships, and culture houses in poorer nations (Galperin 638–39).

At the first meeting of the ministers and secretaries of culture of the member nations, a MERCOSUR *de la Cultura*, or integrated cultural zone, was announced, emphasizing the promotion of Spanish/Portuguese bilingualism in education and other spheres of life, the free circulation of cultural goods and services and a 'cultural cable system for MERCOSUR', largely dedicated to educational and other public programs to familiarize the different countries with each other ('El mercosur de la cultura'). There are, nevertheless, troubling aspects to the cultural integration envisioned at this meeting. In the first place, the basic reason for the creation of a cultural MERCOSUR was the melding of economics and culture, as then Argentine Minister of Culture, Pacho O'Donnell, said. Moreover, trade agreements not only redraw national geographies in ways that exclude certain parts of the member countries (the Brazilian Amazon and Northeast and the Argentine south share little of the dynamism introduced by the agreement), that they also foster the creation of a new imagined community with new constitutive exclusions. Taking the perspective of the new labor migrations in the region, some critics have convincingly argued that the creation of new borders is a retrograde step, sloughing off a southern region from the rest of the South American continent (Grimson 'Comments'), while MERCOSUR's first Visual Arts Biennial in Brazil marked the advent of bilingualism in the south through texts produced in 'portunhol', a mix of Spanish and Portuguese. This hybrid is part of the search for a continental unity, a prerequisite for the legitimacy needed to push for monetary stabilization, regional free trade, and so on.

Given this heterogeneity and competition of interests, is it possible or even desirable to create a Latin American cultural space? Conversations on this topic over the past five years suggest that it is *both* possible *and* desirable, so long as certain pitfalls of national policies are avoided: monopoly by hegemonic centers (i.e. Brazil, Mexico and Argentina; or Spain in the Ibero-American case), minoritization of certain groups and their subordinated incorporation on that basis, and surrender to market imperatives, which should not be understood as synonymous with exclusion of the culture industries, as Getino never tires of pointing out. It should be said that those interested in democratization are quite hesitant about inviting the culture industries to the cultural-policy table. However, they do have the resources that are lacking in the absence of significant government subsidy, and it is also recognized that they have a better track record of attracting 'popular audiences' than the tiny public for the arts or folk culture. It should be remembered that in many Latin American societies, where functional and even complete illiteracy can still reach 30% or more of the population, the authority of public culture passed almost immediately from the oral to the audiovisual 'without crossing the intermediary stage of the written word' (Coelho 19).

As in the US, economic integration has not bettered the conditions for migrant workers, who are minoritized much like Mexican workers in the US or extra-communitarians in the new Europe. This is the case for Bolivian migrants who seek work in Argentina and whose presence, coincident with the waning of class-based politics, has led Argentines to speak publicly of ethnic and racial difference for the first time since the consolidation of an immigrant national identity in the early twentieth century (Grimson *Relator* 177–89). Cultural integration, if taken in a wider sense than the usual showcasing of the arts, as in the MERCOSUR Biennial examined below, would provide a forum for discussion of transborder minoritization and discrimination. As laid out by García Canclini and the architects of Arte Sem Fronteira's integration project, a Latin American cultural space has specific policies for the democratic inclusion of all constituencies.

But most of MERCOSUR's cultural efforts have thus far been concentrated on the arts, for elite showcasing, and on communications, from a business perspective, leaving aside other forms of cultural expression. Indeed, despite the salience of the MERCOSUR Biennial's focus on education, the project is conceived as 'taking culture to the people'. The attention paid to 'community culture' does not necessarily solve the problem of outreach. It may instead institutionalize cultural difference and transform it into an even more instrumentalized resource. In any case, the reason why the business elites from the city of Porto Alegre, capital of the southern-most Brazilian state, sponsored this mega-art event, including over nine hundred works by three hundred artists and costing US$6 million, is that the arts are an excellent form of PR, and in this case, largely at public expense, since the Fundação Bienal de Artes Visuais do Mercosul was able to take advantage of enormous fiscal incentives amounting to over US$3.5 million plus an extra US$1.25 million in Federal funds (Barbosa). Justo Werlang, local businessman, art collector, and President of the Foundation that organized the Biennial, acknowledged that the MERCOSUR trade agreement was a strategy for Southern-Cone competitiveness in global processes that are otherwise led by the US. But economic competition, according to Werlang, is not enough; the economic has to be facilitated by the intermediation of culture. There has to be cultural integration, meaning by this mutual knowledge and respect ('Entrevista'). In other words, the very idea that MERCOSUR is oppositional within (not *to*) the struggle for hegemony in the global economy – for example, in opposition to the Free Trade Area of the Americas (FTAA), disseminated hemispherically by the US and centered in Miami, an analogously emerging art and culture center described in Chapter 2 – has to take root in culture.

Herein lies the gist of Luis Camnitzer's excellent critique, an unusual *rapprochement* of anti-imperialist discourse and neoliberal economic strategies. The three themes of the Biennial – politics, constructivism and cartography – not only provide a platform for an oppositional cultural politics to US and European hegemony but demonstrate that culturally the Southern Cone, and by extension Latin America, does not have any reason to envy the North. Curator-general Federico Morais cites Henry Kissinger at the very beginning of his catalogue essay in order to disprove in what follows the stupid remark that 'nothing important ever came from the South; history is never made in the South' (Morais 12). Of course, the very denial of subordinate status inevitably performs that status. Nevertheless, the political dimension points up the struggle against capital accumulation strategies devised in the North that underdevelop the South, as well as the disparities and injustices that arise due to local dynamics. Morais writes that '[d]aily life in Latin America is contaminated by politics, by social and economic problems. We are always conversing about inflation, recession, corruption, death squads, the extermination of Indians and children, child prostitution, the landless and homeless, kidnappings, political violence, etc. Beyond regional and historical differences, what we have in common is that emerging character of problems. Thus it is often impossible for Latin American artists to abandon their context in the name of a presumably universal, atemporal and ahistorcial language' (Morais 17).

The second theme, the constructivist dimension, points up a different role for Latin American culture *vis-à-vis* Europe and the US. The constructivist legacy, exhibited quite lavishly in the exhibition, demonstrates that Latin American artists, especially from the Southern Cone and Venezuela, not only contributed to that legacy but also took it in directions relatively unexplored elsewhere. On this view, the South has its own expression of modernity. Finally, the focus on alternative cartography, rooted in Joaquín Torres-García's 'Upside-down-map' (1943), a visual expression of the motto *nuestro norte es nuestro sur* ('our North is our South'), conveys the will to displace the hegemonic North.

Camnitzer points out that under Morais' curatorship, the artworks were not grouped by 'national divisions' and were instead 'organiz[ed according to] an expressive fabric in terms of aspects', thus approximating an imagined community thought to be necessary for economic integration. The Bienal would contribute to this imagined community by providing a space for the 'exchange of people, ideas and values that only culture knows how to provide' (Britto). This idea is given clearer expression by the Secretary of Culture of the State of Estado do Rio Grande do Sul: 'This endeavor, by paying tribute to Latin American creativity, places the State of Rio Grande do Sul squarely in the center of the movement to cultural integration that should guide the consolidation of MERCOSUR' (Boeira). The web site for the second edition of the MERCOSUR Biennial in 1999 stresses the 'diversity and plurality, the significant differences in the artistic and cultural production of the countries' to be integrated in the trade agreement ('Bienal do MERCOSUL'). The curator of the second edition, Fábio Magalhães, stresses the idea that globalization forces regions to consolidate in order to survive: 'Some have seen globalization as contributing to the loss of identity, but I believe that even if globalization weakens national political and economic action, it also strengthens regional and local cultures' (Moraes). Magalhães thus maintained the focus on resistance, but deepened the sense of a specific regional identity.

But MERCOSUR may falter alongside the truly 'grand design' of the US to expand NAFTA/TLC into FTAA, and the disastrous impact of privatization on the Argentine economy. Cultural integration is poised to become a major engine of activity and capital accumulation. Founded on the principles of human rights and cultural diversity, as overseen by UNESCO, MERCOSUR and Ibero-Americanism stand as counter-initiatives to US-led trade in cultural production and services. The headway made in these initiatives makes it possible that Latin American countries will not be locked into exclusive arrangements with the US.

EU

'[E]ver closer union among the peoples of Europe' – the goal set out in the Rome and Maastricht Treaties: how to make Europeans of the heterogeneous and traditionally fiercely nationalistic peoples of Europe? – Chris Shore, 1996 ('Transcending' 474)

After the Second World War, anything beyond an economic basis to Western European integration would have been problematic, given the sorry story of Fascism (Lopez 143). But the EU has gradually expanded over the past forty years from its origins as a free-trade agreement towards political integration. The 1993 Treaty on European Union expressed the need for cultural policies to ensure both national diversity and continental identity ('Cultural Policy in the European Union'). Article 128 of its charter commits the Union to 'the flowering of the cultures of the Member States' in the context of 'national and regional diversity' and 'common cultural heritage', putting 'culture and citizenship ... hand in hand' ('Citizens').

Historically, pan-nationalism has not led to political unification, because of cultural differences and communication limitations. The latter problem does not confront Europe today, but the former does, and the period since the mid-1970s has seen the EU turn decisively in the direction of cultural programs, partly for political reasons and partly for economic ones. The dominant definition of the 'new European' favors Judeo-Christian religious beliefs, Hellenistic accounts of polities, arts, and sciences, and Roman jurisprudence. It seeks to distinguish Europe from the World Wars started by capitalistic nationalism, and regards the Cold War split as 'a suspension of the Real'. A heritage is invented that works for a renewed Enlightenment and against Americanization (Borneman and Fowler 488).

But there is much criticism of the fact that this is a top-down definition, with European integration driven by bureaucrats and politicians rather than civil society. Officials seek to prove to Europeans that cultural policies are adding to a shared heritage, not inventing it. This challenge is itself articulated by the EU, which says it seeks to transform 'the technocrats' Europe into a People's Europe' (quoted in Shore 'Transcending' 482). EU directives deploying such logics are increasingly under attack for the partiality of this amalgam and its connection to imperialist tropes that 'other' Asia and Africa (Borneman and Fowler 489–90). Meanwhile, the old notions of state cultural sovereignty that were so crucial to Europe's political traditions are being attenuated by 'bruxellois centralization' from outside and separatist ethnicization (Nathaniel Berman 1515). Critics refer to Eurocrats as 'magisters of culture' (Pieterse 6). On the right, Thatcher always insisted that the EU eschew an 'identikit European personality' on the one hand and a Leviathan-like 'super-state' on the other (quoted in Philip Schlesinger 184). For cultural critics disappointed with a yearning for the authentic, but equally dismissive of pragmatism, this raises 'essentialist and instrumentalist' accusations (Shore 'Transcending' 482). But is this the intention of European literature prizes, museum networks, TV channels and so on? And can a cultural 'leviathan' be organic? For some, there is a link to the Enlightenment that binds Europeans, and this has become part of official ideology. Progress, reason, rationality and humanism are exemplified in the choice of Schiller's 'Ode to Joy' (the lyrics to Beethoven's Ninth Symphony) as the EU's anthem (Shore 'Transcending' 481; Lopez; 'Culture/Audiovisual'). Of course, high culture is not the only terrain of struggle.

After the US had failed to incorporate cultural industries in the 1989 Free Trade Agreement with Canada, its State Department and trade officials had been particularly concerned to thwart EU plans for import quotas on audiovisual texts. The Community's 1989 'Television Without [intra-European] Frontiers' (TWF) directive drew particular ire for its 50% limit on imported texts. TWF was the outcome of years of contumacious debate within the Union. It invited members to reserve the majority of their airtime for European documentaries and features, other than where local quotas necessitated strictly national material (Armand Mattelart 97). Despite 1997 amendments, quotas essentially remain in place, in a form that some critics claim contravenes the GATT. For supporters, television is a cultural service, not a commodity, and TWF is an integral component in the struggle against three GEM effects of satellite intrusion: lower standards, destabilized local media and US domination. TWF was hailed as a bulwark against a totally commodified medium, a means of ensuring diversity. For all this rhetoric, there is a clause that ensures easy access for foreign programming: a 'where practicable' limit on the rule. Attempts to strengthen the wording were unsuccessful in 1996, a year when the EU's audiovisual trade deficit with the US climbed to US$6 billion. At the end of the 1990s, a survey of eighty-eight EU TV stations found that 70% of the films they showed came from Hollywood (Kevin McDonald 1991, 1994–95, 1997, 2001, 2008, 2015). Los Angeles wept reptilian tears.

During the early 1990s, the European Commission's Mésures pour encourager le développement de l'industrie audiovisuelle (Measures to Encourage the Development of the Audiovisual Industry) (MEDIA) program was launched. It aimed to make European film production regionally cohesive in the interests of profitability whilst also being responsive to local cultures – an attempt to blend commerce and culture through the exchange of media within the EU via new forms of distribution, rather than international co-production. The first five years saw annual funding that was less than the cost of producing a single Hollywood blockbuster. The more substantial MEDIA II (US$405 million) ran from 1995 to 2000, adding a particular focus on distribution, development and training plus the global circulation of European texts. As per the first MEDIA, highbrow production was privileged and successful films tended only to travel within their linguistic community of origin, unlike their Hollywood rivals. MEDIA III (MEDIA PLUS) aimed at similar interventions. Its US$355 million budget is predicated on assisting in the creation of 300,000 new jobs in the audiovisual sector between 2001 and 2005 through a link between market success and public subvention, alongside an Internet initiative, e-Europe. The abiding logic of the EU's audiovisual policy is commercial – it favors existing large concerns that can be built upon further. In 1999, Western European theaters were still filled with Hollywood films, which occupied 80% of programming. Of the other 20%, just 5% was imported from other European countries. The goal was to rectify this. Viviane Reding, the key European Commissioner, proclaimed that MEDIA PLUS would generate 'European audiovisual production which no longer relies on its inventiveness and originality, reflecting our cultural diversity, but sets out resolutely to win over European audiences and the rest of the world'. The tactic was a concentration on film distribution rather than production (Theiler 570–71, 576; 'European Commissioner'; Reding quoted in 'Circulation'; Stern 'EC' and 'Reding').

But as we saw in Chapter 2, the NICL has brought into doubt the opposition US:entertainment:Europe:education, with art cinema effectively a 'Euro-American' genre in terms of finance and management (Lev). In this sense, the seeming discontinuity with earlier concerns, when the EU had a primarily economic personality, is misleading: a notion of cultural sovereignty underpins concerns *vis-à-vis* the US, but so too does support for monopoly capital and the larger states inside its own walls (Burgelman and Pauwels).

Sony Entertainment published a report in mid-1994 that argued against EU quotas as inimical to the very producers they are designed to assist, with many commercial TV networks failing to observe national production quotas (Stern 'Film'; Zecchinelli 13; Stern 'Valenti' 1). After years of trying, attempts to bring together the 'quality' stations of the EU to create European drama continue to encounter difficulties with notions of discrete national dramaturgies and fears of creating the ultimate blandness of 'un euro-pudding' that works so hard to include multiple linguistic, audience and production norms that it loses form (although it has at least birthed a program with the best acronym ever: BABEL – Broadcasting Across the Barriers of European Languages) (Ungureit 16; Kevin McDonald 2004; Theiler 570). And away from the attempt to create the alchemical European, how plaintively should French culture maven Jack Lang appeal to national specificity in the language of freedom from media domination when his Ministry worked strenuously to wrest the balance of TV programming away from the US and Britain via the formation of a Latinate audiovisual locale of France, Iberia and Latin America? It may be that the rhetoric of a single Europe is not much more than an attempt to cut the costs of advertising through standardization. In addition, early evidence suggests that the new channels in Europe may have increased the presence of American programs, but that they have also greatly boosted local production by large entertainment groups whilst diminishing the prospect of increased production amongst smaller nations.

The 1992 European Charter on Regional and Minority Languages calls for member-states to permit major regional languages access to the educational curriculum and media time along with place-signage. France has half a dozen principal regional languages. Attempts to introduce some of these rights in 1999 produced a backlash that allied the right and sections of the left. Already concerned by the power of English, critics viewed the Charter as a further erosion of the national language's grandeur and a threat to national identity. France's Constitutional Court ruled, however, that the indivisibility of the republic was compromised by a plurality of languages ('Our Lingo'). At the same time as some constituents of the EU worry away about English, it is the clear correlative of economic forces, with three-quarters of multilingual Western Europeans sharing English (Borneman and Fowler 499).

This contradiction of cultural maintenance versus cultural unification characterizes the EU, as does the blend of privatization and industry policy that colors it economically. Western Europe has seen internal markets opened up to mergers and cultural penetration through continental convergence via commercial priorities, but it has an active cultural policy defined against the rest of the world. The result is internally competitive and externally protective (Beale; Galperin 635).

Conclusion

UNESCO, the GATT/WTO and these regional blocs offer differing perspectives on the neoliberal expansion into culture and the globalization of textual commodities. They veer between free-market models that aid existing power blocs, cultural protectionism that is critical of political and economic domination and continental cultural-industry groupings that reference citizen-consumer debates, pitting loyalty to custom and nation against pleasure in choice, but trying to steer around the ensuing complications by privileging local production where feasible. The US, the most closed cultural market in world history, does this by corporate power. Other nations, infinitely more porous, dedicate political-economic resources to the task.

The newest addition to intergovernmental cooperation on this score is the series of *International Meetings on Cultural Policy* that began in the 1990s. Ministerial-level politicians from all over the world convene (one nation declines to participate – your guess) to discuss: 'cultural diversity and development; the role of culture in global relations; and culture and trade'. And in 1998, the Forum of Latin American and Caribbean Ministers took culture and trade as its annual theme. The next year, Ministers at the *Meetings* formed an International Network on Cultural Policy, which will work with the Organization of American States to develop the first regional cultural plan for its members. Meanwhile, the World Bank established a lending program for development and culture (*Report* 3–4).

Today, culture is not just a problem of political pressure – it is one more category for commodification. In December 2000, Washington sent an official paper to the WTO's Council for Trade in Services on 'Audiovisual and Related Services' that it hoped would give the Organization a framework to assist 'the continued growth of this sector by ensuring an open and predictable environment' that would allegedly enable greater diversity of artistic output. Clearly this was the key to the US' *laissez-faire* politics. But there was now recognition of a countervailing legitimacy, that this environment must pay heed to 'the preservation and promotion of cultural values and identity', just as nations retain control over local prudential rules for their domestic financial systems (United States). It remains to be seen whether this is one more invocation of national concerns on behalf of a *bourgeoisie*, as per the cynical use of culturalism by other countries' media producers in favor of state support for national cinemas and broadcasters. We can see played out here the mix of national-popular ideology and cultural industrialization that has marked the doctrine of ethical incompleteness throughout this volume, with populations construed as needing both care and protection from the buffets of the market as well as schooling in the ways of restructuring economically to meet the needs of post-industrialism.

Conclusion

It was envisioned as a feel-good patriotic festival like the American Bicentennial. But the Brazilian government should have known that its plans to mark the 500th anniversary of the landing of the Portuguese were doomed when an irate Indian chief marched into Congress … drew his bow and arrow and threatened to kill the Senate president. – Larry Rohter ('500')

How can you expect to govern a country that has 246 kinds of cheese? – Charles de Gaulle (quoted in 'How')

I'm aware that it's a lot more glamorous to be on the barricade with a hand-kerchief around your nose than it is to be at the meeting with a briefcase and a bowler hat, but I think that we're getting more done this way. – Bono of U2 (quoted in Dominus)

Brazil's 300,000 Indians and their leaders vowed to struggle against the commemoration of invasion throughout 2000. They were joined in this desire by many Afro-Brazilians, who deemed themselves excluded from the 'celebra-tion', and activists from the Movement of the Landless, who called for agrarian reform. Pelé said he was 'ashamed of Brazil' because of the event. Meanwhile, across the Southern Hemisphere in Australia, a six-week experiment by the New South Wales railway service saw the rate of vandalism on trains cut by 75% – seats were no longer slashed and walls were not painted. Why? The usual suspects were apparently driven away by a relentless onslaught of Western European Enlightenment-era sonatas and concertos played on loudspeakers. Further north, the NEA was continuing to struggle. The newest tactic was to cast itself as standing *in loco parentis* to the US population. The Endowment used the terms '*nurturing*', '*supporting*' and '*fostering*' to describe its goals for the coming century – a kind of non-pharmacological, pre-managed care, non-directive, client-centered Rogerian therapy ('Learn'). In responding to the shocks and doubts of the 1980s and 1990s from critics speaking in the name of family values, US cultural policy had literally *become* a family.

For all that this book was born in a neoliberal era, when global élites and policymakers deride old-style politics, the state remains with us as the *locus classicus* of politics, as exemplified by popular Brazilian revolt and middle-class Australian policing. This is the Janus face to the state, that it subjectifies citizens and residents in a way that makes them its own and it theirs, as well as ushering out those whom it would rather forget or deny. The state monopolizes both violence and national representation, even as its legitimacy depends on a space for its subjects to appeal to it for redress on both these scores.

Nevertheless, the state is seen in much global elite and media discourse as standing in the way of democracy. Rather than politics, the market is said to epitomize freedom. And yet these graceless antinomies, as recent as they are avowedly timeless, are not so far apart as this binary suggests. Just as governments have always facilitated forms of accumulation, so markets have always played a part in allocating political preferences. Just as entrepreneurs have loudly proclaimed the inefficiency of political intervention, so the public routinely calls on parliaments to protect it from untrammeled private investment. And the very notions of limited liability, public education and tax write-offs for research are crucial to successful business innovation. Instead of an uplift model, whereby welfarist doctrines saw governments give money to the arts in order to 'improve' their citizenry, the 1990s model was a cultural-industry one – the state underwrote new market infrastructures, such as art fairs, within which consumer preferences 'determined' the canon (Ardenne 101–02). At the same time, however, as this neoliberal/industry policy *rapprochement* was underway, there were *dirigiste* pressures as well. The US saw repeated assaults on migrants, from the denial of benefits to legal residents, to crackdowns on employed workers without immigration papers. And Europe saw a renewed nationalism that merged anti-immigration rhetoric on the right with the left's call for demographically inclusive national cultural policies (Ingram).

Rather than propose an end to the big state, capital works for the redeployment of state resources in keeping with its own interests. And the global spread of neoliberalism has uneven consequences, diverging as it does between commercial and non-commercial aims, then reconnecting them in aberrant ways. The international art market, valued in late 1999 at US$17 billion a year, is slowly being reorganized, in keeping with norms of monetary valuation via indices that compare art with other investments (especially important given the market's relative autonomy from share fluctuations) ('The Colour'). This represents an attempt to make art calculable according to the norms of the fully-knowledgeable consumer, in the face of a history that cordoned off high culture from mainstream economic indicators. On the other hand, the model of the US philanthropist as a neoliberal benefactor is on export as an alternative to the big state and the unwieldy cultocracy. But it cannot be expected to operate exactly as it has in the US in those countries where wealth is held by traditional families rather than early-generation migrants. In any event, the 1960s US model, whereby Foundations would demonstrate the value of an intervention, then wait for governmental action to come into play, has been succeeded by 'venture philanthropy'. This irksome oxymoron is in a sense an old model of thrift, Victorian improvement by giving, such that angelic high-tech 'venture philanthropists' hand over money without the desire for a financial return – simply that those receiving it will start a business that becomes self-supporting (Cook). The demonstration-effect has shifted from Foundation-state to Foundation-firm, with the individual subject of civil society supposedly empowered by the process.

Through all this, it often seems as though the globalizing force of neoliberalism is a codeword for the extension of the 'American Century', in both temporal and spatial terms, along with that tortured and torturing nation's strange, reluctant notion of statehood. The remainder of our Conclusion will demonstrate the limitation of any approach that stringently separates corporation from state, and either from culture, or hews to an individualist model of socio-cultural theory.

Consider US doctrine over the role played in the Internet by individual North American 'visionaries'. Who invented the Internet? When he's not busy claiming the status of a role model for *Love Story* or working on his post-2000 imper-sonation of Sebastian Cabot, Al Gore sometimes includes this achievement on his CV. He is not alone – chain bookstores feature memoirs by all manner of men making similar assertions. The truth is out there, though, and it's about government policy, not 'individual initiative'. For while Al, his girlfriend Tipper, and his roommate Tommy Lee Jones were padding around Ivy-League dorms during late-night ice-cream feasts, the RAND Corporation was busily devising means of waging the Vietnam War. Its consultancy services didn't end there, of course. Our friends over at the Corporation also addressed the question: what if the Soviet Union managed to strike at the heart of the domestic US com-munications system? A successful attack would leave the country disabled, unless a devolved network could be introduced. The packet system of today originated with that desire to decentralize computing through nodal, semi-autonomous sites. In keeping with those origins – state-driven Cold War consultancies – the Internet grew up nested within public institutions of government and education, and the associated warfare-welfare para-bureaucracy of publicly-funded, but ostensibly independent, research by private universities and firms. How, then, did the myth of individual freedom as the source of the Internet (we call this cybertarianism) emerge? And what is it?

Think back to the early days of radio for some clues. In the US, as in several other countries, the 1920s saw struggles waged between the repressive state apparatus and commerce over radio. The navy and the police asserted the need for exclusive use of the spectrum, while businesses wanted it for them-selves. Government ultimately stepped in as an umpire. For listeners, those early days were a challenge – how clearly could a signal be heard, and from how far away? Stations offered prizes to those who reported the greatest reception distances. Meanwhile, Germany and Australia saw union-owned sta-tions pioneering choral response, two-way radio, a Brechtian dream of worker-actor collaboration across the ether. And speaking of the ether, this mystical substance was given all kinds of bizarre properties by early practitioners, such as contact with the dead and a cure for cancer. Then the system became comprehensively corporatized. Two-way dreams were dispatched to the margins, as the radio set was sealed and the airwaves zoned. Theosophists and oncologists found other sites to ply their trades.

Contemporary radio hams continue the fond memory of a system that broke down the gap between producers and consumers. They are bearers of a largely forgotten myth, if one that resonates in another, contemporary sphere. Libertarian individualists of the US Electronic Frontier Foundation and many other sites, both corporate and not (libertarians need to organize?) today view the Internet as a technologically entrepreneurial zone. It is said to permit human ventriloquism, autonomous subjectivity and a break-up of state power – all thanks to the 'innate' properties of cyberspace. Hence our coining the term 'cybertarian'. Cybertarian mythology rests not only on a flawed, albeit touching, account of the person as a ratiocinative, atomistic individual who can exist outside politics and society. It equally assumes that what was born of warfare consultancies and 'big science', was spread through large institutions, was commodified for a tiny fraction of computer users, and is now moving towards comprehensive corporate control, can be claimed, now or ever, for the wild boys of geekdom. A touching foundation myth, typical of US fantasies about the autonomous subject breathing life into the world.

Of course there *is* a role for the geek in the electronic domain. But today even hackers happily turn up at FBI conventions on Internet security, aiding the state and business to uncover errors and openness in operating systems. The expansion of entertainment conglomerates into the Internet will not, of course, end the technical capacity of web users to make their own sites. But it *will* minimize their significance. Crucial portals take up the traditional corporate role of policing zones and charging tolls. The fastest, easiest, most accessible search systems linked to browsers will direct folks to the 'best' sites – which will not be those of cybertarians. But a far older subject is lurking here – older than the cybertarian, older even than the libertarian. This is, of course, the citizen, who has been a stuttering but persistent presence throughout our investigations.

Whereas the cybertarian is a monad, happily sitting at the controls of his or her life like an idealized consumer, the citizen is intersubjective, keen to link with others in solidarity as well as conflict. As we have seen, citizenship takes three forms: political, economic and cultural. In cyber terms, political citizenship has major implications for the regulation of speech, systems and policing of encryption, privacy, voting and the expression of public opinion. Economic citizenship's Internet significance lies in the push by the IMF and the World Bank for Third World states to get out of telecommunications, leaving the field to private investment. This has dramatically affected the pace and breadth of telephone and Internet access in many countries. Where development comes, it will be driven by corporate targets among the wealthy. Cultural citizenship encompasses discussion groups, ventriloquism, physical space, hardware and access to and for *non*-citizens, such as temporary workers and refugees.

The NICL and the Internet will interact in ways we can only imagine, as cultural labor is internationalized on an uneven basis that will favor North over South and capital over labor. Yet we are seeing signs in the US of a new drive towards unionization. Lapsing cybertarians find an end to vested shares, salaries and health care if they got on board too late, or experience global competition for their jobs. As film and television production go global in search of locations, skills and docile labor, post-production and distribution centralize, thanks to armchair management by computer. Meanwhile, away from the salariat, those affected by the division of labor in manufacturing and agriculture need rights to communication in the new media.

What should be done? First, we need to reconceptualize the three forms of citizenship as interlocking zones, interdependent and equally important. Second, we need to theorize the Internet in terms not just of individual access, but political rights, economic development, cultural norms and tastes. Third, the NICL must be centered in deliberations that look to those who are disenfranchised from citizenship and consumption, via a global statement of worker and citizen rights.

Many other cultural institutions owe their lives, however secretly, to the work of US policy. The chaotic, piecemeal, but discernible outline of US cultural policy and its relationship to the culture industries is beautifully captured in the Hollywood sign. Overlooking LA from Mount Lee in Griffith Park, and visible from Burbank to Santa Monica, the site we now understand as a monument to the cinema started out as a promotion for home sales in a canyon subdivision in 1923 that read 'Hollywoodland'. When the company went bankrupt twenty years later, it handed over both the land and the sign to the City. In 1949 a wind gust destroyed the H letter, encouraging TV executives to metonymize the event as the end of the film industry. Repairs were financed by a blend of governmental and private funds, with the *quid pro quo* that 'Hollywood' stand alone. There was no ongoing maintenance however. In the 1960s, it was declared an historic monument by the City's Cultural Heritage Board, but it seemed done for by the mid-1970s. Then the local Chamber of Commerce patched together funds from Hugh Hefner, Gene Autry, Andy Williams and Alice Cooper in 1978 (an unholy quartet for an unholy decade) to build a new sign, with each man paying for a letter or two (Abramian). Twenty years on, it is one of the most famous signs in the world, its history a quixotic, but in some respects typical, patchwork of public and private interests, their mutuality and contradictoriness hidden, along with years of disrepair, in a historicity of celebration.

Such contradictions are the stuff of cultural policy. In 1994, the French cultural theorist Jean Baudrillard traveled to Australia for a symposium entitled 'The Art of Theory: Baudrillard in the 90s', in order to display fifty of his photographs at various galleries. Now Baudrillard claims that simulation has pervaded the social and artistic world, to the point where originality and authorial signature are no longer noteworthy or even credible, given the culture of the copy. Like reality, art is overrun by signification, such that truth and deception are no longer distinct. But on entering the country, Baudrillard discovered that institutions know the difference: he encountered the Australian Customs Service's Harmonized Commodity Description and Coding System. It did not count photographs as works of art, so 'his' visual texts were liable to import duty (A$16000). This drew the ire of the exhibiting galleries, and much mirth from the Australian media at the way in which Baudrillard's own intellectual position had been instantiated to cost him money (Peter Anderson 'On the Legal'). It also indicated the absence in Baudrillard's atmospheric, impressionistic critique of any sense that concrete institutions and practices determine what counts as art, not some abstract *Zeitgeist*. These mundane knowledges have formed the basis to this book.

Such a complex latticework of forces also applies elsewhere. The meeting of the modern with the colonial, of the traditional and the postcolonial, attains sharp relief in the case of Ghanaian cinema. The Ghana Film Industry Corporation, a state-owned enterprise, has suffered years of inactivity, due to lack of funds. Renowned directors such as King Ampaw and Kwaw Ansah look to former colonial sites for finance, and the cinemas have been dominated by Hong Kong, Indian and Hollywood texts. In the late 1980s, low-budget films, shot on video, started filling local theatres. Instead of addressing officially endorsed themes, such as the emancipation of black thinkers and a return to precolonial custom, these 'guerrilla' genres fixed on the contemporary city, modernization, and the occult, to the alarm of conventional culture-brokers (Birgit Meyer). While in the People's Republic of China, the fiftieth anniversary of the September 1949 socialist revolution saw 100,000 dancers and singers in action as a festival of worker, disabled, regional, and military theatre and opera troupes from around the nation performed local and Western texts, alongside eleven companies run by the Ministry of Culture. This intrication of labor, state and culture went back to Confucianism. The blend of tradition with socialism and Western capitalism was new, however (Melvin).

Clearly, these stories represent historic renegotiations of the citizen-consumer couplet that has exercised us so much here. They signify both new problems and renewed tasks. The problems lie in the push towards commodification by agencies, movements and artists whose defining characteristic has hitherto been their attempt to innovate beyond the borders of market domination. The renewal lies in the fact that the task of binding people to a polity remains, alongside a stubborn faith on the part of both private and public bureaucrats that this can be achieved at the intersection of the aesthetic and anthropological accounts of culture with which we began. The goal must be to avoid the separation of aesthetic awareness from awareness of the history to social division, as García Canclini avows:

> In the presence of the magnificence of a Maya or Inca pyramid, of colonial palaces, indigenous ceramics from three centuries ago, or the work of an internationally recognized national painter, it occurs to almost no one to think about the social contradictions they express. The perennial character of these goods makes us imagine that their value is beyond question and turns them into a source of collective consensus, beyond the divisions among classes, ethnic groups, and other groups that fracture society and differentiate ways of appropriating that patrimony. (108)

This consensual talent derives from fetishising art objects as having their own properties of quality, which become available to the properly schooled observer. The properties of the object, rather than its history of creation and dissemination, then become the proper domain of appreciation, as per our Introduction. But there are other options.

Foucault suggests that pop art offered new ways of appreciating images by its pleasurable commentary on 'the endless circulation of images', rather than through any striking contribution to new aesthetic forms. The newness lay not in innovative ways of painting objects, but innovative ways of painting images *of* those objects ('Photogenic' 90). Twisting that insight a few degrees, with thanks to the Australian Customs Service's Baudrillardian watchdogs, we believe that studying cultural policy can also renew our appreciation of art, albeit not always thanks to pleasurable commentary. Looking at cultural policy through the lens of cultural studies encourages us towards innovative ways of understanding the circulation of texts, how certain forms of cultural expression are privileged and with what effect, such that the systematic inequalities of a society can be both highlighted and countered. Ideally, citizenship can be more than a collection of rights (that are routinely denied to many subjects). Citizenship can be a site for empowering a critique-in-principle of social arrangements, for transcending existing structures of economy and polity by connecting to social movements. Culture has clearly been a key site of critique by those excluded from the bounty of modernity, and its policy seeds need tending by those hopeful for a progressive future.

References

'A Disquieting New Agenda for Trade' *Economist* 332, no. 7872 (1994): 55–56.

'A Panel Discussion: Measuring Changes in National Cultural Behavior Patterns' *Journal of Cultural Economics* 14, no. 1 (1990): 1–17.

'After GATT Pique, Pix Pax Promoted' *Daily Variety* (8 June 1994): 1, 16.

'Art Agency Needs Cleaning Up, Not Scrapping' *New York Times* (13 June 1990): A30.

'Article 128' http://europa.eu.int/en/comm/dg10/culture/en/art128.html.

'Arts, Culture and Condiments' *New York Times* (23 June 1996): 12.

'Australia as a Film Location. Wallaby-wood.' *Economist* (30 May 1998).

'"Baywatch" Goes Out with the Tide.' *Economist* (6 March 1999): 39.

'Boogie Woogie' *Latin Trade* (July 1997). http://www.latintrade.com/archives/july97/tradetalk.html.

'Circulation of Audiovisual Works and Training of Professionals: Commission Adopts its Proposals for the MEDIA PLUS Programme (2001–2005)' Commission of the European Communities RAPID (14 December 1999).

'Citizens' Access to Culture' http://europa.eu.int/en/comm/dg10/culture/en/citizens.html.

'Collaboration of the Press in the Organisation of Peace' *The Global Media Debate: Its Rise, Fall, and Renewal*. Eds George Gerbner, Hamid Mowlana and Kaarle Nordenstreng. Norwood: Ablex (1994): 183.

'The Colour of Money' *Economist* (9 October 1999): 94.

'Comparing Cultural Policies in Various Countries' *Cultures* no. 33 (1983): 67–89.

'Comras Betting on Entertainment Industry', *Miami Herald* 11 August 1998.

'Corporations and the Arts' *ARTnews* 78, no. 5 (1979): 40–68.

'Cultural Export: Re-Orienting Australia' *Media Information Australia* no. 76 (May 1995): 1–81.

'Cultural Policy and Political Philosophy' *Journal of Arts Management and Law* 13, no. 1 (1983): 24–37.

'Cultural Policy in the European Union' http://www.europa.eu.int/pol/cult/en/info.htm.

'Cultural Policy: State of the Art' *Culture and Policy* 7, no. 1 (1996).

'Culture and the State' ICA *Documents* no. 7 (1984).

'Culture Wars' *Economist* (12 September 1998): n. p.

'Culture/Audiovisual Council: Outcome of June 28 Session' *European Report* (30 June 1999).

'Culture/audiovisual Council: Should Culture be Excluded from WTO Millennium Round?' *European Report* (24 July 1999).

'Declaration of Fundamental Principles Concerning the Contribution of the Mass Media to Strengthening Peace and International Understanding, to the Promotion of Human Rights and to Countering Racism, Apartheid and Incitement to War' *The Global Media Debate: Its Rise, Fall, and Renewal*. Eds George Gerbner, Hamid Mowlana and Kaarle Nordenstreng. Norwood: Ablex (1994): 173–78.

'Deja Vu' *Film Journal* 97, no. 6 (1994): 3.

'The Disappearing Czech Intellectual' *Economist* (21 August 1999): 41.

'The Environment for Policy Making' *Journal of Arts Management and Law* 13, no. 1 (1983): 40–87.

'Escuelas vocacionales de arte' http://www.cuba.ru/view/docs/doc_read.php3?idobject=1042&id_rubr=1338.

'European Commissioner Wants More Film Exchange Within EU' *Agene France Presse* (16 December 1999).

'European Community Action in Support of Culture' http://europa.eu.int/en/comm/dg10/culture/en/support/support.html.

'European Film Industry: Worrying Statistix' *Economist* (6 February 1999).

'Final Act of the United Nations Conference on Freedom of Information' *The Global Media Debate: Its Rise, Fall, and Renewal*. Eds. George Gerbner, Hamid Mowlana and Kaarle Nordenstreng. Norwood: Ablex (1994): 179–82.

'The First Amendment and Public Support for the Arts: A Symposium' *Journal of Arts Management and Law* 21, no. 4 (1992): 328–54.

'First Peoples: Cultures, Policies, Politics' *Cultural Studies* 9, no. 1 (1995).

'Foreign Bums on Seats' *Economist* (15 August 1998): n. p.

'Foundation on the Arts and Humanities' *Congressional Quarterly Almanac* no. 21 (1966).

'French Lessons' *Economist* (26 June 1999): 38.

'From Cultural Studies to Cultural Policy' *Culture and Policy* 6, no. 2 (1994).

'GATT Quota Row Puts Muzzle on White Fang' *On Film* no. 11 (1993): 1.

'George Papadopoulos' *Economist* (3 July 1999): 77.

'Giving Something Back' *Economist* (16 June 2001): 15–17.

'The G-Word' *Financial Times* (30 July 1997): 15.

'The Helms Process' *New York Times* (28 July 1989): A26.

'Hollywood Cashes Runaway Checks in Czech Republic.' International Cinematographers Guild (n.d.) www.cameraguild.com/news/global/czech.htm.

'Hollywood on the Vltava.' *Economist* (3 February 2001): 65.

'H'wood Buries Overseas Pix' *Variety* (25–31 January 1999): 1, 90–91.

'How Multilingual is France?' *Economist* (29 April 2000): 46.

'Indian Government Pulls Nude Painting from National Exhibition' *Agence France Presse* (4 September 2000).

'Language on Obscene Art Hangs up Interior Bill' *Congressional Quarterly Almanac* no. 45 (1990).

'Learning About the NEA' http://www.nea.gov/learn/.

'Let's Have Our Treasures Back, Please' *Economist* (10 July 1999): 41.

'Linguistic Human Rights from a Sociolinguistic Perspective' *International Journal of the Sociology of Language* no. 127 (1997).

'The Mexico City Declaration on Cultural Policies' *Cultures* no. 33 (1983): 189–96.

'Monumental Histories' *Representations* no. 35 (Summer 1991).

'Monumental' *Economist* (6 March 1999): 77–78.

'Moving Mummy's Attic' *Economist* (19 February 2000): 83.

'Museums Galore' *Economist* (19 February 2000): 82–85.

'National Endowment for the Arts Question & Answer' http://www.cco.caltech.edu/~ope/nea.html.

'National Foundation on the Arts and the Humanities Act of 1965'

'New Thai Museum Uses Waxworks to Show Horrors of Drugs' *Agence France Presse* (7 September 2000).

'Northern Ireland Film Commission Received Skillset Training Kitemark from Lord Puttnam' M2 Press WIRE (22 February 1999).

'Our Lingo, by Jingo' *Economist* (3 July 1999): 40–41.

'Overview' http://europa.eu.int/en/comm/dg10/culture/en/general.html.

'Panel Discussion' *Journal of Arts Management and Law* 21, no. 4 (1992): 349–54.

'Paying for Culture' *Annals of the American Academy of Political and Social Science* no. 471 (1984).

'Philanthropy, Patronage, Politics' *Daedalus* 116, no. 1 (1987).

'The Policy Moment' *Media Information Australia* no. 73 (August 1994): 3–54.

'The Politics of Culture' *Southern Review* 28, no. 3 (1995).

'The PolyGram Test' *Economist* (15 August 1998): n. p.

'The Poor Give the Hardest' *Time* (24 July 2000): 55.

'Post-Colonial Formations' *Culture and Policy* no. 6 (1994).

'Post-Modern Art and the Death of Obscenity Law' *Yale Law Journal* 99 (1990).

'Power, Objects, and a Voice for Anthropology' *Current Anthropology* no. 37 Supplement (February 1996): S1–S22.

'Protecting Mali's Cultural Heritage' *African Arts* 28, no. 4 (1995): 22–95.

'Public Support for Art: Viewpoints Presented at the Ottawa Meetings' *Journal of Cultural Economics* 13, no. 2 (1989): 1–19.

'Q&A With Gabriel Abaroa' *Latin Music Quarterly* (24 January 1998): LMQ–1 & LMQ–12.

'Research' *Journal of Arts Management and Law* 13, no. 1 (1983): 184–212.

'Shall We, Yawn, Go to a Film?' *Economist* (1 February 1997): n. p.

'Sicilian Town to Open Mafia Museum' *Agence France Presse* (7 September 2000).

'Space*Meaning*Politics' *Continuum* 3, no. 1 (1990).

'Spanish-language Web Sites Specialize.' *Miami Herald* 14 Sep. (1999): 2C

'Studio City: a $100 Million Development Debate Complex Proposed at Washington Ave.' *Miami Herald* 9 August (1998).

'Suite and Sour' *Economist* (13 February 1999): 56–57.

'Superhighway Summit' *Emmy* 16, no. 2 (1994): A1–69.

'Symposium on the Public Benefits of the Arts and Humanities' *Art and the Law* 9, no. 1 (1985).

'Theme: Culture and Urban Regeneration: Some European Examples' *Built Environment* 18, no. 2 (1992).

'Top 100 All-Time Domestic Grossers' *Variety* (17–23 October 1994): M60.

'Two Live Crew, Decoded' *New York Times* (19 June 1990): A23.

'USA: Art Unleashed' *Index on Censorship* 3 (1996): 3–168.

'Where the Gifts Go' *Time* (24 July 2000). 59.

'Who Decides What History Museums Present: Managers, Front-Line Interpreters, Audiences? A Round Table' *Journal of American History* 81, no. 1 (1994): 119–63.

Abbe-Decarroux, François. 'The Perception of Quality and the Demand for Services: Empirical Application to the Peforming Arts' *Journal of Economic Behavior and Organization* 23, no. 1 (1994): 99–107.

Adams, Phillip. 'Response' *Cinema Papers* nos. 44–45 (1984): 70–71.

Ades, Dawn. *Art in Latin America: The Modern Era, 1820–1980.* New Haven: Yale UP. (1989).

Adler, Amy M. 'What's Left?: Hate Speech, Pornography and the Problem for Artistic Expression' *California Law Review* 84 (1996).

Adler, Amy M. 'Why Art is on Trial' *Journal of Arts Management, Law and Society* 22, no. 4 (1993): 322–34.

Adler, Tim. 'A New Script to Save British Film' *Daily Telegraph* (26 February 1999).

Adorno, Rolena. *Guaman Poma: Writing and Resistance in Colonial Peru.* Austin: U of Texas Press (1986).

Afilm.com. http://www.afilm.com/2/01/03/.

Agresto, John. 'Legitimate Restrictions on Federal Arts Funding' *Journal of Arts Management and Law* 21, no. 4 (1992): 333–37.

Akerman, Susan and Raymond L.M. Lee. 'Theory, National Policy and the Management of Minority Cultures' *Southeast Asian Journal of Social Science* 16, no. 2 (1988): 132–42.

Akinnaso, F. Niyi. 'Linguistic Unification and Language Rights' *Applied Linguistics* 15, no. 2 (1994): 139–68.

Alberdi, Juan Bautista. *Bases y puntos de partida para la organización política de la República Argentina*. Buenos Aires: La Cultura Argentina (1915).

Alderson, Evan, Robin Blaser and Harold Coward, Eds *Reflections on Cultural Policy: Past, Present and Future*. Waterloo: Wilfrid Laurier UP (1993).

Alexander, Jane. *Command Performance: An Actress in the Theater of Politics*. New York: Public Affairs (2000).

Alexander, Jane. 'Our Investment in Culture: Art Perfects the Essence of our Common Humanity' *Vital Speeches of the Day* 62, no. 7 (1996): 210–12.

Alexander, N. *Language Policy and National Unity in South Africa/Azania*. Cape Town: Buchu (1989).

Alexander, Victoria D. 'Pictures at an Exhibition: Conflicting Pressures in Museums and the Display of Art' *American Journal of Sociology* 101, no. 4 (1996): 797–839.

Alexander, Victoria D. *Museums and Money: The Impact of Funding on Exhibtions, Scholarship, and Management*. Bloomington: Indiana UP (1996).

Allan, Blaine. 'The State of the State of the Art on TV' *Queen's Quarterly* 95, no. 2 (1988): 318–29.

Allor, Martin and Michelle Gagnon. *L'État de Culture: Généalogie Discursive des Politiques Culturelles Québécoises*. Montréal: Concordia U/U de Montréal (1994).

Althusser, Louis. *For Marx*. Trans. Ben Brewster. Harmondsworth: Penguin (1969).

Alvarez, Sonia E., Evelina Dagnino and Arturo Escobar, Eds *Cultures of Politics, Politics of Cultures. Revisioning Latin American Social Movements*. Boulder: Westview (1998).

American Arts Alliance. 'Economic Impact of Arts and Cultural Institutions in Their Communities' http://www.tmn.com/Oh/Artswire/www/aaa/fact.html.

American Arts Alliance. 'Myths & Facts about National Support of the Arts & Culture' http://www.tmn.com/Oh/Artswire/www/aaa/myth.html.

American Association of Museums. *Code of Ethics for Museums*. Washington (1991).

American Council for the Arts. *The Arts and Humanities Under Fire: New Arguments for Government Support*. New York: American Council for the Arts (1990).

Ames, Michael. *Cannibal Tours and Glass Boxes: The Anthropology of Museums*. Vancouver: U of British Columbia P (1992).

Ames, Michael. *Museums, the Public, and Anthropology: A Study in the Anthropology of Anthropology*. Vancouver: U of British Columbia P (1986).

Amis, Kingsley. 'An Arts Policy?' *Policy Review* 14 (1980): 83–94.

Anderson, Peter. 'On the Legal Limits of Art' *Arts and Entertainment Law Review* 5 (October 1994): 70–76.

Anderson, Peter. 'What the People Want: Government, Arts Funding and the Australia Council' *Australian-Canadian Studies* 7, nos. 1–2 (1989): 127–43.

Anderson, Susan Heller. 'Ever Pragmatic Singapore is Making Art its Business' *New York Times* (25 July 1999): AR6, 23.

Ardenne, P. 'The Art Market in the 1980s' Trans. M. Vale. *International Journal of Political Economy* 25, no. 2 (1995): 100–28.

Arian, Edward A. *Brahms, Beethoven and Bureaucracy*. U of Alabama P (1971).

Arian, Edward A. *The Unfulfilled Promise: Public Subsidy of the Arts in the United States*. Philadelphia: Temple UP (1989).

Arieff, Allison. 'A Different Sort of (P)Reservation: Some Thoughts on the National Museum of the American Indian' *Museum Anthropology* 19, no. 2 (1995): 78–90.

Arnold, Matthew. *Culture & Anarchy*. ed. J. Dover Wilson. Cambridge: Cambridge UP (1971).

Arnoldi, Mary Jo. 'Overcoming a Colonial Legacy: The New National Museum in Mali: 1976 to the Present' *Museum Anthropology* 22, no. 3 (1999): 28–40.

Arts-alert-usa. Association for Theatre in Higher Education. www2.hawaii.edu/athe/ATHEWelcome.html, n. d.

Attali, Jacques. 'Hollywood vs. Europe: The Next Round' *New Perspectives Quarterly* 11, no. 1 (1994): 46–47.

Austen-Smith, David. 'On Justifying Subsidies to the Performing Arts' *Journal of Cultural Economics* 18, no. 3 (1994): 239–49.

Australian Labor Party. *Platform, Resolutions and Rules*. Canberra: Australian Labor Party (1986).

Axtmann, Roland. 'Society, Globalization and the Comparative Method' *History of the Human Sciences* 6, no. 2 (1993): 53–74.

Bale, M. 'Bad Art, Bad Politics' *New York Times Book Review* (28 May 1995): 9.

Balfe, Judith Huggins. 'Artworks as Symbols in International Politics' *International Journal of Politics, Culture and Society* 1 (1987): 195–217.

Balfe, Judith Huggins and Margaret Jane Wyszomirski, Eds. *Art, Ideology, and Politics*. New York: Praeger (1985).

Balfe, Judith Huggins and Margaret Jane Wyszomirski. 'Public Art and Public Policy' *Journal of Arts Management and Law* 15, no. 4 (1986).

Balfe, Judith Huggins, ed. *Paying the Piper: Cases and Consequences of Art Patronage*. Urbana: U of Illinois P (1993).

Balfe, Judith Huggins. 'The Arts and Arts Policy: Issues of Work, Money, and Power' *Contemporary Sociology* 19, no. 4 (1992): 518–20.

Balibar, Etienne. 'What Makes a People a People? Rousseau and Kant' *Masses, Classes and the Public Sphere*. ed. Mike Hill and Warren Montag. London; New York: Verso, (2000): 105–131.

Banfield, Edward C., ed. *The Democratic Muse: Visual Arts and the Public Interest*. New York: Basic (1984).

Bann, Stephen. 'On Living in a New Country' *The New Museology*, ed. Peter Vergo. London: Reaktion, 1991. 99–118.

Barbosa, Luiz Carlos. 'Lastro cultural na Bienal do Mercosul' *Extra Classe* Ano 4, núm. 33 (julho) (1999). http://www.sinpro-rs.org.br/extra/jul99/cultura_l .htm.

Barker, Adele Marie. 'The Culture Factory: Theorizing the Popular in the Old and New Russia' *Consuming Russia: Popular Culture, Sex, and Society since Gorbachev*. ed. Adele Marie Barker. Durham: Duke UP (1999): 12–45.

Barker, Martin 'Sex, violence and videotape' *Sight and Sound* 3, no. 5 (1993) 96–103.

Barr, Alfred H. 'Foreword' Lincoln Kirstein, *The Latin American Collection of the Museum of Modern Art*. New York: The Museum of Modern Art, (1943): 3.

Barr, Malcolm. 'The Labor Party's Policy for the Arts: Is it Socialist?' *Red Letters* no. 19 (1986).

Barreda, Gabino. 'Algunas ideas respecto a instrucción pública' [1875]. In *Opúsculos, discusiones y discursos*. Mexico: Imprenta del Comercio de Dublán y Chávez (1877).

Barrera Bassols, Marco and Ramón Vera Herrera. 'Todo rincón es un centro: Hacia una expansión de la idea del museo' Unpublished manuscript (1996).

Barrett, Wayne. 'Papal Pandering: Rudy Dons Miter in Search of Upstate Colonization' *Village Voice* (12 October 1999): 44–47.

Barshefsky, Charlene. Testimony of the United States Trade Representative Before the House Appropriations Committee Subcommittee on Commerce, Justice, State, the Judiciary and Related Agencies (31 March 1988).

Barthes, Roland. *Mythologies*. Trans. Annette Lavers. London: Paladin (1973).

Bashevkin, Sylvia. 'Does Public Opinion Matter? The Adoption of Federal Royal Commission and Task Force Recommendations on the National Question, 1951–1987' *Canadian Public Administration* 31 no. 1 (1988).

Bator, P. M. *The International Trade in Art*. Chicago: U of Chicago P (1982).

Baumol, William J. and William G. Bowen. *Performing Arts – The Economic Dilemma*. Cambridge, Mass.: MIT P (1966).

Beale, Alison. 'Development and 'Désétatisation' in European Cultural Policy' *Media International Australia incorporating Culture and Policy* no. 90 (February 1999): 91–105.

Beaverstock, J.V. 'Subcontracting the Accountant! Professional Labor Markets, Migration, and Organisational Networks in the Global Accountancy Industry' *Environment and Planning* A 28, no. 2 (1996): 303–26.

Becker, Carol, ed. *The Subversive Imagination: Artists, Society, and Social Responsibility*. New York: Routledge (1994).

Becker, Gary. 'Nobel Lecture: The Economic Way of Looking at Behavior' *Journal of Political Economy* 101, no. 3 (1993): 385–409.

Becker, Howard S. *Art Worlds*. Berkeley: U of California P (1982).

Bell, W.J., Jr. et al. *A Cabinet of Curiosities: Five Episodes in the Evolution of American Museums*. Charlottesville: U of Virginia P (1967).

Bello, Andrés. *Selected Writings of Andrés Bello*. Trans. Frances M. López-Morillas. Ed. and Intro. Iván Jaksić. New York: Oxford University Press (1997).

—— 'Address Delivered at the Inauguration of the University of Chile' (1843). In *Selected Writings*, (1997): 124–37.

—— 'Commentary on 'Historical Sketch of the Constitution of the Govermnent of Chile during the First Period of the Revolution, 1810 to 1814' by José Victorino Lastarria' (1848). In *Selected Writings*, (1997) 169–74.

—— 'The Craft of History.' *Selected Writings of Andres Bello*. Trans. Frances M. Lopez-Morillas. New York and Oxford: Oxford UP (1997): 173–184.

—— 'Government and Society' (1843). In *Selected Writings*, (1997): 287–90.

—— 'On the Aims of Education and the Means of Promoting It' (1836). In *Selected Writings*, (1997): 109–16.

—— 'Prologue: *Grammar of the Spanish Language*' (1847). In *Selected Writings*, (1997): 96–103.

—— 'Prologue: *Ideological Analysis of the Tenses of the Spanish Conjugation*' (1841). In *Selected Writings*, (1997): 85–87.

—— '*El Repertorio Americano*: Prospectus' (1826). In *Selected Writings*, (1997): 3–6.

—— 'Report on the Progress of Public Instruction for the Five-Year Period, 1844–1848' (1848). In *Selected Writings*, (1997): 143–53.

Bello, Andres. 'Las republicas hispanoamericanas: autonomía cultural.; Obras completas. Caracas: La Casa de Bello (1981). Facsimile of edition of Ministerio de Educación de (1951).

Benamou's account in 'Orson Welles's Transcultural Cinema: An Historical/Textual Reconstruction of the Suspended Film, *It's All True*, 1941–1993 Ph.D. Diss, New York University (1997).

Bendizen, Petr. 'Cultural Policy and the Aesthetics of Industrialism' *European Journal of Cultural Policy* 1 (1995).

Benedict, Stephen, ed. *Public Money and the Muse: Essays on Government Funding for the Arts*. New York: Norton (1991).

Benjamin, Walter. 'The Work of Art in the Age of Mechanical Reproduction' *Illuminations*. Trans. Harry Zohn. London: Fontana, (1992): 211–44.

Bennett, Oliver. 'Cultural Policy in the United Kingdom: Collapsing Rationales and the End of a Tradition' *European Journal of Cultural Policy* 1, no. 2 (1995): 199–216.

Bennett, Tony, Gillian Swanson, Toby Miller, and Gordon Tait. 'Youth Cultures and Arts Policies' *Culture and Policy* 2, no. 2–3, no. 1 (1990–91): 135–56.

Bennett, Tony. 'Culture: Theory and Policy' *Culture and Policy* 1, no. 1 (1989): 5–8.

Bennett, Tony. 'Being 'In the True' of Cultural Studies' *Southern Review* 26, no. 2 (1993): 217–38.

Bennett, Tony. 'Culture, Government and the Social' *Culture and Policy* 8, no. 3 (1997): 169–76.

Bennett, Tony. 'Putting Policy into Cultural Studies' *Cultural Studies*. Lawrence Grossberg, Cary Nelson and Paula A. Treichler. New York: Routledge (1992): 23–37.

Bennett, Tony. 'Regulated Restlessness: Museums, Liberal Government and the Historical Sciences' *Economy and Society* 26, no. 2 (1997): 161–90.

Bennett, Tony. 'Useful Culture' *Cultural Studies* 6, no. 3 (1992): 395–408.

Bennett, Tony. *Outside Literature*. London: Routledge (1990).

Bennett, Tony. *The Birth of the Museum: History, Theory, and Politics*. London: Routledge (1995).

Berezin, Mabel. 'Political Belonging: Emotion, Nation, and Identity in Fascist Italy' *State/Culture: State-Formation after the Cultural Turn*. Ed. George Steinmetz. Ithaca: Cornell UP (1999): 355–77.

Berger, Mark T. *Under Northern Eyes: Latin American Studies and U.S. Hegemony in the Americas, 1898–1990*. Bloomington: Indiana University Press (1995).

Berland, Jody and S. Hornstein, eds. *Capital Culture: A Reader on Modernist Legacies, State Institutions and the Value(s) of Art*. Montréal: McGill-Queens UP (1996).

Berman, Nathaniel. 'Nationalism Legal and Linguistic: The Teachings of European Jurisprudence' *New York University Journal of International Law and Politics* 24, no. 4 (1992): 1515–78.

Berman, Ronald. 'Lobbying for Entitlements: Advocacy and Political Action in the Arts' *Journal of Arts Management and Law* 21, no. 3 (1991).

Bernstein, Richard. 'Arts Endowment's Opponents Are Fighting Fire With Fire' *New York Times* (30 May 1990): C13, C15.

Bethell, Leslie, ed. *Latin America. Economy and Society Since 1930*. Cambridge: Cambridge UP (1998).

Bethell, Leslie. *A Cultural History of Latin America. Literature, Music and the Visual Arts in the 19th and 20th Centuries*. Cambridge: Cambridge UP (1998).

Bianchini, Franco and Michael Parkinson, Eds *Cultural Policy and Urban Regeneration: The West European Experience*. Manchester: Manchester UP (1993).

Bianchini, Franco. 'Cultural Policy and Urban Social Movements: The Response of the 'New Left' in Rome (1976–85) and London (1981–86)' *Leisure and Urban Processes: Critical Studies of Leisure Policy in West European Cities*. ed. Peter Bramham et al. London: Routledge (1989).

Bianchini, Franco. 'GLC R.I.P.: Cultural Policies in London 1981–1986' *New Formations* no. 1 (1987).

Binns, Vivienne, ed. *Community and the Arts*. Leichardt: Pluto P (1991).

Birch, David. 'An 'Open' Environment: Asian Case Studies in the Regulation of Public Culture' *Continuum* 12, no. 3 (1998): 335–48.

Birch, David. 'Constructing Asian Values: National Identities and 'Responsible' Citizenship' *Social Semiotics* 8, nos. 2–3 (1998): 177–201.

Black, Samuel. 'Revisionist Liberalism and the Decline of Culture' *Ethics* 102, no. 2 (1992): 244–67.

Blair, Bowen. 'American Indians vs. American Museums' *American Indian Journal* 5, no. 5 (1979): 13–21.

Blau, Judith R. *The Shape of Culture: A Study of Contemporary Cultural Patterns in the United States*. Cambridge: Cambridge UP (1992).

Blaug, Mark and K. King, ed. *The Economics of the Arts*. London: Martin Robertson (1976).

Blaug, Mark and K. King. 'Does the Arts Council Know What it's Doing?' *Encounter* (1973): 6–16.

Bloch-Lainé, Amaya. 'Philanthropie Anglo-Saxonne' *Libération* (3 July 2000): 7.

Blum, Albert A., ed. The Arts: Years of Development, Time of Decision. Austin: U of Texas P (1976).

Boaz, David. 'The Separation of Art and State' Vital Speeches of the Day 61, no. 17 (1995): 541–43.

Boehm, Eric. 'Mixed Reviews on Brit Pic Fund Revise' Variety (15 December 1998): 5, 24.

Boeira, Nelson. Prefáce. 1 Bienal de Artes Visuais do Mercosul, Porto Alegre: Fundação Bienal do Mercosul, 1997 9.

Boime, Albert. 'The Cultural Politics of the Art Academy' The Eighteenth Century 35, no. 3 (1994): 203–22.

Boli, John and George M. Thomas. 'World Culture in the World Polity: A Century of International Non-Governmental Organization' American Sociological Review 62, no. 2 (1997): 171–90.

Bolton, Kingsley and Christopher Hutton. 'Bad and Banned Language: Triad Secret Societies, the Censorship of the Cantonese Vernacular, and Colonial Language Policy in Hong Kong' Language in Society 24, no. 2 (1995): 159–86.

Bolton, Richard, ed. Culture Wars: Documents from the Recent Controversies in the Arts. New York: The New P (1992).

Bonetti, Shane and Chris Madden. 'Utilising a Broad Definition of Cultural Economics' European Journal of Cultural Policy 2, no. 2 (1996): 255–68.

Boniface, Priscilla and Peter J. Fowler. Heritage and Tourism in `the Global Village'. London: Routledge (1993).

Bordowitz, Gregg. Presentation for Conference on Cultural Capital/Cultural Labor, Privatization of Culture Project for Research on Cultural Policy, New York University and New School University, New York City, (1–2 December 2000).

Borneman, John and Nick Fowler. 'Europeanization' Annual Review of Anthropology no. 26 (1997): 487–514.

Boulding, Kenneth. 'Toward the Development of a Cultural Economics' Social Science Quarterly 53 (September 1977): 267–84.

Bourdieu, Pierre, A. Darbel, and D. Schnapper. The Love of Art: European Art Museums and Their Public. Stanford: Stanford UP (1991).

Bourdieu, Pierre. Distinction: A Social Critique of the Judgement of Taste. Trans. Richard Nice. Cambridge, Mass.: Harvard UP (1984).

Bowen, W.G., Nyren, T.I., Turner, S.E., and Duffy, E.A. The Charitable Nonprofits. San Francisco: Jossey-Bass (1994).

Boyd, Don. 'Cowards, Liars, Cultural Despots and Subsidized Cronies: A Portrait of Britain's Film Industry – From the Inside, Naturally.... ' New Statesman (31 October 1997): 34.

Boyle, Mark and George Hughes. 'The Politics of the Representation of 'the real': Discourses from the Left on Glasgow's Role as European City of Culture, 1990' Area 23, no. 3 (1991): 217–28.

Brademas, John. 'The Arts and Politics: A Commentary' Mediterranean Quarterly 1, no. 2 (1990): 93–105.

Braman, Sandra. 'Trade and Information Policy' Media, Culture & Society 12, no. 3 (1990): 361–85.

Bray, Tamara L. and Thomas W. Killion, Eds. Reckoning with the Dead: The Larson Bay Repatriation and the Smithsonian Institution. Washington: Smithsonian Institution P (1994).

Breton, A. 'Nationalism and Language Policies' Canadian Journal of Economics 9, no. 4 (1978): 656–68.

Brett, G. 'Earth and Museum – Local and Global?' Third Text (1989): 89–96.

Brighouse, Harry. 'Neutrality, Publicity, and State Funding of the Arts' Philosophy & Public Affairs 24, no. 1 (1995): 35–63.

Brighton, Andrew. 'Towards a Command Culture: New Labour's Cultural Policy and Soviet Socialist Realism' Critical Quarterly 41, no. 3 (1999): 24–34.

Briller, B.R. 'The Globalization of American TV' Television Quarterly 24, no. 3 (1990): 71–79.

British Council. Making the Connection. (1999).

British Film Commission. http://www.britfilmcom.co.uk/content/filming/site.asp.

Britto, Antônio. (1997) Prefáce. 1 *Bienal de Artes Visuais do Mercosul*. Porto Alegre: Fundação Bienal do Mercosul, 8.

Bronner, Simon J., ed. *Consuming Visions: Accumulation and Display of Goods in America* 1880–1920. New York: WW Norton (1989).

Brooks, Arthur C. 'Toward a Demand-Side Cure for Cost Disease in the Performing Arts' *Journal of Economic Issues* 31, no. 1 (1997): 197–207.

Brooks, David. 'Never for GATT' *American Spectator* 27, no. 1 (1994): 34–37.

Browett, John and Richard, Leaver. 'Shifts in the Global Capitalist Economy and the National Economic Domain' *Australian Geographical Studies* 27, no. 1 (1989): 31–46.

Brown, Chris 'Cultural Diversity and International Political Theory.' *Review of International Studies* 26, no. 2 (2000): 199–213.

Bruce, David. *Scotland the Movie*. Edinburgh: Polygon (1996).

Buchwalter, Andrew., ed. *Culture and Democracy: Social and Ethical Issues in Public Support for the Arts and Humanities*. Boulder: Westview P (1992).

Buck, Elizabeth B. 'Asia and the Global Film Industry' *East-West Film Journal* 6, no. 2 (1992): 116–33.

Buckingham, David. 'News Media, Political Socialization and Popular Citizenship: Towards a New Agenda' *Critical Studies in Mass Communication* 14, no. 4 (1997): 344–66.

Buntinx, Gustavo. (Forthcoming) '"Another Goddamned Gringo Trick": MoMA's Curatorial Construction of 'Latin American Art' (And Some Inverted Mirrors)." *Representing Latinamerican/Latino Art in the New Millennium: Curatorial Issues and Propositions*. ed. Mari Carmen Ramírez. Austin: U of Texas P.

Burgelman, Jean-Claude and Caroline Pauwels. 'Audiovisual Policy and Cultural Identity in Small European States: The Challenge of a Unified Market' *Media, Culture & Society* 14, no. 2 (1992): 169–83.

Burges, Sean W. 'Strength in Numbers: Latin American Trade Blocs, a Free Trade Area of the Americas and the Problem of Economic Development' *Council on Hemispheric Affairs Occasional Paper* no. 2 (April 1998).

Burkholder, Mark A. and Lyman L. Johnson. *Colonial Latin America*. 3rd ed. New York: Oxford UP (1998).

Burt, Richard. '"Degenerate 'Art'": Public Aesthetics and the Simulation of Censorship in Postliberal Los Angeles and Berlin' *The Administration of Aesthetics: Censorship, Political Criticism, and the Public Sphere*. ed. Richard Burt. Minneapolis: U of Minnesota P (1994): 216–59.

Burton, Benedict. *The Anthropology of World's Fairs*. Berkeley (1983).

Burton-Carvajal, Julianne. 'South American Cinema' *World Cinema: Critical Approaches*. ed. John Hill and Pamela Church Gibson. Oxford: Oxford UP (2000): 194–210.

Busch, Noel F. 'Nelson A. Rockefeller' *Life* (27 April 1942): 80–90.

Caivano, Joan M. 'Cuba's Deal with the Dollar' *Dollars, Darkness, and Diplomacy: Three Perspectives on Cuba. Caribe* 6 (July 1994). http://www.georgetown.edu/sfs/programs/clas/Caribe/bp6.htm.

Calder, Angus. 'Review of *Cultural Policy and Urban Regeneration*' *Political Quarterly* 65, no. 4 (1994): 453–55.

Campbell, David. *Writing Security: United States Foreign Policy and the Politics of Identity*. Minneapolis: U of Minnesota P (1992).

Camnitzer, Luis. 'The Biennial of Utopias: The Bienal de la Habana' In BEYOND IDENTITY: *Globalization and Latin American Art*. Eds. Luis Camnitzer and Mari Carmen Ramírez. Minneapolis: University of Minnesota Press (Forthcoming).

Canadian Commission for UNESCO. 'A Working Definition of "Culture"' *Cultures* 4, no. 4 (1977): 78–85.

Canagarajah, A. Suresh. 'The Political Economy of Code Choice in a 'Revolutionary Society': Tamil-English Bilingualism in Jaffna, Sri Lanka' *Language in Society* 24, no. 2 (1995): 187–212.

Cargo, Russell A. 'Cultural Policy in the Era of Shrinking Government' *Policy Studies Review* 14, nos. 1–2 (1995): 215–24.

Carmen, Raff. 'A Cultural Reappraisal of Development: Some Reflections in the Margins of the UN Cultural Development Decennium' *Development* 4 (1995): 32–37.

Carmody, Chi. 'When 'Cultural Identity was not an Issue': Thinking About Canada – Certain Measures Concerning Periodicals' *Law and Policy in International Business* 30, no. 2 (1999): 231–320.

Carr, C. 'The Bad Apple Defense and Other Symptoms of Spinelessness in the Art World' *Village Voice* (12 October 1999): 60.

Carr, C. 'War on Art: The Sexual Politics of Censorship' *Village Voice* (5 June 1990): 25–30.

Carvajal, Doreen with Andrew Ross Sorkin, 'Lycos to Combine With Terra Networks in a $12 Billion Deal.' *New York Times* (online edition) 16 May 2000.

Casonu, Néstor, Regional Managing Director for EMI Music Publishing. (2000) Interview with George Yúdice. Miami Beach, 14 March.

Castel, Robert. 'From Dangerousness to Risk' *The Foucault Effect: Studies in Governmentality.* ed. Graham Burchell et al. Chicago: U of Chicago P (1991).

Castillo, Jose del and Martin F. Murphy. 'Migration, National Identity and Cultural Policy in the Dominican Republic' *Journal of Ethnic Studies* 15, no. 3 (1987): 49–69.

Castro, Fidel. 'Palabras a los intellectuales' (1961). In *Política cultural de la Revolución Cubana. Documentos.* Havana: Editorial de Ciencias Sociales (1977): 16–17.

Catani, Afra nio Mendes. 'Politica Cenematografica nos anos Collor 1990–1992: um arremedo neoliberal' *Imagens*, 3 (December) (1994).

Catlin, Stanton L. 'Traveller-Reporter Artists and the Empirical Tradition in Post-Independence Latin American Art.' In Ades, *Art in Latin America* 41–61 (1989).

Central Committee of the All-Union Communist Party. 'Decree on the Reconstruction of Literary and Artistic Organizations' *Art in Theory 1900–1990: An Anthology of Changing Ideas.* ed. Charles Harrison and Paul Wood. Oxford: Blackwell (1996): 400.

Chandler, Henry P. 'The Attitude of the Law Toward Beauty' *American Bar Association Journal* 8 (1922): 470–74.

Chartrand, Harry Hillman. 'International Cultural Affairs: A Fourteen Country Survey' *Journal of Arts Management, Law and Society* 22, no. 2 (1992): 134–54.

Chartrand, Harry Hillman. 'Subjectivity in an Era of Scientific Imperialism: Shadows in an Age of Reason' *Journal of Arts Management and Law* 18, no. 3 (1988): 5–29.

Chávez, Fermín. (1973) *La cultura en la época de Rosas.* Buenos Aires: Ediciones Theoría.

Cherbo, Joni M. and Margaret J. Wyszomirski. 'Mapping the Public Life of the Arts in America' *The Public Life of the Arts in America.* ed. Joni M. Cherbo and Margaret J. Wyszomirski. New Brunswick: Rutgers UP (2000): 3–21.

Childers, Erskine. 'Old-Boying' *London Review of Books* 16, no. 16 (1994): 3, 5.

Childs, Elizabeth C. 'Museums and the American Indian: Legal Aspects of Repatriation' *Council for Museum Anthropology Newsletter* 4, no. 4 (1980): 4–27.

Chong, Derrick. 'Institutional Identities and National Museums in the United Kingdom' *Journal of Arts Management, Law and Society* 29, no. 4 (2000): 271–89.

Christie, Ian. 'Will Lottery Money Assure the British Film Industry? Or Should Chris Smith be Rediscovering the Virtues of State Intervention?' *New Statesman* (20 June 1997): 38.

Christopherson, Susan and Michael Storper. 'The City as Studio; the World as Back Lot: The Impact of Vertical Disintegration on the Location of the Motion Picture Industry' *Environment and Planning D: Society and Space* 4, no. 3 (1986): 305–20.

Christopherson, Susan. 'Flexibility and Adaptation in Industrial Relations: The Exceptional Case of the U.S. Media Entertainment Industries' *Under the Stars: Essays on Labor Relations in Arts and Entertainment*. ed. L.S. Gray and R.L. Seeber. Ithaca: Cornell UP (1996): 86–112.

Chun, Allen. 'The Culture Industry as National Enterprise: The Politics of Heritage in Contemporary Taiwan' *Culture and Policy* 6, no. 1 (1994): 69–89.

City of South Miami Beach. 'Economic Development Division.' http://www.ci.miami-beach.fl.us/

Clark, David E. and James R. Kahn. 'The Social Benefits of Urban Cultural Amenities' *Journal of Regional Science* 28, no. 3 (1988): 363–77.

Clarke, Hilary. 'Hidden Tax Rises: The Making of the Movies' *Independent on Sunday* (7 March 1999): 3.

Clarke, Tom. 'Made with Passion, Fuelled by Cash' *New Statesman* (17 April 1998): 23.

Clifford, James. 'Four Northwest Coast Museums: Travel Reflections' In Karp & Lavine *Exhibiting Cultures* Washington: Smithsonian Institution P (1991).

Clotfelter, Charles T, ed. *Who Benefits from the Nonprofit Sector?* Chicago: U of Chicago P (1992).

Clotfelter, Charles T. *Federal Tax Policy and Charitable Giving*. Chicago: U of Chicago P (1985).

Cobo, Leila. 'Midem Will Be Here in 2000, If Anywhere' *Miami Herald* 6 Oct. 1999: 1E (1999).

Coelho, Teixeira. (1999) 'From Cultural Policy to Political Culture – Proposals for a Continental Cultural Policy' *Atre Sem Fronteiras: First Forum for Cultural Integration*. ed. Mônica Allende Serra. Saã Paulo: Arte Sem Fronteiras/UNESCO, (1999) 7–34.

Coffey, Mary. 'What Puts the "Culture" in "Multiculturalism"?: An Analysis of Culture, Government, and the Politics of Mexican Identity' *Multicultural Curriculum: New Directions for Social Theory, Practice, and Policy*. Ed. Ram Mahalingam and Cameron McCarthy. New York: Routledge (2001): 37–55.

Cohen, Robin. *Contested Domains: Debates in International Labor Studies*. London: Zed (1991).

Cohen, Roger. 'Aux Armes! France Rallies to Battle Sly and T. Rex' *New York Times* (2 January 1994): H1, 22–3.

Cohen, Roger. 'Exhibiting the Art of History's Dustbin' *New York Times* (17 August 1999): E1, E3.

Cohen, Roger. 'The Sorrows of Goethe: A Creepy East German Tale' *New York Times* (19 March 1999): A3.

Cohen, Roger. 'Trade Pact Still Eludes Negotiators: U.S. Demands Open Technology Market' *The New York Times* (Dec. 7): D1 & D6 (1993).

Coleman, Lawrence Vail. *The Museum in America: A Critical Study*. Washington: American Association of Museums (1979).

Columbia-VLA Journal of Law & the Arts.

'Comras Betting on Entertainment Industry', *Miami Herald* 11 August 1998.

Congressional Record. (10 March 1965): 4594.

Congressional Record. (13 September 1965): 23619.

Congressional Record. (18 May 1989): 85594.

Coombe, Rosemary. *The Cultural Life of Intellectual Properties: Authorship, Approrpiation, and the Law*. Durham: Duke UP (1998).

Coombes, Annie E. *Reinventing Africa: Museums, Material Culture and Popular Imagination in Late Victorian and Edwardian England*. New Haven: Yale UP (1994).

Coombs, P.H. *The Fourth Dimension of Foreign Policy: Educational and Cultural Affairs*. New York: Harper and Row (1964).

Corner, John and Sylvia Harvey, Eds. *Enterprise and Heritage: Crosscurrents of National Culture in the 1980s*. London: Routledge, (1991).

Cornford, James and Kevin Robins. 'Beyond the Last Bastion: Industrial Restructuring and the Labor Force in the British Television Industry' *Global Productions: Labor in the Making of the 'Information Society'*. ed. Gerald Sussman and John A. Lent. Cresskill: Hampton P (1998). 191–212.

Council of Australian Museum Associations. *Previous Possessions, New Obligations: Policies for Museums in Australia and Aboriginal and Torres Strait Islander Peoples*. Melbourne (1993).

Cowan, Matt and Linda Wertheimer. 'Northern Ireland Film Commission' *All Things Considered*, National Public Radio (18 May 1998).

Craik, Jennifer. 'Mapping the Links Between Cultural Studies and Cultural Policy' *Southern Review* 28, no. 2 (1995): 190–207.

Crane, David. 'Real Test of WTO will be Cultural Agreement' *Toronto Star* (2 December 1999).

Crane, Diane. *The Production of Culture: Media and the Urban Arts*. Thousand Oaks: Sage (1992).

Crane, Crane, Nobuko Kawashima, Kenichi Kawasaki, and Rosanne Martorella, eds *Cultural Policies in a global Context: Globalization, and Global Cities*. New York: Routledge (Forthcoming).

Crane, Diane. *The Transformation of the Avant-Garde: The New York Art World, 1940–1985*. Chicago: U of Chicago P (1987).

Crimp, Douglas. *On the Museum's Ruins*. Cambridge, Mass.: MIT P (1993).

Culver, Stuart. 'Whistler v. Ruskin: The Courts, the Public, and Modern Art' *The Administration of Aesthetics: Censorship, Political Criticism, and the Public Sphere*. ed. Richard Burt. Minneapolis: U of Minnesota P (1994): 149–67.

Cummings, Milton C. Jr., 'Government and the Arts: An Overview' *Public Money and the Muse: Essays on Government Funding for the Arts*. Ed. Stephen Benedict. New York: Norton (1991): 49.

Cummings, Milton C. Jr., 'Government and the Arts: Policy Problems in the Fields of Art, Literature and Music' *Policy Studies Journal* 5 (Fall 1976): 114–24.

Cummings, Milton C. Jr., and J. Mark Davidson Schuster, eds *Who's to Pay for the Arts? The International Search for Models of Support*. New York: American Council for the Arts (1989).

Cummings, Milton C. Jr., and Richard S. Katz, eds *The Patron State: Government and the Arts in Europe, North America, and Japan*. New York: Oxford UP (1987).

Cunningham, Stuart and Terry Flew. 'De-Westernizing Australia? Media Systems and Cultural Coordinates' *De-Westernizing Media Studies*. ed. James Curran and Myung-Jin Park. London: Routledge (2000): 237–48.

Cunningham, Stuart and Terry Flew. 'Media Policy' *Government, Politics, Power, & Policy in Australia*, 6th edition. ed. Dennis Woodward, Andrew Parkin, and John Summers. Melbourne: Longman, (1997): 468–85.

Cunnignham, Stuart and Terry Flew. 'Policy' *The Media & Communications in Australia*. ed. Stuart Cunningham and Graeme Turner. Sydney: Allen & Unwin (2002): 48–61.

Cunningham, Stuart and Elizabeth Jacka. *Australian Television and International Mediascapes*. Melbourne: Cambridge UP (1996).

Cunningham, Stuart. 'Cultural Criticism and Policy' *Arena Magazine* no. 7 (October–November 1993): 33–35.

Cunningham, Stuart. *Framing Culture: Criticism and Policy in Australia*. Sydney: Allen and Unwin (1992).

Curtin, Michael. 'Beyond the Vast Wasteland: The Policy of Global Television and the Politics of the American Empire' *Journal of Broadcasting and Electronic Media* 37, no. 2 (1993): 127–46.

Cwi, David. 'Public Support of the Arts: Three Arguments Examined' *Journal of Behavioral Economics* 8 (Summer 1979): 39–68.

DaCosta, Carolina. 'Behind Brazil's Internet Boom' *InfoBrazil.com* II, 55 28 July – August 3 (2000). http://www.InfoBrazil.com

Dahl, Gustavo. "Embrafilme: Present Problems and Future Possibilities." In Johnson and Stam eds, *Brazilian Cinema* expanded edition. New York: Columbia UP. 104–108.

Deleuze, Gilles. (1984) *Kant's Critial Philosophy: the Doctrine of the Faculties.* Trans. Hugh Tomlinson and Barbara Habberjam. Minneapolis: U of Minnesota P.

D'Emilio, John and Estelle B. Freedman. *Intimate Matters: A History of Sexuality in America.* New York: Harper & Row (1988).

Danan, Martine. 'Marketing the Hollywood Blockbuster in France' *Journal of Popular Film and Television* 23, no. 3 (1995): 131–40.

Danto, Arthur C. 'Elitism' and the N.E.A' *The Nation* (17 November 1997): 6–7.

Danziger, Marie. 'Policy Analysis Postmodernized: Some Political and Pedagogical Ramifications' *Policy Studies Journal* 23, no. 3 (1995): 435–50.

Darnton, Robert. 'Censorship, a Comparative View: France, 1789 – East Germany, 1989' *Representations* no. 49 (Winter 1995): 40–60.

Dawtrey, Adam and Benedict Carver. 'Power Trio Ink Int'l Deal' *Daily Variety Gotham* (1 March 1999): 1, 34.

Dawtrey, Adam. 'New Strategy Comes to the 4' *Variety* (8–14 February 1999): 33, 40.

Dawtrey, Adam. 'Parker Tops U.K. Film Council' *Variety* (9–15 August 1999): 16.

Dawtrey, Adam. 'Playing Hollywood's Game: Eurobucks Back Megabiz' *Variety* (7–13 March 1994): 1, 75.

Dawtrey, Adam. 'U.K. Pols Give up Plan for Film Levy' *Daily Variety Gotham* (1 December 1998): 10.

Dawtrey, Adam. 'Woodward to Top U.K. Film Council' *Variety* (4–10 October 1999): 29.

de Grazia, Victoria. 'Mass Culture and Sovereignty: The American Challenge to European Cinemas, 1920–1960' *Journal of Modern History* 61 no. 1 (1989).

deGrazia, Edward. *Girls Lean Back Everywhere: The Law of Obscenity and the Assault on Genius.* New York: Random House (1992).

Department of Commerce. *The Migration of U.S. Film and Television Production,* Washington, D.C. (2001).

Department for Culture, Media and Sport. 'Chris Smith Goes to Hollywood' M2 PressWIRE (27 October 1997).

Dermody, Susan and Elizabeth Jacka. *The Screening of Australia Volume 2: Anatomy of a National Cinema.* Sydney: Currency P (1988).

Derrida, Jacques. '"To Do Justice to Freud": The History of Madness in the Age of Psychoanalysis' Trans. Pascale-Anne Brault and Michael Naas. *Critical Inquiry* 20, no. 2 (1994): 227–66.

Deutsche, Rosalyn. 'Art and Public Space: Questions of Democracy' *Social Text* no. 33 (1992): 34–53.

Deutsche, Rosalyn. 'Uneven Development: Public Art in New York City' *October* no. 47 (Winter 1988): 3–52.

Dicks, Bella. 'Encoding and Decoding the People: Circuits of Communication at a Local Heritage Museum' *European Journal of Communication* 15, no. 1 (2000): 61–78.

Di Girólamo, Claudio. 'Ciudadania cultural: una carta de navegacion hacia el futuro (intervencion en la plenaria). Stockholm, Sweden, 30 March – 2 April (1998). http://www.mineduc.cl/cultura/ciudadania.html.

Dillon, C. Douglas. 'Cross-Cultural Communication Through the Arts' *Columbia Journal of World Business* 6, no. 5 (1971): 31–38.

DiMaggio, Paul J. 'Can Culture Survive the Marketplace?' *Journal of Arts Management and Law* 13, no. 1 (1983): 61–87.

DiMaggio, Paul J. 'Cultural Entrepreneurship in Nineteenth-Century Boston: The Creation of an Organizational Base for High Culture in America' *Media, Culture & Society* 4 (1982): 33–50.

DiMaggio, Paul J. 'Cultural Entrepreneurship in Nineteenth-Century Boston, Part. II: The Classification and Framing of American Art' *Media, Culture & Society* 4 (1982): 303–22.

DiMaggio, Paul J. 'Cultural Policy Studies: What They are and Why We Need Them' *Journal of Arts Management and Law* 13, no. 1 (1983): 241–48.

DiMaggio, Paul J. 'State Expansion and Organizational Fields' *Organizational Theory and Public Policy.* ed. Richard H. Hall and Robert E. Quinn. Beverly Hills: Sage (1983): 147–62.

DiMaggio, Paul J., ed. *Nonprofit Enterprise in the Arts: Studies in Mission and Constraint.* New York: Oxford UP (1986).

DiMaggio, Paul J. and Francie Ostrower. 'Participation in the Arts by Black and White Americans' *Social Forces* 68, no. 3 (1990): 753–78.

DiMaggio, Paul J. and Michael Useem. 'Cultural Democracy in a Period of Cultural Expansion' *Performers and Performances.* ed. Jack B. Kamerman and Rosanne Martarella. South Hadley: Bergin and Garvey, (1983).

DiMaggio, Paul J. and Michael Useem. 'Cultural Property and Public Policy: Emerging Tensions in Government Support for the Arts' *Social Research* 45 (1978): 356–89.

DiMaggio, Paul J. and Michael Useem. 'Social Class and Arts Consumption: The Origin and Consequences of Class Differences in Exposure to the Arts in America' *Theory and Society* 5 (1978): 141–61.

DiMaggio, Paul J. and Walter W. Powell. 'The Iron Cage Revisited: Institutional Isomorphism and Collective Ratinality in Organizationl Fields' *American Sociological Review* 48, no. 2 (1983): 147–60.

DiMaggio, Paul J. and Walter W. Powell, eds *The New Institutionalism in Organizational Analysis.* Chicago: U of Chicago P (1991).

DiMaggio, Paul J., Michael Useem, and Paula Brown. *Audience Studies of the Performing Arts and Museums: A Critical Review.* National Endowment for the Arts, Research Division Report No. 9, (1978).

Dittgen, H. 'The American Debate about Immigration in the 1990s: A New Nationalism After the End of the Cold War?' *Stanford Humanities Review* 5, no. 2 (1997): 256–86.

Dobson, John. 'TNCs and the Corruption of GATT: Free Trade Versus Fair Trade' *Journal of Business Ethics* 12, no. 7 (1993): 573–78.

Dominguez, Virginia R. 'Invoking Culture: The Messy Side of "Cultural Politics"' *South Atlantic Quarterly* 91, no. 1 (1992): 19–42.

Dominus, Susan. 'Relief Pitcher' *New York Times Magazine* (8 October 2000).

Donzelot, Jacques. *The Policing of Families.* Trans. Robert Hurley. New York: Pantheon (1979).

Dorland, Michael, ed. *The Cultural Industries in Canada.* Toronto: James Lorimer & Co. (1996).

Dorland, Michael. 'Policing Culture: Canada, State Rationality, and the Governmentalization of Communication' *Capital Culture: A Reader on Modernist Legacies, State Institutions and the Value(s) of Art.* ed. Jody Berland and S. Hornstein. Montréal: McGill-Queens UP (1996).

Dowd, Maureen. 'Jesse Helms Takes No-Lose Position on Art' *New York Times* (28 July 1989): A1, B6.

Dowler, K. 'The Cultural Industry Policy Apparatus' *Capital Culture: A Reader on Modernist Legacies, State Institutions and the Value(s) of Art.* ed. Michael Dorland. Montréal: McGill-Queens UP (1996).

Drake, William J. and Kalypso Nicolaïdis. 'Ideas, Interests, and Institutionalization: Trade in Services and the Uruguay Round' *International Organization* 46, no. 1 (1992): 37–100.

Draper, Lee. *Museum Audiences Today: Building Constituencies for the Future.* Los Angeles: Museum Educators of Southern California (1987).

Dressayre, P. and N. Garbownik. 'The Imaginary Manager or Illusions in the Public Management of Culture in France' *European Journal of Cultural Policy* 1 (1995): 187–97.

Dubin, Steven C. *Bureaucratising the Muse: Public Funds and the Cultural Worker*. Chicago: U of Chicago P (1987).

Dukeminier, J.J., Jr. 'Zoning for Aesthetic Objectives: A Reappraisal' *Law and Contemporary Problems* 20 (1955): 218–37.

Duncan, Carol. *Civilizing Rituals: Inside Public Art Museums*. London: Routledge (1995).

Durand, Jos Carlos. 'Towards Professionalization of the Administration of Culture: A South American Perspective' *European Journal of Cultural Policy* 2, no. 2 (1996): 281–88.

Dworkin, Ronald. A *Matter of Principle*. Cambridge, Mass.: Harvard UP (1985).

Eco, Umberto. 'Towards a Semiotic Inquiry into the Television Message' Trans. Paola Splendore. *Working Papers in Cultural Studies no.* 3 (1972): 103–21.

Echo-Hawk, Walter. 'Museum Rights vs. Indian Rights: Guidelines for Assessing Competing Legal Interests in Native Cultural Resources' *Review of Law and Social Change* 14 (1986): 437–53.

Economist: 2000. Sins of the Secular Missionaries. *Economist* (29 January 2000): 25–27.

Ellison, Sarah. 'New Tate Museum's Name Pops Up in Some Unlikely Places as Free Plug' *Wall Street Journal* (17 May 2000): B13C.

Elmer, Greg. 'US Cultural Policy and the (De)regulation of the Self' *Continuum* 9, no. 1 (1996): 9–24.

Elsner, John and Roger Cardinal, Eds. *The Cultures of Collecting*. Cambridge, Mass.: Harvard UP (1994).

Evans, Peter. *Dependent Development: The Alliance of Local Capital in Brazil*. Princeton: Princeton UP (1979).

Faber, J.P. and Reese Ewing. 'Cisneros Goes Online', *LatinCEO* (December): (1999) 46–53.

Falicov, Tamara L. 'Argentina's Blockbuster Movies and the Politics of Culture Under Neoliberalism' *Media Culture & Society* 22, no. 3 (2000): 327–42.

Farias, Roberto. *Pra frente Brasil: historia, roteiro e dialogos*. Rio de Janeiro: Alhambra (1983).

Feld, Alan L., Michael O'Hare and J. Mark Davidson Schuster, eds *Patrons Despite Themselves: Taxpayers and Arts Policy*. New York: New York UP (1983).

Feldblum, M. '"Citizenship matters": Contemporary Trends in Europe and the United States' *Stanford Humanities Review* 5, no. 2 (1997): 96–113.

Feldstein, Martin, ed. *The Economics of Art Museums*. Chicago: Chicago UP (1991).

Ferguson, Marjorie. 'The Mythology About Globalization' *European Journal of Communication* 7, no. 1 (1992): 69–93.

Ferme, Valerio C. 'Redefining the Aesthetics of Fascism: The Battle Between the Ancients and the Moderns Revisited' *Symposium* 52 (1998): 67–85.

Field, Heather. 'European Media Regulation: The Increasing Importance of the Supranational' *Media International Australia* no. 95 (2000): 91–105.

Fierlbeck, K. 'The Ambivalent Potential of Cultural Identity' *Canadian Journal of Political Science/Revue canadienne de science politique* 29, no. 1 (1996): 3–22.

Filer, Randall K. 'The "Starving Artist"–Myth or Reality? Earnings of Artists in the United States' *Journal of Political Economy* 94 (1986): 56–75.

Filicko, Therese. 'In What Spirit do Americans Cultivate the Arts? A Review of Survey Questions in the Arts' *Journal of Arts Management, Law and Society* 26, no. 3 (1996): 221–46.

Finlayson, Bruce. 'EDUCATION AND TRAINING OF GRADUATE STUDENTS.' Meeting of the Council for Chemical Research (CCR). January (1996). http://www.chem.purdue.edu/ccr/news/jan96/news2.html.

Finney, Angus. *The State of European Cinema: A New Dose of Reality*. London: Cassell (1996).

Fisher, David H. 'Public Art and Public Space' *Soundings* 79, nos. 1–2 (1996): 40–57.

Fisher, John H. 'A Language Policy for Lancastrian England' PMLA 107, no. 5 (1992): 1168–80.

Fitzgerald, Michael. 'Inside Sydney: Harboring Hollywood.' *Time International* (31 July 2000): 48.

Fitzpatrick, Sheila. *The Cultural Front: Power and Culture in Revolutionary Russia*. Ithaca: Cornell UP (1992).

Fogel, Aaron. 'The Prose of Populations and the Magic of Demography' *Western Humanities Review* 47, no. 4 (1993): 312–37.

Forbes, Jill. 'Cultural Policy: The Soul of Man Under Socialism' *Mitterand's France*. ed. Sonia Mazey and Michael Newman. London: Croom Helm (1987): 131–65.

Foster, Arnold W. and Judith R. Blau, Eds. *Art and Society: Readings in the Sociology of the Arts*. Albany: State U of New York P (1989).

Foucault, Michel. 'Conversation with Michel Foucault' *The Threepenny Review* Winter/Spring (1980): 4–5.

Foucault, Michel. 'Governmentality' Trans. Pasquale Pasquino. *The Foucault Effect: Studies in Governmentality*. ed. Graham Burchell, Colin Gordon, and Peter Miller. London: Harvester Wheatsheaf (1991): 87–104.

Foucault, Michel. 'Photogenic Painting' Trans. Dafydd Roberts. *Gérard Fromanger: Photogenic Painting*. ed. Sarah Wilson. London: Black Dog (1999): 83–104.

Foucault, Michel. 'Politics and the Study of Discourse' Trans. A.M. Nazzaro. Rev. C. Gordon. *Ideology and Consciousness* no. 3 (1978): 7–26.

Foucault, Michel. 'Problematics: Excerpts from Conversations' *Crash: Nostalgia for the Absence of Cyberspace*. ed. Robert Reynolds and Thomas Zummer. New York: Third Waxing Space (1994). 121–27.

Foucault, Michel. Lecture, Collège de France, (4 April 1979).

Foucault, Michel. *The History of Sexuality: An Introduction*. Trans. Robert Hurley. Harmondsworth: Penguin (1984).

Fox, Daniel M. *Engines of Culture: Philanthropy and Art Museums*. New Brunswick: Transaction (1995).

Fox, Elizabeth. 'Media and Culture in Latin America' *International Media Research: A Critical Survey*. ed. John Corner, Philip Schlesinger, and Roger Silverstone. London: Routledge (1997): 184–205.

Franco, Jean. *Plotting Women: Gender and Representation in Mexico*. New York: Colombia UP (1989).

Fraser, Andrea. 'Museum Highlights: A Gallery Talk' *A Companion to Cultural Studies*. ed. Toby Miller. Oxford: Blackwell (2001): 391–406.

Freedman, Samuel G. 'Where the Arts Still Sustain the Social Compact' *New York Times* (3 September 2000): 1, 18–19.

Fremantle Prison. http://www.cams.wa.gov.au/web/cams.nsf/web/freoprison.

French, S. 'Letter to the Editor' *Policy Review: The Journal of American Citizenship* 84 (1997): 4–5.

Frey, Bruno S. and Werner W. Pommerehne. 'Art Investment: An Empirical Inquiry' *Southern Economic Journal* 56, no. 2 (1989): 396–409.

Frey, Bruno S. and Werner W. Pommerehne. *Muses and Markets: Explorations in the Economics of the Arts*. Oxford: Basil Blackwell (1989).

Friedman, Sandra. 'Racing With Catastrophe: Representations of the Holocaust and American Jewish Anxiety' Ph.D. Dissertation, New York University, March (2001).

Frith, Simon. 'Knowing One's Place: The Culture of Cultural Industries' *Cultural Studies Birmingham* no. 1 (1991): 134–55.

Fröbel, Folker, Jürgen, Heinrichs, and Otto, Kreye. *The New International Division of Labor: Structural Unemployment in Industrialised Countries and Industrialisation in Developing Countries*. Trans. P. Burgess. Cambridge: Cambridge UP; Paris: Éditions de la Maison des Sciences de l'Homme (1980).

Frow, John. 'Class and Culture: Funding the Arts' *Meanjin* 45, no. 1 (1986): 118–28.

Fullerton, Don. 'On Justifications for Public Support of the Arts' *Journal of Cultural Economics* 15, no. 2 (1991): 67–82.

Gabler, Neal. 'Win Now, or Lose Forever' *The New York Times* 3 May (2000).

Galperin, Hernan. 'Cultural Industries Policy in Regional Trade Agreements: The Cases of NAFTA, the European Union and MERCOSUR' *Media Culture & Society* 21, no. 5 (1999): 627–48.

Gamarekian, Barbara. 'White House Opposes Restrictions on Arts Grants' New York Times (22 March 1990): A1, B4.

Gamson, Zelda F. 'The Stratification of the Academy' Social Text 51 (Summer 1997): 68.

Gans, Herbert J. Popular Culture and High Culture: An Analysis and Evaluation of Taste. New York: Basic, 1974.

Gapinski, James H. 'The Economic Right Triangle of Nonprofit Theatre' Social Science Quarterly 69 (September 1988): 756–63.

Gapinski, James H. 'The Economics of Performing Shakespeare' American Economic Review 74 (May 1983): 458–66.

Granado, Bruno del. Interview with George Yúdice, Miami Beach, 13 March (2000).

García, Beatrice E. 'Entertainment Industry Survey Is Off the Mark' Miami Herald (online edition) 5 December 1998: IC.

García Canclini, Néstor. Hybrid Cultures: Strategies for Entering and Leaving Modernity. Trans. Christopher L. Chiappari and Silvia L. López. Minneapolis: U of Minnesota P (1995).

Garnham, Nicholas. 'Concepts of Culture: Public Policy and the Cultural Industries' Cultural Studies 1, no. 1 (1987): 23–37.

Garton-Smith, Jennifer. 'The Prison Wall: Interpretation Problems for Prison Museums' Open Museum Journal 2 (n. d.).

Graser, Marc. '"Silicon Barrio" getting Latin America online', Variety, 1–7 November (1999): M32–M33.

Gates, Henry Louis, Jr.. '2 Live Crew, Deconded. Rap Music Group's Use of Street Language in Context of Afro-American Cultural Heritage Analyzed' New York Times 19 June: (1990) A15(N), A23(L).

Gee, Constance Bumgarner. 'Four More Years–So What?' Arts Education Policy Review 98, no. 6 (1997): 8–13.

Gellman, Ernest F. Good Neighbor Policy. United States Policies in Latin America, 1933–1945. Baltimore: The Johns Hopkins UP (1979).

Gendron, Richard. 'Arts and Craft: Implementing an Arts-Based Development Strategy in a "Controlled Growth" County' Sociological Perspectives 39, no. 4 (1996): 539–55.

Gerbi, Antonello. (1973) The Dispute of the New World; the History of a Polemic, 1750–1900. Rev. ed., trans. Jeremy Moyle. Pittsburgh: U of Pittsburgh P.

Gies, D.L. J.S. Ott, and J.M. Shafritz, eds., The Nonprofit Organizations: Essential Readings. Pacific Grove: Brooks/Cole (1989).

Gilmore, Samuel. 'Minorities and Distributional Equity at the National Endowment for the Arts' Journal of Arts Management, Law, and Society 23, no. 2 (1993): 137–73.

Gingrich, Arnold. Business and the Arts: An Answer to Tomorrow. New York: Eriksson (1969).

Ginsburg, Faye. 'Embedded Aesthetics: Creating a Discursive Space for Indigenous Media' Cultural Anthropology 9, no. 3 (1994): 365–82.

Girard, Augustin. 'Policy and the Arts: The Forgotten Cultural Industries' Journal of Comparative Economics 5, no. 1 (1981): 61–68.

Girard, Augustin. Cultural Development: Experiences and Policies. Paris: UNESCO (1982).

Glaser, Jane R. and Artemis A. Zenetou, Eds Gender Perspectives: Essays on Women in Museums. Washington: Smithsonian Institution P (1994).

Glueck, Grace. 'Senate Vote Prompts Anger, but some Approval, in the Art World' New York Times (28 July 1989): B 6.

Gold, Sonia S. 'Policy and Administative Change in the Arts in Australia' Prometheus 5, no. 1 (1987): 146–54.

Goldfarb, Alice Marquis. *Art Lessons: Learning from the Rise and Fall of Public Arts Funding*. New York: Basic (1995).

Golodner, Jack. 'The Downside of Protectionism' *New York Times* (27 February 1994): H6.

Goodwin, Philip L. 'Foreword' *Brazil Builds: Architecture New and Old 1652–1942*. New York: The Museum of Modern Art (1943).

Goodwin, Steven. 'Screen Revival for Scotland's Forgotten Film Collection' *Independent* (13 August 1998): 6.

Gorman, Clem. 'Do the Arts Need Massive Subsidy?' *Quadrant* 38, no. 9 (1994): 51–54.

Graham, Gordon. 'The Politics of Culture: Art in a Free Society' *History of European Ideas* 13, no. 6 (1991): 763–74.

Grampp, William D. 'Rent-Seeking in Arts Policy' *Public Choice* 60 (February 1989): 113–21.

Grampp, William D. *Pricing the Priceless: Art, Artists, and Economics*. London: Basic (1989).

Gramsci, Antonio. (1971) *Selections from the Prison Notebooks*. Ed. and trans. Quintin Hoare and Geoffrey Nowell Smith. New York: International Publishers.

Gran Fury. 'International AIDS Information' *The Act* 2, no. 1 (1990): 5–9.

Granado, Bruno del. Interview with George Yúdice, Miami Beach (13 March 2000).

Graser, Marc. '"Silicon Barrio" Getting Latin America Online.' *Variety* (1–7 November 1999): M32-M33.

Gray, Clive. 'Comparing Cultural Policy: A Reformulation' *European Journal of Cultural Policy* 2, no. 2 (1996): 213–22.

Gray, Clive. 'The Commodification of Cultural Policy in Britain' *Contemporary Political Studies*. ed. J. Lovenduski and J. Stanyer. Belfast: Political Studies Association of the United Kingdom (1995): 307–15.

Gray, Jerry. 'Cuts to the Arts Would Hit New York Hardest' *New York Times* (2 October 1997): A14.

Gray, Jerry. 'House Approves Measure to Kill Arts Endowment' *New York Times* (16 July 1997): A15.

Gray, L. and Seeber, R. 'Introduction' *Under the Stars: Essays on Labor Relations in Arts and Entertainment*. ed. L.S. Gray and R.L. Seeber. Ithaca: Cornell UP (1996): 1–13.

Gray, L. and Seeber, R. 'The Industry and the Unions: An Overview' *Under the Stars: Essays on Labor Relations in Arts and Entertainment*. ed. L.S. Gray and R.L. Seeber. Ithaca: Cornell UP (1996): 15–49.

Greenblatt, Stephen. *Learning to Curse: Essays in Early Modern Culture*. New York: Routledge, 1990.

Greenblatt, Stephen. 'Resonance and Wonder' *Exhibiting Cultures: The Poetics and Politics of Museum Display*. ed. Ivan Karp and Steven C. Lavine. Washington: Smithsonian Institution P, 1991. 42–56.

Greenfeld, Karl Taro. 'A New Way of Giving' *Time* (24 July 2000): 49–51.

Greenfield, Jeannette. *The Return of Cultural Treasures*. Cambridge: Cambridge UP (1989).

Greenhalgh, Paul. *Ephemeral Vistas: The Expositions Universelles, Great Exhibitions and World's Fairs, 1851–1939*. Manchester: Manchester UP (1988).

Grey, Rodney de C. *Concepts of Trade Diplomacy and Trade in Services*. Hemel Hempstead: Harvester Wheatsheaf (1990).

Griffiths, Ron. 'The Politics of Cultural Policy in Urban Regeneration Strategies' *Policy and Politics* 21, no. 1 (1993): 39–46.

Gritten, David. 'The Other Ireland Unreels: After Watching the Republic Become a Movie Mecca, the Northern Ireland Film Industry is Growing Under Today's Relatively Tranquil Conditions' *Los Angeles Times* (1 February 1998): 4.

Grimson, Alejandro. Comments on the Cultural Policies of MERCOSUL, International Seminar on 'Economic Integration and the Culture Industries in Latin America and the Caribbean, Buenos Aires, 30–31 July (1998).

————. *Relatos de la diferencia y de la igualdad: Los bolivianos en Buenos Aires*. Buenos Aires: Eudeba/Felafacs (1999).

Grosfoguel Romón 'World Cities in the Caribbean: The Rise of Miami and San Juan.' *Review* 17, 3 (Summer): (1994) 351–381.

Gross, David. 'Critical Synthesis on Urban Knowledge: Remembering and Forgetting in the Modern City' *Social Epistemology* 4, no. 1 (1990): 3–9.

Grossman, Philip J. and Peter Kenyon. 'Artists' Subsidy of the Arts: A Comment' *Australian Economic Papers* 28, no. 53 (1989): 280–87.

Grosman, Ernesto Livon. (2000) 'Patagonia: narrativas de viaje y nacion.' Ph.D. Diss. New York University.

Groves, Don. 'A Major Force O'seas' *Variety* (12–18 April 1999): 9.

Groves, Don. 'O'seas B.O. Power Saluted at Confab' *Variety* 356, no. 4 (1994): 18.

Groys, Boris. 'The Struggle Against the Museum: Or, the Display of Art in Totaliarian Space' Trans. Thomas Seifrid. *Museum Culture: Histories, Discourses, Spectacles.* ed. Daniel J. Sherman and Irit Rogoff. Minneapolis: U of Minnesota P, (1994): 144–62.

Grueso, Libia, Caralos Rosero, and Arturo Escobar. The Pocess of Black Community Organizing in the Southern Pacific Coast Region of Colombia' In Alverez, Dagnino and Escodar *Cultures of Politics, Politics of Cultures*, Boulder: Westview (1998). 196–219.

Guback, Thomas H. 'Cultural Identity and Film in the European Economic Community' *Cinema Journal* 14, no. 1 (1974): 2–17.

Guback, Thomas H. 'Government Support to the Film Industry in the United States' *Current Research in Film: Audiences, Economics and Law vol.* 3. ed. Bruce A. Austin. Norwood: Ablex (1987): 88–104.

Guback, Thomas H. 'International Circulation of U.S. Theatrical Films and Television Programming' *World Communications: A Handbook.* ed. George Gerbner and Marsha Siefert. New York: Longman (1984): 153–63.

Gubernick, Lisa and Joel Millman. 'El Sur is the Promised Land' *Forbes* 153, no. 7 (1994): 94–95.

Guerra, Rui. 'Popular Cinema and the State' In Johnson and Stam *Brazilian Cinema*. Expanded edition. New York: Columbia UP (1995). 101–103.

Guilbaut, Serge. *How New York Stole the Idea of Modern Art: Abstract Expressionism, Freedom, and the Cold War*. Chicago: U of Chicago P (1983).

Gunew, Sneja and Fazal Rizvi, Eds *Culture, Difference and the Arts*. Sydney: Allen and Unwin (1994).

Guttridge, Peter. 'Our Green and Profitable Land' *Independent* (11 July 1996): 8 9.

Habermas, Jurgen. The Structural Transformation of the Public Sphere: An Inquiry into a Category of Bourgeois Society. Trans. Thomas, Cambridge, MA.: MIT P (1989).

Habermas, Jürgen. 'Modern and Postmodern Architecture' *The New Conservatism: Cultural Criticism and the Historians' Debate*. ed. and Trans. Shierry Weber Nicholsen. Cambridge, Mass.: MIT P (1989).

Hall, James B. and Barry Ulanov, Eds *Modern Culture and the Arts*. New York: McGraw-Hill (1967).

Halperin Donghi, Tulio. *The Contemporary History of Latin America*. Durham: Duke UP (1993).

Hamelink, Cees. 'Information Imbalance: Core and Periphery' *Questioning the Media: A Critical Introduction.* ed. John H. Downing, Ali Mohammadi, and Annabelle Sreberny-Mohammadi. Newbury Park: Sage (1990).

Hames, Peter. 'Czech Cinema: From State Industry to Competition.' *Canadian Slavonic Papers* 42, no. 1 (2000): 63–85.

Hamilton, Marci A. 'Art Speech' *Vanderbilt Law Review* 49 (1996): 73–122.

Hammack, David. 'Think Tanks and the Invention of Policy Studies' *Nonprofit and Voluntary Service Quarterly* 24, no. 2 (1995): 173–81.

Hammer, John. 'On the Potential Impact of Rust v. Sullivan as a Model for Content-Based Restrictions on Federal Arts and Humanities Funding' PS: *Political Science and Politics* 25, no. 1 (1992).

Hanrahan, John. 'Studios Busy with all Aspects of Production.' *Variety* (4–10 December 2000): 58.

Hansen, T. 'Measuring the Value of Culture' *European Journal of Cultural Policy* 1, no. 2 (1995): 309–22.

Hansmann, Henry B. 'Nonprofit Enterprise in the Performing Arts' *Rand Journal of Economics* 12 (Autumn 1981): 341–61.

Harkavy, Ward. 'Statues of Limitations' *Village Voice* (29 August 2000): 23.

Harmon, Louise. 'Law, Art, and the Killing Jar' *Iowa Law Review* 79 (1994).

Harris, Jonathan. *Federal Art and National Culture: The Politics of Identity in New Deal America*. Cambridge: Cambridge UP (1995).

Harris, Leo J. 'From the Collector's Perspective: The Legality of Importing Pre-Columbian Art and Artifacts' *The Ethics of Collecting: Whose Culture? Whose Property?*, 2nd edition. ed. Phyllis Mauch Messenger. Albuquerque: U of New Mexico P (1999): 155–75.

Harris, Neil. *Cultural Excursions: Marketing Appetites and Cultural Tastes in Modern America*. Chicago: U of Chicago P (1990).

Hartley, John. *Popular Reality: Journalism, Modernity, Popular Culture*. London: Arnold (1996).

Harvey, Sylvia. Review of *Framing Culture. Media, Culture & Society* 16, no. 1 (1994): 170–73.

Hart Dávalos, Armando. *Cambiar las reglas del juego*. ed. and interview by Luis Báez. Havana: Letras Cubanas (1983).

Hawkins, Gay. *From Nimbin to Mardi Gras: Constructing Community Arts*. Sydney: Allen and Unwin (1993).

Hayward, Susan. 'State, Culture and the Cinema: Jack Lang's Strategies for the French Film Industry' *Screen* 34, no. 4 (1993): 382–91.

Healy, Patrick. 'In Final Budget, Clinton Tries Again for Big Boost for Cultural Endowments' *Chronicle of Higher Education* (18 February 2000): A40.

Heilbrun, James and Charles M. Gray. *The Economics of Art and Culture: An American Perspective*. Cambridge: Cambridge UP (1993).

Heilemann, John. 'A Survey of Television: Feeling for the Future' *Economist* 330, no. 7850 (1994): SURVEY 1–18.

Hejma, Ondrej. 'Quality Filmmakers Turn to Prague When They Can't Afford Hollywood.' *Columbian* (22 September 2000): Weekend.

Hendon, William S. and James L. Shanahan, eds *Economics of Cultural Decisions*. Cambridge, Mass.: Abt (1983).

Hendon, William S., Frank Costa and Robert A. Rosenberg. 'The General Public and the Art Museum' *American Journal of Economics and Sociology* 48 (April 1989): 132–43.

Hendon, William S., James L. Shanahan and Alice J. MacDonald. *Economic Policy for the Arts*. Cambridge, Mass.: Abt (1980).

Hendon, William S., Nancy K. Grant and Douglas V. Shaw, Eds *The Economics of Cultural Industries*. Akron: Association for Cultural Economics (1984).

Henley, Jon. 'The Battle for France's History' *Guardian* (9 May 2001).

Hennenberger, Melinda. 'Italy Plans to Have Private Sector Run Museums' *New York Times* (3 December 2001): E1, E3.

Herodutus. *The Histories*. Trans. Aubrey de Sélincourt. Harmondsworth: Penguin, 1974.

Herscher, Ellen. 'International Control Efforts: Are There Any Good Solutions?' *The Ethics of Collecting: Whose Culture? Whose Property?*, 2nd edition. ed. Phyllis Mauch Messenger. Albuquerque: U of New Mexico P (1999): 117–28.

Herscovici, Alain. 'Globalización, sistema de redes y estructuración del espaio: un análisis económico' In Mastrini and Bolaña *Globalizacióny monopolios en la comunicación en Amêricia Latina. Hacia una economía política de in communicación*. Buenos Aires: Editorial Biblos. (1999) 49–60.

Hibbin, Sally. 'Britain has a New Film Establishment and it is Leading us Towards Disaster' *New Statesman*, (27 March 1998) p. 40.

Hill, John. 'British Film Policy' *Film Policy*. ed. Albert Moran. London: Routledge (1996).

Hill, John. 'British Television and Film: The Making of a Relationship' *Big Picture Small Screen*. ed. John Hill and Martin McLoone. Luton: U of Luton P (1997).

Hill, John. 'Introduction' *Border Crossing: Film in Ireland, Britain and Europe*. ed. John Hill, Martin McLoone, and Paul Hainsworth. Belfast: Institute of Irish Studies (1994): 1–7.

Hills, Jill. 'Dependency Theory and its Relevance Today: International Institutions in Telecommunications and Structural Power' *Review of International Studies* 20, no. 2 (1994): 169–86.

Himmelstein, Jerome L. and Mayer Zald. 'American Conservatism and Government Funding of the Social Sciences and Arts' *Sociological Inquiry* 54, no. 2 (1984): 171–87.

Hindess, Barry. 'Divide and Rule: The International Character of Citizenship' *European Journal of Social Theory* 1, no. 1 (1998): 57–70.

Hingston, Ann Guthrie. 'U.S. Implementation of the UNESCO Cultural Property Convention' *The Ethics of Collecting: Whose Culture? Whose Property?*, 2nd edition. ed. Phyllis Mauch Messenger. Albuquerque: U of New Mexico P (1999): 129–47.

Hirsch, S. 'Letter to the Editor' *Policy Review: The Journal of American Citizenship* 84 (1997): 4.

Hiscock, John. 'Hollywood Backs British Film Drive' *Daily Telegraph* (24 July 1998): 19.

Hitchens, Christopher. 'Who's Sorry Now?' *Nation* (29 May 2000): 9.

Hitler, Adolf. 'Speech Inaugurating the "Great Exhibition of German Art"' *Art in Theory 1900–1990: An Anthology of Changing Ideas*. ed. Charles Harrison and Paul Wood. Oxford: Blackwell (1996): 423–26.

Hoekman, Bernard M. and Michel M. Kostecki. *The Political Economy of the World Trading System: From GATT to WTO*. Oxford: Oxford UP (1995).

Hoggart, Richard. *Speaking to Each Other. Volume One: About Society*. Harmondsworth: Penguin Books (1973).

Holley, David. 'Prague: AKA 'Hollywood East'.' *Bergen Record* (27 August 2000).

Home Affairs Bureau. 'Long Term Culture Policy' http://www.info.gov.hk.

Home Affairs Bureau. 'Response of the Administration to Written Submissions to the Legislative Council Panel on Home Affairs' http://www.info.gov.hk.

Home Affairs Bureau. 'Structure of Arts and Culture in Overseas Countries' http://www.info.gov.hk.

Hong Kong Cultural Policy Study Group. *In Search of Cultural Policy '93*. Hong Kong: Zuni Icosahedron (1994).

Honig, Bonnie. 'Immigrant America? How Foreignness "Solves" Democracy's Problems' *Social Text* no. 56 (1998): 1–27.

Hooper-Greenhil, Eilean. *Museums and the Shaping of Knowledge*. New York: Routledge (1992).

Hooper-Greenhil, Eilean. 'Museums, Exhibitions, and Communities: Cultural Politics' *Semiotica* 108, nos. 1–2 (1996): 177–87.

Hoover, Deborah A. 'Developing a Cultural Policy in The Gambia: Problems and Progress' *Journal of Arts Management and Law* 18, no. 3 (1988): 31–39.

Hope, Sam. 'A Critique: The Continuing Crisis Distills an Old Idea' *Journal of Arts Management and Law* 20, no. 3 (1990).

Horne, Donald. *The Great Museum: The Re-Presentation of History*. London: Pluto P (1984).

Horne, Donald. *The Public Culture*. Sydney: Pluto P (1986).

Horyn, Cathy. 'The Met Cancels Exhibit on Chanel' *New York Times* (20 May 2000): B3.

Hoskins, Colin, Stuart McFadyen, and Adam Finn. *Global Television and Film: An Introduction to the Economics of the Business*. Oxford: Clarendon (1997).

Hudson, Kenneth. *Museums of Influence*. Cambridge: Cambridge UP (1987).

Hufford, Mary, ed. *Conserving Culture: A New Discourse on Heritage*. Champaign: U of Illinois P (1994).

Hughes, Gordon. 'Measuring the Economic Value of the Arts' *Policy Studies* 9, no. 3 (1989): 33–45.

Hughes, Robert. 'The Case for Élitist Do-Gooders' *New Yorker* (27 May 1996): n. p.

Hunter, Ian, David Saunders and Dugald Williamson. *On Pornography: Literature, Sexuality and Obscenity Law*. London: Macmillan (1993).

Hunter, Ian. 'Accounting for the Humanities' *Meanjin* 48, no. 3 (1989): 438–48.

Hunter, Ian. 'Setting Limits to Culture' *New Formations* no. 4 (Spring 1988): 103–23.

Hunter, Ian. 'The Humanities Without Humanism' *Meanjin* 51, no. 3 (1992): 479–90.

Hunter, Ian. *Culture and Government: The Emergence of Literary Education*. London: Macmillan (1988).

Hunter, Ian. *Rethinking the School: Subjectivity, Bureaucracy, Criticism*. Sydney: Allen and Unwin (1994).

Hunter, J.D. *Culture Wars*. New York: Basic (1989).

Hurtado, Shannon Hunter. 'The Promotion of the Visual Arts in Britain, 1835–1860' *Canadian Journal of History* 28, no. 1 (1993): 60–80.

Hutter, Michael and Ilde Rizzo, Eds *Economic Perspectives on Cultural Heritage*. London: Macmillan (1997).

Huyssen, Andreas. *After the Great Divide: Modernism, Mass Culture and Postmodernism*. London: Macmillan, 1988.

I'Anson-Sparks, Justin. 'Hollywood Goes Even Further East' *Independent* 3 August (2000).

Ingram, M. 'A Nationalist Turn in French Cultural Policy' *The French Review* 71, no. 5 (1998): 797–808.

Interim Report of the Film Committee, Australian Council for the Arts. An Australian Film Reader. ed. Albert Moran and Tom O'Regan. Sydney: Currency P: (1969) 171.

International Journal of Museum Management and Curatorship.

Ip, D., C. Inglis, and C.T. Wu. 'Concepts of Citizenship and Identity Among Recent Asian Immigrants to Australia' *Asian and Pacific Migration Journal* 6, nos. 3–4 (1997): 363–84.

Irvine, Judith. *Sound Politics: Speaking, Writing, and Printing in Early Colonial Africa*. Unpublished mimeo (1997).

Ismayr, Wolfgang. 'Cultural Federalism and Public Support for the Arts in the Federal Republic of Germany' Trans. J. C. Laursen. *The Patron State: Government and the Arts in Europe, North America, and Japan*. ed. Milton C. Cummings, Jr. and Richard S. Katz. New York: Oxford UP (1987): 45–67.

Ivey, Bill. Statement to the House Interior Appropriations Committee Regarding Appropriation of the National Endowment for the Arts (23 March 2000). http://wwws.elibray.com/getdoc.cgi?id=174...@HCS_20001002_04&dtype=0~&dinst=.

Jacka, Elizabeth. 'Australian Cinema: An Anachronism in the '80s?' *The Imaginary Industry: Australian Film in the Late '80s*. ed. Susan Dermody and Elizabeth Jacka. Sydney: Australian Film, Television & Radio School (1988).

Jacka, Elizabeth. 'Film' *The Media in Australia: Industries, Texts, Audiences*, 2nd edition. ed. Stuart Cunningham and Graeme Turner. Sydney: Allen & Unwin (1997): 70–89.

Jäckel, Anne. 'European Co-Production Strategies: The Case of France and Britain' *Film Policy*. ed. Albert Moran. London: Routledge (1996): 85–97.

Jackson, V., ed. *Art Museums of the World*. Westport: Greenwood P (1987).

Jacques, R. 'The Work of the Council for the Encouragement of Music and the Arts' *Journal of the Royal Society of Arts* (April 1945): 276–84.

Jameson, Fredric. *Postmodernism, or, the Cultural Logic of Late Capitalism*. London: Verso (1991).

Jarvie, Ian. 'Free Trade as Cultural Threat: American Film and TV Exports in the Post-War Period' *Hollywood and Europe: Economics, Culture, National Identity: 1945–95*. ed. Geoffrey Nowell-Smith and Steven Ricci. London: BFI (1998): 34–46.

Jaszi, Peter and Martha Woodmansee. 'The Ethical Reaches of Authorship' *South Atlantic Quarterly* 95, no. 4 (1996): 947–77.

Jensen, Joli. 'Democratic Culture and the Arts: Constructing a Usable Past' *Journal of Arts Management, Law, and Society* 23, no. 2 (1993): 110–20.

Jensen, Richard. 'The Culture Wars, 1965–1995: A Historian's Map' *Journal of Social History* 29 (1996): 17–38.

Jobert, Bruno. 'The Normative Frameworks of Public Policy' *Political Studies* 37, no. 3 (1989): 376–86.

Johnson, Randal and Robert Stam, eds *Brazilian Cinema*. Expanded edition. New York: Columbia University Press (1995).

Jordanova, Ludmilla. 'Objects of Knowledge: A Historical Perspective on Museums' *The New Museology*. ed. Peter Vergo. London: Reaktion, 1991. 22–40.

Johnson, Randal. 'Film Policy in Latin America' *Film Policy: International, National and Regional Perspectives*. ed. Albert Moran. London: Routledge (1996): 128–47.

Johnston, Sheila. 'Was 'British Invasion' Boon or Bane for Foreign?' *Variety* (22–28 February 1999): A10.

Jones, Anna Laura. 'Exploding Canons: The Anthropology of Museums' *Annual Review of Anthropology* no. 22 (1993): 201–20.

Jones, Peter. 'Museums and the Meanings of Their Contents' *New Literary History* 23, no. 4 (1992): 911–21.

Joseph, May. 'Diaspora, New Hybrid Identities, and the Performance of Citizenship' *Women and Performance* 7, no. 2–8, no. 1 (1995): 3–13.

Joyce, Michael S. 'The National Endowments for the Humanities and Arts' *Mandate for Leadership*. ed. Charles Heatherly. Washington: Heritage Foundation (1981): 1039–56.

Julien, Isaac. 'Burning Rubber's Perfume' *Remote Control: Dilemmas of Black Intervention in British Film & TV*. ed. June Givanni. London: BFI (1995).

Jury, Louise. 'Mission Possible: Red Tape Cut to Boost Film Industry' *Independent* (4 July 1996): 3.

Kahn, David. 'Domesticating a Foreign Import: Museums in Asia' *Curator* 41, no. 4 (1998): 226–28.

Kahn Jr., E. J. *Jock! The Life and Times of John Hay Whitney*. Garden City, NY: Doubleday (1981).

Kammen, Michael. 'Culture and the State in America' *Journal of American History* 83, no. 3 (1996): 791–814.

Kaplan, Flora E. S., ed. *Museums and the Making of 'Ourselves': The Role of Objects in National Identity*. Leicester: Leicester UP (1994).

Kant, Immanuel. 'The Doctrine of Right' *Metaphysics of Morals* (1797). ed. Raymond Geuss. Trans. Mary Gregor. Cambridge: Cambridge UP (1991).

———. 'The Character of Nations' In *Anthropology from a Pragmatic Point of View*. Trans. Victor L. Dowdell. Illinois: Illinois UP (1978).

Karlen, Peter H. 'Legal Aesthetics' *British Journal of Aesthetics* 19 (1979): 195–212.

Karlen, Peter H. 'What is Art?: A Sketch or a Legal Definition' *Law Quarterly Review* 94 (1978): 383–407.

Karnoouh, Claude. 'The End of National Culture in Eastern Europe' Trans. Wayne Hayes and Valerie Marchal. *Telos* no. 89 (Fall 1991): 132–37.

Karp, Ivan and Steven C. Lavine. *Exhibiting Cultures: The Poetics and Politics of Museum Display*. Washington: Smithsonian Institution P (1991).

Karp, Ivan, Christine Mullen Kreamer, and Steven D. Lavine, Eds *Museums and Communities: The Politics of Public Culture*. Washington: Smithsonian Institution P (1992).

Katel, Peter. 'El futuro de Miami mira hacia el sur' *El Nuevo Herald*, 1 January (2000): 1A.

Katz, Jonathan. 'Decentralization and the Arts: Principles, Practice, and Policy' *Journal of Arts Management and Law* 13 (Spring 1983): 109–20.

Kavanagh, Gaynor. *Museums and the First World War: A Social History*. Leicester: Leicester UP (1994).

Kawashima, N. 'Comparing Cultural Policy: Towards the Development of Comparative Study' *European Journal of Cultural Policy* 1 (1995): 289–307.

Keane, Michael. 'Cultural Policy in China: Emerging Research Agendas' *Cultural Policy* 6, no. 2 (2000): 243–58.

Keller, Anthony S. 'Cultural Policy and Educational Change in the 1990s' *Education and Urban Society* 22, no. 4 (1990): 413–24.

Kennedy, Maeve. 'Local Museums Facing a Slow Death by a Thousand Budget Cuts' *Guardian* (29 August 2000).

Keppel, F.P. *The Foundation: Its Place in American Life*. New Brunswick: Transaction (1989).

Kerr, James Semple. *Fremantle Prison: A Policy for its Conservation*. Perth: Building Management Authority of Western Australia, 1992.

Kessler, Kirsten L. 'Protecting Free Trade in Audiovisual Entertainment: A Proposal for Counteracting the European Union's Trade Barriers to the U.S. Entertainment Industry's Exports' *Law and Policy in International Business* 26, no. 2 (1995): 563–611.

Keynes, J.M. *The General Theory of Employment Interest and Money*. London: Macmillan; New York: St. Martin's P (1957).

Kilborn, Peter. 'Miami Beach Clubgoers Creating New, Unwanted Image', *New York Times* 27 February (2000).

Kim, Kong Ki. 'Cultural Diversity in Enjoyment and Cultural Policy in Evaluation: The South Korean State of the Art' *Culture and Policy* 7, no. 2 (1996): 43–60.

Kimbis, Thomas Peter. 'Surviving the Storm: How the National Endowment for the Arts Restructured Itself to Serve a New Constituency' *Journal of Arts Management, Law and Society* 27, no. 2 (1997): 139–58.

Kimmelman, Michael. 'What D'Ya Call a House of Sex? A Museum. Oh' *New York Times* (18 January 2000): E1, E9.

King, John. 'Cinema.' In Bethell *Latin America. Economy and Society Since* 1930. Cambridge: Cambridge UP. (1998) 455–518.

Kirstein, Lincoln. *The Latin American Collection of the Museum of Modern Art*. New York: The Museum of Modern Art (1943).

Kirshenblatt-Gimblett, Barbara. 'Objects of Ethnography' *Exhibiting Cultures: The Poetics and Politics of Museum Display*. ed. Ivan Karp and steven C. Lavine. Washington: Smithsonian Institution P, (1991): 386–443.

Klamer, A., ed. *The Value of Culture*. Ann Arbor: U of Michigan P (1997).

KPMG. *Film Financing and Television Programming: A Taxation Guide*. Amsterdam: KPMG (1996).

Kramer, Hilton. 'Is Art Above the Laws of Decency?' *New York Times* (2 July 1989): H1.

Kreidler, John. 'Leverage Lost: The Nonprofit Arts in the Post-Ford Era' *Journal of Arts Management, Law, and Society* 26, no. 2 (1996): 79–100.

Krischke, Paulo J. 'Problems in the Study of Democratization in Latin America: Regime Analysis vs Cultural Studies' *International Sociology* 15, no. 1 (2000): 107–25.

Kristeva, Julia. 'Postmodernism?' *Bucknell Review* 25 no. 2 (1980): 138.

Krosnar, Katka, Adam Piore, and Stefan Theil. 'Take One: Prague.' *Newsweek International* (19 March 2001): 40.

Kruger, Loren. 'Attending (to) the National Spectacle: Instituting National (Popular) Theater in England and France' *Macropolitics of Nineteenth-Century Literature: Nationalism, Exoticism, Imperialism*. ed. Jonathan Arac and Harriet Ritvo. Philadelphia: U of Pennsylvania P (1991).

Kuhn, Michael. 'How Can Europe Benefit from the Digital Revolution?' Presentation to the European Audiovisual Conference, Birmingham (6–8 April 1998).

Kurin, Richard. 'Cultural Policy Through Public Display' *Journal of Popular Culture* 29, no. 1 (1995): 2–14.

Lacarrieu, Mónica. 'Construcción de imaginarios locales e identidades culturales en la mundialización.' Ponencia presentada en el Seminario Nuevos retos y estrategias de las políticas culturales frente a la globalización, Instituto d'Estudis Catalans, Barcelona, (22 a 25 de nov 2000).

LaFranchi, Howard. 'Mexifilms vs. Mickey Mouse.' *Christian Science Monitor* (5 January 1999).

Lambropoulos, Vassilis. 'Violence and the Liberal Imagination: The Representation of Hellenism in Matthew Arnold.' *The Violence of Representation: Literature and the History of Violence.* ed. Nancy Armstrong and Leonard Tennenhouse. London: Routledge (1989): 171–93.

Lang, Beryl and Forest Williams, eds *Marxism and Art: Writings in Asthetics and Criticism.* New York: McKay (1972).

Lang, Gladys Engel and Kurt Lang. 'Public Opinion and the Helms Amendment' *Journal of Arts Management and Law* 21, no. 2 (1991): 127–39.

Lang, Tim and Colin Hines. *The New Protectionism: Protecting the Future Against Free Trade.* New York: New P (1993).

Langsted, Jorn. 'Double Strategies in a Modern Cultural Policy' *Journal of Arts Management and Law* 19, no. 4 (1990): 53–71.

Language Problems & Language Planning.

Larson, Gary O. *American Canvas.* Washington, D.C.: National Endowment for the Arts (1997).

Larson, Gary O. *The Reluctant Patron: The United States Government and the Arts, 1943–1965.* Philadelphia: U of Pennsylvania P (1983).

Lasch, Christopher. *The Culture of Narcissism: American Life in An Age of Diminishing Expectations.* New York: Norton (1978).

Lawson, Sylvia. 'General Editor's Preface' *Images and Influence.* Albert Moran. Sydney: Curency P, (1985): 6.

Lawson, Sylvia. 'Not for the Likes of Us' *An Australian Film Reader.* ed. Albert Moran and Tom O'Regan. Sydney: Currency P (1985): 154–55.

LeClaire, Jennifer. 'Latin America Makes Miami Major Entertainment Player. "Hollywood East" is now third-largest production hub.' *Christian Science Monitor* (17 August 1998).

Lee, Benjamin. 'Hong Kong Arts Policy' http://www.info.gov.hk.

Lee, Terence. 'Freedom to Regulate: The Internet in Singapore' *Media & Culture Review* no. 1 (May 2000): 4–5.

Lenin, Vladimir Ilyich. 'On Proletarian Culture' *Art in Theory 1900–1990: An Anthology of Changing Ideas.* ed. Charles Harrison and Paul Wood. Oxford: Blackwell (1996): 383–87.

Lenin, Vladimir Ilyich. 'Party Organization and Party Literature' *Marxism and Art: Essays Classic and Contemporary.* ed. Maynard Solomon. Brighton: Harvester P (1979): 179–83.

Lenin, Vladimir Ilyich. *On Literature and Art.* Moscow: Progress (1967).

Lent, John A. 'The Animation Industry and its Offshore Factories' *Global Productions: Labor in the Making of the 'Information Society'* ed. Gerald Sussman and John A. Lent. Cresskill: Hampton P (1998): 239–54.

Leon, Warren and Roy Rosenzweig, eds *History Museums in the United States: A Critical Assessment.* Urbana: U of Illinois P (1989).

Lev, Peter. *The Euro-American Cinema.* Austin: U of Texas P (1993).

Leventhal, F.M. '"The Best for the Most": CEMA and State Sponsorship of the Arts in Wartime, 1939–1945' *Twentieth Century British History* 1, no. 3 (1990): 289–317.

Lever M., Elsa. 'Televisión y Educación al final de milenio' *Fem* no. 190 (January 1999): 22–26.

Levy, Bronwen. 'Ruffling the Feathers of the Cultural Polity' *Meanjin* 51, no. 3 (1992): 552–55.

Lewis, Geoffrey. *For Instruction and Recreation – A Century History of the Museums Association.* London: Quiller P (1989).

Lewontin, R.C. 'The Cold War and the Transformation of the Academy' *The Cold War and the University: Toward an Intellectual History of the Postwar Years*. ed. Noam Chomsky. New York: New P (1997).

Leyva, Dennis. Inteview with George Yúdice, Office of City of Miami Beach, 14 March (2000).

Lievrouw, Leah A. 'Communication and the "Culture Wars"' *Journal of Communication* 46, no. 1 (1996): 169–78.

Lingle, Christopher. 'Interest Groups and Cultural Protectionism: Apartheid and Public Arts Policies' *International Journal of Social Economics* 18, no. 4 (1991): 4–13.

Lister, David and Nonie Niesewand. 'Admission Charges Strike Discordant Note in Minister's Museum Fanfare' *Independent* (21 January 2000): 3.

Llewellyn, K.N. 'On the Good, the True, the Beautiful, in the Law' *University of Chicago Law Review* 9 (1942): 224–50.

Lloyd, David and Paul Thomas. 'Culture and Society or "Culture and the State"?' *Social Text* 30 (1992): 49–78.

Lloyd, David and Paul Thomas. *Culture and the State.* New York: Routledge (1998).

Lopez, Susana. 'The Cultural Policy of the European Community and its Influence on Museums' *Museum Management and Curatorship* 12, no. 2 (1993): 143–57.

Lovell, Alan. 'The British Cinema: The Known Cinema?' *The British Cinema Book.* ed. Robert Murphy. London: BFI (1997).

Low, Kee Hong. 'The Singapore Culture Inc.: Promises of a "New Asian Renaissance"' Paper to the Workshop on Cultural Policy, Singapore Art Museum (21 March 1998).

Lowry, W. McNeil, ed. *The Arts and Public Policy in the United States.* Englewood Cliffs: Prentice-Hall (1984).

Lumley, R., ed. *The Museum Time Machine: Putting Cultures on Display.* London: Routledge (1988).

Lury, Celia. *Cultural Rights: Technology, Legality, and Personality.* London: Routledge (1993).

Lyotard, Jean-François. *La Condition Postmoderne: Rapport sur le Savoir.* Paris: Les Éditions de Minuit (1988).

MacBride, Sean and Colleen Roach. 'The New International Information Order' *The Global Media Debate: Its Rise, Fall, and Renewal,* eds George Gerbner, Hamid Mowlana and Kaarle Nordenstreng. Norwood: Ablex (1994). 3–11.

MacCabe, Colin. 'A Post-National European Cinema: A Consideration of Derek Jarman's *The Tempest* and *Edward II*' *Dissolving Views: Key Writings on British Cinema.* ed. Andrew Higson. London: Cassell (1996): 191–201.

MacCabe, Colin. 'Preface' *Remote Control: Dilemmas of Black Intervention in British Film & TV.* Ed. June Givanni. London: BFI (1995): ix–x.

MacCallum, Mungo. 'Drama' *Ten Years of Television.* ed. Mungo MacCallum. Melbourne: Sun, (1968).

Macdonnell, Justin. *Arts, Minister? Government Policy and the Arts.* Sydney: Currency P (1992).

Mackey, Eva. 'Postmodernism and Cultural Politics in a Multicultural Nation: Contests over Truth in the Into the Heart of Africa Controversy' *Public Culture* 7, no. 2 (1995): 403–31.

Mackey, William F. 'Language Diversity, Language Policy and the Sovereign State' *History of European Ideas* 13, nos. 1–2 (1991): 51–61.

Maffi, Luisa. 'Toward the Integrated Protection of Language and Knowledge as a Part of Indigenous Peoples' Cultural Heritage' *Cultural Survival* 24, no. 4 (2001): 32–36.

Magat, R., ed. *Philanthropic Giving: Studies in Varieties and Goals.* New York: Oxford UP (1989).

Mahmud, Tayyab. 'Migration, Identity, & the Colonial Encounter' *Oregon Law Review* 76, no. 3 (1997): 633–690.

Malaro, Marie C. *Museum Governance: Mission, Ethics, Policy.* Washington: Smithsonian Institution P (1994).

Mally, Lynn. *Culture of the Future: The Proletkult Movement in Revolutionary Russia*. Berkeley: U of California P (1990).

Mankin, Lawrence D. 'The National Endowment for the Arts: The Biddle Years and After' *Journal of Arts Management and Law* 14, no. 2 (1984).

Mansfield, Alan. 'Cultural Policy Theory and Practice: A New Constellation' *Continuum* 4, no. 1 (1990): 204–14.

Mantell, Edmund H. 'If Art is Resold, Should the Artist Profit?' *The American Economist* 39, no. 1 (1995): 23–31.

Mao Tse-Tung. *Mao Tse-Tung Unrehearsed: Talks and Letters: 1956–71*. Trans. John Chinnery and Tieyun. ed. Stuart Schram. Harmondsworth: Penguin, (1974).

Marable, Manning. 'In Pursuit of Cultural Democracy' *Journal of Arts Management and Law* 13 (1983): 28–31.

Marcus, George E. and Fred R. Myers, eds *The Traffic in Culture: Refiguring Art and Anthropology*. Berkeley: U of California P (1995).

Margalit, Avishai and Moshe Halbertal. 'Liberalism and the Right to Culture' *Social Research* 61, no. 3 (1994): 491–510.

Marinetto, M. 'The Historical Development of Business Philanthropy: Social Responsibility in the New Corporate Economy' *Business History* 41, no. 4 (1999): 1–20.

Mark, Charles Christopher. *Reluctant Bureaucrats: The Struggle to Establish the National Endowment for the Arts*. Dubuque: Kendall/Hunt (1991).

Markoff, John and Verónica Montecinos. 'The Ubiquitous Rise of Economists' *Journal of Public Policy* 13, no. 1 (1993): 37–68.

Marshall, T.H. 'The Nature and Determinants of Social Status.' *Sociological Perspectives: Selected Readings*. ed. Kenneth Thompson and Jeremy Tunstall. Harmondsworth: Penguin Books (1976): 288–98.

Marshall, T.H. *Class, Citizenship, and Social Development: Essays by T. H. Marshall*. ed. Seymour Martin Lipset. Chicago: U of Chicago P (1964).

Martin, Lydia. 'Studio Miami How Does an Entertainment Capital Rise from the Ground Up? Cash, Connections and Cool' *Miami Herald* (13 December 1998): 1I.

Martin, Randy. *Critical Moves: Dance Studies in Theory and Politics*. Durham: Duke UP (1998).

Martin, Randy. *Socialist Ensembles: Theater and State in Cuba and Nicaragua*. Minneapolis: U of Minnesota P (1994).

Martorella, Rosanne, ed. *Art and Business: An International Perspective on Sponsorship*. Westport: Greenwood P (1996).

Martorella, Rosanne. *Corporate Art*. New Brunswick: Rutgers UP (1990).

Marvasti, A. 'International Trade in Cultural Goods: A Cross-Sectional Analysis' *Journal of Cultural Economics* 18, no. 2 (1994): 135–48.

Marx, Karl. *The Eighteenth Brumaire of Louis Bonaparte*. Peking: Foreign Language P (1978).

Marx, Karl. *The Grundrisse*. Trans. and ed. David McLellan. New York: Harper Torchbooks (1971).

Marx, Karl. *Karl Marx on colonialism and modernization; his despatches [sic] and other writings on China, India, Mexico, the Middle East and North Africa*. Edited with an introd. by Shlomo Avineri. Garden City, N.Y.: Doubleday (1968).

Marquis, Alice Goldfarb. *Art Lessons: Learning from the Rise and Fall of Public Arts Funding*. New York: Basic Books (1995).

Mastrini, Guillermo y César Bolaño, eds *Globalizacióny monopolios en la comunicación en América Latina. Hacia una economía política de la comunicación*. Buenos Aires: Editorial Biblos (1999).

Mattelart, Armand and Michéle Mattelart. *Theories of Communication: A Short Introduction*. Trans. Susan Gruenheck Taponier and James A. Cohen. London: Sage (1998).

Mattelart, Armand. 'European Film Policy and the Response to Hollywood' *World Cinema: Critical Approaches.* ed. John Hill and Pamela Church Gibson. Oxford: Oxford UP (2000). 94–101.

Mattelart, Michèle. 'Can Industrial Culture Be a Culture of Difference: A Reflection on France's Confrontation with the U.S. Model of Serialized Cultural Production' Trans. Stanley Gray and Nelly Mitchell. *Marxism and the Interpretation of Culture.* ed. Cary Nelson and Lawrence Grossberg. Urbana: U of Illinois P (1988).

Mattson, Kevin. 'Populism and the NEA' *Telos* no. 89 (Fall 1991): 115–20.

Masiello, Francine. *Between Civilization and Barbarism. Women, Nation, and Literary Culture in Modern Argentina.* Lincoln: U of Nebraska P (1992).

Mato, Daniel. 'Culture, Development, and Indigenous Peoples in the Age of Globalization: The 1994 Smithsonian's Folklife Festival and the Transnational Making of Representations.' *Cultural Studies* 12, no. 2 (1998): 193–209.

———. 'Miami en la transnacionalización de la industria de la telenovela: Sobre la territorialidad de los procesos de globalización.' Paper presented panel on Global Cities and Cultural Capitals I: Media and Culture Industries, XXII Congreso de la Latin American Studies Association, Hyatt Regency Hotel, Miami, (16–18 March 2000).

Maxwell, Richard. 'Model for European TV and National Identity: Assembly Instructions not Included' *Jump Cut* no. 40 (1996): 89–95.

Maxwell, Richard. 'Out of Kindness and Into Difference: The Value of Global Market Research' *Media, Culture & Society* 18, no. 1 (1996): 105–26.

May, Anthony. 'The Magnetics of Policy: Stuart Cunningham's *Framing Culture*' *New Researcher* nos. 1–2 (1992): 116–21.

Mayer, Gerald M. 'American Motion Pictures in World Trade' *Annals of the American Academy of Political and Social Science* no. 254 (1947): 31–36.

Mayer, J.P. *Sociology of Film: Studies and Documents.* London: Faber & Faber (1946).

Mayrhofer, Debra. 'Media Briefs' *Media Information Australia* no. 74 (1994): 126–42.

Mazama, Ama. 'An Afrocentric Approach to Language Planning' *Journal of Black Studies* 25, no. 1 (1994): 3–19.

Mazrui, Ali A. *Cultural Forces in World Politics.* London: James Currey; Nairobi: Heinemann Kenya (1990).

McArthur, Colin. 'The Cultural Necessity of a Poor Celtic Cinema' *Border Crossing: Film in Ireland, Britain and Europe.* Ed. John Hill, Martin McLoone and Paul Hainsworth. Institute of Irish Studies, Queen's U of Belfast, U of Ulster, and the BFI (1994).

McCann, Paul. 'Hollywood Film-makers Desert UK' *Independent* (14 August 1998): 7.

McCarthy, Kathleen D. *Women's Culture: American Philanthropy and Art, 1830–1930.* Chicago: U of Chicago P (1991).

McClintock, Anne. *Imperial Leather: Race, Gender and Sexuality in the Colonial Contest.* New York: Routledge (1995).

McCormack, Thelma. 'Culture and the State' *Canadian Public Policy* 10, no. 3 (1984): 267–77.

McDonald, Kevin M. 'How Would You Like Your Television: With or Without Borders and With or Without Culture–A New Approach to Media Regulation in the European Union' *Fordham International Law Journal* 22 (1999): 1991–2023.

McDonald, William F. *Federal Relief Administration and the Arts.* Cleveland: Ohio UP (1969).

McGuigan, Jim. *Culture and the Public Sphere.* London: Routledge (1996).

McIntyre, Steve. 'Art and Industry: Regional Film and Video Policy in the UK' *Film Policy.* ed. Albert Moran. London: Routledge (1996): 215–33.

McIntyre, Steve. 'Vanishing Point: Feature Film Production in a Small Country' *Border Crossing: Film in Ireland, Britain and Europe.* ed. John Hill, Martin McLoone, and Paul Hainsworth. Institute of Irish Studies, Queen's U of Belfast, U of Ulster, and the BFI (1994).

McKay, Jim. 'Hegemonic Masculinity, the State and the Politics of Gender Equity Policy Research' *Culture and Policy* 5 (1993): 233–40.

McKinnon, K.R. 'Australian Cultural Policy Issues' *Public Policies in Two Federal Countries: Canada and Australia* (1982): 249–65.

McKinzie, R.D. *The New Deal for Artists*. Princeton: Princeton UP (1973).

McLaren, John. 'Cultural Independence for Australia: The Need for a National Literature' *Australian Studies* 14 (1990).

McNaughton, Patrick R. 'Malian Antiquities and Contemporary Desire' *African Arts* 28, no. 4 (1995): 22–27.

McQuail, Denis. 'Media Policy Research: Conditions for Progress' *Mass Communication Research: On Problems and Policies: The Art of Asking the Right Questions. In Honor of James D. Halloran*. ed. Cees J. Hamelink and Olga Linn. Norwood: Ablex Publishing (1994): 39–51.

Mda, Zakes. *The Role of Culture in the Process of Reconciliation in South Africa*. Centre for the Study of Violence and Reconciliation, U of Witwatersrand. Seminar no. 9 (1994).

Meils, Cathy. 'Prague Studio Steels for Future.' *Variety* (22–28 June 1998): 46.

Meils, Cathy. 'More Pix Say 'Czech, Please.' *Variety* (1–7 May 2000): 88.

Meils, Cathy. 'Milk & Honey Cuts in with *Blade 2* Prod'n.' *Daily Variety* (28 November 2000): 38.

Meils, Cathy. 'Czech It Out: Studio Biz Good, Sale Is On.' *Daily Variety* (22 December 2000): 8.

Meisel, John. 'Political Culture and the Politics of Culture' *Canadian Journal of Political Science* 7, no. 4 (1974): 601–15.

Melvin, Sheila. 'On a Golden Anniversary, a Leaden Yoke of Ideology' *New York Times* (26 September 1999): 1, 38.

Mennell, Stephen. 'Cultural Policy and Models of Society' *Loisir et Société* 4, no. 2 (1981): 213–27.

Mennell, Stephen. 'Theoretical Considerations on the Study of Cultural Needs' *Sociology* 13, no. 2 (1979): 235–57.

Mera, Jorge and Carlos Ruiz. 'Freedom of the Press: Censorship and Cultural Policy in Chile' *Studies in Communications* 4 (1990): 21–38.

Meredith, Robyn. 'Another Art Battle, as Detroit Museum Closes an Exhibit Early' *New York Times* (23 November 1999): A14.

Messenger, Phyllis Mauch. 'Preface to the Second Edition' *The Ethics of Collecting: Whose Culture? Whose Property?*, 2nd edition. ed. Phyllis Mauch Messenger. Albuquerque: U of New Mexico P (1999): xv–xvii.

Meyer, Birgit. 'Popular Ghanaian Cinema and "African Heritage"' *Africa Today* 46, no. 2 (1999): 92–114.

Meyer, Karl E. *The Art Museum: Power, Money, Ethics*. New York: Morrow (1979).

Meyrick, Julian. 'Accounting for the Arts in the Nineties: The Growth of Performing Arts Administration in Australia, 1975–1995' *Journal of Arts Management, Law and Society* 26, no. 4 (1997): 285–307.

Michalski, Sergiusz. *Public Monuments: Art in Political Bondage 1870–1997*. London: Reaktion (1998).

Miège, Bernard. *The Capitalization of Cultural Production*. Trans. J. Hay, N. Garnham and UNESCO. New York: International General (1989).

Mignolo, Walter. *The Darker Side of the Renaissance: Literacy, Territoriality, and Colonization*. Ann Arbor: U of Michigan P (1994).

Millea, Michael. 'Czech Privatization: The Case of Fimove Studio Barrandov.' *Journal of International Affairs* 50, no. 2 (1997): 489–505.

Mill, John Stuart. *On Liberty*. Harmondsworth: Penguin (1974).

Miller, J.D.B. *Norman Angell and the Futility of War: Peace and the Public Mind*. Basingstoke: Macmillan (1986).

Miller, Judith. 'Alexander Plans to Resign As Leader of Arts Agency,' New York Times (8 October 1997): A12.

Miller, Toby. 'Hollywood and the World' The Oxford Guide to Film Studies. ed. John Hill and Pamela Church Gibson. Oxford: Oxford UP (1998): 371–81.

Miller, Toby. 'National Policy and the Traded Image' National Identity and Europe: The Television Revolution. ed. Phillip Drummond, Richard Paterson and Janet Willis. London: BFI (1993): 95–109.

Miller, Toby. 'The Crime of Monsieur Lang: GATT, the Screen and the New International Division of Cultural Labor' Film Policy. ed. Albert Moran. London: Routledge (1996): 72–84.

Miller, Toby. 'The NEA in the 1990s: A "Black Eye on the Arts"?' American Behavioral Scientist (2000).

Miller, Toby. Technologies of Truth: Cultural Citizenship and the Popular Media. Minneapolis: U of Minnesota P (1998).

Millea, Mechael. 'Czech Privatization: The Case of Fimove Studio Barrandov' Journal of International Affairs 50, no. 2: (1997) 489–505.

Miller, Toby. The Well-Tempered Self: Citizenship, Culture, and the Postmodern Subject. Baltimore: The Johns Hopkins UP (1993).

Miller, Toby, Nitin Govil, John McMurria, and Richard Maxwell. Global Hollywood. London: BFI (2001).

Mills, C. Wright. 'Culture and Politics' Power, Politics and People: The Collected Essays of C. Wright Mills. ed. Irving Louis Horowitz. London: Oxford UP (1970).

Minihan, J. The Nationalization of Culture: The Development of State Subsidies to the Arts in Great Britain. London: Hamish Hamilton (1977).

Mitchell, Clare J.A. and Geoffrey Wall. 'The Arts and Employment: A Case Study of the Stratford Festival' Growth and Change 20, no. 4 (1989): 31–40.

Mitchell, J.M. International Cultural Relations. London: Allen and Unwin (1986).

Mitchell, Paul. 'Britain: Labour Government Outlines the Next Stage in its Assault on the Arts' World Socialist Web Site (10 April 2001). www.wsws.org/articles/2001/apr2001/arts-a10_prn.shtml.

Mitchell, Timothy. Colonising Egypt. Cambridge: Cambridge UP (1988).

Mitter, Rana. 'Behind the Scenes at the Museum: Nationalism, History and Memory in the Beijing War of Resistance Museum, 1987–1997' China Quarterly no. 161 (2000): 279–93.

Moen, Matthew C. 'Congress and the National Endowment for the Arts: Institutional Patterns and Arts Funding, 1965–1994' Social Science Journal 34, no. 2 (1997): 185–200.

Moen, Matthew C. The Christian Right and Congress. Philadelphia: Temple UP (1989).

Mokia, Rosemary Ntumnyuy. 'Publishers, United States Foreign Policy and the Third World, 1960–1967' Publishing Research Quarterly 11, no. 2 (1995): 36–51.

Mokwa, Michael and William Dawson, eds. Marketing and the Arts. New York: Praeger (1979).

Molotsky, Irvin. 'Donations May be Sought to Send U.S. Arts Abroad' New York Times (29 November 2000): E3.

Moncrieff Arrarte, Anne. 'Region Emerges as Entertainment Capital', Miami Herald 25 June: 1A (1998).

Monitor. U.S. Runaway Film and Television Production Study Report (1999).

Moore, Kevin, ed. Museum Management. London: Routledge (1994).

Moore, Thomas Gale. The Economics of the American Theater. Durham: Duke UP (1968).

Moraes, Angélica de. 'Fábio Magalhães conta como será a Bienal do Mercosul.' O Estado de São Paulo 28 July (1998). http://www.estado.estadao.com.br/edicao/pano/98/07/27/ ca2606.html

Monitor. U.S. Runaway Film and Television Production Study Report (1999).

Moran, Albert, ed. Film Policy: International, National and Regional Perspectives. London: Routledge (1996).

Morais, Federico. 'Reescrevendo a historia da arte latino-americana.' I Bienal de Artes Visuais do Mercosul. Porto Alegre: Fundação Bienal do Mercosul (1997), 12–20.

221

Morales-Moreno, Luis Gerardo. 'History and Patriotism in the National Museum of Mexico.' *Museums and the Making of 'Ourselves': The Role of Objects in National Identity* ed. Flora Kaplan, London: Leicester UP (1994) 171–191.

Moran, Albert. *Copycat TV: Globalisation, Program Formats and Cultural Identity.* Luton: U of Luton P (1998).

Moran, Albert. *Images and Industry: Television Drama Production in Australia.* Sydney: Currency P (1985).

Morrison, William G. and Edwin G. West. 'Subsidies for the Performing Arts: Evidence on Voter Preferences' *Journal of Behavioral Economics* 15 (Fall 1986): 57–72.

Mossetto, Gianfranco. *Aesthetics and Economics.* Dordrecht: Kluwer (1993).

Moulin, Raymonde. *The French Art Market: A Sociological View.* Trans. Arthur Goldhammer. New Brunswick: Rutgers UP (1987).

Mulcahy, Kevin V. 'Ideology and Public Culture' *Journal of Aesthetic Education* 16 (1982): 11–24.

Mulcahy, Kevin V. 'Official Culture and Cultural Repression' *Journal of Aesthetic Education* 18 (1984): 69–83.

Mulcahy, Kevin V. 'Public Support for the Arts in the United States, Western Europe and Canada: Polities, Policies, Politics' Commissioned by the American Assembly. New York: Columbia U (1997).

Mulcahy, Kevin V. 'The Arts and Their Economic Impact: The Values of Utility' *Journal of Arts Management and Law* 16 (Autumn 1986): 33–48.

Mulcahy, Kevin V. 'Cultural Policy and Kulturkampf' *Journal of Aesthetic Education* 14 (October 1980): 48–53.

Mulcahy, Kevin V. 'The Public Interest in Public Culture' *Journal of Arts Management and Law* 21, no. 1 (1991): 9–23.

Mulcahy, Kevin V. and C. Richard Swaim, eds. *Public Policy and the Arts.* Bolder: Westview P (1982).

Mulcahy, Kevin V. and Harold F. Kendrick. 'Congress and Culture: Legislative Reauthorization and the Arts Endowment' *Journal of Arts Management and Law* 17, no. 4 (1988).

Murdoch, Rupert. Presentation Prepared for the European Audiovisual Conference. Birmingham (6–8 April 1998).

Murdock, Graham. 'Across the Great Divide: Cultural Analysis and the Condition of Democracy' *Critical Studies in Mass Communication* 12, no. 1 (1995): 89–95.

Nahmod, Sheldon. 'Artistic Expression and Aesthetic Theory: The Beautiful, the Sublime, and the First Amendment' *Wisconsin Law Review* 221 (1987).

National Endowment for the Arts. *International Data on Government Spending on the Arts.* Research Note no. 74. Washington, D.C.: National Endowment for the Arts (2000).

National Endowment for the Arts Question & Answer. http://www.cco.caltech.edu/--ope/nea.html.

National Endowment for the Arts. *Toward Civilization: A Report on Arts Education.* Washington, D.C.: National Endowment for the Arts (1988).

Netzer, Dick. *The Subsidized Muse: Public Support for the Arts in the United States.* Cambridge: Cambridge UP (1978).

Newcomb, Horace. 'Other People's Fictions: Cultural Appropriation, Cultural Integrity, and International Media Struggles' *Mass Media and Free Trade: NAFTA and the Cultural Industries.* ed. Emile G. McAnany and Kenton T. Wilkinson. Austin: U of Texas P (1996): 92–109.

Newland, Carlos. *Buenos Aires no es pampa: La educación elemental porteóa 1820–1860.* Buenos Aires: Grupo Editor Latinoamericano (1992).

Nichols, Deborah L., Anthony L. Klesert, and Roger Anyon. 'Ancestral Sites, Shrines, and Graves: Native American Perspectives on the Ethics of Collecting Cultural Properties' *The Ethics of Collecting: Whose Culture? Whose Property?,* 2nd ed. Ed. Phyllis Mauch Messenger. Albuquerque: U of New Mexico P (1999): 27–38.

Ninkovich, Frank. A. *The Diplomacy of Ideas: US Foreign Policy and Cultural Relations.* Cambridge: Cambridge UP (1981).

Ninkovich, Frank. U.S. *Information Policy and Cultural Diplomacy*. New York: Foreign Policy Association (1996).

Nisbet, Robert A. 'Project Camelot: An Autopsy' *On Intellectuals: Theoretical Studies. Case Studies*. ed. Philip Rieff. New York: Anchor, 1970: 307–39.

Nowell-Smith, Geoffrey. 'Prefatory Statement' *Fires Were Started: British Cinema and Thatcherism* ed. Lester Friedman. Minneapolis: U of Minnesota P (1993).

Nulens, Gert and Leo Van Audenhove. An Information Society in Africa? An Analysis of the Information Society Policy of the World Bank, ITU and ECA. *Gazette* 6, no. 16 (1999) 451–71.

O'Conner, J. and D. Wynne. 'The Uses and Abuses of Popular Culture: Cultural Policy and Popular Culture' *Loisir et Société* 14, no. 2 (1991): 465–82.

O'Connor, F.V., ed. *Art for the Millions: Essays from the 1930s by Artists and Administrators of the WPA Federal Art Project*. Boston: New York Graphic Society (1973).

O'Connor, Timothy Edward. *The Politics of Soviet Culture: Anatolii Lunacharskii*. Ann Arbor: UMI Research P (1983).

Ochoa Gautier, Ana María. 'Listening to the State: Power, Culture, and Cultural Policy in Colombia.' *Companion to Cultural Studies*. Toby Miller, ed. Boston: Blackwell, (2001) 375–90.

Odendahl, Teresa, ed. *America's Wealthy and the Future of Foundations*. New York: Foundation Center (1987).

O'Hagan, John W. 'Access to and Participation in the Arts: The Case of Those with Low Incomes/Educational Attainment' *Journal of Cultural Economics* 20, no. 4 (1996): 269–82.

Opondo, Patricia A. 'Cultural Policies in Kenya' *Arts Education Policy Review* 101, no. 5 (2000): 18–24.

O'Regan, Tom. '"Knowing the Processes but not the Outcomes": Australian Cinema Faces the Millennium' *Culture in Australia: Policies, Publics and Programs*. ed. Tony Bennett and David Carter. Cambridge: Cambridge UP (2001): 18–45.

O'Regan, Tom. '(Mis)taking Policy: Notes on the Cultural Policy Debate' *Australian Cultural Studies: A Reader*. ed. John Frow and Meaghan Morris. Sydney: Allen and Unwin (1993): 192–206.

O'Regan, Tom. *Australian National Cinema*. London: Routledge (1996).

Ortiz, Fernando. *Cuban Counterpoint: Tobacco and Sugar* (1940). Trans. Harriet de Onis. Intro. Bronislaw Malinowski. New intro. Fernando Coronil. Chapel Hill: Duke University Press (1995).

Ortiz, Renato. *Cultura brasileira e identidade nacional*. São Paulo: Brasiliense (1985).

Ooi, Vicki. 'The Best Cultural Policy is no Cultural Policy: Cultural Policy in Hong Kong' *Cultural Policy* 1, no. 2 (1995): http://www.info.gov.hk.

Orosz, J.J. *Curators and Culture: The Museum Movement in America, 1773–1870*. Tuscaloosa: U of Alabama P (1990).

Ostrower, Francie. *Why the Wealthy Give: The Culture of Elite Philanthropy*. Princeton: Princeton UP (1997).

Ottmann, Goetz. 'Cultura é um Bom Negócio.' Unpublished ms.

Palma, Giuseppe and Guido Clemente di San Luca. 'State Intervention in the Arts in Italy from 1945 to 1982' Trans. G. Falcone. *The Patron State: Government and the Arts in Europe, North America, and Japan*. ed. Milton C. Cummings, Jr. and Richard S. Katz. New York: Oxford UP (1987): 68–104.

Pankratz, David B. 'Toward an Integrated Study of Cultural and Educational Policy' *Journal of Arts Management and Law* 18, no. 3 (1988): 63–80.

Pankratz, David B. and Valerie B. Morris, Eds *The Future of the Arts: Public Policy and Arts Research*. New York: Praeger (1990).

Pankratz, David B. *Multiculturalism and Public Arts Policy*. Westport: Bergin and Garvey (1993).

Pannell, Sandra. 'Mabo and Museums: "The Indigenous (Re)Appropriation of Indigenous Things"' *Oceania* 65 (1994): 18–39.

Park, M. and G. E. Markowitz. *Democratic Vista: Post Offices and Public Art in the New Deal*. Philadelpia: Temple UP (1984).

Parker, Richard A. 'The Guise of the Propagandist: Governmental Classification of Foreign Political Films' *Current Research in Film: Audiences, Economics and Law vol. 5.* ed. Bruce A. Austin. Norwood: Ablex (1991): 135–46.

Parsons, Philip, ed. *Shooting the Pianist: The Role of Government in the Arts.* Sydney: Currency P (1987).

Payne, Richard J. *The Clash with Distant Cultures: Values, Interests, and Force in American Foreign Policy.* Albany: State U of New York P (1996).

Paz, Octavio. 'The Power of Ancient Mexican Art.' *New York Review of Books* (Dec. 6) 1990.

Peacock, Alan and Ilde Rizzo, Eds. *Cultural Economics and Cultural Policies.* Dordrecht: Kluwer Academic (1994).

Peacock, Alan. 'Economics, Cultural Values and Cultural Policies' *Journal of Cultural Economics* 15, no. 2 (1991): 1–18.

Pearce, Susan M. *Museums, Objects, and Collections: A Cultural Study.* Washington: Smithsonian Institution P (1992).

Pearce, Susan M., ed. *Museum Studies in Material Culture.* Leicester: Leicester UP (1989).

Pearson, N. *The State and the Visual Arts: A Discussion of State Intervention in the Visual Arts in Britain,* 1760–1981. Milton Keynes: Open UP (1982).

Pendakur, Manjunath. 'Dynamics of Cultural Policy Making: The US Film Industry in India' *Journal of Communication* 35, no. 4 (1987): 52–72.

Pendakur, Manjunath. 'Hollywood North: Film and TV Production in Canada' *Global Productions: Labor in the Making of the 'Information Society'.* ed. Gerald Sussman and John A. Lent. Cresskill: Hampton P (1998): 213–38.

Peterson, Richard A. 'Foreword: Beyond the Production of Culture' *Art, Ideology, and Politics.* ed. Judith H. Balfe and Margaret Jane Wyszomirski. New York: Praeger, 1985. iii–v.

Persick, L.J. 'The Continuing Development of United States Policy Concerning the International Movement of Cultural Property' *Dickinson Journal of International Law* 4, no. 1 (1985): 89–112.

Petras, James. 'The CIA and the Cultural Cold War Revisited' *Monthly Review* 51, no. 6 (1999): 47–56.

Petropoulos, Jonathan. *Art as Politics in the Third Reich.* Chapel Hill: U of North Carolina P (1996).

Pfister, Bonnie. 'Movie May Help, Hurt Mexican Village.' *San Diego Union-Tribune* (31 May 2000).

Phillips, A.A. 'Culture and Canberra' *Meanjin Papers: A Quarterly of Literature and Art* 5, no. 2 (1946): 99–103.

Phillipson, Robert. 'English Language Spread Policy' *International Journal of the Sociology of Language* no. 107 (1994): 7–24.

Pick, John. *Managing the Arts? The British Experience.* London: Rhinegold (1986).

Pick, John. *The Arts in a State.* Bristol: Bristol Classical P (1988).

Pieterse, Jan Nederveen. 'Fictions of Europe' *Race & Class* 32, no. 3 (1991).

Ping-hui, Lao. 'Chinese Nationalism or Taiwanese Localism?' *Culture and Policy* 7, no. 2 (1996): 75–92.

Piven, Frances Fox and Richard Cloward. *Regulating the Poor: The Functions of Public Welfare,* rev. ed. New York: Vintage/Random House (1993).

Plagens, P. 'Squishy Defenses by its Supporters Don't Help the Endowment' *Chronicle of Higher Education* (24 July 1998): B4–B5.

Pointon, Marcia, ed. *Art Apart: Art Institutions and Ideology Across England and North America.* Manchester: Manchester UP (1994).

Policy.com. 'Issue of the week: Defunding the NEA' (1997): http://www.policy.com/issuewk/0721/072197b.html 1–3.

Political & Economic Planning. *The British Film Industry.* London: PEP (1952).

Pollock, Barbara. 'Jockeying for Position in the Culture Wars' *Village Voice* (12 October 1999): 50–53.

Pommerehne, Werner W. and Bruno S. Frey. 'Public Promotion of the Arts: A Survey of Means' *Journal of Cultural Economics* 14, no. 2 (1990): 73–93.

Porter, Eduardo. 'Hispanic Actors Await End of Strike.' *Wall Street Journal* (22 September 2000): B3.

Posner, Richard. 'Art for Law's Sake' *American Scholar* (Autumn 1989): 513–20.

Potts, Jackie. 'Lincoln Road Revitalized.' *Variety* 1–7 November (1999): M25–M26.

Powell, Walter W., ed. *The Handbook of Non-Profit Organizations*. New Haven: Yale UP (1987).

Pratten, Stephen and Simon Deakin. 'Competitiveness Policy and Economic Organization: The Case of the British Film Industry' *Screen* 41, no. 2 (2000): 217–37.

Pendergast, David M. and Elizabeth Graham. 'The Battle for the Maya Past: The Effects of International Looting and Collecting in Belize' *The Ethics of Collecting: Whose Culture? Whose Property?*, 2nd edition. ed. Phyllis Mauch Messenger. Albuquerque: U of New Mexico P (1999): 51–60.

President's Committee on the Arts and Humanities. *Creative America: A Report to the President*. Washington (1997).

Preuss, U.K. 'Migration – A Challenge to Modern Citizenship' *Constellations* 4, no. 3 (1998): 307–19.

Price, Clement Alexander. *Many Voices Many Opportunities: Cultural Pluralism and American Arts Policy*. New York: American Council for the Arts/Allworth P (1994).

Price, Monroe E. 'Controlling Imagery: The Fight Over Using Art to Change Society' *American Art* 7, no. 3 (1993): 2–13.

Price, Richard and Sally Price. 'Executing Culture: Musée, Museo, Museum' *American Anthropologist* 97, no. 1 (1995): 97–109.

Price, Sally. *Primitive Art in Civilized Places*. Chicago: U of Chicago P (1989).

Public Affairs Quarterly 8 (April 1994).

Public Law 89–209. 'National Foundation on the Arts and the Humanities Act of 1965' Public Law 89–209. Cited in President's Committee on the Arts and the Humanities, 23.

Puplick, Christopher and Tony Bennett. 'Arts National' Programme on Museums: A Discussion with Christopher Puplick and Tony Bennett Held Following the Delivery of 'Thanks for the Memories,' August 1989' *Culture and Policy* 1, no. 2 (1990): 67–74.

Puttnam, David with Neil Watson. *Movies and Money*. New York: Alfred A. Knopf (1998).

Pye, Lucian W. 'Introduction: Political Culture and Political Development' *Political Culture and Political Development*. ed. Lucian W. Pye and Sidney Verba. Princeton: Princeton UP, 1965. 3–26.

Quester, George H. *The International Politics of Television*. Lexington, Mass.: Lexington (1990).

Radbourne, Jennifer. 'Creative Nation–A Policy for Leaders or Followers? An Evaluation of Australia's 1994 Cultural Policy Statement' *Journal of Arts Management, Law and Society* 26, no. 4 (1997): 271–83.

Rama, Angel. *The Lettered City*. Trans. John Chasteen. Durham: Duke University Press (1996).

Ramos, Julio. *Divergent Modernities: Culture and Politics in Nineteenth Century Latin America*. Trans. John D. Blanco. Durham and London: Duke University Press.

Rankin, Elizabeth and Carolyn Hamilton. 'Revision; Reaction; Re-Vision: The Role of Museums in (a) Transforming South Africa' *Museum Anthropology* 22, no. 3 (1999): 3–13.

Raphael, Alison. *Samba and Social Control: Popular Culture and Racial Democracy in Rio de Janeiro*. Ph.D. Diss. Columbia University (1980).

Ratman, Niru. 'Chris Ofili and the Limits of Hybridity' *New Left Review* no. 235 (May-June 1999): 153–59.

Reeves, Geoffrey. *Communications and the 'Third World'* London: Routledge, 1993.

Regen, Richard. 'Flinching and Fear. Is the Art World Doing Jesse Helms' Work For Him?' *Village Voice* (17 October 1989): 29.

Report of the International Meeting on Cultural Policy: Putting Culture on the World Stage. (1999).

Rhoades, Gary and Sheila Slaughter. 'Academic Capitalism, Managed Professionals, and Supply Side Higher Education' *Social Text* no. 51 (Summer 1997): 9–38.

Rice, William Craig. 'I Hear America Singing: The Arts will Flower without the NEA' *Policy Review: The Journal of American Citizenship* no. 82 (March-April 1997): 37–45.

Rich, B. Ruby. 'Dissed and Disconnected: Notes on Present Ills and Future Dreams' *Transition* no. 62 (1993): 27–47.

Richards, Jeffrey. 'British Film Censorship' *The British Cinema Book*. ed. Robert Murphy. London: BFI (1997).

Riddell, Janice B. 'The Political Climate and Arts Education' *Arts Education Policy Review* 98, no. 5 (1997): 2–8.

Riding, Alan. 'Art in Germany Crosses the Borders' *New York Times* (2 December 1999): E1, E5.

Ridler, Neil B. 'Cultural Identity and Public Policy: An Economic Analysis' *Journal of Cultural Economics* 10, no. 2 (1986): 45–56.

Ridley, F.F. 'Cultural Economics and the Culture of Economists' *Journal of Cultural Economics* 7, no. 1 (1983): 1–17.

Rieff, Philip. 'The Case of Dr Oppenheimer' *On Intellectuals: Theoretical Studies. Case Studies*. ed. Philip Rieff. New York: Anchor, (1970). 341–69.

Riggins, Stephen H. and Khoa Pham. 'Democratizing the Arts: France in an Era of Austerity' *Queen's Quarterly* 93, no. 1 (1986): 149–61.

Riely, Michael. 'Producers Find Magic in Mexico.' *Houston Chronicle* (3 December 1999).

Rivera-Lyles, Jeannette. 'FIU hacia la elite iniversitaria de EU' *El Nuevo Herald* 4 January (2000).

Roane, Kit R. 'Buchanan Visits Art Exhibit in Brooklyn and Doesn't Like It' *New York Times* (6 November 1999): B5.

Robbins, Lord. *Politics and Economics: Essays in Political Economy*. London: Macmillan (1963).

Robinson, J.P., ed. *Social Science and the Arts*. Lanham: UP of Americas (1985).

Rodda, Clinton. 'The Accomplishment of Aesthetic Purposes Under the Police Power' *Southern California Law Review* 27 (1954): 149–79.

Roddick, Nick. 'A Hard Sell: The State of Documentary Film Marketing' *Dox* no. 2 (1994): 30–32.

Rodríguez, Roberto and Patrisia Gónzales. 'Bring Me the Foot of Oñate' *ColorLines* 3, no. 1 (2000): 8–10.

Rohter, Larry. '500 Years Later, Brazil Looks its Past in the Face' *New York Times* (25 April 2000): A3.

Rohter, Larry. 'Miami, the Hollywood of Latin America' *New York Times News Service* (1996): http://www.latinolink.com/art/0818aho1.htm.

Rorty, Amélie Oksenberg. 'Rights: Educational, Not Cultural' *Social Research* 62, no. 1 (1995): 161–70.

Rosaldo, Renato. 'Cultural Citizenship and Educational Democracy' *Cultural Anthropology* 9, no. 3 (1994): 402–11.

Rose, Joseph B. 'Landmarks Preservation in New York' *The Public Face of Architecture: Civic Culture and Public Spaces*. ed. Nathan Glazer and Mark Lilla. New York: Free P; London: Collier Macmillan (1987): 428–42.

Rose, Nikolas and Peter Miller. 'Political Power Beyond the State: Problematics of Government' *British Journal of Sociology* 43, no. 2 (1992): 173–205.

Rose, Nikolas. *Powers of Freedom: Reframing Political Thought*. Cambridge; New York: Cambridge University Press (1999).

Rosenberg, Carol. 'Miami attracting celebrity exiles: Famous flee Colombia for life on quieter, safer South Florida', *The Miami Herald*, 3 April (2000).

Rosenthal, Andrew. 'Bush's Balancing Act Over Financing of Arts' *New York Times* (19 June 1990): C14.

Rousseau, Jean-Jacques *The Social Contract and Discourses*. Trans. G.D.H. Cole. London: J.M. Dent (1975).

Rowe, David and Peter Brown. 'Promoting Women's Sport: Theory, Policy and Practice' *Leisure Studies* 13, no. 2 (1994): 97–110.

Rowse, Tim. 'Cultural Policy and Social Theory' *Media Information Australia* no. 53 (August 1989): 13–22.

Rowse, Tim. *Arguing the Arts*. Melbourne: Penguin (1985).

Rubinstein, A.J., William J. Baumol, and Hilda Baumol. 'On the Economics of the Performing Arts in the Soviet Union and the USA: A Comparison of Data' *Journal of Cultural Economics* 16, no. 2 (1992): 1–23.

Rueschemeyer, Marilyn. 'State Patronage in the German Democratic Republic: Artistic and Political Change in a State Socialist Society' *Journal of Arts Management and Law* 20, no. 4 (1991): 31–55.

Rydell, Robert W. 'Museums and Cultural History: A Review Article' *Comparative Studies in Society and History* 34, no. 2 (1992): 242–47.

Rydell, Robert W. *All the World's a Fair: Visions of Empire at American International Expositions, 1876–1916*. Chicago: U of Chicago P (1984).

Rydon, Joan and Diane Mackay. 'Federalism and the Arts' *Australian Cultural History* no. 3 (1984): 87–99.

Ryerson, André. 'Abolish the NEA: Government is Incapable of Detecting Artistic Genius' *Policy Review* 104 (Fall 1990): 32–37.

Sabonis-Chafee, Theresa. 'Communism as Kitsch: Soviet Symbols in Post-Soviet Society' *Consuming Russia: Popular Culture, Sex, and Society since Gorbachev*. Ed. Adele Marie Barker. Durham: Duke UP (1999): 362–82.

Salz, Jerry. 'At 'Sensation,' Transgression Prevails Over Insight' *Village Voice* (12 October 1999): 59.

Salz, Jerry. 'Man in the Middle' *Village Voice* (12 October 1999): 48.

Sankowski, Edward. 'Ethics, Art, and Museums' *Journal of Aesthetic Education* 26, no. 3 (1992): 1–15.

Santana, Elcior. (1999) Remarks at Meeting on the Transnationalization of Support for Culture in a Globalizing World, Bellagio Study and Conference Center, Villa Serbelloni, Bellagio, Italy, 6 to 10 December.

Sarmiento, Domingo Faustino. *Educion popular* (1849). Buenos Aires: Banco de la Provincia de Córdoba (1989).

———. 'Ejercicios populares de la lengua castellana' (1842). *Sarmiento en el destierro.* ed. Armando Duroio. Buenos Aires: M. Gleizer (1927).

———. 'Raro descubrimiento!' (1842) In *Sarmiento en el destierro.* ed. Armando Duroio. Buenos Aires: M. Gleizer (1927).

———. *Facundo, or, civilization and barbarism* (1845). Trans. Mary Mann. (1998) New York: Penguin Books, 1998.

———. *Obras completas iv: Ortografia, instrucción pública*, 1841–1854. Buenos Aires: Editorial Luz del Día (1948).

Saunders, Frances Stonor. *Cultural Cold War: The CIA and the World of Arts and Letters*. New York: The New Press (1999).

Savage, James D. 'Populism, Decentralization, and Arts Policy in California: The Jerry Brown Years and Afterward' *Administration and Society* 20, no. 4 (1989): 446–64.

Schatz, Thomas. *The Genius of the System: Hollywood Filmmaking in the Studio Era*. New York: Pantheon (1988).

Schechner, Richard. 'Bon Voyage, NEA' *The Drama Review* 40, no. 1 (1996): 7–9.

Schiller, Herbert I. 'Transnational Media: Creating Consumers Worldwide' *Journal of International Affairs* 47, no. 1 (1993): 47–58.

Schiller, Herbert I. *Culture, Inc.: The Corporate Takeover of Public Expression*. New York: Oxford UP (1989).

Schlesinger, Arthur. *The Vital Center: The Politics of Freedom*. Cambridge, Mass: Harvard UP (1949).

Schlesinger, Philip. *Media, State and Nation: Political Violence and Collective Identities*. London: Sage (1991).

Schmidt, Ronald, Sr. *Language Policy and Identity Politics in the United States*. Philadelphia: Temple UP (2000).

Schuster, J. Mark Davidson. 'Funding the Arts and Culture Through Dedicated State Lotteries–Part I' *European Journal of Cultural Policy* 1, no. 1 (1995): 21–41.

Schuster, J. Mark Davidson. 'Funding the Arts and Culture Through Dedicated State Lotteries–Part II' *European Journal of Cultural Policy* 1, no. 2 (1995): 329–54.

Schuster, J. Mark Davidson. 'Making Compromises to Make Comparisons in Cross-National Arts Policy Research' *Journal of Cultural Economics* 11, no. 2 (1987): 1–36.

Schuster, J. Mark Davidson. 'The Interrelationships Between Public and Private Funding of the Arts in the United States' *Journal of Arts Management and Law* 14 (Winter 1985): 77–105.

Schwab, S. 'Television in the 90's: Revolution or Confusion?' *Tenth Joseph I. Lubin Memorial Lecture*. New York U (1 March 1994).

Schwarz, Roberto. *Misplaced Ideas: Essays On Brazilian Culture*. London and New York: Verso (1992).

Seelye, K.Q. 'For Election Year, House Approves Arts Financing' *New York Times* (22 July 1998): A1, A14.

Sellars, Richard West. *Preserving Nature in the National Parks: A History*. New Haven: Yale UP (1997).

Selle, Per and Lars Svasand. 'Cultural Policy, Leisure and Voluntary Organizations in Norway' *Leisure Studies* 6, no. 3 (1987): 347–64.

Senghor, Léopold Sédar. 'The African Road to Socialism' *On African Socialism*. Trans. Mercer Cook. New York: Frederick A. Praeger (1964): 67–103.

Senie, Harriet F. and Sally Webster, eds. *Critical Issues in Public Art: Content, Context, and Controversy*. New York: Iconeditions (1992).

Sewell, James P. 'UNESCO: Pluralism Rampant' *The Anatomy of Influence: Decision Making in International Organization*. Ed. Robert W. Cox and Harold K. Jacobson. New Haven: Yale UP (1974): 139–74.

Shafir, G. 'Introduction: The Evolving Traditions of Citizenship' *The Citizenship Debates: A Reader*. ed. G. Shafir. Minneapolis: U of Minnesota P (1998): 1–28.

Shapiro, Michael J. *Reading 'Adam Smith': Desire, History and Value*. Newbury Park: Sage (1993).

Shapiro, Michael J. *Reading the Postmodern: Political Theory as Textual Practice*. Minneapolis: U of Minnesota P (1992).

Shaw, Douglas V., William S. Hendon, and C. Richard Waits, Eds *Artists and Cultural Consumers*. Akron: Association for Cultural Economics (1986).

Shaw, Douglas V., William S. Hendon, and Virginia Lee Owen, Eds *Cultural Economics 8: An American Perspective*. Akron: Association for Cultural Economics, (1988).

Shen, Zhilong and Chunmei Zhao. 'Aesthetic Education in China' *Journal of Multicultural and Cross-Cultural Research in Art Education* 17 (1999): 91–102.

Sherman, Daniel J. and Irit Rogoff, eds. *Museum Culture: Histories, Discourses, Spectacles*. Minneapolis: U of Minnesota P (1994).

Shipley, Kim M. 'The Politicization of Art: The National Endowment for the Arts, the First Amendment, and Senator Helms' *Emory Law Journal* 40 (1991).

Sholle, David. 'Resisting Disciplines: Repositioning Media Studies in the University' *Communication Theory* 5, no. 2 (1995): 130–43.

Shore, Chris. 'Transcending the Nation-State?: The European Commission and the (Re)-Discovery of Europe' *Journal of Historical Sociology* 9, no. 4 (1996): 473–96.

Short, David. 'Pearson Resists Pressure for a Focus on Television.' *European* (21 March 1996): 24.

Sierra, Justo. (1948) *La educación nacional; artículos, actuaciones y documentos*. ed. Agustin Yáñez. México: Universidad Nacional Autónoma de México.

Simmel, Georg. 'The Metropolis and Mental Life.' Trans. Kurt H. Wolff. *Sociological Perspectives: Selected Readings*. ed. Kenneth Thompson and Jeremy Tunstall. Harmondsworth: Penguin Books (1976): 82–93.

Simpson, Christopher. *Science of Coercion: Communication Research and Psychological Warfare 1945–1960.* New York: Oxford UP, 1994.

Sinclair, Andrew. *Arts and Cultures: The History of the 50 Years of the Arts Council of Great Britain.* London: Sinclair-Stevenson (1995).

Singer, Daniel. 'GATT and the Shape of Our Dreams' *The Nation* 258, no. 2 (1994): 54–6.

Sjolander, Claire Turner. 'Unilateralism and Multilateralism: The United States and the Negotiation of the GATS' *International Journal* 48, no. 1 (1992–3): 52–79.

Smejkalová-Strickland, Jirina. 'Censoring Canons: Transitions and Prospects of Literary Institutions in Czechoslovakia' *The Administration of Aesthetics: Censorship, Political Criticism, and the Public Sphere.* ed. Richard Burt. Minneapolis: U of Minnesota P (1994): 195–215.

Smith, Paul. 'A Memory of Marxism' *Polygraph* nos. 6–7 (1993): 98–105.

Smith, Ralph A. and Alan Simpson, Eds *Aesthetics and Arts Education.* Urbana: U of Illinois P (1991).

Smith, Ralph A. and Ronald Berman, Eds *Public Policy and the Aesthetic Interest: Critical Essays on Defining Cultural and Educational Relations.* Urbana: U of Illinois P (1992).

Smith, Roberta. 'Waging Guerilla Warfare Against the Art World' *New York Times* (17 June 1990): H1, H31.

Smolensky, Eugene. 'Municipal Financing of the U.S. Fine Art Museum: A Historical Rationale' *Journal of Economic History* 46, no. 4 (1986): 757–68.

Snow, Nancy. *Propaganda, Inc.: Selling America's Culture to the World.* New York: Seven Stories P (1998).

Sofoulis, Zoë. 'Position-Envy and the Subsumption of Feminism: Some Hypotheses' *Cultural Studies: Pluralism and Theory.* ed. David Bennett. Melbourne: Melbourne U Department of English (1993): 213–20.

Sorensen, Colin. 'Theme Parks and Time Machnies' *The New Museology.* ed. Peter Vergo. London: Reaktion, (1991): 60–73.

Soren, Barbara. 'The Museum as Curricular Site' *Journal of Aesthetic Education* 26, no. 3 (1992): 91–101.

Sorlin, Pierre. *European Cinemas, European Societies 1939–1990.* London: Routledge (1991).

Southwick, Ron. 'Budget Will Rise for Arts and Humanities Endowments' *Chronicle of Higher Education* (10 November 2000): A29.

Southwick, Ron. 'House Panel Votes Down Spending Increases for NEH and NEA' *Chronicle of Higher Education* (18 May 2000): 3.

Sparshott, Francis. 'Why Artworks Have no Right to Have Rights' *Journal of Aesthetics and Art Criticism* 42 (1983): 5–15.

Spurgeon, Christina. 'National Culture, Communications and the Information Economy' *Media International Australia* no. 87 (May 1998): 23–34.

Stahler, Gerald J. and William R. Tash. 'Centers and Institutes in the Research University: Issues, Problems, and Prospects' *Journal of Higher Education* 65, no. 5 (1994): 540–54.

Stalin, J.V. *Marxism and Problems of Linguistics.* Peking: Foreign Languages P (1972).

Stark, Andrew. '"Political-Discourse" Analysis and the Debate over Canada's Lobbying Legislation' *Canadian Journal of Political Science* 25, no. 3 (1992): 513–34.

Stehle, Vincent. 'The Competitive Disadvantage of Foundation Giving' *Grantmakers in the Arts* 11, no. 1 (2000): 18–20.

Stern, Andy. 'EC Funnels $355 Mil to Boost Pix' *Variety* (20 December 1999–2 January 2000): 20.

Stern, Andy. 'Film/TV Future Tops Confab Agenda' *Variety* (27 June–3 July 1994): 39.

Stern, Andy. 'Reding Plans More Green for Distrib'n' *Variety* (1–7 November 1999): 18.

Stern, Andy. 'Valenti Denies Euro TV Crisis' *Daily Variety* (23 June 1994): 1, 17.

Stevenson, Richard W. 'Lights! Camera! Europe!' *New York Times* (6 February 1994): 1, 6.

Stimpson, Catharine R. 'Federal Papers' *October* no. 53 (1990): 24–39.

Stocking, G., ed. *Objects and Others: Essays on Museums and Material Culture.* Madison: U of Wisconsin P (1985).

Stoklund, Bjarne. 'The Role of the International Exhibitions in the Construction of National Cultures in the 19th Century' *Ethnologia Europaea* 24, no. 1 (1994): 35–44.

Stone, Marla Susan. *The Patron State: Culture & Politics in Fascist Italy*. Princeton: Princeton UP (1998).

Stonor Saunders, Frances. *Cultural Cold War: The CIA and the World of Arts and Letters*. New York: New P (1999).

Straight, Michael. *Twigs for an Eagle's Nest: Government and the Arts, 1965–1978*. New York: Devon P (1979).

Strange, Susan. 'The Limits of Politics' *Government and Opposition* 30, no. 3 (1995): 291–311.

Street, Sarah. *British National Cinema*. London: Routledge (1997).

Streeter, Thomas. *Selling the Air: A Critique of the Policy of Commercial Broadcasting in the United States*. Chicago: U of Chicago P (1996).

Sullivan, Martin. 'A Museum Perspective on Repatriation: Issues and Opportunities' *Arizona Law Journal* 71 (1992): 40–44.

Sutter, Mary. 'Viva Mexico!–Hollywood Heads South of the Border' *Kempos* 21–27 December: 1, 4–5 (1998a).

Sutter, Mary. 'Woman on Top in a Macho Man's Union' *Kempos* 21–27 December: 8 (1998b).

Swarns, Rachel L. 'Oppression in Black and White' *New York Times* (10 December 2001): E1, E3.

Swift, Brent. 'Film and Television Action Committee Past & Present' (1999) http://www.ftac.net/about.html.

Synnott, Anthony. *The Body Social: Symbolism, Self and Society*. London: Routledge, (1993).

Tagg, John. 'A Discourse (With Shape of Reason Missing)' *Art History* 15, no. 3 (1992): 351–73.

Taylor, Andrew. 'How Political is the Arts Council?' *Political Quarterly* 66, no. 2 (1995): 184–96.

Taylor, Fannie and Anthony L. Barresi. *The Arts at a New Frontier: The National Endowment for the Arts*. New York: Plenum P (1984).

Tedesco, Juan Carlos. *Educación y sociedad en la Argentina (1880–1900)*. Buenos Aires: Centro Editor de América Latina (1982).

Tegel, Simeon. 'Hollywood Gets Last Word in Mexican Dubs' *Variety* 13 March (2000).

Tegel, Simeon. 'Sand and Stardust' *Business Mexico* 1 February (2001).

Theiler, Tobias. 'Viewers into Europeans?: How the European Union Tried to Europeanize the Audiovisual Sector, and Why it Failed' *Canadian Journal of Communication* 24, no. 4 (1999): 557–87.

Thelen, David. 'History after the Enola Gay Controversy: An Introduction' *Journal of American History* 82, no. 3 (1995): 1029–35.

Thøgersen, Stig. 'Cultural Life and Cultural Control in Rural China: Where is the Party?' *China Journal* 44 (2000): 129–41.

Thompson, Kristin. *Exporting Entertainment: America in the World Film Market 1907–1934*. London: BFI (1985).

Thorp, Rosemary. 'The Latin American Economies, 1939–c. 1950' In Bethell ed., *Latin America. Economy and Society Since 1930* Cambridge: Cambridge UP (1998).

Throsby, C. David and Glen A. Withers. 'Strategic Bias and Demand for Public Goods: Theory and an Application to the Arts' *Journal of Public Economics* 31 (December 1986): 307–27.

Throsby, C. David and Glen A. Withers. *The Economics of the Performing Arts*. New York: St. Martin's P (1979).

Throsby, C. David. 'The Production and Consumption of the Arts: A View of Cultural Economics' *Journal of Economic Literature* 32, no. 1 (1994): 1–29.

Toepler, Stefan. 'From Communism to Civil Society? The Arts and the Nonprofit Sector in Central and Eastern Europe' *Journal of Arts Management, Law and Society* 30, no. 1 (2000): 7–18.

Toffler, Alvin. *The Culture Consumers: A Study of Art and Affluence in America*. New York: St. Martin's P (1964).

Tomaselli, Keyan G. and Alum Mpofu. 'The Rearticulation of Meaning of National Monuments: Beyond Apartheid' *Culture and Policy* 8, no. 3 (1997): 57–76.

Tonkin, Boyd. 'Will Lottery Funding Help Mike Leigh or Ken Loach Make More and Better Films? Not if David Puttnam and his Friends Have Anything to do with it' *New Statesman* (23 May 1997): 38.

Tovar y de Teresa, Rafael. *Modernizacion y polícica cultural: Una visión de la modernización de México*. México: Fondo de Cultura Económica (1994).

Towse, Ruth and Abdul Khakee, eds. *Cultural Economics*. Berlin: Springer-Verlag (1992).

Towse, Ruth and Mark Crain. 'Editorial: The Culture of Cultural Economics' *Journal of Cultural Economics* 18, no. 1 (1994): 1–2.

Trend, David. *Cultural Pedagogy: Art/Education/Politics*. New York: Bergin and Garvey (1992).

Tribe, K.W. 'Government Support for the Arts – Practices, Principles and Proposals' *Australian Cultural History* no. 7 (1988): 18–36.

Trotsky, Leon. *Literature and Revolution*. Trans. Rose Strunsky. Ann Arbor: U of Michigan P (1968).

Tsang, Susan. 'Arts More Cake than Icing' *Variety* (15–21 June 1998): 97.

Tsang, Susan. 'Intl. Festival of Arts Finds its Feet' *Variety* (15–21 June 1998): 98.

Tunstall, Jeremy and David Machin. *The Anglo-American Media Connection* Oxford University Press (1999).

Turim, Maureen. 'The Retraction of State Funding of Film and Video Arts and its Effects on Future Practice' *Cinema Histories Cinema Practices*. ed. Patricia Mellencamp and Philip Rosen. Los Angeles: AFI, 1984. 132–41.

Turnbull, Robert. 'Reconstructing Khmer Classics from Zero' *New York Times* (25 July 1999): AR6, 24.

Turner, Graeme. 'Cultural Policy and National Culture' *Nation, Culture, Text: Australian Cultural and Media Studies*. Ed. Graeme Turner. London: Routledge (1993): 67–71.

Turner, Graeme. *Making it National: Nationalism and Australian Popular Culture*. Sydney: Allen and Unwin, 1994.

UNESCO. *Background Document*. Intergovernmental Conference on Cultural Policies for Development. Stockholm (30 March–2 April (1998).

UNESCO. *Final Report of World Conference on Cultural Policies*. Mexico City and Paris: UNESCO (1982).

United States Government. 'Government. 'Communication from the United States: Audiovisual and Related Services.' World Trade Organization. Council for Trade in Services Special Session, S/CSS/W/21 (18 December 2000).

Ungureit, Heinz. 'Le Groupement Européen de Production: Rassembler les Forces du Service Public ...' *Dossiers de l'Audiovisuel* no. 35 (1991).

Urice, John K. 'Planning at the National Endowment for the Arts: A Review of the Plan and Planning Documents, 1978–1984' *Journal of Arts Management and Law* 15 (Summer 1985): 79–91.

Urice, John K. 'Using Research to Determine, Challenge, or Validate Public Arts Policy' *Journal of Arts Management and Law* 13 (Spring 1983): 199–220.

Urla, Jacqueline. 'Cultural Politics in an Age of Statistics: Numbers, Nations, and the Making of Identity' *American Ethnologist* 20, no. 4 (1993): 818–43.

USIA. '1997 National Trade Estimate Report – European Union' M2 Press Wire (1997).

Van Camp, Julie. 'Freedom of Expression at the National Endowment for the Arts: An Opportunity for Interdisciplinary Education' *Journal of Aesthetic Education* 30, no. 3 (1996): 43–65.

Van Camp, Julie. 'The Philosophy of Art Law' *Metaphilosophy* 25, no. 1 (1994): 60–70.

van den Haag, Ernest. 'Should the Government Subsidize the Arts?' *Policy Review* 10 (Fall 1979).

Van Elteren, Mel. 'Conceptualizing the Impact of US Popular Culture Globally' *Journal of Popular Culture* 30, no. 1 (1996): 47–89.

Van Elteren, Mel. 'GATT and Beyond: World Trade, the Arts and American Popular Culture in Western Europe' *Journal of American Culture* 19, no. 3 (1996): 59–73.

van Krieken, Robert. 'Proto-Governmentalization and the Historical Formation of Organizational Subjectivity' *Economy and Society* 25, no. 2 (1996): 195–221.

Vance, Carol. 'Misunderstanding Obscenity' *Art in America* (May 1990): 49–55.

Vasey, Ruth. *The World According to Hollywood, 1918–1939.* Madison: U of Wisconsin P (1997).

Vattimo, Gianni. 'Postmodernity and New Monumentality' *Res* no. 28 (Autumn 1995): 39–46.

Venturelli, Shalini. 'Cultural Rights and World Trade Agreements in the Information Society' *Gazette* 60, no. 1 (1998): 47–76.

Vergo, Peter, ed. *The New Museology.* London: Reaktion (1991).

Vestheim, G. 'Instrumental Cultural Policy in Scandinavian Countries: A Critical Historical Perspective' *European Journal of Cultural Policy* 1 (1995): 57–71.

Vianna, Hermano. *The Mystery of Samba: Popular Music and National Identity on Brazil.* ed. and trans. John Chasteen. Chapel Hill and London: University of North Carolina Press (1999).

Vitanyi, Ivan. 'Typology and Effects of Cultural Policies' *Cultures* no. 33 (1983): 97–106.

Volkerling, Michael. 'Death or Transfiguration: The Future for Cultural Policy in New Zealand' *Culture and Policy* 6, no. 1 (1994): 7–28.

Volkerling, Michael. 'Deconstructing the Difference-Engine: A Theory of Cultural Policy' *European Journal of Cultural Policy* 2, no. 2 (1996): 189–212.

Volos inov, V.N. *Marxism and the Philosophy of Language,* trans. Ladislav Matejka and I.R. Titunik. New York: Seminar P (1973).

Wachtel, D. *Cultural Policy and Socialist France.* Westport: Greenwood P (1987).

Wagnleitner, Reinhold. 'American Cultural Diplomacy, Hollywood, and the Cold War in Central Europe' *Rethinking MARXISM* 7, no. 1 (1994): 31–47.

Wagnleitner, Reinhold. 'Propagating the American Dream: Cultural Policies as Means of Integration' *American Studies International* 24, no. 1 (1986): 60–84.

Waisbord, Silvio. 'Media in South America: Between the Rock of the State and the Hard Place of the Market' *De-Westernizing Media Studies.* ed. James Curran and Myung-Jin Park. London: Routledge, (2000): 50–62.

Wallerstein, Immanuel. 'Culture as the Ideological Battleground of the Modern World-System' *Hitotsubashi Journal of Social Studies* 21, no. 1 (1989): 5–22.

Wallis, Brian. 'Public Funding and Alternative Spaces' Unpublished ms. (Dec. 1998).

Wallis, Roger and Krister Malm. *Media Policy and Music Activity.* London: Routledge (1993).

Warren, Karen J. 'Introduction: A Philosophical Perspective on the Ethics and Resoltuion of Cultural Properties Issues' *The Ethics of Collecting: Whose Culture? Whose Property?,* 2nd edition. Phyllis Mauch Messenger. Albuquerque: U of New Mexico P (1999): 1–25.

Washington, Paul. '"Being Post-Colonial": Culture, Policy and Government' *Southern Review* 28, no. 3 (1995): 273–82.

Wasko, Janet. 'Challenges to Hollywood's Labor Force in the 1990s' *Global Productions: Labor in the Making of the 'Information Society'.* ed. Gerald Sussman and John A. Lent. Cresskill: Hampton P (1998): 173–89.

Wasko, Janet. *Hollywood in the Information Age: Beyond the Silver Screen.* Cambridge: Polity P (1994).

Wasko, Janet. *Movies and Money: Financing the American Film Industry.* Norwood: Ablex (1982).

Wasser, Frederick. 'Is Hollywood America? The Trans-nationalization of the American Film Industry' *Critical Studies in Mass Communication* 12, no. 4 (1995): 423–37.

Waxman, Sharon. 'Location, Location: hollywood Loses Films to Cheaper Climes,' *Washington Post* (25 June 1999): C1.

Webb, Natalie J. 'Tax and Government Policy Implications for Corporate Foundation Giving' *Nonprofit and Voluntary Sector Quarterly* 23, no. 1 (1994): 41–67.

232

Weber, Max. *General Economic History*. Trans. Frank H. Knight. New York: Collier, (1961).

Wedell, George. 'Prospects for Television in Europe' *Government and Opposition* 29, no. 3 (1994): 315–31.

Weil, Stephen E. *A Cabinet of Curiosities: Inquiries into Museums and Their Prospects*. Washington: Smithsonian Institution P (1995).

Weiler, Betty and Colin Michael Hall, Eds *Special Interest Tourism*. London: Belhaven P; New York: Halstead P (1992).

Weinraub, Bernard. 'Directors Battle Over GATT's Final Cut and Print' *New York Times* (12 December 1993): L24.

Weir, Tom. 'No Daydreams of Our Own: The Film as National Self-Expression' *An Australian Film Reader*. ed. Albert Moran and Tom O'Regan. Sydney: Currency P (1985): 144.

Weisberg, Jacob. 'A Well-Staged Scandal' *New York Times Magazine* (10 October 1999): 56–57.

Welch, L.S. and Luostarinen, R. 'Internationalization: Evolution of a Concept' *Journal of General Management* 14, no. 2 (1988): 34–55.

Welles, Sumner. *Pan American Coopoeration*. Washington, D.C.: U.S. Government Printing Office, Department of State Publication no. 692, Latin American Series no. 9 (1935).

West, Edwin G. 'Art Vouchers to Replace Grants' *Economic Affairs* 6, no. 3 (1986): 9–11, 16.

Whisnant, David E. *Rascally Signs in Sacred Places: The Politics of Culture in Nicaragua*. Chapel Hill: U of North Carolina P (1995).

White, E.W. *The Arts Council of Great Britain*. London: Davis-Poynter (1975).

White, Geoffrey M. 'Culture Talk in the 90s' *Culture and Policy* 6, no. 2 (1994): 5–22.

Whitelaw, Anne. 'Statistical Imperatives: Representing the Nation in Exhibitions of Contemporary Art' *Topia* no. 1 (Spring 1997): 22–41.

Whitt, J. Allen and Allen J. Share. 'The Performing Arts as an Urban Development Strategy: Transforming the Central City' *Research in Politics and Society* vol. 3 (1988): 155–72.

Whitt, J. Allen and John Lammers. 'The Art of Growth: Ties Between Development Organizations and the Performing Arts' *Urban Affairs Quarterly* 26 (1991): 376–93.

Whitt, J. Allen. 'Mozart in the Metropolis: The Arts Coalition and the Urban Growth Machine' *Urban Affairs Quarterly* 23, no. 1 (1987): 15–36.

Whitt, J. Allen. 'The Role of the Performing Arts in Urban Competition and Growth' *Business Elites and Urban Development: Case Studies and Critical Perspectives*. Ed. S. Cummings. Albany: State U of New York P (1988): 49–69.

Wieck, R. *Ignorance Abroad: American Educational and Cultural Foreign Policy and the Office of Assistant Secretary of State*. Westport: Praeger (1992).

Wilkins, Geraldine. 'Film Production in Northern Ireland' *Border Crossing: Film in Ireland, Britain and Europe*. ed. John Hill, Martin McLoone, and Paul Hainsworth. Institute of Irish Studies, Queen's U of Belfast, U of Ulster, and the BFI (1994).

Williams, J.J. 'Report of the Arts and Culture Task Group Presented to the Minister of Arts, Culture, Science and Technology, June 1995' *Critical Arts* 10, no. 1 (1996): 107–22.

Williams, Michael. 'Euros Bury Dinos, Fete 'List' Auteur' *Variety* (7–13 March 1994): 55–56.

Williams, Michael. 'Lines Drawn for Trade Talks' *Variety* (1–7 November 1999): 27.

Williams, Raymond. *Sources of Hope*. ed. Robin Gable. London: Verso (1989).

Williams, Raymond. *The Politics of Modernism: Against the New Conformists*. ed. Tony Pinkney. London: Verso (1989).

Williams, Robert J. 'Culture in the Service of the State: Canadian and Australian International Cultural Policy' *Australian Canadian Studies* 5, no. 1 (1987): 49–60.

Williams, Robert J. 'International Cultural Programmes: Canada and Australia Compared' *Contemporary Affairs* no. 50 (1985): 83–111.

Williamson, David. 'Arts 1: Aussie Content At Risk' *Australian* (9 November 1989): 16.

Wilson, Elizabeth. *The Sphinx in the City: Urban Life, the Control of Disorder, and Women*. London: Virago P (1991).

Wilson, Woodrow. 'Life Comes from the Soil' *Virginia Reader: A Treasury of Writings from the First Voyages to the Present*. ed. Francis Coleman Rosenberger. New York: Octagon (1972).

Wineland, John. 'Rethinking the Philanthropic Ogre: The Privatization of Museums and Exhibitions in Mexico and Brazil' In *Representing Latinamerican/Latino Art in the New Millennium: Curatorial Issues and Propositions*. ed. Mari Carmen Ramirez. Austin: U of Texas P (Forthcoming).

Winer, L. 'So What's Next, a Mustard Ballet?' *Newsday* (28 June 1996): B3.

Withers, Glen A. 'Principles of Government Support to the Arts' *Meanjin* 40 (December 1981): 442–60.

Wolfson, Richard F. 'Aesthetics in and About the Law' *Kentucky Law Review* 33 (1944): 33–47.

Wong, Edward. 'China's New Culture Starting to Take Shape, Minister Says' *New York Times* (8 September 2000): A13.

Woods, Mark. 'Foreign Pix Bring Life to Biz' *Variety* (3–9 May 1999): 37, 44, 46, 59.

Woods, Mark. 'That Championship Season' *Variety* (11–17 January 1999): 9, 16.

Woolf, Marie. 'Why the Next English Patient Will be British' *Independent on Sunday* (20 December 1998): 9.

World Commission on Culture and Development, *Our Creative Diversity: Report of the World Commission on Culture and Development*. Paris: UNESCO (1995).

World Trade Organization. 'Audiovisual Services: Background Note by the Secretariat' S/C/W/40 of 15 June 1998.

World Bank. *Culture Counts: Financing, Resources, and the Economics of Culture in Sustainable Development. Proceedings of the Conference*. Washington, D.C. (1999). http://WBLN0018.Worldbank.org/-Networks/ESSD/icdb.nsf/D4856F112E805DF4852566C9007C27A6/4D4D56F007815BD1852568 C8006741DF

———. *Culture and Sustainable Development: A Framework Action*. Washington, D.C. http://Inweb18.worldbank.org/essd/essd.nsf/9b1cfc683a76bt71852567cb0076a25e/fa8a463ac24a486 685668525684600720ce7?OpenDocument (1999).

Wyszomirski, Margaret Jane and Kevin V. Mulcahy, Eds *America's Commitment to Culture: Government and the Arts*. Boulder: Westview P (1995).

Wyszomirski, Margaret Jane and Pat Clubb, eds *The Cost of Culture: Patterns and Prospects of Private Art Patronage*. New York: American Council for the Arts, (1989).

Wyszomirski, Margaret Jane, ed. *Congress and the Arts: A Precarious Alliance*. New York: American Council for the Arts (1988).

Wyszomirski, Margaret Jane. 'Arts Policymaking and Interest-Group Politics' *Journal of Aesthetic Education* 14 (October 1980): 28–34.

Wyszomirski, Margaret Jane. 'Federal Cultural Support: Toward a New Paradigm?' *Journal of Arts Management, Law, and Society* 25, no. 1 (1995): 69–83.

Wyszomirski, Margaret Jane. 'Philanthropy, the Arts, and Public Policy' *Journal of Arts Management and Law* 16 (Winter 1987): 5–29.

Wyszomirski, Margaret Jane. 'Policy Communities and Policy Influence: Securing a Government Role in Cultural Policy for the Twenty-First Century' *Journal of Arts Management, Law, and Society* 25, no. 3 (1995): 192–205.

Wyszomirski, Margaret Jane. 'The Politics of Art: Nancy Hanks and the National Endowment for the Arts' *Leadership and Innovation: Entrepreneurs in Government*. ed. Jameson W. Doig and Erwin C. Hargrove. Baltimore: The Johns Hopkins UP (1990).

Wythe, George. *The United States and Inter-American Relations: a Contemporary Appraisal*. Gainesville: University of Florida Press (1964).

Yang, Danielle. 'MOFA Says Cultural Exchanges can Help Foreign Policy' http://ww3.sinanet.com/-news/0613news/4_E.html (n. d.)

Yencken, David. 'The Deep Dung of Cash: Cultural Policy in Australia' *Overland* no. 88 (July 1982): 5–11.

Yim Hak Soon. The Role and Limit of the Local Government and Nonprofit Organizations in the Development of Regional Culture in Korea. Paper delivered to Institute for Cultural Policy Studies Conference 'Cultural Policy: State of the Art' (29 June 1995).

Young, James E. 'Holocaust Memorials in America: Public Art as Process' *Critical Issues in Public Art: Content, Contest, and Controversy*. ed. Harriet F. Senie and Sally Webster. New York: Iconeditions, 1992. 57–70.

Yúdice, George. 'Civil Society, Consumption, and Governmentality in an Age of Global Restructuring: An Introduction' *Social Text* 13, no. 4 (1995): 1–25.

Yúdice, George. 'La industria de la música en la integración America Latina-Estados Unidos', ed. Néstor Garcia Canclini and Carlos Moneta, Eds., *Las industrias culturales en la integración Iltinoamericana*, Buenos Aires, Eudeba/SELA (1999): 115–161.

Yúdice, George. 'For a Practical Aesthetics' *Social Text*, no. 25/26 (1990): 129–45.

Zea, Leopoldo. *Positivism in Mexico* (1943). Austin: U of Texas P (1974).

Zecchinelli, Cecilia. 'Gaps Seen for EU TV Meet' *Daily Variety* (26 June 1994): 13.

Zeigler, Joseph Wesley. 'The Tiny Endowment: Radical Differences in Public and Private Sectors' *Journal of Arts Management, Law and Society* 24, no. 4 (1995): 345–52.

Zel, Antoinette, Executive Vice President and Director General of MTV Latin America. Interview with George Yúdice. Miami Beach, 14 March (2000).

Zhdanov, Andrei. 'Speech to the Congress of Soviet Writers' *Art in Theory 1900–1990: An Anthology of Changing Ideas*. ed. Charles Harrison and Paul Wood. Oxford: Blackwell (1996): 409–12.

Zimmer, Annette and Stefan Toppler. 'Cultural Policies and the Welfare State: The Cases of Sweden, Germany, and the United States' *Journal of Arts Management, Law and Society* 26, no. 3 (1996): 167–93.

Zolberg, Vera L. 'Conflicting Visions in American Art Museums' *Theory and Society* 10 (1981): 103–25.

Zolberg, Vera L. 'Museum Culture and the Threat to National Identity in the Age of the GATT' *Journal of Arts Management, Law and Society* 25, no. 1 (1995): 5–16.

Zolberg, Vera L. 'Paying for Art: The Temptations of Privatization à l'Américaine' *International Sociology* 11, no. 4 (1996): 395–408.

Zolberg, Vera L. *Constructing a Sociology of the Arts*. Cambridge: Cambridge UP (1990).

Zolov, Eric. *Refried Elvis: the rise of the Mexican counterculture*.Berkeley: U of California P (1999).

Index